How the West Was Lost

How the West Was Lost

Theft and Usurpation of State's
Property Rights

———

America's Frontier: 1776-2000
Our Public Land—Who Really Owns It

by

William C. Hayward

ISBN: 1-55517-486-8
v.1

Library of Congress Card Number: 00-109634

Published by Bonneville Books

Distributed by:
925 North Main, Springville, UT 84663 • 801/489-4084

CFI | Publishing and
Distribution Since 1986

Cedar Fort, Incorporated
CFI Distribution • CFI Books • Inside Cougar Report

Typeset by Virginia Reeder
Cover design by Adam Ford
Cover design © 2000 by Lyle Mortimer

Printed in the United States of America

"AUTOGRAPHED EDITION"
Limited to five hundred numbered copies
of which this is
Number_____

AN EXPLANATION
AND MY GRATITUDE

It seems that nothing really starts out as anything other than a simple project. This book was no exception. In the years of dealing with the Forest Service, one of the larger federal custodians of real estate, on whose custodial lands I built and operated the June Mountain Ski in the California Sierra mountains, I became more than casually knowledgeable about the operation and management of the Forest Service. And, more to the point, I watched a sort of metamorphic change take place over the nearly 30 years of my involvement. I was involved in those changes; they affected me personally, for I was a permittee on Forest Service land for those years. I was a part of many of the things I have written about. In short, I could not help but develop an ongoing curiosity and interest about how our public land in the different states was managed and by whose authority. Where and how did it all start? Where did the authority for its management come from? How did the federal government gain title to the land? At that time, like almost everyone else in the country, I thought that this land was owned by the federal government, and as such was, in truth, federal land. I believe now that that assumption was in error, but I did not reach that conclusion until I had done a considerable amount of research. How I got started on that research was a different story altogether; it was almost by happenstance.

I had no idea when it happened that a casual comment by a friend, Mary Mead, a Wyoming rancher, would start it all. But it did—eight years ago. I thought that she would find some interest in things that I had been exposed to and learned over the years inasmuch as she, too, was a permittee on Forest Service land. This that follows started out as a simple letter, perhaps longer than a usual one, but none the less, a letter. As you can see, it turned into more than that. One thing led to another.

Aside from my own experiences and personal knowledge, there were many others that contributed theirs as well. Many of them sent me material, or told me where to look and what to look for, as well as giving me sound, thoughtful advise. As a result, I don't feel that I can take credit for much more than being a chronicler, because this book, in many ways, is a compilation and combination of their experiences and knowledge as well. Also, as I got involved, I found that each of them had been involved in a far more personal and dramatic way than had I. They knew far more than I. In fact, I think they still do, each in his or her area of interest or knowledge. To each of them, in different ways, I—or perhaps we—owe a debt of gratitude: Wayne Hage, Dick Carver, Ed Presley, Zane Miles, Bill Schaeffer, Glade Hall, Cliff Gardner, and many others. Clearly, this book would not have been written if I had not had the advantage of their prior research and effort. The effort was not all my own, even though over the eight year period, I spent countless hours in our local Orange County law library researching, copying, reading, looking up, checking on, or tracking down fragments of information. I could not have done it without their guidance. Of course, I discovered books and cases on my own, but it is to them that I am eternally grateful for getting me going—reading, listening and digesting whatever it was they sent or told me. In all truthfulness, were it not for them, I would still be trying to figure out if a door swung in or out. They were all immensely helpful—and yes—encouraging.

In addition, I am most grateful to the National Geographic Society for their permission to use the two maps that appear between Part One and Part Two of this book. Those maps show at a glance what a lot more than a thousand words could ever do: The differences in the land masses that are encompassed within the borders of these United States; their topographical and physical nature.

Further I am grateful to the Economist Newspaper Group, Inc. for the use of their map entitled, "Expanding westward," that shows the different parcels, both large and small, that ultimately became a part of these United States by purchase or by war.

To a large extent, these maps show the core of what this book is all about. They give it understandability, and, I hope, more clarity.

Santa Ana, California, March 1, 2000

DEDICATION

When I read a dedication of a book, usually it seems it goes to some unidentifiable person who seems to have only a first name. This one goes to a lot of children, most of whom will never read this; some don't know how to yet. This book is dedicated to all the grandchildren of those persons previously named—and my own.

INTRODUCTION

The history of our public lands is far more complex than would appear on the surface. That history is punctuated by all sorts of events and changing moods of the time. This that follows is an attempt to give, in broad-brush form, a brief history of these public lands that now compose, on an apparently permanent basis, nearly one third of these United States. These circumstances were not always that way. The "why" of that statement is based more in the time and mood of the past, which, like almost all history, is best reviewed with benefit of considerable hindsight. In just over 200 years there is much to draw upon in terms of influencing events and dynamic mood swings that directly affected the status, disposition or retention of the public land as well as our perception of its legal status.

With respect to our public land, its management and control, it is altogether obvious that certain inequities exist; that breaches of faith have occurred on the part of the federal government; that constitutional provisions have either been overlooked or simply ignored; that court decisions leave less than a straight pathway and that even they have been ignored, distorted or overlooked—intentionally or accidentally; that our founding fathers would be appalled to the point of incredulity by the twists and bends in the interpretation of their insuring document, the United States Constitution, with respect to the separation of powers between the federal and the state government; and last but by no means least, a collectivism mentality that has—and still is—garnering more and more finite control over these same public (now called federal) lands as well as over our individual lives.

First off, from time to time I may call these public lands, "federal lands," when in reality they are public lands and at times past were called public domain lands subject to homestead, settlement and/or sale. The name "federal lands," is a name acquired by just over 100 years of usage; it is an assumed name, born out of constant usage and, perhaps, an intent to give the land a meaning that it never had in the first place, a purpose not intended by our forefathers, and last but not least, a connotation of ownership that goes by implication and association with the name: federal. This is not to say that there was not a time when, indeed, this public land was in federal ownership. There was. The time: When this land was in a territorial state of being, prior to each state's joining the Union—except in the case of the original 13 colonies—a pivotal fact that you will want to remember. We have been taught, by usage alone, to call all of it federal lands when in actuality, public land is the accurate nomenclature. But then, even the shift in name is a part of the history that will unfold in what follows.

This book is divided into two distinct parts. The two parts are not inseparable, but one does lead to the other and is supportive. In Part One, I have accepted whatever happened as an established fact, with no real question or doubt cast upon whatever inconsistency I saw as to its adherence to the Constitution or to Supreme Court decisions. Further, in Part One I have not challenged the constitutionality of federal ownership of this land, nor any of the federal authority exercised over it today by any of the federal bureaus. Rather, it has been my objective to focus upon the historical background of our public lands and shed some light on how they came into being, how they came to be called federal land, how they were disposed of and why, how the motivation to dispose of the land changed with the times, where these public (now called federal) lands are located today, how they are administered and by what department or bureau of the federal government, how much land is involved, the vested interests of private property that existed and still exist on that same public (now called federal) land, the extent of some of the legislation affecting this land, a cursory view of the laws that impact this land or control its use, the conflicts that are apparent in the treatment of private property rights, how they came into being and what is being done about and with it today.

Today, the federal government has stated unequivocally that it owns the public lands, a statement I emphatically dispute. Part Two is focused upon the legal foundation, or lack of it, upon which the claim of federal ownership of the public land is based, as well as the authority, control and power sources that keep and maintain that base. Part Two is more of a legal brief wherein the departure from the Constitution, various inconsistencies, acts and actions taken by the different agencies or bureaus of the federal government are pointed out and challenged. These inconsistencies, acts and actions are profound, serious and far-reaching.

With respect to our public land, I did not fully realize the extent and magnitude of all the things that I have written about until I had done considerable research. Nor, for that matter, was I fully aware of the inequities that still exist today; it is all a part of the history which I have tried to relate.

Tracing the history from whence it all came is of primary importance, for, as George Santayana once said, "Those who cannot remember the past are condemned to repeat it." What to do about these inequities and the expansion of federal power and control is another matter. However, knowing its extent and how it got there in the first place is the first step toward finding a solution.

TABLE OF CONTENTS

PART I
AMERICA'S FRONTIER: 1776-2000

PART II
OUR PUBLIC LAND — WHO REALLY OWNS IT?

SUMMARY AND CONCLUSION

APPENDIX

PART I

AMERICA'S FRONTIER: 1776-2000
AN HISTORICAL REVIEW OF OUR PUBLIC LAND,
ITS ORIGIN, DISPOSITION, AND LATER
RETENTION AS FEDERAL LAND

THE BEGINNING

Following the American Revolution, seven of the original thirteen colonies laid claim to all of the land adjacent to their western borders—all the way to the Mississippi River. The Mississippi River was to be the western border of the freed Colonies, in conformance with the Treaty of Paris in 1783, the final document of independence freeing the American Colonies from Great Britain. These western lands were largely unsettled and only sparsely occupied by Indians, whose nomadic way of life was not considered to be of much importance as far as land ownership was concerned. Even though the term "Manifest Destiny"[1] would wait over 50 years to be uttered, its seeds in fact and intent were being clearly sown.

The mentality of that day was one of nation and possessed Colonies. Great Britain had her colonies—Australia, part of Canada and India; the American colonies were simply no longer among them. Other nations—Belgium, Holland, France, Italy, Spain—had their colonies too.

To those nations, the colonies were to be used—and developed—by their parent for their raw materials and natural resources, as well as to become a source of income or developing wealth for the parent country or its citizenry. This was the mind-set of the time. This mind-set existed in the new freed colonies as well, and was to have a material effect upon the development of the eleven Western states long after their population growth (60,000 minimum) was sufficient to make them eligible for statehood. To a burgeoning federal establishment, largely controlled at that time by the populated eastern states, this mentality was to have the effect of treating the West as though it were not of age and still was a collection of "colonies" even

---

1- "Manifest Destiny" was the coinage of journalist John O'Sullivan in 1850.

1

though the names had all been changed to "Territories." A few had actually been admitted to the Union as states. Yet this mentality, constriction or restriction, still existed.

By virtue of the vast land holdings retained as federal lands, public lands or Public Domain as they were referred to in the earlier days, a hold was retained over the growth and development of this western land. It was to be developed differently from that of the East, the South and the Midwest. Almost all of the land that composes the East, the Midwest, the South, and even some of the more easterly of the western states was in private owner-ship—perhaps well over 95 percent. The 11 western states, plus Alaska, were—and still are—in the opposite circumstance, wherein what is now claimed to be federal land is by far the major component—probably 60 percent or more.

It makes little or no difference if this change in disposition of land came about by intent; whether it was overt, covert, done with malice of fore-thought or out of ignorance, the western land was subjected to controls—a withholding from sale or transfer into private ownership—that had never been imposed on all of the other lands to the east.

It was not always so. It all started right after the Revolutionary War, and there were major policy shifts that took place as well on the part of the federal government over a wide span of years. At first the federal govern-ment made every effort to get rid of these vast lands, even making outright gifts. As time went on the strings of attachment, stringency and possession took over, and the federal government was literally loath to part with a single acre. This later change to retention effected the eleven western states (plus Alaska) in particular. federal lands, as they are commonly called today, constitute most of the land of these western states. (See the map at the end of Part I.)

Major historical events also influenced this seeming policy shift as well. Were it not for these events there would never have been any land to give away or hold west of the Mississippi River: The Louisiana Purchase in 1803, the War of 1812 between the United States and Great Britain, the Florida Purchase in 1819, The Texas Annexation in 1845, the Oregon Territory settlement in 1846, the Mexican War of 1846, the Gadsden Purchase (from Mexico) in 1853, the Civil War in 1861, the purchase of Alaska in 1867, and the Spanish American War of 1898. The United States was expanding to the west—into lands that it either purchased or took as the spoils of war. It is interesting and important to note that all purchases of land were finalized by treaties. Treaties are specifically mentioned and afforded special importance in Article VI, Clause 2 of the United States Constitution.[2]

In 1783, before the Confederacy was confirmed, one thing was clear: The federal government did not own the land; it belonged to the seven claiming states. However, it was this claimed ownership that prevented the formation of the Confederacy. The other six states could not accept this fact, and it was not until a year later, in 1784, that the Virginia Act of Cession ceded Virginia's western "territory" to the United States to "be considered as common fund"[3] for the use and benefit of the United States upon its formation. The other six claiming states did the same. The Confederacy could now pay in land, as it had promised to its Revolutionary Army in conformance with an act of the Continental Congress in 1776, to wit: 100 to 500 acres, depending upon rank. Without this land in federal ownership, the Confederation—now the United States—had no land with which to pay. It had no money. But the debt to the soldiers of the American Revolution was not the only debt; the United States and/or the component several states owed millions of dollars to other creditors as well. However, this land was not given to the federal government-to-be; it was conveyed in the form of a trust. There were strings attached. The land was conveyed to the United States for enumerated purposes, all of which were connected with the payment of the Revolutionary War debt. The following quotations from Virginia's "Cession of Western Lands to the United States, December 20, 1783" are noteworthy:

> "[The land is to be conveyed to the United States] Upon condition that the territory so ceded shall be laid out and formed into states,...and the States so formed shall be distinct republican States, and admitted members of the Federal Union, having the same rights of sovereignty, freedom, and independence as the other States...."

> "That all the lands within the territory so ceded to the United States, and not reserved for or appropriated to any of the before-mentioned purposes [payment of expenses in subduing British posts, land as payment to certain officers, and soldiers of the Revolutionary War] shall be considered as a common fund for use and benefit of such of the United States...***and shall be faithfully and bona fide disposed of for that purpose, and for no other use or purpose whatsoever***...(Italics added for emphasis)

2- "....all treaties made or which shall be made, under the authority of the United States, shall be the supreme law of the land..."

3-Virginia Act of Cession, March 1, 1784.

Two foundation points in the trust are laid here: One, the foundation for the Equal Footing Doctrine, which is discussed in detail later; and two, the simple fact that the land was to be disposed 0f—it was not to be held in perpetuity by the United States.

This was the beginning of federal ownership of our public land. It was not the intention of the federal government at that time to keep this land in federal ownership. Indeed, it was to be disposed of as rapidly and in as orderly a manner as was possible—preferably for money. The largest single parcel was 1,500,000 acres, sold for $1,000,000 to The Ohio Company, a group of former Revolutionary soldiers. They in turn resold it in smaller plots. That 1,500,000 acres is now what is today a part of the state of Ohio.

THE ORIGINAL DISPOSITION OF LAND

The new Continental Congress in 1785 set up procedures for the sale of the federal land. It was to be properly surveyed into 640 acre lots, each lot to be a part of a township of 36 such lots (no change to this date) and auctioned off at a minimum bid of $1.00 per acre. Half of this land was to be auctioned off in parcels of 640 acres (one square mile) while the other half was to be sold in parcels of one entire township (36 square miles). The expression "Doing a land office business" must surely have had its roots in that time. Many large parcels were purchased, divided and then resold in smaller plots. It was common practice. However, no land was actually sold until 1787, the date of the ratification of the Constitution of the United States. Public land came into being only after the ratification of the Constitution.

A euphoria developed about this available "cheap" land to the west. It was advertised, promoted, and it was sold. This euphoria was a fearful thing to those who did not want to "pull up stakes and move." This exodus was a drain on labor, skilled and otherwise. It was a threat to an accepted way of life. This threat weighed heavily upon the established entrepreneur who had, by custom, been paying wages that kept the underprivileged underprivileged. And it was this same entrepreneur who had the ear of the government. In short, for all intents and purposes, he was the government. It would take nearly 150 years for this government/entrepreneur relationship to completely reverse into an adversarial role. However, the dream of owning one's own place, owning one's own land, being one's own boss, starting afresh, was compelling, to say the least. And many were compelled.

The federal government had its own problems too. It had a large war debt incurred by the American Revolution,[4] a country to build—to develop—and it had no money. But it did have land to sell! Lots of it.

And sell it it did—at first in large parcels, but Congress at later dates changed the amount of land a person could purchase to a maximum amount of land per person. In 1800, the size was reduced to 320 acres. In 1804 the size was further reduced to 160 acres, and at a still later date down to 40 acres. The brakes of growth and development were starting to be applied—and relatively soon at that.

Why was there a reduction in the maximum amount of land that one could buy, reducing it in fits and starts down to 40 acres? Was the exodus to the west that heavy and that costly? Not entirely, but it did attract most of the settlers. From 1815 to around 1850 rapid westward expansion resulted in more than twice the population increase west of the Appalachians than in the original thirteen colonies. Experts in that day determined that 160 and then down to 40 acres was enough land to provide a living for a farmer. Jefferson used the Old English term, "yeomen," meaning farmer. He envisioned settlers composed of yeomen, each contributing his worth to the United States. I doubt that he ever envisioned the parsimonious disposition of these vast lands in such small plots. And small they were. Somehow these experts determined, as time went on, that 30 inches of annual rainfall were also necessary for farming. Grazing live-stock on large tracts of arid land was, for all intents and purposes, unheard of as a valid use of land; arid land was not encountered in those early days—certainly not in the East. Farmers existed. Ranchers did not—yet. Further, these experts determined that it was at just about the 98th meridian where land to the west of that line received less than 30 inches of annual rainfall. In short, somewhere out there beyond the 100th meridian, farming 40 acres was not practical except in widely scattered plots where springs, streams

---

4-Not well known is the fact that the war debt incurred by the American Revolution was fully paid by the sale of land—that land known as the Northwest Territory as well as land acquired by purchase from France in 1803, the Louisiana Purchase, by the year 1835. There was no national debt as of that year. It had all been paid off. Even so, I have found no record where the federal government conveyed back to the original thirteen colonies, now states, the remaining unsold or unappropriated land of the Northwest Territory held "as a common fund" in trust for the payment of this war debt. The Northwest Territory land was special. It was terri-torial land ceded to the United States for the express purpose of paying off debts of the United States. The territory referred to in the U. S. Constitution is this same territory, there was no other. Part Two covers this issue in detail.

or seeps existed. But this land still had use and value for something other than tilling the soil. This was grazing land. And these vast stretches of land, rolling hills, were to become known as grazing land—the land of the buffalo and antelope—semi-arid rangelands: Land you could not farm, but land upon which cattle and sheep could graze.

Interestingly, Congress never made any provision for any of this grazing land to become private even though two other significant groups were provided for: Namely, the miner and the farmer, who could gain title to their land by either registering their "claim" to the land with the General Land Office (later through the process provided for in the Homestead Act of 1862, which limited the size of homestead land to 160 acres) or the patent process[5] of the Mining Act of 1872. Privatizing this grazing land by selling it in larger than 40 to 160-acre plots was proposed by proponents of such action—largely western ranchers. There was some support in Washington, but never enough, so nothing was done until many years later[6]—too late for the rancher of earlier years, well after the Forest Reserve Act of 1891 was passed that was a pivotal change for the West, but later for that. Efforts were made, even as late as 1878 by Major John Wesley Powell, to specify 2,560 acres (four square miles) as the amount of land necessary for ranching (grazing as it was called in those days) and to have this amount of land approved for acquisition by the ranchers.[7] To no avail. Congress stuck to the smaller acreage. Even though Washington Irving's description of the West was the popular belief, "...undulating and treeless plains, and desolate sandy wastes, wearisome to the eye from their extent and monotony," the concept of farming on smaller plots won out. Some in Congress were moved to keep the size small because they thought of larger plots as a "land grab" effort. The rancher either did not exist, or it was felt that he was some kind of high-bred farmer who could "manage" under the then existing circumstances of land ownership. The idea of disposing of large amounts of land to private people was too much for Congress to stomach. Then too, parsimonious disposition of land was a growing attitude.

5-The issuance of a certificate evidencing the grant of land by a government.

6-The Desert Land Act of 1877 provided for a claim of homestead for 640 acres—later changed to 320 acres by the Act of 1890. The Enlarged Homestead Act of 1909 reestablished 320 acres as the amount that could be patented. Later still, the Grazing Homestead Act (a.k.a. The Stock Raising Act of 1916) provided 640 acres as patentable. This act had some limitations, the most notable of which was one claim per one man, and when patented, his rights to homestead were extinguished.

7-"Report on the Lands of The Arid Region of the United States," by John Wesley Powell (1878).

There were other concerns as well that bothered Congress. The Pacific Northwest was somewhat disputed territory between Great Britain, the United States, and the burgeoning independence of Canada. Whose land was it? Where were its borders? If settlers occupied it, who was there to defend their safety or interests? If guarantees of occupation were to be extended by the United States into Oregon Territory, would that aggravate Great Britain? Just how far could "Manifest Destiny" be pushed? Could not the limiting of the size of the land upon which a settlement could be authorized by the United States be less aggravating? Justifiable concerns.

These concerns were by no means the only ones; there were other motivating factors as well. One authority, Wayne Hage,[8] attributes much, if not all, of this reluctance to increase the size of the land to be conveyed into private ownership to avarice and greed on the part of eastern financialists. He contends that by this time the value of the natural resources of the West was becoming well known: Timber, minerals and even the grass for the grazing of vast herds of cattle. By keeping the West in "public" ownership, Hage contends, at least there was a chance to exploit its value, while such an opportunity would be lost if it became private land. As open range it could be used free. And "used" it was by the extremely large cattle combines of those early days, right along with the smaller private ranchers, whose herds were dwarfed by comparison. On the part of some ranchers, there was little or no concern for overgrazing—and it was overgrazed in many areas. However, it would be wrong to imply that a lack of concern included all settlers for it did not. For many a rancher, this was his home, his land, and he was no more interested in damaging his land than in shooting his favorite horse!

But Congress did give away huge blocks of land for its own quid pro quo purposes. The rancher, to Congress, was on the "take" end only. The railroad men were not. To them, every other section was given that varied from 10 to 40 miles on each side of the railroad. The Illinois Central Act of 1850 was the beginning of the land grant to railroads era, and it provided that alternating sections of land be granted to the railroad for 6 miles on each side of the railroad line. In some areas, to other railroads, this distance varied up to 40 miles on each side. It was a subsidy for the purpose of pro-

8- Storm Over Rangelands, by Wayne Hage. Mr. Hage earned a masters degree from the University of Nevada, Reno; he is a rancher, and has served as Chairman of the Agriculture Land Use Committee of the California State Chamber of Commerce. He is a member of the American Society of Farm Managers and Rural Appraisers of the Nevada Agriculture Foundation; he is a board member of the Mountain States Legal Foundation, and he is a trustee of the University of Nevada Foundation.

viding transportation within the different states. The quid pro quo? Construct the railroad to provide transportation between the states and transport government shipments at 50 percent of the going freight rate. To these same railroad men huge low interest loans were given—so much a mile. So, in a way, building the railroad did become a sort of "gift"—an unbelievable financial opportunity for the not so daring "boys" on the inside track! On the other hand, over the years this 50 percent discount has amounted to a huge sum in "payment" for the land that in parts of the arid West had little or no real value...at least at that time.

As the first of the two enclosed maps between Part One and Part Two show, the difference in the amount of federal land to the east of about the 103rd meridian—the border line between Montana and Wyoming on the west and North Dakota, South Dakota and Nebraska on the east extended southward is startling. Quite obviously, the federal government stopped selling land or conveying title somewhere along this north-south line. There was a change in policy, and it was not just because there was less rainfall, or, as the second map shows, a distinct difference in the topography of the western land. Is Hage right? Was this an overt effort to "control"? Did it just "happen"? Was this simply an example of Parkinson's Law[9] in action? Perhaps all in varying degrees and at different times.

With all of his fears set aside, the eastern entrepreneur saw the West grow and grow. Land was sold, transferred, resold, purchased and accumulated. In fact, the boom of "cheap" land was so compelling that the land could not be processed—conveyed to the land holder or squatter, as he was known in those times—fast enough, and these squatters demanded Preemptive Rights.[10] Congress authorized these squatters to remain as temporary tenants—if they obtained permission from the local land officers —and passed acts in 1830 and in 1834 recognizing this Preemptive Right. This is an important fact to remember later: Congress did, finally, authorize and approve Preemptive Rights. The General Land Office eventually caught up with the squatters and properly registered their claims, but it took years to do so. The preemptive process was established and this became the primary method by which settlers actually obtained most of the public lands (Public Domain). They simply got there first and acquired for themselves

---

9-In oversimplified terms, Parkinson's Law states that a conscientious person or bureaucrat believes that he can do a better and better job if he continues to have more and more money with which to do it.

10-The right to claim land inasmuch as they were occupying the land and ostensibly the first to do so.

the amount of land allotted by the federal government regulation in force then at that time.

It is not illogical at all to wonder why it took so long for the General Land Office to process land claims. It did take a long time because the land had to be surveyed first. The Continental Congress, in 1785, stipulated how the land was to be sold off. There was much discussion as to whether a description of claimed land should be by metes and bounds from some local, prominent geographical location or surveyed and sold as a known plot. The Continental Congress chose the survey method.[11] The survey took years and years to accomplish. In the meantime, the claimant to the land simply occupied the land and waited for the survey to catch up with him. As a matter of interest, it was not until 1861 that the first survey of Nevada creased that state, around Gardnerville, and even then only two townships were surveyed.[12] In spite of the time delay, the survey had to be performed first before the issuance of a patent was possible. The squatter had to wait to locate his parcel as near as he could to the land he was occupying. It didn't always fit! In the west the misfit could be a disaster, for the shift could place the squatter partially or wholly away from an irrigable valley within which his "spread" was located. Or the law could change. And it did. The Pre-Emption Act of 1841 was repealed in 1891, when a massive change in policy occurred. But later for that change.

Was the acceptance, authorization and approval by Congress of this Preemptive Right to initial ownership of land the only way? At the time it

---

11-A note about surveys as authorized by the Continental Congress: From some base location the survey starts. In Northern California, this base location is Mt. Diablo, just south of San Francisco. From this single point, in a true east-west and north-south direction, each mile is carefully measured. These mile-long measurements are pin-pointed, staked and identified as section corners. A grid pattern is thus established into a large square make up of 36 sections called townships—6 sections in each direction (a section is 640 acres). The legal description or 40 acres could be as follows: The NW 1/4 of the NW 1/4, Section 10, Township 3 East, 2 South of the Mt. Diablo meridian.

12-*Golden Fleece In Nevada*, by Judge Clel Georgetta, p. 69. Judge Georgetta took seven years of research before writing this book. He was a District Court Judge in Nevada, a trial attorney for 30 years who handled many range and water rights cases, and an owner of the Triune Ranch in Eastern Nevada.

was. Unlike today, where we have a large number of government employees in reasonably far-flung locations across these United States, whether they be Forest Service or Bureau of Land Management personnel to perform their assigned duties, the General Land Office was not staffed all the time. Further, they were overwhelmed by the mountain of paperwork and record keeping—all of which had to be done by hand. It took time—far more than we would consider prudent today. The equity of the circumstances could only be maintained by the acceptance of the intent of Congress in the first instance: Namely, to dispose of the land by claim of "first come first serve." Authorization and approval by Congress of this preemptive right created new law. It was basic, and it passed the oldest of common tests: It was fair.

Then too, Congress was still paying its soldiers, in addition to their regular pay, such as it was, in land warrants. Congressional intent was clear: Settle the Public Domain. Congress went further in recognizing and authorizing this preemptive right and passed the Act of 1866, which in effect recognized the rights of appropriation—squatter's rights.[13] Further, it recognized the rights of miners— "first come, first served" doctrine. The act took cognizance of the custom and usages that had grown up on public lands under state and territorial sanction. More than that, it constituted recognition of a **preexisting right** "...rather a voluntary recognition of a pre-existing right of possession, constituting a valid claim to its continued use, than the establishment of a new one."[14] In effect, it became a private right that had grown up under the government's tacit consent and approval.
(Emphasis added)

WATER CLAIMS ON THE PUBLIC LAND AND THE BEGINNING OF THE SPLIT ESTATE

As these easterners plunged west and occupied unoccupied land, they laid claim to the water, for, after all, if there was no water, there would be no crop, there would be no way to survive, there would be no way to extract gold from the rock, there would be no water for cattle or sheep. Water was all important. Before long every seep, spring or stream was claimed. The Act of 1866 authenticated these early claims of prior usage.

13-Taken quite literally this was the right to appropriate— "take for your own use"— land you selected. It became known later as "Squatter's Rights."

14-U.S. Supreme Court

But with whom did they register their claim to the water? They used the water because it was needed for their grazing of cattle or sheep. It was, to them, a part of the land and as such it was theirs. They thought, justifiably, that their building of a house and their clearing and tilling the soil of the land they claimed gave them the water as well. On their own parcel, it did, but in almost all cases this parcel was not large enough for grazing alone as a source of income sufficient to support a family, so they used the adjoining Public Domain land as well. They simply appropriated it for their own use even though they knew that the maximum amount of land they could have at that time in "fee-simple" was 320, 160, or 40 acres,[15] depending upon the vagaries of Congress. On this adjacent land they did claim the water; this they could do with the territorial or state government office and they did. It was "custom and practice" of the time. Could they register their claim to the water on adjacent federal land with the General Land Office? Many probably tried to, but the General Land Office dealt in land only—federal (territorial) land. Further, the General Land Office was, for the most part, an agency set up to register preempted, appropriated land sold at auction, or, later, homestead land. Disputes over water were handled by the territorial government, or later by its successor, the state government. Within a very short time there was a standard of operation for each settler: File your claim to the land with the General Land Office and file your claim to the water with the territorial or state government even if the water is on adjacent federal land—and much of it was. All of this was done in conformance with and protected by different laws, statutes or court decisions.

The arid climate of the West occasioned the need for the appropriation of water on adjacent land beyond the limits of acreage available within a potential homestead. Rainfall did not produce a lush grass for year-round grazing. What water there was had to be husbanded, saved, and developed. Ditches were built, tanks were dug and seeps were enlarged. Water was the key to survival inasmuch as the amount or number of sheep or cattle necessary for the support of a family was dependant directly upon water. This number in the arid West could not be sustained by the water on the homestead alone; it had to come from the adjacent land—public land. In many cases this water was transported a long distance in ditches to land suitable for irrigation purposes.[16]

This, then, became the beginning of what was later to be called the split estate. The land was federal if the land was still in a territorial state of

---

15-There was a short while when this arid land could be claimed in as much as 640 acre plots.

16-Simplified, there are essentially two rules of law with respect to water rights: One, being, while the water claimed was subject to the territorial or state government—two separate entities. Title to the land (in an amount consistent with the existing Federal Law) could be obtained from the federal government, while the state or territorial government controlled the disposition or regulation of the water on the land. An interesting distinction arises here. Water could be claimed on land that was outside of the boundaries of the preempted, appropriated or homesteaded land claimed. There was only one string: You had to use it for your own use. Further, you had to be the first to use it. It was appropriated in most cases by the homesteader who was using the adjacent land as a part of his "spread" for grazing cattle or sheep. The term "beneficial use" comes into play here: The water had to be used for the "beneficial use" of the claimer. This fact was crucial to his right to its continued usage. In fact, this became the basis for law.

What I have outlined as split-estate interests is really quite fundamental. In actuality there is today a plethora of different laws and statutes that establish, protect and insure rights of not just the federal government or the state, but rights of exploration for minerals, petroleum, timber harvesting, wildlife, endangered species and even wild horses and burros. In many cases it is a different law with different rights. In other words, on this same land, ownership interests are subject to continuing rights of others—a split interest—Hence the term "split estate."

The split-estate did not just erupt, it developed over a continuous, long period of time without challenge or change.

An understanding of the split-estate does not end there—federal versus state. One does not receive title to water or minerals; one receives a right—a right to use the water or extract the minerals until a patent (title) has been obtained on the land, if and when granted. This right is personal property and subject to all laws relative to personal property. It can easily be seen that the land can remain in federal ownership while the water or minerals can belong to an individual. This is the essence of the split estate: Two parties with a valid interest in the land: one may be the government (state or federal) who owns or controls the land, and the second, an indi-

---

(16 continued)—riparian, wherein the water goes with the land and the title to it is a part of the land. This, generally, is in effect in the eastern states. Second, water that is appropriated—water that is claimed by an individual on Public Domain land to which a certificate of ownership or the right to use it is issued by the state. Prior to statehood, this certificate or right to use the water was issued by the territorial government. This condition is generally in effect in the West. The case of Kansas v. Colorado (1906) 206 U.S. 46 adjudicated this separation.

vidual who has a valid interest in its contents—water or minerals—and thus, by implication, the land. This was to become the law of the land.

Water—the claim to the usage of water, its appropriation (use for oneself) or preemption (first to claim or use)—was all-controlling for the occupation, settlement and development of the arid West. The Act of 1866 recognized the obligation of the government to respect private rights, including water—an outgrowth of the government's tacit consent and approval.

Later, the Act of 1870 clarified an issue—namely, that any patent (title to the land), preemption or homestead right granted or allowed to a settler was subject to **already vested water rights**. It was just like an easement or mineral right today: Someone else had rights over or under land that was not owned. These rights were and are private property that is separate and apart from the land itself—one part of the split estate.

Further clarification occurred with the passage of the Desert Land Act of 1877. This act limited the amount of the water rights on desert (arid) land to that of the bona fide *prior* appropriation. Excess over this amount was to be held free for further appropriation (by others).

It is interesting to note that it was not until 1935 that the United States Supreme Court ruled that the Desert Land Act of 1877 **severed the water from the public lands** and left any remaining unappropriated water open for further appropriation "...under the laws of the several states and territories." This is another distinct split of interest, this time, federal from state.

State and territorial sanction established the validity of claims or settled arguments as to who should or did own or have rights to this water. The miners set the early pattern in their own way—by the establishment of mining districts which had their own rules and regulations that were, surprisingly, remarkably uniform from one district to another. "First come, first served" was the rule. This became law that was later upheld by the territorial or state government. Note, however, that the land was owned by the federal government, while the water was under the jurisdiction, control or disposition of the territory or state. Private rights to this water and usage of land were upheld. And for years—until 1891—nothing was ever done to change this fact. This same "rule of law" was in effect for the farmer as well; if the farmer or rancher had appropriated the water, and most important of all, was using it, it was his—so long as he used it. If he ceased to use it, it could be claimed by someone else, or he could lose it altogether. Ranchers gained title to the water and thereby, albeit tacitly, the right of usage of this Public Domain land. It became a part of his range. The Act of 1866 confirmed this. Their claiming the water on Public Domain land gave them control of the grazing lands within the distance that stock would travel for water in a day. This became the limit of the rancher's preemptive right of appropriation, and this right was accepted throughout the west by 1875. This right, too, was upheld by the different states and territories. The federal government acquiesced in this use. The titular ownership did not change; it remained as a part of the Public Domain (federal lands); sovereign immunity remained intact. Ownership of the land cannot be preempted without the sovereign's consent, and wasn't—only its use.

This Act of 1866 was actually the legal beginning of the "Split Estate:" water rights were "property," owned individually, and could be taxed as such. They were and still are. The IRS considers water rights today as personal property (as well as Taylor Grazing Rights and National Forest Grazing Permits, which will be covered later). The transfer of these rights are possibly, if not probably, a taxable event.

The split-estate property right of usage, in simplified terms, is much like a lien, an easement, a right that is a prior, valid claim—an encumbrance upon the land that goes with the land itself. This property right can be transferred, sold and conveyed. It goes with the land even though the land is public. The private property right of usage is a private property right. It is private property—at least those rights that predate 1890, a most important date to remember. But later for that.

Aside from the acquisition of western land through purchase (Louisiana Purchase in 1803 from France, the Florida Purchase from Spain in 1819, the Gadsden Purchase from Mexico in 1853 and Alaska from Russia in 1867), by war (Mexican War of 1846 and the Spanish American War of 1898), or border disputes resolved by treaty (the Red River Basin in 1810, the Oregon Territory in 1846), the Civil War in 1861-65 played an important part as well. The western movement was one that attracted southerners as well as northerners. The issue of free or slave states reared its head in the West, and the West had discovered gold and silver in both California and Nevada. Both warring sides wanted it. Without going into detail, the Northern influence won out, and the states of California and Nevada were admitted to the Union—California with a population of just over 100,000 and Nevada with less than the minimum of 60,000 population. Lincoln needed the additional votes in the Senate—and he got them. The Enabling Acts[17] admitting both states were the same as far as the unclaimed land was

17-Enabling Acts were those that set forth the conditions under which a territory

concerned. It simply became public land within the border of the separate states while still remaining under federal control as to its disposition. Keep in mind that this did not negate the right of usage that was even at that time taking place on parts of this public land. There was still no way the rancher could claim more land for his eventual ownership in fee simple than the maximum amount of land authorized by the current governmental regulation. For his kind of use in this semi-arid western land, it was way less than adequate. But he did claim that small piece of ranch land anyway. That "patch" of land was his base from which he roamed his cattle or sheep on the adjacent public land. However, the ultimate control or regulation of use of this land still remained in federal hands. But the pressure was on. The rancher wanted to have some valid claim to this land that he was using without charge. This land was vital to his survival as a rancher. He wanted title to this land—land upon which he had probably already filed claim to the water (springs, seeps or stream) in accordance with state or territorial law—land upon which he had made improvements from time to time such as dams, wells, ditches, corrals, out-buildings and even barns. He could not make a living farming his small homestead—his "patch." It was simply too small.

THE HOMESTEAD ACT OF 1862
AND ITS EFFECT ON THE WEST

The westerners were to lose again to the easterners, who really did not understand their situation and basic needs. But this time the westerner was used! The Civil War was raging, and right in the middle of it Congress passed the Homestead Act of 1862. It required that no one could acquire land under the Homestead Act who was not a citizen of the United States—meaning, of course, a "northerner." To the westerner, who needed more than a patch of land for his survival as a rancher, it was a blow in another important respect: The Homestead Act set a limit of 160 acres as the maximum amount of land that could be claimed. The eastern congressmen never really understood that the westerner needed not just 160 acres but sections of this arid land in order to make a living. A section is 640 acres. Worst of all, this lack of understanding of the westerner's real needs started the conflict between the rancher and the federal government as to the grazing rights.

Preemptive rights of the squatter were approved by Congress in 1830 and again in 1834 and reinforced in 1866. To what extent did this

(17 continued)—could be admitted to the Union as a state.

approval now apply to the rancher? Did he have any rights? That now became the issue, inasmuch as he was using far more than the 160-acre allotment to which he could eventually gain title under the Homestead Act of 1862. Further, the rancher honestly believed that he could and would gain title to the rest of the rangelands he was using by virtue of his **Preemptive Right or Rights of Appropriation**. He was willing to buy it as well. Problem: It was not available for purchase. He still thought that one day it would be his. And why not, he reasoned. After all, that is the way almost all of the other land in the United States had been acquired in the past. And it had!

The issue of ownership was now translated into prescriptive right.[18] Prescriptive rights cannot be asserted against a sovereign, but if the sovereign elects to recognize a preemptive right, *it can lead* to the patent of the land in fee-simple title. This the rancher knew and this was what he expected. After all, the entire Eastern land had been transferred into private ownership in this manner. Was it not now reasonable to assume that this would continue in the West? He did have the right to expect this outcome—it was historical **modus operandi**. How wrong he was! But then he did not know it at the time. The rancher started to fence off the land he used—public land—federal land—Public Domain land. In that day and age, all three names were somewhat homogenous or interchangeable. He did this not just to hold his herd or flock in—which he did—but to keep others out! Others wanted to use the land too. To the others it was "public" land and free for their use as well; it was simply there for the taking. Further, there were no restraints employed by the federal establishment to prevent their using it—yet. To some, the ruthless opportunists, this was land that only needed someone strong enough to simply occupy it. Many an American movie of the old west has been scripted around these ruthless land robbers. Fortunately, these land robbers were the exception and not the rule. The rule of the "six gun" was really more the figment of movie making imagination than real. It was there, of course—Wyatt Earp and others like him were real people. Even so, lawlessness was the exception and not the rule.

To the average rancher, the problem was simple. The rancher did have rights to the water; he had been using it in most cases for years for his "beneficial use." And as for the land, he thought he had every right to expect this land to be his some day in the future by virtue of a patent. But the intruder had to have this water too, or he could not graze his herd or flock. The mind-set of the West was simple—and acknowledged: He who owns the water owns the land. And the rancher did own the water. It was his private property. Under the circumstances, fencing his land was a "must," and fence it he did.

18-A right acquired by the long exercise of some power. Use, in this case.

THE ANTI-FENCING LAW OF 1885 AND THE MOVEMENT OF LARGE HERDS

Once again the rancher was to lose out, for in 1885, after many conflicts over usage, Congress passed a law that required the removal of all fences. Also an issue, but not stated, was the threat of preemptive property rights. The fence had to go: It might later become a prescriptive right. And those fences did go, at times with the aid of federal troops.

It is not hard to imagine the disillusion of the rancher on this arid land. Why was he being badgered? Why was he being singled out for what seemed like ruthless constriction? Why were his legitimate rights being ignored? Why could he not get title to his land like everyone else? Congress passed the Mining Law in 1872 that allowed mining claims to become private property in full fee simple. Wasn't he, the rancher, going to get the same treatment? He had been led to think so, but the rancher was clearly outside the loop! Congress always thought he wanted too much land and never really understood why. Then too, the conflicts of use of this public land were ruthlessly fought over. While the bloody and violent cattle war waged against the sheep-men in Wyoming continued for several years around 1905, it was by no means singular. That sort of thing had been going on for the previous 50 years. Isolated though they might have been, bloody conflicts did arise over usage and ownership—two words that hazily melded into one another, for one meant very nearly the same thing as the other to the rancher. In any event, his image was not always the best. This kind of conflict did not help the rancher's cause in Washington. There were reasons for this conflict that were compelling. They were real. Simply put, large herds of cattle and sheep were trailed both east and west from the western states. By the mid 1870's, nearly three quarters of a million sheep alone had been herded across Nevada in either direction to market: to California, and even from California to eastern markets of Omaha, Nebraska or even Chicago. Squatters had settled upon most of the seeps, springs, meadowland or streams in the West. Inasmuch as a herd of sheep will eat nearly everything that grows in its path, much of the land was fenced to preserve the arable land of the squatter. The sheep or cattle decimated the unfenced land the squatter was dependent upon for a living. At first an unwritten law was respected that a trail-herd must remain 6 miles from a settlement. Later a Nevada statute reduced this unwritten law to a law in fact: A trail-herd must remain 3 miles from a settlement, thus protecting the squatter or small rancher. Without doubt, fencing was an issue and an impediment to the trail-herds who were grazing while passing through free-to-use Public Domain land.[19] As mentioned before, the result was the anti-fencing Federal Law of 1885. Public domain land was not to be fenced. The squatter could fence only his own land, not the adjacent Public Domain land he was using.

The rancher really needed to have his rights defined. And they finally were in 1890!

PREEMPTION RIGHTS ARE FINALLY RECOGNIZED

It came about in the Supreme Court case of Buford v. Houtz:[20]

"We are of the opinion that there is an implied license, growing out of the custom of nearly a hundred years that the public land of the United States, especially those in which the native grasses are adapted to the growing and fattening of domestic animals, shall be free to people who seek to use them where they are left open and uninclosed and no act of government forbids this use...The government of the United States, in all its branches has known of this use, has never forbidden it, nor taken any steps to arrest it. No doubt it may be safely stated that this has been done with the consent of all branches of the government and, as we shall attempt to show, with its direct encouragement.

"The whole system of control of the public land of the United States as it has been conducted by the government, under acts of Congress, shows liberality in regard to their use which has been uniform and remarkable. They have always been open to sale at a very cheap prices. Laws have been enacted authorizing persons to settle upon them and to cultivate them, before they acquire any title to them. While in the incipiency of the settlement of these lands, by persons entering upon them, the permission to do so was a tacit one, the exercise of this permission became so important that Congress by a system of laws called the **Preemption Laws**, recognized this right so far as to confer a priority of the right to purchase on the persons who settled upon and cultivated any part of this Public Domain. During the time the

---

19-*Golden Fleece In Nevada*, by Judge Clel Georgetta, chapters 3, 4, and 5.

20-Buford v. Houtz., 133 U.S. 618 (1890)

settler was perfecting his title...both he and all other persons who desired to do so had full liberty to graze their stock upon the grasses of the prairies and upon other nutritious substances found upon the soil." (Emphasis added)

The Supreme Court used the treatment of mining claims as an example:

"....and while this remained for many years as a right resting upon the tacit assent of government, the principle has been since incorporated in the positive legislation of Congress, and today the larger part of the valuable mines of the United States are held by individuals under the claim of discovery...."

There you have it spelled out: prior appropriation and preemptive rights were real.

THE END OF PREEMPTION RIGHTS
AND THE BEGINNING OF FEDERALISM

But it didn't last long—a year to be exact—for in 1891 another law was passed that put an end to this chapter. This law, called the "Creative Act of 1891" or "The Forest Reserve Act of 1891," did, among other things, put an end to preemptive law. This law has had a far-reaching effect upon all who use the public land by permit today. Other subsequent legislation has had its effect, but this was the beginning of *real* federal stewardship of the public lands and the initial basis for the claim of federal ownership of the public lands that would surface later—irrespective of other claims.

For the rancher, while he may not have known it at the time, this law meant the end of any real possibility of gaining title to the land he had been using for years. The wheels had been put into motion; federal stewardship of the public lands would become the watchword of the future. Outright sale to those who had been using the land would no longer be a viable possibility. The law did not say that, but "custom and practice" that developed as a result of that momentous act did. The Forest Service can really date its beginning, in mind-set, to that date even though its actual beginning was later (1905). The Bureau of Land Management, a name change from the old General Land Office, got reinforcement as well.

THE BEGINNING OF SET ASIDE LAND: SECTION 24 OF THE FOREST RESERVE ACT OF 1891

Where did this beginning of federal stewardship come from? It came from a short rider to this legislation, Section 24:

> "That the president of the United States may, from time to time, *set apart and reserve*, in any state or territory having public land bearing forest, in any part of the public lands wholly or in part covered with timber or undergrowth, whether of commercial value or not, as *public reservations*; and the president shall, by *public proclamation*, declare the establishment of such *reservation* and limits thereof." (Emphasis added)

Any further act of Congress was no longer necessary. The President could handle it alone. And he did.

The real objective of Section 24 was to add more land to Yellowstone National Park; the Yellowstone Timber Reserve was promptly set aside by President Harrison to accomplish this end. The fact that the Public Domain could be taken over for effective control by the General Land Office—later to become the Bureau of Land Management (BLM)—and the then-to-be Forest Service was overlooked. Couple this oversight with Parkinson's Law[21] and the picture becomes clearer. Federal bureaus would henceforth handle the public lands as they acquired control piece by piece. It made no difference, it seems, whether the Public Domain land was inside the border of a given state or still in a territorial state of being. The land was to remain federal, and as time went on it slowly took on the exclusive name, "federal land." Part Two deals with this issue in detail.

These public lands really aren't that public at all, even though we refer to them that way today. They are riddled with valid legal claims: Water rights, easements, grazing rights, mining claims, oil and gas rights, etc. Some of these rights, Taylor Grazing Rights and Forest Service grazing permits, are in truth attached to the adjacent property and are in actuality a part of the value of that adjacent property. If you take away those rights upon the public land owned by the adjacent property owner without paying for it, you have *taken without compensation* something of value that is attached to the private land. This is a violation of the Fifth Amendment.[22]

21-Parkinson's Law has a number of satirical truisms: Work expands to fill the time available for its completion. Another: A conscientious worker believes that the only thing that separates his department from doing a better job is the lack of additional funds.

More later on these grazing permits and how they were "modified" to make them un-compensable for a cancellation, reduction or limitation of use—a "taking."

It is reasonably moot that it was not until 1897 that the so-called "kinks" were worked out to implement Section 24 of this 1891 Act, for there was no provision prior to 1897 for the administration and appropriation measure for this act. There simply was no money voted for its implementation. Life was breathed into the Forest Reserve Act of 1891 in 1897 by voting sufficient funds for its administration. However, this "life" did not prevent the immediate setting-aside of vast stretches of the Public Domain into forest reserves. From 1891 to 1893 fifteen different forest reserves were set aside. At that early date they were controlled by the General Land Office, a bureau within the Department of Interior. The Secretary of Interior had complete autocratic control of these reserves. (It was not until later that these forest reserves were all turned over to the Department of Agriculture's bureau, the Forest Service.) Land within these reserves was withdrawn from any future settlement; all livestock was prohibited from grazing on any part of these set-aside reserves. (This grazing prohibition was changed later.) The reserves did not just contain forested land only. A great deal of it contained no timber at all but was suitable for grazing. Grazing violators were prosecuted as trespassers. This prohibition from grazing was a severe blow to the livestock men who had been using it for summer range.[23] More on this subject later. In those six intervening years all sides just vied for position, so to speak—the central power advocates against the limit-of-power advocates. We tend to think of this philosophical difference of opinion as to central power versus states' rights or limited power with respect to our United States government as reasonably recent. It isn't at all. Its seeds were sown centuries ago and its fruit has been bitter or sweet ever since—depending upon your persuasion. However, one thing is clear: Central power has grown and Parkinson was right. The 1891 Act and the measures of 1897 were simply a few more nails in the coffin of states' rights.

By 1897, teeth were more than forming in the mouth of the federal establishment. Grazing on public land was considered to be trespassing, and ranchers with their claims to ownership of the water on these lands by virtue of "Beneficial Use" of the water and implied right to *use* the land were the prime target. Note again the words, "Beneficial Use." Simply put: The water was yours as long as you used the water for a beneficial use. If you did not, you lost it. Later, the bureaus would use means at their disposal—not always

22-Excerpt from the 5th Amendment of the U.S. Constitution: "...nor shall private property be taken for public use, without just compensation."

23-*Golden Fleece In Nevada*, Clel Georgetta, pp. 172-174.

with approval—to prevent this use and thereby attempt to invalidate this prior claim with its implied use of the land. Despicable, but true. The cattlemen's Associations in the West have records of such actions taken by the federal government to invalidate, impinge or prevent the use of water by a permittee and thus render his certificated water right null and void by reason of his failure to use the water for his "beneficial use"—a thing he must continue to do in order to retain his right to its usage: The "use it or lose it" doctrine. In such a case, the water right would then revert back to the federal government. Is this done with malice of forethought? Some ranchers say yes.

This 1891 Act was used by Presidents Harrison, Cleveland and Teddy Roosevelt. This one-sentence rider of this act gave to the president a new, far reaching authority to unilaterally, by decree, establish reserve land—land to be known later as forest reserves. They withdrew millions and millions of acres of the West's hills and mountain ranges from public settlement. This was done in the name of conservation. Thus the National Forests began, as did the precedent of set aside land. As we know it today, these millions and millions of acres of set aside public lands that found their beginning in 1891 are under the administrative control of the BLM, the National Park Service, the Forest Service, the Fish & Wildlife Service, the Bureau of Indian Affairs and the Department of Defense. In more recent years parts of these public lands were further designated as "wilderness" by the Wilderness Act. 38 million acres have been set aside as wilderness. 85 percent of this land is in the state of Alaska. While it is well known that no motorized vehicles are permitted within wilderness areas, little known is the fact that any and all natural resources of all kinds are likewise set aside: mining, timber harvesting, etc. are precluded from exploitation or use.[24] There is an exception, however: mining claims that were in existence inside a plot of land that was later placed in a "wilderness" category, were "grandfathered;" i.e. those claims would remain in full force and effect irrespective of their location inside the wilderness area. However, new mining claims were precluded. The land was, and is, off limits.[25]

In those relatively early days, conservation was not a new word, and it wasn't a new thought either. In the name of conservation, Yellowstone national park, set aside in 1872, became the first of what are today 364 National parks, monuments, or reserves—far more than most people realize. Oddly enough, it was Yellowstone National Park that provided the impetus

[24]-National Park System, Sierra Club booklet, May, 1991, 2nd edition.

[25]-There are some instances where "grandfathered" claims have been challenged, where access to the site is either prevented or impeded. Two such cases exist in the Anza National Forest.

for the legislation that was the foundation of today's public lands. Section 24 of the 1891 Act allowed the head of the camel to enter the tent; the entire camel was soon to follow.

Presidents since Teddy Roosevelt have set aside public land by their personal edict and without further authority from Congress. President Carter did so as well in the only place Public Domain remained of any consequence—Alaska. Today, Alaskans are still bitter over this huge reserve established by a single decree of President Jimmy Carter. Alaskans were upset. They still are! Among other things, their bitterness is over the proposal by the federal government that any new oil royalties will be shared on a 50 percent-50 percent basis rather than the present 90 percent-10 percent basis. The oil is under Forest Reserve land. Not surprising; the composition of Alaska land is as follows: 59 percent federal, 28 percent state (which came from the federal lands as a trust for education), 12 percent Alaskan native, leaving 1 percent in private ownership. They were upset enough to circulate a referendum in the late 1980s to secede from the Union. There were insufficient signatures to place the measure on the ballot. The unrest is still there and its core theme is states rights versus federal rights. Governor Walter J. Hickel took the problem to Washington D.C. and filed a claim for 29 billion dollars for, in essence, breach of contract of the Alaskan Enabling Act, which breach, he claims, prevents Alaska from developing its natural resources. He has proposed turning over the federal land in Alaska to the state. Further, even he has voiced secession. Today these reserves, along with the other set-aside land, constitute a third of the nation.

One could surely ask how an act such as the Forest Reserve Act of 1891, whose constitutionality must surely have crossed more than one congressman's or senator's mind, could have been passed. If the issue of constitutionality was brought up, little has been said about it. The paramount issue, therefore, must have been the simple need, in their minds, for preservative legislation. From a historical point of view, the Forest Reserve Act of 1891 was the culmination of a mounting concern for the preservation and wise *use* of the nation's natural resources as well as the *preservation in perpetuity* of natural, scenic wonders such as Yosemite and Yellowstone. This concern was voiced and debated across the nation. The media for this debate were a number of magazines, such as **Atlantic Monthly, North American Review, Review of Reviews, Yale Review** and a number of others. The West was captivating to the Easterner; he could enjoy its adventure and grandeur vicariously. The mystique of the West was captivating. Artists such as Remington and Russell gave spice and verve to this presentation of the West with their illustrations and art. Conservationists such as John Muir presented their verbal picture as well; all appeared in these and other early magazines, tabloids and journals.

EXPANSION TO THE WEST: RUNNING OUT OF LAND, OR SO THEY THOUGHT

Another factor was quietly increasing in importance: the expansion to the West itself. And the census reports every ten years reflected this movement—ever westward. In each census report the Western frontier was traced as though it were a waterline of a rising tide. Its line moved inexorably westward, leaving the reader with the impression or certain knowledge that land was running out. The census reports even included maps indicating the uninhabited land of the United States and its territories. Writers such as Henry George, Thomas Donaldson, Thomas Gill, Josiah Strong, Owen Wister, Frederick Jackson Turner, Francis A. Walker and many others, each in his own way, sounded the alarm—not always the same to each of them. As they saw it, land was definitely running out. Some even spoke of the need to annex Canada; others simply lamented the dwindling supply of additional land for a population that was still bulging with immigrants; a few even espoused an expansionist agenda to ensure a supply of land for the future.[26] The U.S. population was, indeed, exploding. The 1870 census marked a population of 39 million. By 1890 that figure had ballooned to 63 million—a 62 percent increase in population in just 20 years. In what later was declared to be erroneous, Thomas Donaldson, a member of the newly formed Public Land Commission, and, as such, a vocal voice directed close at hand toward the Congress, declared in the supplementary edition of the census in 1884 that only five million acres of agricultural lands remained in public ownership.[27]

Such misstatements were compounded by claims that loggers "simply burned over twenty-five million acres of forest each year and managed to cut four-fifths of it in less than a century."[28] The message was plain: Waste! It is quite likely that figures used were for effect rather than fact:[29] More important and compounding, the 1890 census no longer featured a frontier line of settlement; a line no longer existed because of the

---

26-*The End Of American Exceptionalism*, David M. Wrobel, (University Press of Kansas, 1993), Parts 1, 2, and 3.

27-Ibid.

28-Ibid., p. 45

29-Twenty-five million acres burned every year is a rather preposterous number to swallow: A million acres is a plot of land 30 miles by 52 miles.

bodies of the broken up lines of population. Officially, this fact of omission marked the end of the frontier. To most, this was the signal marking the end of settlement on public lands. Moreover, it marked the beginning of a perceived need for saving and conserving the land that was left. The fact that there still remained a great deal of it is simply incidental. This they never knew. Little heeded, read or heard were the words of John B. Weber, United States Commissioner of Immigrations, and Charles S. Smith, president of the New York Chamber of Commerce, that the nation's resources had "hardly been touched," and that "the point of exhaustion" had "certainly...not been approached."[30] Incongruous as it may seem in light of the above, Indian reservation land was taken back and opened up for settlement. The famous Oklahoma land rush into reclaimed Indian land in 1893 was the result. Back-filling was taking place. According to the Census Bureau reports, the westerly expansion had reached the Pacific Ocean. The westward expansion was over. It was a fait accompli.

This was the stage-setting for the pivotal Forest Reserve Act of 1891. Something had to be done about waste and abuse and Congress was ready to do just that. The Westerner didn't have a chance, for the East was the center of communications, commerce and commitment. Further, the population centers were concentrated in the northeastern states, giving numerical superiority in the House of Representatives to those manufacturing-oriented states. For most representatives, their understanding and judgments were based upon what they read or heard. And it was romanticized or negatively exaggerated! But part of it was real. By 1891 the mind-set was reasonably firm: Waste and abuse had to be stopped. Commitment to this end was a reasonably foregone conclusion. The nearly sole voice of John Wesley Powell was not enough to sway the East and Congress; supposed waste must be stopped; natural resources must be preserved and husbanded; land must be retained. After all, they were told, there was very little left!

Conservation of scenic wonders had already taken place. Yosemite and Yellowstone had been set aside as National parks. The precedent had been set; land could be set aside as a national objective. To my knowledge, the constitutionality of such an act was never raised. Congress simply must have assumed that the power was theirs. Congress must have thought, Why not set aside additional resource land for national preservation? After all, they must have reasoned, it is being decimated, abused and wasted—and parts of it were—by an irresponsible westerner who to them was a cowboy embodied in a Remington illustration; a visitor to fashionable New York such as "Baby Doe" accompanied by Horace Tabor, who were lavishly

30-Ibid., p. 51

spending their wealth from their Matchless Mine in Leadville, Colorado; visits to the East by such western tycoons as Crocker, Stanford, Huntington and Hopkins. Even "Buffalo Bill" Cody and his "Wild West" show were instrumental in portraying the image of the West as rough and tumble, barely subdued and slightly more than scarcely civilized. To most easterners—and surely to Congress—the West was a land of opportunity just passed. It was now time to look at this West in a new light and to save it from itself.

The fact that very few of those that passed the Act of 1891 ever saw the West is just incidental.

It has not been my intent to leave out the effect that the treatment of the American Indians had upon the West. It has been profound. However, suffice it to say, this effect is so vast that it cannot be touched upon in any other manner than in very general terms in this review and very brief history of our public lands. In short, the American Indians possessed the land. It was taken away from them by a culture that was 1000 years more advanced than theirs. They were overrun and their land was simply confiscated. In reality, the land became the spoils that went to the victor in this overrunning or ongoing war with the Indians. The culture, as "advanced" as it was supposed to be, was ruthless, crafty, dishonest and warlike at its worst and apologetic, remorseful and sorrowful at its best—in general, the former attitude prior to the confiscation of the land and the latter attitude years and years after the "taking" was a fact. "Taking" is a word I shall deal with later. In a strict sense, "taking," as used here, is not quite accurate with respect to Indian land. "Taking," as used later, is confiscation without compensation *without* use of force. The Indian land was taken *with* the use of force: an act of war. In the intervening years the American Indians' tales of suffering fell on deaf ears—they were, after all, very little, if any, different from savages in the minds of too many Americans. To term their treatment as brutal would be flattery. Famous men such as Custer and Kit Carson were deeply involved as well in their participation in mindless, inhuman brutality. Custer's first "Battle of the Washita" is little known. It could better be called a massacre first clouded by Custer's deceit and trickery; the outcome was foregone: Annihilation of 112 in all, of which only 10 were warriors. The rest were women and children. Later, the annihilation of Custer's forces at the Little Big Horn, and still later the Massacre at Wounded Knee all had a common denominator: The Seventh Cavalry—Custer's outfit!

Kit Carson, a dutiful colonel, was a participant in the literal herding of Navajo Indians from Arizona to Texas in the depth of winter. [I draw no distinction between the Navajo and the Apache, in that the two tribes were culturally very, very close.] The deaths along the way were staggering.[31] Efforts toward justice, fairness and equity were there, but communications were at best very difficult; information was easily twisted by fear-driven settlers or the army personnel stationed in the various forts to protect these same settlers from these savages. Military personnel of those days were far from sterling, and some of their motives were just as suspect. It was a dark era—not a proud one—and it wasn't until relatively recently that Congress enacted legislation that compensated the American Indians for this "taking"—meager though it was. Nonetheless, it was a gesture. As we shall see later, this same benevolence was not to be extended to the possessor of private property and its accompanying rights on public lands. Instead, efforts would be made by federal bureaus to interpret these rights as cancelable and non-compensable. In other words, confiscation *without* compensation. Later for this. The American Indian did start a precedent, however. He does possess Indian Reservation land that is, for the sake of comparison, included in the tables that follow.

PUBLIC (FEDERAL) LAND MANAGED BY THE FEDERAL GOVERNMENT

Today the public (federal) and Indian reservation lands are managed by the following agencies, bureaus or departments:

AGENCY OR BUREAU	PERCENT OF FED. LAND MANAGED	PERCENT OF U.S.
Bureau of Land Management	43 percent	1 4 percent
Forest Service	25 percent	8 percent
Fish & Wild Life Service	12 percent	4 percent
National Parks	10 percent	3 . 3 percent
Bureau of Indian Affairs	7 percent	2 percent
Department of Defense	3 percent	1 percent

PUBLIC (FEDERAL) LAND OF THE WEST: PERCENT OF EACH STATE

The massive bulk of this federal land under the control of the above agencies or bureaus is borne by the western states and Alaska almost in its

31-*The Memoirs Of Chief Red Fox*, Chief Red Fox.

entirety. The following table indicates the amount of public (federal) land (including Indian reservations) in each of these states today:

STATE	ESTIMATED PERCENTAGE OF FEDERAL & INDIAN RES. LAND
Nevada	86 percent
Utah	75 percent
Oregon	75 percent
Idaho	75 percent
Alaska	71 percent
Wyoming	65 percent
New Mexico	60 percent
California	55 percent
Colorado	50 percent
Arizona	45 percent
Montana	45 percent
Washington	40 percent

Source: National Geographic Society.

Alaska is quite unique; as pointed out earlier, only 1 percent of its land is in private ownership. 28 percent, not shown in the table above, is state of Alaska Educational Trust land and is available for homestead—40 acres of non-agricultural land and 160 acres of agricultural land per individual homestead. This land was granted to the State of Alaska by the federal government for the purpose of providing funds for educational purposes. Problem: The lack of roads in Alaska makes most of the land inaccessible.[32]

A referral to the map enclosed shows graphically where all or most of the public (federal) lands are today—in the eleven western states plus Alaska where the average of public (federal) lands is approximately 60 percent of the total land. Note that there are even some states that show *no* public (federal) lands. This is an obvious and substantial disparity, which fact alone gives rise to a claim of inequality with the original thirteen colonies. This is discussed at length in Part Two. One could surely ask, "Who is the better steward?"

32-Source: *The Alaska Almanac*, 16th edition.

TEXAS: A STATE IN CONTRAST

Texas, as an additional state admitted to the Union, is an interesting story in contrast. Texas, when it became a part of the United States, was just as sparsely populated as others in the West; its land in western Texas was very nearly just as arid as that to the west, yet it came into the Union with *none* of its land reverting to federal ownership. How did that happen? Oversimplified, wily Sam Houston had formed an independent "country" and it was this "country" that was admitted to the Union by treaty! As a separate country, the vast stretches of unsettled land were not parsimoniously dished out in 320, 160 or 40 acre plots as territorial land was elsewhere, but in huge parcels encompassing hundreds of square miles. For all practical purposes, Texas, as we know it today, came into the Union without giving up any land to the federal government.[33] In fact, Sam Houston expressly demanded that. As a condition of Texas becoming a state, no land in Texas would become federal Land.[34] Texas is privately owned today. One may well wonder just how Texas would look today if it had been admitted to the Union by way of an Enabling Act used for admission of the other 12 Western States. This makes for interesting conjecture. In Part Two, the details of how all of this took place is discussed in the section entitled, THE ANNEXATION OF TEXAS: CONGRESSIONAL INTENT FOR THE PUBLIC LAND.

In any event, federal management of these set aside National Forest Reserve Lands after 1897, was the accepted way of life. Now to manage them better!

MANAGEMENT OF THE WESTERN LAND

In 1905, the Forest Service came into being about the same time as the war between the sheep-men and cattlemen of Wyoming—a war basically over who had prior preemptive rights to the water and thus the land. Prior to that date the Department of Interior or the Department of Agriculture simply operated or handled the Forest Reserve Lands. And "handle" them they did. In 1894, after the Forest Reserves had been turned over to them

33-Texas did deed over a strip of land extending northwesterly. This was disputed land being also claimed by Mexico.

34-Texas does have a relatively small amount of federal land today: Big Bend National Park and four small National Forests, all of which total probably less than one percent of its total land

from the Department of Interior, the Department of Agriculture issued its first official statement of administrative policy on the Forest Reserve land (now a huge percentage of the entire country): a total halt to all grazing! Appropriated water rights and preemptive rights to the *use* of land whose legality had, according to some, come down from ancient Roman law all be damned! The new policy prohibited the "...driving, feeding, grazing, pasturing or herding of cattle, sheep, or other livestock."[35] To the rancher, this was no nail in the coffin, it was a spike! The use of the land would now come as a result of permits issued by the federal government via its bureaus. This was, in fact, a bold departure from the "old ways." Even the Department of Agriculture agreed with this definition:

> "This action flew in the face of accepted ideas regarding the functions of the federal government. It involved a reversal of the course which had been pursued with relation to the Public Domain from the foundation of the Union. It conflicted with the whole American tradition of individualism and preference for private property ownership."[36]

In just over 100 years, nothing has been brought before the Supreme Court to clear up this conflict of interest. Buford v. Houtz remains the Supreme Court's decision on the issue of appropriation and preemptive rights, but this case does not address the issue of the **right to use land or not use land** by virtue of **water rights**. Some claim that this use of the land had become a prescriptive right and was not cancelable without compensation by the implementation of the Taylor Grazing Rights in 1934 and their accompanying permit issuance for use. Prescriptive rights to use the land were authenticated by the Supreme Court. This use was private property—it was an asset. The problematic crux of the issue was raised later when those who had been, historically, using the land (and had been using its water for beneficial use—another tie-in) were issued a grazing permit in recognition of their prior existing rights on the land. Did the grazing permit completely take the place of the prior right? In other words, did the user of the land forego his claim or right to his usage by accepting the grazing permit? Did he give up his private property—which was his use—when he accepted the grazing permit? What was to happen when his grazing permit was altered or canceled? Would he be compensated for the "taking" in conformance with the 5th Amendment to the Constitution? These questions are still largely unresolved. The issue is still there.

35-U.S. Department of Agriculture, Division of Forestry Bulletin no. 15, page 10.

36-*National Plan For American Forestry*, U.S. Department of Agriculture, Washington, D.C., 1933, p. 746.

1907 brought still more change. This time it was semantic. What had been referred to in the past as Public Domain with all the lands' past usage-history of "open to the public for their **use and settlement**" were now to be called National Forests and withdrawn from settlement and its use strictly controlled. It seems like such a little thing! But, as it turned out, it was not that simple. The implication was clear and later to be taken as hardened concrete: These lands were to remain under federal control and— as it has turned out—in perpetuity. federal ownership was never relinquished even though state jurisdiction was present after statehood. Was this by intent or did it just happen? It doesn't make any difference. The mind-set was to gradually shift more and more to ownership forever as a national treasure and not to provide for use other than that which was clearly defined by one or more of the later-to-become-powerful bureaus.

And Congress went along with this too: They agreed. In 1915 Congress passed the Term Permit Act, giving the Forest Service a broad definition of its authority. The fact that the Forest Service is trying to exceed that authority today is simply incidental.[37]

If Congress had stopped there the problem might just not be as great as it is today, but they have gone on and on. These national lands are clearly national in mind-set today on the part of not only Congress but all of the so-called conservation and environmental concern groups who are today accused by some of being mindlessly myopic with little or no peripheral vision. Strong words!

THE TAYLOR GRAZING ACT OF 1934

The Taylor Grazing Act of 1934 was and is pivotal. This act provided that the federal government would now, by permit, allow those ranchers with prior-use rights the use of the remaining non-forest Public Domain. Those who qualified would be issued grazing permits. Those grazing rights were to become private property. They could be secured only by the owner of adjacent or nearby private (range) land. They were then and are now

37-Current Term Special Use Permits for cabins on Forest Service land (there are 16,000 of them), include authority for actions not included in this 1915 Act—namely the establishment of a Forest Plan after public input. However, when push comes to shove, there is nothing that precludes the Forest Service from doing whatever it pleases. The language is palliative, not compelling. The result: Unilateral authority is still with the local Forest Ranger to determine the continued use of private property interests, improvements or structures on National Forest land.

bought and sold, encumbered and transferred: They were and are private property. Grazing permits or rights were treated like all other private property, which when impinged, interfered with, abrogated or restricted, ***except for environmental reasons to protect the land***, compensation for such interference, restrictive action or "taking" was lawfully due under the provisions of the 5th Amendment. Or so the recipients thought.

In the early 1930's ranchers felt they had an ownership interest in the range. Efforts by the Hoover administration to privatize the western rangelands (not to be confused with Forest Reserve land) failed. These lands would remain under federal control. Prior appropriation doctrine had been upheld as had the states' sovereignty of forest land.[38] On the other hand, courts did uphold the federal government's right to regulate.[39] The result was the recognition of the split estate: Ownership of land by the federal government on the one hand and ownership of the right to use the same land by private parties on the other.

The rancher still wanted title to the land he had been using. Even at this seemingly late date, he still thought that he would eventually get it, too. After all, the rest of the Public Domain had been disposed of at a fair price to those who had been using it. Why should he expect to be treated any differently? He didn't!

On the other side of this same coin was the thought by the now growing power centers of the federal bureaucracy: Could there ever be a legal preemptive right of ownership claimed on any part of these vast stretches of land? Was the prior appropriation doctrine going to effectively splinter the Public Lands and the Forest Reserves? These were the problems facing the now burgeoning bureaus of the federal government as well as the federal centrists. Certainly, control and regulation by these same bureaus was an issue. If the Supreme Court should rule that preemptive right claims were valid and that a "Taking" had occurred—and that likelihood was real— damage claims against the federal government could be enormous and similar in effect to that which was later to be successfully argued—and collected—by the various Indian tribes.

How could they get around it?

38-Kansas v. Colorado, 206 U.S. 46 (1906)

39-Light v. United States, 220 U.S. 523; 55 L.Ed. 570; 31 Sup. Ct. Rep. 485 (1911) and Shannon v. United States, 160 F, 870 (9th Cir. 1908)

THE "TAKING" ISSUE AND THE 5TH AMENDMENT

Without some change, "taking" could be compensable—this time potentially on a grand scale. The original intentions of the Taylor Grazing Act may have been varied—to forestall a "taking" issue, charge for the use of this free land or some other intention—but however it may have been, in 1934 this act was enacted. The Taylor Grazing Act did cloud the "taking" issue, it did charge for the use of the land, it did put an end to any *future* preemptive challenges to the use of the land by virtue of water rights alone. How? The act granted permits for use of the public (federal) rangelands. It should be noted that these permits were well defined as to the limit of usage, the number of cattle or sheep per acre as well as protective clauses for damage to the land. And probably most important of all, they could be changed at the will of the government. These changes—and many have taken place—are arguably a form of *taking*. Most important to the rancher at the time was a palliative clause in the Taylor Grazing Act that preemptive rights would eventually be given recognition. Or so he thought. These preemptive rights were his. The term, "*final disposition*," was used.[40] And of course, to the rancher, this "final disposition" meant that he would get to buy the land. It would be his! Wrong again. The federal bureaus that administrated these grazing rights would later claim, vociferously, that another phrase in The Taylor Grazing Act was restrictive and limiting, to wit;

> "...shall not create any right, title, interest, or estate in or to the lands."

To the bureau this phrase literally meant that the rancher had no right, title, interest, or estate in or to the land. This phrase, however, is somewhat taken out of context. This latter statement is in reference to the establishment of a *grazing district* or the *issuance* of a permit. If the land had been used prior to the issuance of a grazing permit, the rancher could, and did, claim that the phrase "final disposition" was an indication of Congressional intent—and it probably was—regarding his eventual owner-ship of this land that he had already been using. But moods swing.

There was a catch. The Taylor Grazing Rights and Forest Grazing Permits are issued on an annual basis even though some are renewable, annually, for a longer period of time. This "catch" was to prove critical later

---

40-The opening words of Section 1 of the Taylor Grazing Act: "That in order to promote the highest use of the public lands *pending its final disposal*, the Secretary of the Interior is authorized, in his discretion..."—(Emphasis added)

when cancellation of the permit was to occur—and it did. There was no compensation for the "taking."

In the arid west, it is axiomatic that if one does not have water, or access to it, he cannot effectively use the land—if at all. Water was and is the controlling factor thus making water-rights on public land in the west of the utmost importance.

Not many years ago, the Bureau of Land Management, as best I can determine, on their own, implemented a change in their permit procedure. Permits for upgrading existing water sources and the development of new water sources were to include a provision whereby the water on the permitted land was to be applied for by the permittee and the federal government on a 50 percent basis. This has "taking" written all over it. The rancher who must have the use of the land to survive will lose the water when and if his permit is not renewed for some reason. Was there an ulterior motive? The rancher surely thinks so. In a not-too-well disguised way, this is coercion: If you want to use the land, you have to include us in the water right. If a program of this kind went unchecked, it could eventually give the federal government complete autonomous control of the public lands within a state. Private property on the public land would no longer exist as far as the rancher was concerned.

However, in this instance, the federal government was thwarted—at least in Nevada. During the legislative session of 1997, Nevada passed a law that defined the meaning of "beneficial use" of the water—the ingredient that qualifies one for a water-right on the public land under state of Nevada law. In their definition they precluded the federal government from qualifying as a "beneficial user." But it didn't end there. The Attorney General for the state of Nevada redefined the meaning of the intent of the law and stated in an opinion that the law only pertained to BLM land—leaving the Forest Service land outside of the definition.

The Forest Service is involved as well as the BLM in a plan to control water on the public lands. The following information came as a result of a Freedom of Information Request (FOIA). As a result of that request from the Elko County Task Force in a letter dated April 18, 1995, the Forest Service responded that in the Toiyabe National Forest alone, that agency had filed on 624 water sources, of which 390 were for stock water.

In the case of U.S. v. the State of New Mexico (1978),[41] Justice Rehnquist, in writing the opinion of the court, said,

41-U.S. v. The State of New Mexico (1978), 438 US 696.

"The United States contends that, since Congress clearly foresaw stock watering on National Forests, reserved rights [to water to the United States] must be recognized for this purpose. New Mexico Courts disagreed and held that any stock watering rights must be allocated under State Law to individual stock waterers. We agree."

Continuing, he adds,

"The District Court concluded that...any water rights arising from cattle grazing by permittees on the forest should be adjudicated 'to the permittee under the law of prior appropriation and not to the United States.'"

It is interesting to note that at no time during the history of the public land has Congress directed either the Forest Service or the Bureau of Land Management to acquire stock water rights. Here we see both agencies doing exactly that independently on their own, long after Justice Rehnquist's opinion in U.S. v. the State of New Mexico in 1978 confirmed that water rights are to be held under state law by stock waterers—the permittee.

As is usually the case, very little is overwhelmingly one-sided. Even in that time, well over one hundred years ago, one side wanted this Public Domain land to be federal land and as such, to be under the control of the federal government in perpetuity, while the other wanted it to be developed and used with less restriction placed upon the imaginative, inventive resourcefulness of human effort. With so much land under federal control (and/or de facto ownership) in the West, many a county has been hard pressed to meet its minimal financial obligations, many of which are federally mandated. Mono County in California is an interesting case in point. The private land in Mono County is not quite ten percent of the total land, yet the county is larger than the state of Rhode Island with a population of about 10,000 people. That is a mighty big parcel of land which does not contribute to the sustenance of its occupants. It is off the tax roles; federal lands are not taxable—a provision in all of the Enabling Acts for admission to the Union. Further, its economic growth—its ability to create jobs—is hampered by federal control that is unwilling to pass this land into private ownership for growth and development. Federal land within the National Forests can only be acquired for private ownership or development by exchanging it for another parcel of land the government wants or needs. This situation is fraught with problems that are simply too numerous to count. The exchange process can take many years; land values are distorted by a short supply occasioned by monopolistic, federal ownership. Revolutions have been fought over issues no more complex than this alone! In some cases the exchange process has been known to take over 10 years to accomplish. Moreover, there is no real desire on the part of any bureau to privatize the land under its control. To the contrary, history has demonstrated that these bureaus want more, not less land to control.

THE BACKGROUND OF THE TAYLOR GRAZING ACT

The Taylor Grazing Act of 1934 is so pivotal that it requires greater explanation and exposure. This act was written by the Department of Interior and given to Congressman Taylor of Colorado to propose for enactment.[42]

This act was really the culmination of efforts that began in 1878 when the first bill, very much like the Taylor Grazing Act, was drafted and introduced by the Interior Department to regulate grazing on the Public Domain land.[43] Passage of the Taylor Grazing Act took many years, but it finally occurred in 1934; grazing was to be regulated on the remaining Public Domain land. Grazing was already regulated by this time on Forest Reserve land. Its passage was not easy, earlier attempts had failed, but this time it was really an act of coercion that turned the tide. Secretary Ickes let it be known to Congress that President Roosevelt already had the power to withdraw any and all of the Public Domain from entry and set up grazing districts without any further legislation. The fact that the livestock men had already, on their own, set up grazing districts was just incidental to Ickes; he wanted to be in control. The president's authority, he claimed, came from the Act of 1910 (36 Stat. 847). Also, he claimed, court cases (Caha v. U.S.; 152 U.S. 211 and Roughton v. Knight; 219 U.S. 537) would uphold such a withdrawal.[44] There was little doubt in any congressman's or senator's mind that such a withdrawal by the president, ostensibly authorized by this Act of 1910, would be upheld by the Supreme Court. A valiant fight was put up by western senators and congressmen—and even the governor of Wyoming. The most caustic—and truthful—remarks were reserved to Congressman Vince Carter from Wyoming:

"The title [to this bill] should read: 'A bill to take away from the livestock industry of the west the free use of 173,000,000 acres

---

42-*Golden Fleece In Nevada*, Clel Georgetta, p. 207.

43-Ibid., p. 202, p. 211.

44-Ibid., p. 225.

of Public Domain, abolish the 640 acre homestead and desert entry laws, and retard the political and economic growth of the west.'"[45]

The act finally passed, largely intact, and—most important of all to the Department of Interior—it contained, without limitation, the provision for the Department of Interior to make any and all rules and regulations with respect to the use of the Public Domain—henceforth to be known as federal land—that was to be under their exclusive control. The following excerpt from the Taylor Grazing Act is most noteworthy:

"Preference shall be given in the issuance of grazing permits to those within or near a district who are landowners engaged in the livestock business, bona fide occupants, or settlers, or owners of water or water rights as may be necessary to permit the proper use of lands, owned, occupied or leased by them..."

This statement was added as an amendment! It was not a part of the original draft of the bill prepared by the Department of Interior![46] Without prodding, the Department of Interior had no intention of recognizing any prior appropriation or use of the land. As Judge Clel Georgetta put it, "grab" was the action word! Further, the first draft of the bill was to take in all the Public Domain—about 173,000,000 acres. By amendment, this was reduced to 80,000,000 acres. This limitation was finally removed completely in 1954. As of June 1966, the Bureau of Land Management (the bureau under the Department of Interior) controlled 175,003,898 acres in the lower 48 states plus another 282,008,300 acres in Alaska.[47] Another clause in the Taylor Grazing Act provides the Secretary of Interior the authority to designate suitable lands for homesteads. Other than the provision for plots of two and one-half acres relatively close to population centers, no real amount of this federal land has been made available for "settlement" as provided for in the Homestead Act.

"The Taylor Grazing Act dealt the first blow which has eventually spelled the death of the Homestead Act, and all the other land laws by which Public Domain passed into private ownership, and reached the tax rolls of the states."[48]

Originally, there was a safeguard that was contained in earlier bills and, as such, was contained in the first draft of the Taylor Grazing Act. This

45-Ibid., p. 214.

46-Ibid., p. 227.

47-Ibid., p. 239.

48-Ibid., p. 240.

was called section thirteen and it provided that the act would not become effective in any state until 60 days after the state legislature had accepted its operation. This provision was deleted from the enacted bill. The states were outside of the loop!

All told, the Taylor Grazing Act was a compromise. President Roosevelt, according to Ikes, was prepared to withdraw all the Public Domain in any **event**. Those senators and congressmen who opposed the bill finally gave in. They believed it would be better to have a law with some limitations in it rather than a blanket withdrawal of all the Public Domain without any Congressional input. As it turned out, they might just as well have saved their breath or effort, for the Department of Interior paid little attention to the safeguards that were included in the bill.[49]

F. R. Carpenter, U.S. Director of Grazing in 1935, said:

> "The Act was passed on an unsuspecting West. Just how it got by is one of those miracles of legislation."

He was not gloating. He sympathized with the livestock men and had this to say:

> "I am of the philosophy that the quicker land is put under private ownership, the better off the state **to which it belongs** will be. I am in favor of turning the government land over to the states and thence to the citizens as rapidly as possible."[50]
> (Emphasis added)

Prior to the Taylor Grazing Act or the Forest Reserve Act of 1891, the anti-fencing law on Forest Reserve Land enacted in 1885 created havoc by encouraging common use of these free lands by all comers—not just by those who had homesteads on adjacent land and water rights on the public (now called federal) lands. The grazing rights stopped this too. Fences are common today. Many different grazing areas are fenced off one from the other.

49-Ibid., p. 224.

50-Ibid., p. 234

THE RIGHT TO GOVERN SUPPORTED BY SUPREME COURT DECISIONS[51]

The issue is still largely unresolved as to prior to 1891 water rights and the collaterally implied land use that went with it. The federal bureaus claim that no such right to use the land exists by virtue of water rights or water usage, and they cite one or more of the cases that are listed below as their authority to deny any compensation when this usage is altered or terminated. In other words, the federal bureau's position is that there is no connection, implied or otherwise, between water rights (usage) and land usage; that there is no ongoing right to use the land for grazing purposes even though the water rights do not belong to the federal government; that any right to use the land is subject wholly to the unilateral determination of the bureau; that no compensation is due for the termination, modification, reduction or change of use of the land, at the whole discretion of the bureau. Why? Because the permits now all contain the following clause that is taken from the Taylor Grazing Act:

"By the terms of the [Taylor Grazing] Act, the issuance of a permit does not 'create any right, title, interest, or estate in or to the land.'"

The above quotation comes directly from United States v. Fuller (p. 495)

Why did the ranchers sign such a restrictive permit in the first place when it clearly took away an element of their private property—the right to use the land as they had been? Simple. Either sign it or give up being a rancher. They all signed!

Mollohand v. Gray, 412 F. 2d 349 (1969)
Acton v. United States, 401 F 2d 896 (1968)
United States v. Cox, 190 F. 2d 293 (1951)
Oman v. United States, 179 F. 2d 738 (1949)
Bowman v. Udall, 243 F. Supp. 672 (1965)
Placer County Water Agency v. Jonas, 275 Cal. App. 2nd 691.80 Cal.   Rptr. (1969)
Fauske v. Dean, 101 N.W. 2d 769. (1960)
United States v. Fuller, 409 U.S. 488 (1973)

51-Part II deals with the limits of these decisions and how they have been interpreted to mean what is not there.

In general, these cases deny compensation for the cancellation of grazing permits, holding, generally, that an annual permit, when not renewed, has no compensable value regardless of how many years it has been used or to what extent it impinges privately owned property (ranches) to which, in reality, it is attached.

It should be noted that the court was not entirely one-sided on the issue. In the case of United States v. Fuller, the court was split 5 to 4. The dissenting opinion is worth reading in that it questions the federal government's power to put its land to another use without paying for the damages this change in use creates. Of equal importance, this dissenting opinion points out clearly that permitted grazing land does impact and is a part of the value of the fee property to which it is attached: Take away the permitted grazing land and you will have taken value away from the fee property itself.

It is interesting to note that none of these cases deal with ***preemptive water rights*** as an underlying right to use the land, nor, for that matter, do they even mention the private property of water rights that were confiscated, such water rights having their basis prior to 1891 and having been successively transferred and handed down to following generations of owners. These water rights are on most of the rangelands in use today. Further, these cases do not refer in any way to ***proof*** of "beneficial use" of the water; there is no discussion of the prior appropriation doctrine or, for that matter, any vested or accrued rights under existing law validly affecting the public land. In fact, to my knowledge, no demand was made in any of these cases for the "taking" of the water rights on these same lands—and I am sure those water rights were there.[52]

EARLY EFFORTS TO PRIVATIZE THE PUBLIC LAND

Centralization of authority and power was well under way, and Washington's powerful bureaus were growing right with it; they would now

---

[52] It is interesting conjecture to note in the case of Placer County Water Agency v. Jonas a recital on page 697 refers to Seaboard Air Lines R.R. Co. v. County of Crisp of the State of Georgia. in which the following is stated:

"The court held that the license granted to a county by the federal Power Commission to build a dam made the county liable for damages to property rights **held under state law**." (Emphasis added)

Water rights *are* under state law. It would appear that a critical element of the damages was omitted by the plaintive.

be the controllers of all public (federal) lands, which, before long, would come to be considered as national land. Privatizing this land would never have its seeds of possibility sown in any of these powerful bureaus. Outside of these bureaus privatization has crossed the mind of many a person as desirable. James Watt, former Secretary of the Interior, was only one of these. Few know it, but President Herbert Hoover was another. A commission he formed recommended that all remaining Public Domain be officially turned over to the states in which it was located.[53] The report also recommended that all major decisions of the agencies should be subject to judicial review. Laws were even proposed for this purpose. They all died for lack of enough support. Or, as Judge Clel Georgetta points out, enough lobbying or pressure was applied by the Department of Interior, the department whose land was to be virtually eliminated, to kill the bills. In reading over the record of testimony relative to the Taylor Grazing Act, this "pressure" focused largely upon the lack of need for any bills to insure that the Public Domain remained intact, unchanged in nature and still available for settlement. At one point, Secretary of Interior Ickes testified,

> "It should first be borne in mind, however, that in this bill, if passed, ***it makes no disposition of the Public Domain. It merely regulates a use to which it is now being put***. A cession to the states of these lands would require a congressional act, and there is nothing in the provisions of this bill which would preclude or embarrass such action by Congress if and when it deems it desirable." (Emphasis added)

A rather remarkable palliative. As finally written, the Taylor Grazing Act left it up to the sole determination of the Secretary of Interior as to what was or was not going to be "available for settlement." It would be fair to say that this has not been done. The land is held in "perpetuity," so to speak.

The Taylor Grazing Act gave the Department of Interior the right and power to regulate grazing of livestock; it had been managing nearly everything else without any real authority.[54]

53-One section of the Hoover Commission report states:

"The transfer of the public lands to the states would mean that each state would be charged with the solid obligation of conserving and using the range. The experiences of the public-land states in dealing with the large areas now owned by those states, and suitable for range, show that in many instances this administration has been effective and salutary."

54-*Golden Fleece In Nevada*, Clel Georgetta, p. 249

In the eyes of the Department of Interior, the Taylor Grazing Act did not go far enough in establishing permanent control over the Public Domain. It took a number of years—until 1964 to be exact—for Congress to pass more far-reaching acts that directly affected the federal lands: The Multiple Use Act, The Public Sales Act and the Public Land Law Review Commission Act. These acts would fill in the chinks.

The Multiple Use Act sounds reasonable enough. It gave the Secretary of Interior the authority as follows:

> "...to classify certain lands...in order to provide for their ***disposal of interim management*** under principles of multiple use and to produce a sustained yield of products and services, and for *other purposes.*" (Emphasis added)

Further, it had a time limit—a sort of lets-see-how-it-works limit. That time limit was until 1969. But it could be extended. And it has been...for 30 years!

The term "classify" is general. Classify for what? How? Classify for sale or "multiple use?" As we have seen, nothing of any consequence has been classified for sale. Classified for "multiple use" is another story. Georgetta puts it succinctly:

> "The Secretary of Interior and his Bureau of Land Management contend that when land is 'withdrawn' for 'retention in Federal ownership' for 'multiple use' that is 'permanent'."[55]

This act removed all the safety provisions that had been put in the Taylor Grazing Act, (few as they were), that had been hard fought for by the westerners. While the act seems to provide protection in the first part of Section 7, what it went on to say was that this protection was valid until such time as the Secretary of Interior took any action to the contrary. Sub-section (b) went even further. In effect it said that the land laws passed by Congress would be effective until the Secretary of Interior repealed them by with-drawing the Public Domain for "Multiple Use."[56] So far, over 154,400,000 acres have been withdrawn for "Multiple Use."

55-Ibid., p. 242.7,

56-Ibid., p. 243.

THE PUBLIC SALES ACT OF 1964 AND THE PUBLIC LAND LAW REVIEW COMMISSION

The Public Sales Act of 1964 gives the Secretary of Interior the authority to sell land he has classified as required for orderly growth and development of a community; again, a discretionary authority.

The Public Land Law Review Commission Act set up a commission to make recommendations. The commission was composed of largely "federalist" persuasion—vixen to look after the hen house, and their recommendation reflected this viewpoint. Their report in 1970 stated the following:

"...no additional grants should be made to any of the fifty states."[57]

Some of the recommendation were pleasing to livestock men of the West. While chastising the BLM for haphazard withdrawals, it said little about what to do about it other than the following recommendation:

"[The restrictions should be] periodically reviewed and either re-justified or modified."[58]

It did recommend that some grazing land be sold into private ownership.[59] To my knowledge, that has not occurred. Recommendations are one thing, action is another, and there was no compulsion to act.

After these acts were passed, it would now be fair to say that the use of the term "federal lands" was no longer ambiguous. The nomenclature change was now completed: Public lands were to be known as federal lands. The knot had been tied firmly. All bridges to the past had been burned. That land which our founding fathers planned for eventual settlement, that land which was to become a part of a separate state, that land whose mineral content was available for exploration and use, became federal land and under the exclusive control of one bureau or another. The "grab" had been completed. Moreover, from that time on, the names "Public Domain" or "public lands" would virtually cease to exist, and in their stead the name "federal lands" would be superimposed.

57-Ibid,. Recommendation 104, p. 243.

58-Ibid., Recommendation 9, p. 56.

59-Ibid., Recommendation 42, p. 115.

Parkinson's Law and the powerful incentive to control, exercised by the bureaus, are massive deterrents to privatizing this land or, for that matter, any part thereof. Is there a need to hold such vast stretches of land in a public trust? Most environmental groups say yes. There is a genuine concern for the environment and endangered species, even though knowledge on both of these subjects seems for the most part to be somewhat embryonic.

THE 1930's AND BEYOND: THE DAWNING OF A NEW DAY

The Great Depression of the early 1930's spawned a new day in management of our public (federal) lands. New agencies and bureaus were either created or expanded to absorb the unemployed. Many acts have since been passed by Congress that impact, regulate or control the use of these public (federal) lands. The Employment Act of 1946 simply gave expansion of government agencies and bureaus a stamp of approval. In a way, it gave tenure.

Following World War II, 1946 was a year of consolidation. The General Land Office and Taylor Grazing Office were combined into one. The Bureau of Land Management would now, in that single office, control, manage and administer 14 percent of the entire United States as its sovereign.

This is a huge area of the United States. To compound the problem, it is not all contiguous. To further compound the problem, the Bureau of Land Management cannot operate under just one set of laws; there are twelve different states involved in which most of the land is located. Furthermore, even in a single state the parcels of public land are not necessarily adjacent one to the other. This tends to make different areas autonomous in their own right.

It is little known or a matter to which little or no attention is paid by the federal bureaus. A business or enterprise conducted on federal land in a state is subject first to the laws of that state (generally). And the laws of that state take precedence over the Federal Law as far as the conduct of that business is concerned. [60] Aside from this, space and distance offer a huge,

60-This is a provision of the 10th Amendment to the U.S. Constitution. However, to get around the problem of a possible conflict with or provision of state law, language is inserted into many Use Permits as follows: "In case of conflict between the terms of this permit and the terms of any document or State law...the permit terms shall control."

almost insurmountable problem of management consistency. The local "controller" is very nearly the sovereign himself. And he has the vast authority of the law behind him to back him up. The penchant to back up a subordinate is clearly there too...even if he is wrong! There are, of course, exceptions to this near-automatic back-up, but they are rare and not the rule. It would seem that the "system" itself breeds this penchant for automatic endorsement of the action of a subordinate. Sad, but true.

ADMINISTRATIVE LAW

Administrative Law, a genuine effort to offer an appeal procedure for the aggrieved, has been turned around and is used almost as often by the federal government as a tool to "beat" the aggrieved. It would seem that it is almost like a game where "winning" becomes more important than justice. There are multiple layers in the administrative process wherein each layer, on its own, "finds" its conclusion. A self-protective layer above the initial first layer is hard pressed to "find" a conflicting conclusion. It is like the sea anemone: "Tickle one of my tentacles and I will close around you in order to protect one of my own." The entire administrative law process has been described by some—with considerable accuracy—as designating the fox as the keeper of the hen house.

Only after exhausting all of the administrative law process can the aggrieved have an audience before a judge. Further, it takes time. By the time the administrative law process is exhausted, the problem is, at times, moot; it is too late to salvage or correct anything. This is a far cry from what our founding fathers had in mind.

A SENSE OF PERSPECTIVE: YESTERDAY AND TODAY

The public lands have become national lands by assumption and are used for a variety of purposes. There are, however, conflicts of interest that will prove to be clear and unmistakable later. In 1960 Congress passed the Multiple Use and the Sustained Yield Acts. Congress wanted the land to be used for more than just a few uses; Congress wanted it used for many uses. These acts not only gave rise to many uses of the public (now federal)

(60-continued)- In other words, the permittee either gives up rights he may have under state law or he does not get the Use Permit. This is a form of coercion.

land but they were also directed toward the ***protection*** of the watershed as well as wildlife. There is no question that the rancher felt, in the name of these two things, that he was the camel with too many straws, wondering if the next would be one too many.

The owner of any property who allows another the use of that property has the continuing right to protect that property from damage. For the national land, the sovereign had, has, and will continue to have the right to protect that property from damage—real or perceived. This protection can be and is extended to what flora and fauna live on the land as well—not just erosion or overgrazing.

A sense of perspective is really necessary at this point. Old photographs are a perfect way to illustrate part of it. Yosemite Valley is an ideal example. In the days of John Muir,[61] pictures of that valley show relatively few trees, but today it is almost covered with the encroachment of many, many more trees into what at one time were much larger meadows. In the not-too-distant past, National Park Service personnel selectively cut down trees that blocked the view of Yosemite Falls, the highest—if not the most spectacular—waterfall in the valley. Over time, the trees had grown to such an extent that they literally blocked the view! Yosemite is not unique. That same process of growth has been going on all over the United States. These lands have not stopped growing trees, bushes, shrubs or grasses. The change is apparent in some of those old pictures. You would scarcely recognize the hills behind Elko, Nevada, for the increased number of trees and shrubs—and this is typical of the arid West. Unfortunately, our own life span, short by comparison to longer lasting trees, bushes and shrubs, forces us, subliminally, to judge by our own "short" viewpoint; we don't see change, it all looks so much the same as it did "years" ago.

This same shortsightedness of ours is not just limited to the flora. Fauna is included as well. Much credit for the increase of fauna on these federal lands should go to the rancher. He is the one who developed the water, the seeps, the springs and drilled the countless thousands of wells on these lands so that he could fill a trough, a ditch or a pond with water for his livestock. To think that his herd or flock is the only user of that water is absurd. Wildlife, birds, as well as wild animals of many kinds, use it too. And they have flourished as well. In fact, their very presence has created a vast new problem. The multiple use doctrine established the basis, and a flood of new laws emerged to protect this man-made increase in wildlife as well as some endangered species. Not many understand that much of this increase

61-A great naturalist whose principal efforts were largely responsible for making

Yosemite a National Park

in use by wildlife is the direct result of man-made improvement of the water. And these improvements did not get there without cost; they are a part of the private property interests held by the rancher—legitimately, with precedent. They are his private property. If they are to be taken away from him, they are subject to the provision of the 5th Amendment, notwithstanding any contrary view by the different bureaus. Some claim that this "contrary view" by the different bureaus is promulgated by the Office of Management and Budget (OMB). The view of the OMB? We don't have the funds or, it will cost too much! The rebuttal? One adamant person said the government does not need money so badly that it must steal to get it and that "fair is fair."

PRESERVATION AND PROTECTION ACTS

The passage of the Wilderness Act of 1964 and the federal Land Policy and Management Act of 1976 reinforced an already mounting concern for preservation and protection. Conservation groups—the Sierra Club, the National Audubon Society, the Environmental Defense Fund, the National Center for Appropriate Technology, Friends of the Earth, the Natural Resources Defense Council, the Center for Renewable Resources and even Earth First, to name some of many—each with its own agenda, have one thing in common: Preservation and protection of our natural resources. Not a bad philosophy at all. But is there a sense of balance? Some would and could argue successfully to the contrary. Environmental groups have enormous political clout even though they probably represent less that 2 to 3 percent of the population, collectively, of the United States. Are their concerns an expression of their own singular interest to the exclusion of those of the broader population base? Some would argue this point in the affirmative. Environmental concerns have been addressed and laws passed in recent years that are for all intents and purposes a plethora of directed protective measures. A new agency of the federal government was established to oversee their administration: The Environmental Protection Agency.

Some of those laws or acts are listed below:

Wilderness Act of 1964
The federal Land Policy and Management Act of 1976
Wild Free-Roaming Horse and Burro Act of 1971
Multiple Use, Sustained Yield Act of 1964
National Forest Management Act
Endangered Species Act

Environmental Policy Act

These same laws also dictate that the Bureau of Land Management, the Forest Service, the Fish & Wildlife Service, the Army Corp of Engineers, and the Environmental Protection Agency shall enforce these laws as well— and enforce them they do. That is one of their jobs. Further, to ensure the management and direction of these directorships, the Resources Planning Act was passed. The public interests are to be taken into consideration through the process of public hearings—an opportunity for the views of the public to be heard. The law requires the hearing, but it does not require that the bureau listen! Many years ago, access to public lands were literally cut off by the Roadless Area Review (RARE I & II). Today, the BLM and the Forest Service have gates that they say allow them to better "manage" the land under their jurisdiction. They manage it all right. You can't get onto it unless you walk. The land around Sedona, Arizona is fenced; land in Mono county is gated. It would seem that an Orwellian society has developed— some are more equal than others. One person asked the simple question: If you cannot get onto the land, cannot see it, what are we saving it for? For those of us who used to roam the west fifty or more years ago, unfenced, un-gated and un-regimented, we have seen a huge change. We question if it is all necessary.

OUR ENDANGERED SPECIES: A PERSPECTIVE

It is appropriate to put into perspective what the passage of time— centuries, no less—have done to and for endangered species. The truth of the matter is that ever since Pithecanthropus Erectus stood up, species have been endangered, they have mutated or have died off—one of the three. The environment in which we live is simply in a constant state of change. Our problem is that in our life span we don't see it. We only read about it, hear about it on the radio or see a program on TV about it. To us, time is static; to us the dynamic sense of slowness of change is lost, when in reality our life span is literally nothing more than a flicker of an eyelid in time. We tend to think of it as "all there is." Wrong! One authority at the University of California at Davis estimated that 2000 different species die off every century as a result of their failure to adapt. With that sense of proportion, how realistic is it really to preserve in perpetuity some of those species that cannot adapt or compete? Further, in some cases we don't even know that they cannot!

It would appear as though a definite conflict of interest or use is being generated. On the one hand we have, for example, ranchers who have a right—a prior right—to use the land, and on the other we have laws that proclaim that this same land **shall** be the home for burros or wild horses who, in many cases, surely would not be able to survive were it not for the prior development of the water. See the findings in the cases of Fallini v. Hodel.[62] This is an excellent case in point for several reasons: Fallini developed the water; wild horses drank it all, leaving little or none for his cattle; Fallini prevented the wild horses from having access to his water while still allowing his cattle to use the water (an ingenious and yet simple method: fence the spring, seep or trough with a fence whose lowest rung in just high enough for cattle to go under, but is too low for burros or horses); the BLM canceled Fallini's grazing permit because he prevented the wild horses from drinking his water; the number of wild horses on his range exceeded the carrying capacity of the rangelands; Fallini claimed an unlawful taking.

Fallini finally prevailed after a number of years in pursuit of justice at considerable expense and loss of time; Fallini won his case and recovered his attorney's fees—that's all; hardly enough to create a deterrent for a similar action in the future. But he did make a point.

This case shows:

1.   The lengthy process required for administrative law to finally be exhausted and for the case to be heard, finally, by a Federal Court. Note the dates and passage of time: six years.

2.   The unspecified costs to carry a legal action this far into the U.S. District Court in order to finally secure a favorable decision consistent with the U.S. Constitution—surely not a process affordable by many. The cost issue is used time and time again as a weapon by the bureaus to further an agenda, albeit inconsistent with the intent of the law.

3.   The length to which administrative government agencies or bureaus can and will go to in order to press their perception of the law or their agenda.

62-Fallini v. Hodel, 783 F. 2d 1343 (9th Cir. 1986); Fallini V. Hodel, 783 F. Supp. 1113 (D. Nev. 1989); Fallini v. Hodel, 963 F. 2d 275 (9th Cir. 1992)

THE ISSUE OF "TAKING"

500 wild horses will consume just as much of the forage as 500 cattle. To mandate or allow these co-users is a form of "***taking***." If there is only so much land that is under grazing rights, insistence upon a lesser use of the land than that which existed before, or was customarily used, is a form of "***taking***". This "use" to the rancher is known as AUM's, Animal Units per Month. This AUM has been on a steady decline for decades. Is it because there is overgrazing going on? Is it because, in the opinion and (perhaps even unsubstantiated by facts or supportable evidence) of a district manager or ranger that "less is better" by definition? There are cases where this is so. Most cattlemen's associations know them by heart and are alarmed. Overgrazing has been used for years as the primary reason for reducing the AUMs. It is clear to the rancher that there is competition for the land he uses...with a valid federal permit; it is his to use by virtue of his grazing rights. Besides, all the water belongs to the rancher: it is his private property. Taylor Grazing Rights and National Forest Grazing permits are private property.

Some further historical explanation is in order with regard to Taylor Grazing Rights and National Forest Grazing Permits. These rights were not bestowed upon just anyone. Prior to 1934 there were really no restrictions of merit prohibiting the use of the open range other than the fact that prior use gave priority, or a sort of possessory interest in its use, or that the water had already been claimed and was the private property of the user of the open range. To control or administer this open range after 1934, the Bureau of Land Management or the Forest Service issued what they called "privileged" grazing permits. There were strings attached to their issuance: the rancher had to prove prior usage ***as well*** as prove that he owned range land of his own. Many a rancher who had been grazing his livestock on the open range was unable to continue to do so, inasmuch as he either could not prove prior usage, or, more probably, that he did not own range land of his own.[63]

The term "privileged," as it was originally used in 1934, was applicable only to those who had already been grazing their herd on the public land and owned adjacent property—two requirements in order to be "privileged." In other words, the grazing permit was granted to certain qualified persons, not to just anyone. It was an entitlement to those who qualified. In

---

63-Example: Loyd Sorensen did not have any range land that he owned but was grazing livestock on the Arizona Strip. He was compelled to sell his livestock. He could not qualify for Taylor Grazing Rights

no way was the term "privileged" an arbitrary determination by either the Forest Service or the BLM. The Forest Service and the BLM today claim that this term, "privileged," is a benevolent gesture of magnanimity on the part of the federal government without apparent regard for prerequisite, qualifying requirements. This is a complete reversal of meaning.

The federal government's position: The term "privileged" simply meant that the grazing permits were issued or granted to a privileged few. In other words, there were no other requirements for the issuance of a grazing permit—its issuance was a matter of arbitrary choice on the part of the issuer. It follows, then, that as such it could be canceled as non-renewable at the option of the federal government, and, further, that the right of cancellation was inherent in the original act itself, in that it was issued at the convenience and/or pleasure of the federal government to a privileged—not necessarily equal—few. Under this interpretation, no compensation would be due upon cancellation. Understandably, the holder of these grazing rights says "Not so." Is it possible that much of this is some form of a twist to avoid payment for a "taking"? That thought has crossed many a mind.

Inasmuch as these (private property) grazing permits "go with the land" (now called federal land), they substantially enhance the value of the nearby, private rangelands whose ownership in fee simple made it possible to secure the Taylor Grazing Rights or National Forest Grazing Permit on federal land in the first place. Without the addition of Taylor Grazing Rights or National Forest Grazing Permits on federal lands adjacent or near the private rangelands, the total operational rangelands—private and public (now federal) land combined—is vastly reduced, and, as such, so is the value of the private rangeland and its improvements, inasmuch as the lesser amount of land will accommodate fewer cattle. The court has denied this value enhancement based upon the annual renewal provision of these permits.

In a way, confiscation now became "legal."

Finally, the bureaus had found a way to eliminate one "taking" issue: Eliminate the longevity of the permits.

These rangelands were used as open range prior to 1934 without compensation to the federal government. (Keep in mind that the rancher had always wanted to buy this open range, but he was precluded from doing so: The amount of land he could actually purchase in his own name was limited by the then-in-effect homestead law—40 to 640 acres depending upon the time.) The rangelands were used in the same manner as **custom**

and practice had dictated their use for as much as a hundred years prior to 1934. Taylor Grazing Rights only formalized this usage, except that there would now be a charge for such usage. The rancher could and did recite prior appropriation of use as a valid claim to usage of the land. He never claimed that a charge for this use was not called for. He has argued vociferously that any increase in the charge for the animal Units per Month (AUM) may put him out of the business of using the public (now federal) land and, as such, "out of business" altogether because he could no longer feed enough sheep or cattle on his fee land to support his family. In short, an uneconomic unit is arbitrarily established by governmental decree or regulation. And it did put many a livestock man out of business completely. Recently, a doubling of the price was considered ("dictated" is a better word) by the Secretary of Interior, Bruce Babbitt. That fight, as of this date, is not really over—it may be more apropos to simply say that it has been set aside.

Taylor Grazing Rights and National Forest Grazing Permits are private property. When this is modified arbitrarily or capriciously, a "taking" is involved and compensation is due—that is, if you read and pay any attention to Executive Order 12630. Executive Order 12630 is focused upon this very issue and is a directive to the various agencies and bureaus. Executive Order 12630, signed by President Reagan on March 15, 1988, is a directive to all federal government agencies reinforcing the 5th Amendment provision that "taking" is a compensable act; that private property, when impinged, devalued by acts of the federal government, destroyed or confiscated is a form of "taking."

Certain recent laws have generated their own conflict. You cannot drill a well within 1000 yards of a nesting hawk (1000 yards is over a half a mile); you are restricted from using the land when you have, by custom, been using it; you must share it with wild horses or burros. In short, you have a conflict. This conflict is a restriction or limit placed upon the prior customary use of the land. This restriction or limit is a form of "taking" and as such is arguably compensable in accordance with the 5th Amendment.[64] Further, in most cases this very same land contains some improvements that are the private property of the rancher, such as wells, troughs, ditches, ponds, corrals, barns and shelters.[65]

64-Extract from the 5th Amendment: "...nor shall private property be taken for public use, without just compensation."

65-The House of Representatives has recently passed a proposed regulation that would define and require compensation for a "taking" in connection with the Clean Water Act and the Endangered Species Act only. Unfortunately, "takings" are not limited to these two acts. Just how this legislation turns out remains to be seen. Concern, however, seems apparent.

GRAZING PERMITS ARE CANCELABLE WITHOUT COMPENSATION

The federal government has taken the position, albeit inconsistently, that these grazing rights are cancelable without compensation. For example, Fort Lewis in Washington had a need for additional training grounds at its ancillary training base at Yakima, Washington. This need was fulfilled by purchasing 65,000 acres of private land and securing 6,000 acres of BLM land upon which Taylor Grazing Rights did exist as private property of ranchers. These grazing rights were to continue for two years, after which time they would be "taken" without compensation to the holder of these Taylor Grazing Rights. On the other hand, land that was acquired for the expansion of the Naval Air Station in Dixie Valley, near Fallon, Nevada, again upon which Taylor Grazing Rights existed, payment was made upon cancellation of these grazing rights. An inconsistency.

The first question one should ask is this: Is a "taking" issue involved in the cancellation of the grazing rights at Yakima? It would appear so. To clarify the question of a "taking," because it had come up before, President Reagan issued Executive Order 12630 in 1989 as a guide for all governmental agencies and bureaus as to what constituted a "taking." While more information that covers Executive Order 12630 follows shortly, a short explanation is in order at this time.

Executive Order 12630 is a long definitive explanation of what constitutes a "taking." The 5th Amendment of the U.S. Constitution, in the last phrase states: "...nor shall private property be taken for public use, without just compensation." Executive Order 12630 tells what it is.

The issue of a "taking" is far from clear, all efforts toward clarity to the contrary. The federal government has taken the position that these grazing rights are cancelable without compensation and cites one or more of the following cases as their authority:

> McNeil v. Seaton, 281 F. 2d 931 (1960)
> Hatahley v. United States, 351 U.S. 173 (1956)
> United States v. Fuller, 409 U.S. 488 (1973)
> Red Canyon Sheep Company v. Ickes, 98 F. 2d 308 (1938)
> Osborn v. United States, 145 2d 892 (1944)
> Oman v. United States, 179 F. 2d 738 (1949)

Case law has repeatedly asserted that the permit to graze granted by the federal government is revocable and non-compensable. However, here is the catch:

> "While it remains un-revoked, it is something of value and ***the Federal agency has an obligation, not only to not interfere in its use, but is obligated to defend that use from interference by third parties***."[66] (Emphasis added)

Where do friends of the court actions filed by environmental groups fit into this picture? Should they fit? What duty does the government have in light of its defined obligation above? What happens if the interfering third party is shown to be an agent of the federal government, as was shown in the case of Oman v. United States? Is it possible that less use or non-use is envisioned by the federal government and its agents as viable, if not desirable, options? It certainly is an objective of most of the environmental groups. Is that objective of the environmental groups being parroted by the government overtly or covertly? If so, is it fair or legal?

GOVERNMENT JUSTIFICATION FOR REDUCED USE OF ITS NOW FEDERAL LAND

The sovereign has the right to look after the proper care of his property. And it is this issue of "care" upon which most of the additional restrictions the rancher and other permittees on federal land face when modification of use is involved—be it less AUMs or other restrictions. In the case of the rancher, it usually is a case of accused overgrazing. To say or do otherwise is to invite the "taking" issue. As a result, environmental concerns are usually the basis for reductions in AUMs to the rancher. This is not a violation of the law. To arbitrarily reduce the AUMs could be!

EXECUTIVE ORDER 12630 AND THE 5TH AMENDMENT

Old court decisions, and, specifically, the 5th Amendment to the Constitution, were reinforced by Executive Order 12630. The Attorney General's guidelines for the application of Executive Order 12630 are a gut gut shot at the "Taking" issue:

66-Red Canyon Sheep Company v. Ickes and United States v. Fuller

"Any policy or action to which the executive order applies that, upon examination by the decision-maker...appear to have an effect on private property *sufficiently severe as effectively deny economically viable use or any distinct legally protected property interest to its owner, or to have the effect of, or result in, a permanent or temporary physical occupation, invasion, or deprivation, shall be deemed to have a taking implication for the purposes of the executive order and these guidelines*." (Emphasis added)

The guidelines go on to say:

"The fact that the government's actions are otherwise constitutionally authorized does not mean that those actions cannot effect a taking."

Paraphrased it simply means this: The government may do whatever it deems appropriate (provided it is a constitutional act), including mandating wild horses and burros on public land—even those public lands on which Use Permits exist. However, in so doing, if the federal government "takes" for public use or even deprives a person of his right to use his personal property, the government must pay for it.

Sadly, however, in the summer of 1994, the Office of Management and Budget notified all agencies that they no longer needed to consider Executive Order 12630 in their deliberations relative to rules and regulations. The basis: Adequate redress was contained in the 5th Amendment itself. In other words, go ahead and do what you please. If there is opposition, that opposition could take it to Federal Court...if they had enough time, resources or tenacity.

One could justifiable ask: is an executive order the same thing as an act of law? The answer is, no, it is not. An Executive Order is an instruction by the executive branch of the federal government to its subordinate division. It does not have the same force of law at all as a rule or regulation that a bureau or agency of the federal government might develop that is written and then printed in the federal register. Such a written rule or regulation, after the proper comment period of time has expired, becomes an enforceable, binding law. This subject is addressed in more detail in the section entitled, FEDERAL LAW ON OUR PUBLIC (FEDERAL) LAND: UNITED STATES CODE & CODE OF FEDERAL REGULATIONS.

To my knowledge, Executive Order 12630 has not been rescinded. The Bureau of OMB simply blunted its effectiveness. They did not eliminate it.

In the case of the Forest Service and its nearly 16,000 cabins on Forest Service land by Use Permit, when the Forest Service wishes to cancel a permit and use the land for "a higher and better use," a ten year extension of the Use Permit is given as well as notice at that same time that the Use Permit will not be renewed. The Forest Service mistakenly believes that in so doing they are somehow allowing the permittee to recover his or her loss of their private property—in this case a cabin. The Forest Service believes that amortizing this loss over a 10 year period is the same thing to the permittee as payment for the private property.[67] Not so at all. If, for example, a cabin has a value of $100,000—and many do—and it is to be taken as a capital loss, the owner has a $100,000 capital loss. The tax code allows a maximum deduction of $3,000 per year on a capital loss. The permittee, in this case, must live over 30 more years to get paid for his loss or "taking," plus, in the meantime, endure the loss of his invested capital, plus its inflationary loss over that same period of years. Is it possible that all of this is done so that the "taking" issue is circumvented? There are many who believe that it is and that it is unfair. And I happen to be one of them!

In accordance with Executive Order 12630, in one way or another, a "taking" could include the following:

1. An increase in grazing fees. (Not economically viable.)

2. The sharing of this land with wild horses. (Diluting the use by the rancher.)

3. The delay of use from that which was enjoyed earlier. (Deprivation of use by virtue of time delay.)

4. The prohibition from drilling a well. (Invasion of use.)

A REVIEW: TODAY

In just over 200 years the federal government has swung from selling, as well as giving, its land away as fast as it could to reserving it to non-use in the name of preservation.

Parkinson's Law has played a major role in the shaping of this

[67] I Know this because this is what the Forest Service told me, personally.

husbanding and control. Central control has surely won out for the moment, and it would seem to have done so at the expense of private property interests that are prior and are legally constituted, though this is argued to the contrary by government bureaus, irrespective of shaky legal ground.

None of this would seem out of place were it not for the fact that "confiscation **without** compensation" is being tried as a viable method of regaining all or some of these rights conveyed in the past to private parties. The method? Cancel the permit and force the aggrieved or injured party into the administrative law process, delay as long as legally possible, then fight it out in the Federal Court system. The stakes would have to be mighty high before someone could consider the enormous financial outlay to be worth the eventual outcome of fair compensation. Our founding fathers would be justified if they turned over in their graves; their view of equity and fairness never encompassed this kind of action.

There is simply too much of this kind of thing going on for confiscation without compensation to be without malice of forethought even though part of it can be explained by ignorance and a confrontational attitude.

It would be wrong to picture all actions of federal bureaus and departments or their personnel as insidious, underhanded, heavy-handed or privately fostering their own agenda. Some do and some do not. Some are power-hungry while others think their ideas are simply better than anyone else's and as a result consider themselves better qualified to make decisions for the many. Some confuse the purpose of government in these United States: Namely, to do for the people those things they are unable to do for themselves, not those things they are **unwilling** to do for themselves.

Where does all this seemingly headlong plunge toward more and more control and at times heavy handed—and even devious—power come from? Aside from a rather basic facet of human nature on the part of many managers whose egos cannot be satiated without more and more power, it boils down to two words, in my view: ignorance and loyalty—two strange words to use here.

Ignorance: Ignorance of the law, ignorance of intent, ignorance on the part of some who should know better that is passed down the line to a subordinate by dictum.

Loyalty: Loyalty to an employer, loyalty to a supervisor or boss, loyalty to a set of values obtained by osmosis or loyalty to a modus operandi—a that's-the-way-we-have-always-done-it syndrome.

Why has all this action been taking place in the past and why is it still continuing today?

This is not too difficult to answer. Some simply do not know better; some simply do not understand from whence freedom comes and the place our government, in accordance with our Constitution, is supposed to play in the assurance of continued freedom; some simply lack the fortitude and courage of their conviction to object; some simply fear that their involvement will, among other things, cost them their jobs; some simply fervently believe that that which is taking place is not only philosophically correct, but just—an honest difference of opinion; and tragically last, some believe our Constitution is antiquated and in need of reform or modification, thus allowing them to take onto themselves the assumed right to act—or support the acts of others—in contradiction to the provisions of the U.S. Constitution. Or, perhaps it is a combination of the above.

Sadly, too many who should have read the Constitution have not.

Governments are by no means the only ones subject to most of the maladies above. All organizations or business have the same problems. How they deal with them differs.

This brings on the next question: why is this situation tolerated? In most cases, among other things, it is tolerated for exactly the same reasons as outlined above—ignorance and loyalty. But there is another reason that is far, far more compelling: Expense! If you are the aggrieved as a result of some bureau's edict or rule that you believe is wrong, your ultimate recourse is not a happy one—it will be *very* costly and ***take a very long time***. Will you, or do you, have both the time and money? In most cases, this is the end of the line: there is not enough of one or the other! Recourse is simply beyond reach. Paraphrased, confronting our governmental bureaus or departments is a little like playing no-limit poker with the sultan of Brunei! The federal government can and may run you out of chips...or time! It would be a big mistake to believe that this is unknown or overlooked by the different governmental bureaus or departments. It is a formidable weapon, and they know it!

QUESTIONS FOR TOMORROW

Questions that must be asked certainly include the following:

Does this nation no longer have a need for natural resources on and under the ground of this or proposed future reserve or wilderness land?

Will the best interests of this entire nation be best served by taking these lands out of the inventory of viable and usable natural resources?

How will the private property claimants be paid for the confiscation of their property?

Does anyone know the extent of what these claims might be?

Do the advocates of non-use constitute a majority of opinion or are they simply a vocal minority out of proportion to their numbers?

Are the advocates of non-use accurate about their claims of damage to the environment and renewable resources?

The matter is far from settled. Public lands are subject to a vast number of legitimate claims that are somebody's private property. Confiscation or "taking" of private property without compensation is a violation of the 5th Amendment.

Equity and fairness dictate better treatment than any effort to circumnavigate the rather basic laws of human behavior.

And last but not least, who really owns these public (now federal) lands anyway! That is the subject of Part Two.

INTRODUCTION TO
PART II

In Part One, I accepted the historical background of our public lands without any question as to any conflict I saw in various or different rules and regulations developed by the bureaus of the federal government or even different acts of Congress as to their conformance to the U. S. Constitution. I did not question their legality; what was done was done. I did not want to confuse the history of its being with the nagging and lingering question of its appropriateness or legality. It was therefore, historically, with some emphasis, focused upon the effectual change this history has had upon private property and private property rights. That, in and of itself, I thought, was enough!

However, PART Two is another matter. It is the same subject but this time where its history and metamorphosis conflicted with the provisions of the Constitution or the intent of the founding fathers, I have tried to point out these conflicts created by bureau developed rules and regulations and acts of Congress, where and how they conflict, as well as cite the authority in both the U.S. Constitution and controlling Supreme Court cases that impact the subject matter.

From time to time I may call these public lands by a different name, federal lands. The reason is simple enough; that is what nearly 100 percent of the people of these United States have been led to believe—erroneously— that all public lands are federally owned. That simply is not so. Part Two is the basis for that statement even though the federal bureaus steadfastly adhere to the notion of exclusive ownership. Not surprising: most of these far-flung bureau administrators, have never, ever read the Constitution— certainly not since their graduation for high school! Certainly not the Supreme Court cases that uphold or define the meaning of the Constitution. These bureaus have simply **assumed** federal ownership and control to be correct; but then, so have the rest of us. We have all been calling these lands "federal" lands for so many years that the sequential mental gymnastics is easy. Gertrude Stein said a rose is a rose is a rose. The name takes on the character of what we think it to be, and if we are told what it is often enough, even though it be wrong, we come to believe that which is not true to be truth itself.

This is not to say that the federal bureaus have done a poor or a good job of managing the public land. Part Two is really about the usurpation of sovereignty, dominion, jurisdiction, power and authority by the federal government over this same land; usurped by assumption and not by constitutional means or delegated constitutional authority.

The name federal land had no real meaning prior to 1891, when vast areas of the West were set-aside as forest reserves. Slowly but surely, after that date, the nomenclature of forest reserves, a portion of the then Public Domain, was shifted to the name of federal land or National Forest. When all the remaining Public Domain land was "withdrawn" from settlement or sale, the name here was also changed to federal public land. Across the western United States, the only place where such land existed, highway signs now emblazon that title of identification: Federal public land. It is no wonder that to most of us it is an accepted fact...federal land, National Forests, or federal public land are federally owned. It is this accepted fact, which isn't a fact at all, that Part Two is all about. Our federal (public) lands are not federal at all.

There are a few people in the various bureaus that know better— that the federal land, by all of the names above are really not federal at all. After reading what follows, I hope that there will be even more.

Justice Sandra Day O'Connor reminds us in New York v. United States (quoting United States v. Butler):

"The question is not what power the federal government ought to have but what powers in fact have been given by the people."

And then she reminds us, directly:

"But the Constitution protects us from our own best intentions; it divides power among sovereigns and among branches of government precisely so that we may resist the temptation to concentrate power in one location as the expedient solution to the crisis of the day."

William C. Hayward

PART II

OUR PUBLIC LAND
WHO REALLY OWNS IT?

DEFINITION OF DIFFERENT LANDS

How did our federal government lay claim to land that the U.S. Constitution says it cannot own?

For the sake of clarity I may from time to time continue to call all the land that was acquired by purchase, treaty or the spoils of war (solemnized later by treaty) and seemingly withheld from the western states when they entered the Union, federal lands, even though, as you shall see, that term is too all-inclusive in that this implies a singularity of interest exclusive of any other ownership interests. Except when the land was in a territorial state of being prior to statehood, that simply is not so. When it comes to land, very little of its exclusive ownership can now be called federal at all— that is, if its ownership is to be governed by the definitions and limitations stated in the U.S. Constitution. In general I have inserted, in parenthesis, the name federal, after the initial name public, i.e. public (federal) land.

The following definitions of land status are rather fundamental and helpful in understanding the different forms and kinds of land either owned or controlled.

Federally owned land: Land held by the federal government in accordance with Article 1, Section 8, Clause 17 of the United States Constitution (this is quoted later in its entirety in the following section entitle, JURISDICTION: FEDERAL OR STATE?) in which the federal government has both ownership rights and exclusive legislative jurisdiction.

Federally controlled land: Land occupied by the federal government after a state has been accepted into the Union of the United

63

States.

Split estate land: Land in which the several estates (different interests or ownership rights) are divided between two or more owners—including combinations of state and private.

Private land: Land held in exclusive private ownership.

Public land:

1. Public domain: Land owned by the government (state or federal) and available to the public for purchase and/or settlement, upon which different interest or ownership rights may exist. (There is no more Public Domain land owned by the federal government within the borders of any of the United States.)

2. Land owned by the government (state or federal) upon which different interests or ownership rights may or may not exist.

State land: Land owned by the government of a separate state to the exclusion of other ownership interests.

As can be seen in the maps, between Part One and Part Two, federal land encompasses nearly 60 percent of the western states, while little or none of the land east of the 100th meridian is federal at all. How, contrary to all the intents of our founding fathers, did this land come to be conclusively considered as under federal ownership in perpetuity? How did it all get turned around and stay that way? How did it come to be that most people today think this land is indeed in federal ownership? How did it stay that way for so many decades? Why wasn't something done about it if it was in fact an unconstitutional retention? Even if the doctrine of that's-the-way-we-have-been-doing-it-for-years (a prescriptive law of sorts) is well in place by custom and usage on the part of our governmental departments and bureaus, is this the end of the trail? Can this assumed ownership and control of our public lands by the federal government be challenged? Is anyone doing anything about it now, and if so, what? And what has been the outcome? Those are the questions.

CONSTITUTIONALLY AUTHORIZED
FEDERAL LAND OWNERSHIP

Certainly one of the first questions to ask is fundamental enough: Why can't the federal government own the land? The answer is basic: the U.S. Constitution details what the federal government *can* own. It does not say what it cannot own, but this is implied by limiting, specifically, what the federal government can own. And make no mistake about it, this is defined in the Constitution. Our founding fathers were mightily concerned about limiting the size, scope and control that seems to go with all governments. Their recent experiences had not been dimmed. They had all just fought a long, hard war with Great Britain for their freedom and independence and could see, at that time, the overwhelming power and control King George III had over the American colonies. They wanted no part of this, and they framed a constitution that preserved their freedom and liberties, part of which was to *grossly limit* the power of government. Even a casual examination of the U.S. Constitution reveals that their major concern was that of *limiting* government rather than guaranteeing individual freedoms or rights. The guarantees did not come until the addition of the first ten amendments—an act that followed the ratification of the Constitution by all of the original thirteen colonies. Specifically stating what property and land the federal government could own was a part of this limitation.

Article 1, Section 8, Clause 17 of the U.S. Constitution:

"To exercise exclusive legislation in all cases whatsoever over such district (not exceeding ten square miles) as may, by cession of particular states and the acceptance of Congress, become the seat of government of the United States and to exercise like authority over all places purchased, by the consent of the legislature of the state in which the same shall be, for the *erection of Forts, Magazines, Arsenals, dock-Yards, and other needful Buildings*." (Emphasis added)

MEANING AND LIMITATIONS OF "TERRITORY"

However, there was, at the time of the ratification of the Constitution by the thirteen original states, a huge quantity of land west of the western border of seven of the original colonies—all the way to the Mississippi River—that did not belong to anyone. It was unclaimed. It was unused. It was unoccupied except by the Indians. It was, to them, at the time, waste-land. Upon ratification of the U.S. Constitution in 1787, this land became "Territory:" land owned by the United States, to be used "for a common fund." All of this land, even though it was not northwest of very many new states, had another common name: "Northwest Territory." It is true that it did not remain "territory" land long, for it was auctioned off, subdivided and sold in smaller plots, and even given away. A very important fact to remember is that ***this land was the only land that bore the title of "territory"*** as far as the framers of the Constitution were concerned. It was not necessarily the only land owned by the new federal government. Some unclaimed or unsettled land was inside the boundary of the new states. This land, formerly crown land, was ceded to the **states** or **colonies** by the Treaty of Paris. It ***was not*** ceded to the United States. All claim to the land was "relinquished" to the "sovereign and independent" States. The United States had not been formed yet and would not be formed for another four years! It could not possibly be federal land. It was the colony's or independent state's land by treaty.[68] This is a fact to remember, for it will surface as a part of the "Equal Footing Doctrine" later. However, at this point, one could surely ask how we can be so sure that the term "territory," as defined in Article IV, the Property Clause of the Constitution, has limited meaning and that it does not include all future land called by the same name but acquired later by purchase, treaty or as the spoils of war? This that follows defines and limits this meaning.

"TERRITORY" DEFINED: DRED SCOTT V. SANDFORD

The Dred Scott decision is a defining case of momentous proportion that was brought before the Supreme Court many, many years ago. It is extremely long inasmuch as each justice wrote his own separate opinion in addition to that which Chief Justice J. Taney wrote as the collective finding of the Supreme Court. It is despicable in one regard, in that it found that a slave was, indeed, private property. It was defining in a most important way in that it goes into lengthy detail to define in no uncertain terms the Property Court (Article IV) of the Constitution. It is this second part of this decision about which we are interested, agreeing all the while that the first part was indeed despicable. But then, under the laws of the time, there was

68-Treaty of Peace with Great Britain: Art. I.; "His Britannic Majesty acknowledges the United States, [each are named separately]...to be *free, sovereign and independent States*; that he treats with them as such, and for himself, his heirs and successors, relinquishes all claims to the Government, proprietary and territorial rights of the same, and every part thereof."

little else the justices could do: Slavery, and the possession of slaves was an accepted part of human behavior at the time—albeit greatly lessening, but nonetheless accepted. In the Unites States, it would take a great civil war and an amendment to our constitution (the 13th Amendment) to alter this fact.

The case of Dred Scott v. Sandford[69] goes into a lengthy recitation of the history of the creation of the "territory" and what lands were meant by the term "territory," inasmuch as the resolution of this case depended upon jurisdiction of the court—federal jurisdiction (Admiralty Law) or state jurisdiction (laws of the individual state in which the act or acts occurred). The court states the reason for a territory's being, the circumstances that made its creation necessary, and what and how it was to be used. The Dred Scott decision was rendered long after the Louisiana Purchase and even after the Treaty of Guadalupe Hidalgo, two events that created the major part of the land that now composes the lower 48 states—a time when much of this additional land was called "Territory." The following quotations are of particular note in that they definitely limit the term "territory," as used in the Constitution to that of the territory ceded to the colonies by Great Britain.

> "...that article in the Constitution [Article IV, Sec. 3] which confers on Congress the power 'to dispose of and make all needful rules and regulations respecting the *territory* or *other property* belonging to the United States;'...in the judgment of the court...is confined, and was intended to be confined, to the territory which at that time belonged to, or was claimed by, the United States, and was within their boundaries as settled by the Treaty of Great Britain, and can have no influence upon territory afterwards acquired from a foreign government. *It was a special provision for a known and particular Territory, and to meet a present emergency, and nothing more*." (Emphasis added)

Further:

> "The language used in the clause [Article IV, Sec. 3.],[70] the arrangement and combination of the powers, and the somewhat unusual phraseology it uses, when it speaks of the political power to

69-Dred Scott v. Sandford: (1856) 60 U.S. (19 HOW) 393.

70- "...The Congress shall have Power to dispose of and make all needful Rules and Regulations respecting Territory or other Property belonging to the United States; and nothing in this Constitution shall be so construed as to Prejudice any Claim of the Unites States, or of any particular State."

be exercised in the government of the territory, all indicate the design and meaning of the clause to be such as we have mentioned. *It does not speak of Territory, nor of Territories, but uses language which, according to its legitimate meaning, points to a particular thing. The power is given in relation only to the territory of the United States—that is, to a Territory then in existence, and then known or claimed as the territory of the United States*....[the Article] then gives the power which was necessarily associated with disposition and sale of the lands—that is, the power of making needful rules and regulations respecting the Territory. And whatever construction may now be given to these words, everyone, we think, must admit that they are not the words usually employed by statesmen in giving supreme power to legislation. They are certainly very unlike the words used in the power granted to legislate over territory which the new government might afterwards itself obtain by cession from a state, either for its seat of government, or for forts, magazines, arsenals, dockyards, and other needful buildings.""

"And the same power of making needful rules respecting Territory is, in precisely the same language, applied to the other property belonging to the United States—associating the power over the Territory in this respect with the power over movable or personal property."

With respect to "other property belonging to the United States," the court continues:

"Nor can it [Article IV, Sec. 3,], upon any fair construction, be applied to any property *but* that which the new government was *about to receive* from the confederated states. And if this be true as to this property, *it must be equally true and limited as to the territory*, which is so carefully and precisely coupled with it— and like it referred to as property in the power granted." (Emphasis added)

There is, however, more to this case than just that which is discussed and quoted above. This case defines the reasons for the Property Clause of the Constitution (Article IV) in a finite way. On page 436 of the decision:

"...there were many articles of value besides this property in land [territory], such as arms, military stores, munitions, and ships of war, which were the common property of the States, when acting in their independent characters as confederates,...and it was to place these things under the guardianship and protection of the new government, and to clothe it with the necessary powers, that the clause was inserted in the Constitution which gives Congress the power 'to dispose of and make all needful rules and regulations respecting the territory or other property belonging to the United States.' It was intended for a specific purpose, *to provide for the things we have mentioned*. It was to transfer to the new government the property then held in common by the States, and to give to that government the power to apply it to the objects for which it had been destined by mutual agreement among the States before their league was dissolved. *It applies only to the property which the States held in common at that time, and has no reference whatever to any territory or other property which the new sovereignty might afterwards itself acquire*." (Emphasis added)

Chief Justice Taney continues on page 437:

"And the same power of making needful rules respecting the Territory is, in precisely the same language, applied to the other property belonging to the United States—associating the power over the Territory in this respect with the power over movable or personal property—that is, the ships, arms, and munitions of war, which then belonged in common to the State sovereignties. And it will hardly be said, that this power, in relation to the last mentioned objects, was deemed necessary to be this specially given to the new government, in order to authorize it to make needful rules and regulations respecting the ships it might itself build, or arms and munitions of war it might itself manufacture or provide for the public service [in the future].

"No one, it is believed, would think a moment of deriving the power of Congress to make needful rules and regulations in relation to property of this kind [ships, arms, etc.] from this clause of the Constitution. Nor can it, upon any fair construction, be applied to any property but that which the new government was about to receive from the confederated States. And if this be true as to this property, it must be equally true and limited as to the territory, which is so carefully and precisely coupled with it— and like it referred to as property in the power granted. The concluding words of the clause appear to render this construction irresistible; for, after the provisions we have mentioned, it proceeds to say, 'that nothing in the Constitution shall be so construed as to prejudice any claims of the United States, or of any particular State.'"

Justice Taney explains, why:

"...all of the States except North Carolina and Georgia, had made the cession before the Constitution was adopted.... The Claims of other States that the unappropriated lands in these two States should be applied to the common benefit, in like manner, was still insisted on but refused by the States [North Carolina and Georgia]. And this member of the clause in question evidently applies to them and can apply to nothing else. It was to exclude the conclusion that either party, by adopting the Constitution, would surrender what they deemed their rights."

On page 438 Justice Taney supports this argument:

"...it is impossible, by any just rule of construction, to make the first provision general, and extend to all territories, which the Federal Government might in any way afterwards acquire, when the latter is plainly and unequivocally confined to a particular territory; which was a part of the same controversy, and involved in the same dispute, and depended upon the same principles. The union of the two provisions in the same clause shows that they were kindred subjects, and that the whole clause is local, and relates only to lands, within the limits of the United States which had been or then were claimed by a State; and that no other Territory was in the mind of the framers of the Constitution, or intended to be embraced in it."

On page 440, Justice Taney continues:

"The words, "rules and regulations" are usually employed in the Constitution in speaking of some particular specific power which it means to confer on the government, and not, as we have seen, when granting general powers of legislation. *And to construe the words of which we are speaking as a general and unlimited grant of sovereignty over territories which the government might afterwards acquire, is to use them in a sense and for a purpose for which they*

were not used in any other part of the instrument [U.S. Constitution]. But is confined to a particular territory in which a government and laws had already been established, but which would require some alterations to adapt it to the new government, the words are peculiarly applicable and appropriate for that purpose." (Emphasis added)

Justice Taney goes on to explain why this entire Article was necessary at all: The new Union would gather no power at all from the Confederation after the Union of States was formed, and therefore, it all had to be stated in the Constitution all over again in specific detail—which was done.

On page 441, Justice Taney states:

"Assembled together, special provisions were indispensable to transfer to the new government the property and rights which at that time they held in common;...and this power could only be given to it by special provisions in the Constitution.

"The clause in relation to the territory and other property of the United Stated provide for the first, and the clause last quoted provided for the other. They have no connection with the general powers and rights of sovereignty delegated to the new government, and can neither enlarge nor diminish them. They were inserted to meet a present emergency, and not to regulate its powers as a government."

Taney states that the following clause with respect to treaties is likewise limited to existing territory at that time. [This fact should be of particular interest to those that believe that treaties have no limits at all. They do, and this is discussed later.]

On page 442, he finalizes his observations:

"Consequently, the power which Congress may have lawfully exercised in this territory, while it remained under territorial government, and which may have been sanctioned by judicial decision, ***can furnish no justification and no argument to support a similar exercise of power over territory afterwards acquired by the Federal Government.***" (Emphasis added)

When taken as a whole, the quotations above appear, if anything, to be repetitive and somewhat redundant. Justice Taney says it plainly first, and then states it again with his explanation as to why and how. It is pretty hard to believe, after reading the above quotations, that there could be any possibility that some reader could construe the meaning of "territory" to extend to any and all territory that the United States could afterward acquire, such as the Louisiana Purchase and the western land from Mexico via the Treaty of Guadalupe Hidalgo. Yet, many jurists and lawyers do, and in doing so, they necessarily grant to Congress vast powers it does not in fact possess.

How could it be that they could ignore something so plain? There are two possible reasons.

First, one could simply say that such a despicable finding (a human being could be the private property of another human being), should be ignored completely and that, surely, such a finding should never be granted the dignity of any lasting importance.

Second, and perhaps more compelling, this decision speaks of more than just a slave as personal property; it speaks to and defines the meaning of the Property Court of the U. S. Constitution. Further, it defines the meaning of the term "territory," as used in the Property Court. Because this case speaks to more than personal property, the essential thrust of the case, we can ignore this second part, because it is dicta and therefore not a part of the decision at all. Being dicta, it is not law at all! Right? Wrong!

Now, as to why it is not dicta.

Justice Taney cited excerpts in length from a case decided by one of our most renown and respected justices, Chief Justice Marshall: American and The Ocean Insurance Co. v. Canter. [71] Justice Taney makes this point:

"There is, however, not the slightest conflict between *the opinion now given and the one referred to*; (American and The Ocean Insurance Co. v. Canter)." (Emphasis added)

Justice Taney is stating that what he is saying is an opinion of the court. As such it is not dicta at all, but a decision.

71-American and The Ocean Insurance Company v. 356 Bales of Cotton, David Canter. (1828) 1 Pet. 511; 7 L. Ed. 242.

After quoting a lengthy paragraph, Justice Taney makes the following statement about what the Marshall court found:

> "They do not decide that the power in Congress is unquestionable, and in this we entirely concur, *and nothing will be found in this opinion to the contrary*."
> (Emphasis added)

Here again, Justice Taney refers to "this opinion."

Then, finally, after quoting at length from the lower court from which the American and The Ocean Insurance Co. v. Canter was appealed, Justice Taney makes this statement:

> "No one, we presume, will question the correctness of that opinion; nor is there anything in conflict with it *in the opinion now given*." (Emphasis added)

There you have it, not once but three times. Justice Taney considered what he was saying to be an opinion of the court. As such, it cannot be construed to be dicta. It is a finding of the court and as such is law—and it is...until reversed. And that has not happened.

With respect to this "territory," the Constitution details what is to become of it after each defined area attains a population of 60,000 inhabitants: It could become, upon application, a separate state. The method of becoming a state is embodied in an enabling act. This enabling act details those conditions for admission to the Union. In the case of the western states, (and almost all other states) these enabling acts grant to the federal government all rights and title to all **unclaimed** or **non-homestead** lands. Among other things or for other purposes which are discussed later, this becomes an estoppel[72] of all pending or unfiled claims based upon either preemptive or appropriated rights; no longer could you appropriate land in that territorial area. In a way, you could say that this was the beginning of a clear title. And it was. All land that was to be included within the border of a new state was to have no prior encumbrance, such as a claim to ownership by virtue of an un-filed homestead or simply a squatter who "might get around to filing some day." This was the beginning. Further, any claim to the title of any of this land by Indians or a foreign country was to be cleared by an act of the United States—a patent.

72-Webster: "The stopping of a person from making a claim or denial which contradicts his prior acts or allegations."

DICTA: WHAT IT IS AND WHY IT IS NO BASIS FOR LAW

In the preceding section, the term "dicta" was used. Inasmuch as it will continue to be used in future sections, an explanation as to what it is and what is meant by that word is in order.

The term, obiter dicta, or dicta, is a legal phrase that identifies information, a thought, a fact, that is not directly related to the subject matter of a given case, inasmuch as it was not necessary to the decision of the case. It is important, however, in that it gives background—history even—upon which a decision is based. It is an important part of a decision even though it cannot be used as a basis for law. That is not to say that it has not been taken as a basis for law, for it definitely has been. In fact, almost all of the cases that are related later as the basis of the federal government's claim that they are the owners of all public land has its foundation firmly anchored in dicta. Generally speaking, this basis for law is taken by lower courts in their findings of law because it gives them direction as to how and what the Supreme Court has thought. The important fact of the matter is that a case or decision is about a specific act or subject; the case has a finite subject and the court limits its specific findings to the finite subject. All other observations by the court are dicta—even the history they may or may not relate.

For example: If the determination of the strength of reading glasses was the subject of a law suit, an observation by the court that the eyes were blue would not be a matter of law even if it were a fact. What the court had to say about the strength of the lenses would be. The observation by the court that the eyes were blue would be dicta.

Why? Because the color of the eyes was not a subject of the law suit. The color of the eyes was not necessary in determining the opinion and it was not argued. No facts or argument relating to the color of the eyes was presented.

Quite obviously, it is important to know exactly what the subject matter of a case is all about, for it is that exact subject matter—and nothing else—that is the basis of law. The other observations and even conclusions the court comes to are a matter of dicta.

If it was not argued, it is not law.

CALIFORNIA AND NEVADA ENABLING ACTS

The California Enabling Act is reasonably typical of all the other western states (except Nevada)[73] and is quoted in part. Both parts of the California Enabling Act, quoted below, are extremely important for two very different reasons.

The first reason has to do with "Equal Footing":

> "...That the State of California shall be one, and is hereby declared to be one, of the United States of America, and admitted into the Union **on an Equal Footing with the original States in all respects whatever**." (Emphasis added)

Read the emphasized part again and note the words, "Equal Footing," and "all respects." This is pivotal. This is a lawful act of Congress which is in strict conformance to the U.S. Constitution. The Constitution states the following in Article IV, Section 3: "New States may be admitted by the Congress into the Union." The California Enabling Act, typical of all the other enabling acts, states **how** Congress shall admit the new state and under what conditions: "on an Equal Footing with the **original** states in all respects whatever." Simply put, this statement in the enabling acts of nearly all the states requires that each state admitted to the Union **be** on an Equal Footing with the original thirteen states, not just equal to another state admitted after the original thirteen colonies formed the United States. The measuring stick was and is the original thirteen states, no other.

The second reason has to do with a disclaimer of the "title...to," disposition, control, etc. of the "public lands" within the limits of the about-to-be new state. (Note the words "about-to-be" new state. This is important later.) This, on the surface, would seem to run contrary to the Constitution in that it appears to allow the federal government the right to retain ownership of the territorial land after statehood. But look further.

> "...That the said State of California is admitted into the Union upon the express condition that the people of said State, through their **legislature** or otherwise, shall never interfere with the primary disposal of **public lands** within its limits,

---

73-The Nevada Enabling Act of 1864 is directed toward and constrains "the inhabitants of...the **territory** of Nevada" rather than the state of Nevada later formed. Note the difference between this disclaimer and that which is quoted in the California Enabling Act later.

and shall pass no law and do no act whereby the title of the United States to, and right to dispose of, the same shall be impaired or questioned; and that they shall never lay any tax or assessment of any description whatsoever upon the Public Domain of the United States..." (Emphasis added)

The Nevada Enabling Act of 1864 seems to want to say the same thing in a different way. This "different way" is quoted as follows:

Nevada Enabling Act of 1864, Sec. 4. Third:

> "That **the people inhabiting said territory** do agree and declare that they forever disclaim all right and title to the unappropriated public lands lying within said territory, and that the same shall be and remain at the sole and entire disposition of the United States;" (Emphasis added)

Note that it is "the people inhabiting said territory," not the state of Nevada that is to do the disclaiming. I find this distinction quite interesting. In the instance of California, it was the "primary disposal of the public land" that California as a state was to forego, as well as not impair the United States' title to the land. In the case of Nevada, the *title* to the land was to be disclaimed...forever...by the inhabitant of the **Nevada territory**. Does this mean that the state of Nevada, through its legislature—being a different body, could later enact legislation affecting the title of the land? Perhaps.

In the case of Pollard v. Hagan (1845),[74] state disclaimers were declared unconstitutional. Quoting from Pollard v. Hagan, (p.571):

> "We, therefore, think the United States hold the public lands within the new States by force of the deeds of cession, [Georgia to the U.S. of which Alabama was a part] and the statutes connected with them, **and not by any municipal sovereignty which it may be supposed they possess, or have received by compact with the new States, for that particular purpose. The provisions of the Constitution above referred to show that no such power can be exercised by the United States within a State**." (Emphasis added)

In other words, the United States (federal government) can only hold the public land or gain title to it by force of a deed of cession from the state legislature after a state is formed.

74-Pollard v. Hagan: (1845) 44 U.S., 3 How, 212, 11 L. Ed. 565.

As a matter of interest, note that no such state disclaimer was included in the Nevada Enabling Act.

According to at least one authority, Clel Georgetta,[75] this opinion respecting the disclaimer has never been overturned. More later on that subject.

Further, the Enabling Act of California authorized the citizens of the territory to hold a Constitutional Convention, the residual purpose of which was the formation and adoption of a state constitution (which had to be approved by the federal government) and to apply for admission to the Union. As far as the West was concerned, some interpret these same enabling acts to be a hammer to the head, a do-it-or-else dictum to those same states: You either grant all unclaimed or un-appropriated land to the federal government or forget about becoming a state! This was a condition of entry into the Union. Even Alabama, a state formed from what had been formerly a part of Georgia, had the same condition.[76] So, for the West it was not a new and unexpected demand. There was one unexpected event, however: The West never did get any of it back while all of the land of the Northwest Territory, and most of the land from the Louisiana Purchase was either transferred into state ownership for specific purposes or appropriated by a homesteader and later purchased at or above their minimum price per acre. It became, in time, private land. Not so with the land acquired by the Treaty of Guadalupe Hidalgo—a rather clear impingement of the Equal Footing Doctrine, which is discussed later. Each territorial convention, in turn, adopted an ordinance granting to the United States all such land. This disclaimer refers to all "territorial" land in the about-to-become new state. Up until the state joined the Union as "one of the United States," this "territorial" land was in federal ownership for the express purpose of holding it in trust until it could be disposed of in accordance with the then-in-place laws of homestead, appropriation, preemption, etc. or until it was transferred to the new state. This last item never happened.

Nothing in the Constitution allows the federal government to retain land inside a state after it becomes a state UNLESS the *state legislature* approves such transfer.[77] Such transfers have taken place to accommodate the establishment of national parks. Yosemite National Park is an interesting case in point. Yosemite Valley was conveyed by the federal government to the State of California for a state park in 1864 by Act of

75-*Golden Fleece In Nevada*, Clel Georgetta, p. 168, 169.

76-Georgia ceded its "wasteland" in 1803, long after the other seven colonies had done so.

77-See Article I, Sec. 8, Clause 17 of the U. S. Constitution.

Congress when a trust was created and granted for such a purpose. But this conveyance did not include the surrounding High Sierra mountains. After extensive lobbying by John Muir, it became a national park—including the surrounding High Sierra mountains. California deeded the land to the United States, and Congress accepted the grant—all exactly in the manner prescribed by Article I, Sec. 8, Clause 17 of the Constitution, and in the Act of 1891 (St. 1891, p 262):

> "The State of California hereby cedes to the United States of America exclusive jurisdiction over such piece or parcel of land as may have been or may be hereafter ceded or conveyed to the United States..." [78]

Thus the State of California consented to the federal ownership of Yosemite. Note that all of this was done **exactly** in accordance with the Constitution, which required such action on the part of the separate state's legislatures.

How could it be that the Congress could adhere strictly to the Constitution in one instance and in the next one declare federal jurisdiction and ownership to land that the Constitution implies by indirection that it cannot own **after a state is accepted into the Union**? Some claim that Congress did no such thing and that it was simply reserving to itself the right to do whatever it pleased with the property it was lawfully entitled to own, namely, "forts, magazines, arsenals, dock-yards, and other needful buildings," as well as provide the new state with a clear title to the land. Besides, they also claim, the disclaimer of ownership to this same land contained in the Enabling Acts after a territory became a state allowed the federal government the exclusive right to dispose of this land. They cite that this disclaimer contained in the enabling acts was originally a part of The Northwest Ordinance of 1787. And it was. That section is quoted:

> "The legislatures of those districts or new States, shall never interfere with the primary disposal of the soil by the United States in Congress assembled...."

More on The Northwest Ordinance of 1787 later.

One thing was clear, however. The federal government did not relinquish its authority and control over the territorial land, as it had done in the past. For the first time, the Equal Footing Doctrine was ignored. This was no accident.

78-Standard Oil Co. of California v. Johnson. 76 P.R. 2d S. p. 118

THE DISCLAIMER CLAUSE IN THE ENABLING ACTS

The earliest reference to a disclaimer of land ownership by a state can be found in the Northwest Ordinance of 1787. There was a reason for its being there. The Northwest Ordinance was the primary act that was to take the land east of the borders of the original thirteen colonies in trust, and sell that land for the purpose of paying off the debt incurred by the American Revolutionary War. As such, no state would be permitted to interfere with the disposal of that same land inasmuch as the proceeds were, by agreement, to be used as a "common fund" for the repayment of that debt.

The requirement for each new state to disclaim title to the Public Domain at the time of its joining the Union was a requirement that seemed to grow with the exigency of creeping time. As might well be expected, those states that were formed from the Northwest Territory each had, in a different way, a disclaimer. Ohio, one of those, had a metes and bounds description of the land, within which the federal government retained disposal rights to the land:

> "...in conformance with the 5th article of compact between the original states."[79]

On the other hand, Louisiana, a state formed from the Louisiana Purchase, had no disclaimer at all. The state of Louisiana received all the land within its borders.[80] There was no need to do otherwise: There was no formal trust that governed the disposal of this land as there had been with the original thirteen States.

The Enabling Acts drafted before 1812 were far from consistent. Kentucky and Vermont had no mention of "on an Equal Footing."[81] After 1812, the disclaimer of land seemed to be a constant and relatively uniform requirement.

79-7th Congress, Sess. 1, Ch. 40, 1802

80-12th Congress, Sess. 1, Ch. 50, 1812

81-Kentucky: 1st Congress, Sess. III, Ch. 4, 1791;
Vermont: 1st Congress, Sess. III, Ch. 7, 1791

THE DISCLAIMER CLAUSE:
AN EXCLUSIVE SALES CONTRACT

Another reason for the disclaimer clause is quite simple, direct and understandable. If the federal government (the United States) retained the title to the land, the proceeds would continue to go into the federal treasury and not the state's, even after all purchase monies had been paid back by the sale of the land. An examination of the source of all funds that flowed into the federal treasury reveals that the proceeds from the sale of the public land was much smaller than the funds derived from customs and internal Revenue.[82] Nonetheless, it was substantial enough to make it an important source of revenue. The sale of Indian land was also an additional source of revenue. This fact raises another entirely different important reason for the Disclaimer Clause. The reason: Almost all Indian land was the subject matter covered in one way or another by treaties with the hundreds of different Indian tribes across the length and breadth of the entire United States and its territories. Even though there probably were some exceptions, the tribes did not feel that they were bound by any treaties signed by Great Britain, France or Spain which conveyed the sovereignty of their land to the United States. They considered the land to be theirs, and originally it was. To them, the European "conquerors" were not their sovereign.

Our concern, here, is that the land of these three European nations (within the present boundary of the United States) eventually became that of the thirteen original colonies and/or that of the United States (as a sovereign nation) as the spoils of war or by purchase. Later, after 1789, the continual and increasing pressure of the westward movement of people into land the Indian tribes considered to be theirs, motivated treaties between the different Indian tribes and the United States as the sovereign. In essence, the Indian tribes became the wards of the United States. Exactly where the United States secured the authority to sell Indian land, I don't know, but sell it the United States did—a lot of it. In fact, there was scarcely a year during which time the sale of Indian land did not appear as a source of federal revenue. The sale of Indian land constituted almost 20 percent of the total amount of land sold.[83] And this went on for years.

The question that concerns us here is this: If a state acquires formerly territorial land as a result of conveyance that the Equal Footing

---

82-*Historical Statistics, Colonial Times to 1970* (Bicentennial Edition) page 1106. U.S. Printing Office: Stock No. 003-024-00120-9.

83-*Annual Report of the Commissioner of the General Land Office to the Secretary of the Interior* in 1929.

Doctrine indicates is in order upon statehood, how does the state convey title to another of this former Indian land that has been declared to be available for homestead under Federal Law? The simple answer is that it can't do so easily without creating a cloud upon the title. Why not? Because the United States was the sovereign up until statehood, and it was the United States that entered into the treaty agreement with the Indian tribe or tribes, not the state. (Forget, for the moment, that the federal government broke many many Indian treaties almost at will.[84]) As far as Indian land was concerned, the Disclaimer Clause in each of the Enabling Acts was an answer: The federal government would retain title to the state land after statehood in a de facto trust, and when the land was homesteaded, the United States would convey a clear title by issuing a patent—and keep the proceeds of the sale! The sale of both the public and Indian lands were sources of federal revenue. And the federal government wanted to keep it that way. They did so by relying upon the Disclaimer Clause in the Enabling Acts. However that may be, all this places another light upon the Disclaimer Clause in the Enabling Acts: The Disclaimer Clause was there for the purpose of raising money, and, additionally, to convey a clear (federally assured) title to former Indian land.

The state's disclaimer of the public land within their borders after statehood amounted to an exclusive sales contract between the state and the federal government; the state possessed or owned the land after statehood, but the federal government retained the right to sell the land for the state. And while this selling was in process, the federal government would retain the titular ownership of state land in this de facto trust, so that when sold, the federal government could keep the money and convey, by patent, a clear title. This scenario leads to the reinforcement of the existence of a trustor-trustee relationship between the state and federal government. (As an aside, it had to be this way in order to comply with the Equal Footing Doctrine that

---

84-The early treatment of the Indians certainly commands the question, even though it is not really a part of our concern here as the subject matter of this book: How could we treat the Indians in such a manner? In an earlier time, without a lot of detail, the Indians were for the most part considered to be brutal, uncivilized heathens. As early as Columbus, they were thought to have no soul by many. This concept lingered on. Ultimately, the Indians were subjugated—conquered is a better word. They were driven to reservations and kept there. They became the wards of the conqueror. Their former land became that of the conqueror, and treaties notwithstanding it was literally taken and sold. This was not done peacefully. The discovery of gold in the Black Hills of South Dakota "negated" one treaty and gold did it elsewhere as well. But almost as compelling was the thought that land was needed for settlement. Settlement was the reason for the Oklahoma land rush in 1905 wherein all hopeful settlers were lined up, and at the firing of a starter's gun, the rush was on to stake out your plot of ground for homestead on formerly Indian land.

demanded that each new state be equal in all respects whatever with the original thirteen states.

There was even more justification for the Disclaimer Clause. The federal government was managing the General Land Office, handling all the sales and recording all the preempted land locations for homestead. But the location of the homestead land was not readily ascertained; the land had to be properly surveyed. This took many years in most cases. In addition, Congress, all the while, was continually appropriating more and more funds for its operation. Besides, the debt incurred by the American Revolution had not been paid off yet by the sale of land from either the Northwest Territory or the Louisiana Purchase. Further, the purchase-money for the Louisiana Purchase was a long term obligation that was ongoing with payments extending over a number of years. Surely, one could assume, the United States were entitled to reimbursement of this expense, for, after all, these were general treasury funds from which the purchase-money came.

Meanwhile, the westward movement was in full swing; cheap land, now two dollars an acre, was available toward the West by homestead; settlement of that new land was an objective of the United States. Time delays were a constant problem. The General Land Office did not keep regular hours; the offices were not always easy to get to for some of the far-flung settlers; the settlers did not always record their homesteads promptly. Moreover, the lands claimed were not always contiguous to one another. There were blank spaces in between. Errors were common, and Congress often had to define how different claimants to the same land would settle their differences. Maintaining and keeping a clear title became an ongoing problem. If, as each state entered the Union, title were to pass immediately from the federal government to the state prior to the actual issuance of the patent to the claimed land by the federal government, a cloud on the title would be an immediate result. This, too, had been Indian land whose title to the land was literally cleared off by the homestead occupant and the following patent issued by the federal government. Bluntly, the Indian land was taken as the spoils of war with the Indians. As the spoils of war, its title was cleared by one treaty or another with the Indians. Treaty-making was and is a federal function, and the patent process was in reality an assurance of title by the federal government, clearing any Indian claim to the land.

The disclaimer of title by the state was a solution to alleviate the problem of time-delay in conveying the land to a settler. This was a seemingly simple solution, and it worked. Each state which entered the Union after 1812 disclaimed title to the Public Domain. At that time there was no intent to do anything other than continue to dispose of the land in an orderly fashion. As the new state entered the Union, the land was, in effect, the property of the state and held in trust by the federal government. Obviously, the benefit to the federal government in doing this was not overlooked; the proceeds from the sale of this land went into the general treasury of the United States. Eventually, the land was sold, preempted or appropriated, for which a patent was issued by the federal government.

Again, look at the maps between Part One and Part Two. Nothing changed until after the war with Mexico brought in the western territorial lands. Why was the Equal Footing Doctrine ignored at that time? Why did the federal government fail to relinquish title to the Public Domain or cease to sell it as it had always done up until that time? Was this permanent retention really the intention of Congress? No, it was not, at least as late as 1845.

With benefit of hindsight, it appears as though the passage of the 16th Amendment to the U.S. Constitution in 1913 was the end of any real effort to sell off the public land. This amendment was the authorization to collect income taxes. Another source of revenue had been found! The sale of the public land was no longer necessary. A look at the statistics compiled in *Historical Statistics, Colonial Times to 1970,* (p. 1106) clearly indicates that the sale of public land was slowly choked off. By 1937 the revenue derived from the sale of public land brought in a mere $37,000. More compelling however, was the impact of the two federal government agencies, the Forest Service and the Bureau of Land Management, whose joint and several policy was this: Public land of the United States should be kept in perpetuity and preserved under federal control. Quite obviously, these two bureaus were not concerned that this policy shredded the Equal Footing Doctrine. After all, they must have reasoned, that was not their problem; that was up to Congress.

This policy was not the original intent of Congress. The original intent of Congress can best be garnered from an examination of the annexation documents admitting Texas into the Union. See THE ANNEXATION OF TEXAS: CONGRESSIONAL INTENT FOR THE PUBLIC LAND in Part II.

TERRITORIAL CONVENTIONS, NOT STATES, ADOPT DISCLAIMERS

For the sake of argument, let's adopt the view that Congress was laying claim to the land the federal government held in trust. This does not and cannot, in a rather technical way, hold water. Why? Because it was the territorial convention of the territory that adopted the ordinance of admission to statehood, with all its conditions and restrictions, not the state. Remember, in accordance with Article I, Section 8, Clause 17 of the U. S. Constitution, it is the state legislature alone that can and must approve any land within its borders that is to become or remain as federal land. The state had not been formed yet, which of course, meant that there was no such thing as a state legislature! If the state legislature approved such a withholding of this land after joining the Union, that would have been another matter. But this they did not do.

But let's now look at exactly what is said in conformance to the U.S. Constitution. The Constitution states specifically what the federal government *can* own. It says nothing about any land other than that which is for "forts, magazines, arsenals, dock-yards, and other needful buildings." Can it be that this disclaimer is outside the authority of the Constitution? If not, and it should be assumed that Congress was not blatantly intending to operate outside the authority of the Constitution, then that which is referred to are these same "forts, magazines, arsenals, dock-yards, and other needful buildings." There is really no other interpretation that is consistent with the Constitution. To interpret otherwise is to admit that Congress intended to operate outside the limits of the Constitution.

ENABLING ACTS

With respect to a Territorial Assembly committing a state government that is not in existence yet, the following should be noted: It is a rather basic fact of common law that one party cannot bargain or give away rights that belong to another. Simply put, it is not theirs to give. In this case, the territory cannot encumber, give away or grant to another land that they do not own. One could argue: What's the difference? They are the same people as a territory whom they are as a state, and at about the same time. Regardless of this argument, they are two different bodies, and the one cannot bargain for the other. As a result thereof, short of a consent by the state legislature, the individual constitution of the state must govern. ***None of the state constitutions*** contain any such grant of the unappropriated federal lands to the United States. In fact, rather to the contrary, the California constitution frowns upon holding large tracts of land that are unimproved. Presumably, this would include federal lands as well. Article XVII, Section 2 and 3 of the California constitution follows:

"Sec. 2. The holding of large tracts of land, uncultivated and unimproved, by individuals or corporations, is against the public interest, and should be discouraged by all means not inconsistent with the rights of private property."

"Sec. 3. Lands belonging to this State, which are suitable for cultivation, shall be granted only to actual settlers, and in quantities not exceeding 320 acres to each settler, under such conditions as shall be prescribed by law."

There is another important factor that is reinforced by the case of Permoli v. First Municipalities.[85] This was a case that argued that a clause in the Enabling Act for the territory of Orleans had been violated. The court found that no such violation occurred, in that the state constitution had no such provision contained in it that defined the action as a violation. In other words, Congress accepted that which was a fact at the time of the ratification by Congress of the state's constitution, and by so doing forgave or accepted the status quo at that time. Result: No violation. In that case, Justice Catron said:

"The instrument [State Constitution] having been duly formed, and presented, it was for the national legislature to judge whether it contained the proper principles, and to accept it if it did; or reject it if it did not. Having accepted the constitution and admitted the state 'on an Equal Footing with the original States in all respects whatever,' Congress was concluded [settled finally] from assuming that the instructions contained in the Act of 1811 had not been complied with."[86]

Put another way, the state constitution must reiterate provisions in the Enabling Act or those provisions in the Enabling Act that are not in the state constitution are moot: Retention of ownership of the land by the federal government after statehood is not in conformance to the requirement of the U.S. Constitution. Art.1 Sec.8 Cl 17, requires the approval of the legislature of the state. Bluntly: No approval, no land.

85-Permoli v. First Municipality, 3 How. 589, 609.

86-Ibid.

A quotation from New York v. United States, which is discussed in more detail later, is particularly appropriate at this juncture:

> "The constitutional authority of Congress cannot be expanded by the 'consent' of the governmental unit whose domain is thereby narrowed, whether that unit is the Executive Branch or the States."

These are the facts: While still a territory, the territorial land belonged to the United States in trust. It was, indeed, federal land as "territory." (These lands could have been called by some other name to differentiate them from the "Northwest Territory," but they were not. A similar name was in fact picked for land of an entirely different nature.) Once the land became a part of a separate state, the land became state land (in trust)—a part of the separate state, and as such, public land of the state with all of their separate split estates intact and in full force and effect.[87]

Restated again, it is the state and not the territory that can grant this consent to federal ownership of the land. That binding consent cannot be given by a territory on and behalf of a state that did not exist.

Congress retained the right to approve the constitution of the new state; this, the Constitution requires. Congress must guarantee to "every State in this Union a republican form of government."[88]

With some limitations, the U.S. Constitution states: "New States may be admitted by the Congress into this Union."[89] The limitations have to do with the prohibition of forming a state within another state, or combining two or more states into a single state without the consent of both the legislature of the state or states and Congress. That's all the Constitution says directly. But there is the other requirement laid down by the Northwest Ordinance of 1787: The state is to be admitted into the Union on an Equal Footing with the other states—specifically, with the original thirteen states. This is discussed later.

In the case of Coyle v. Smith[90], Justice Lurton had a number of things to say about Enabling Acts, Equal Footing and the new state disclaiming title to public lands. The following are noteworthy quotations:

87-The split estate interests—largely private property interests—are discussed in Part I.

88-Art. IV, Sec. 4 of the U.S. Constitution

89- Art. IV, Sec. 3 (1).

90-Coyle v. Smith: (1911) 221 US 559

"The argument that Congress derives from the duty of 'guaranteeing to each State in this Union a republican form of government,' power to impose restrictions upon a new State which deprives it of equality with other members of the Union has no merit. It may imply the duty of such new State to provide itself with such state government, and impose upon Congress the duty of seeing that such form is not changed to one anti-republican, *but it obviously does not confer power to admit a new State which shall be any less a State than those which compose the Union*." (Emphasis added)

With respect to new states disclaiming title to the public lands, Justice Lurton had this to say:

"Whatever force such provisions have after admission of the State may be attributed to the power of Congress over the subjects, [are] derived from other provisions of the Constitution, rather than from any consent by or compact with the State."

In other words, if the federal government has the power to deprive the state of ownership of the land after statehood, this power does not come from the disclaimer. It comes from some other power. He doesn't say from what other power or that that power does or does not exist.

The court quotes Pollard v. Hagan:[91]

"Full power is given to Congress 'to make all needful rules and regulations respecting the territory or other property of the United States.' This authorized the passage of all laws necessary to secure the rights of the United States to the public lands, and *to provide for their sale*, and to protect them from taxation." (Emphasis added)

Keep in mind that the court is talking about land ceded by Georgia, one of the original colonies, to the United States for a "common fund" to pay off debt. This land differs from later acquired land commonly called by the same name.

Further:

"Every **constitutional** act of Congress is passed by the will of the people of the United States, expressed through their

91-Pollard v. Hagan: 11 L. Ed. 565.

representatives, on the subject-matter of the enactment; and when so passed it becomes the supreme law of the land, and operates by its own force on the subject-matter, in whatever State or Territory it may happen to be. The proposition, therefor that such a law cannot operate upon the subject-matter of its enactment, without the express consent of the people of the new State, where it may happen to be, contains its own refutation."

(Emphasis added)

This certainly seems to give the federal government the right to retain ownership and control of territorial land and thus, under the guise of rules and regulations, retain the title to the land after it became a state. Not so, except in a narrow context. Rules and regulations, in this instance, are restricted to territory. Dred Scott v. Sandford, discussed earlier, defined territory; it was that land ceded by the seven colonies to the United States for "a common fund." The narrow context is that the federal government could retain title to the land as "a common fund" until the conditions of the trust in which it was placed as "a common fund" were fulfilled. Secondly, there is no argument about the validity of every *constitutional* act of Congress becoming the supreme law of the land. It is. But what about unconstitutional acts of Congress? **Unconstitutional** acts of Congress are not enforceable and of no force and effect. The above quotation does not apply to unconstitutional acts of Congress.

Justice Lurton, in Coyle v. Smith cites Escanaba Co. v. Chicago[92] as follows:

"Whatever the limitation upon her powers as a government whilst in a territorial condition, whether from the ordinance of 1787 or the legislation of Congress, it ceased to have any operative force, except as voluntarily adopted by her [the state], after she became a State of Union. ***On her admission she at once became entitled to and possessed of all the rights of dominion[93] and sovereignty[94] which belonged to the original States***. She was admitted, and could be admitted, only...'on an Equal Footing with the original States in all respects whatever.'"

92-Escanaba Co. v. Chicago: 107 US 678.

93-Black's Law Dictionary: "Dominion. Generally accepted definition of 'dominion' is perfect control in *right of ownership*. The word implies both *title and possession* and appears to require a complete *retention of control over disposition*. Eastex Aviation, Inc. v. Sperry & Hutchinson Co.., C.A. Tex., 522 F 2d 1299, 1307. Title to an article of property which arises from the power of disposition and the right of claiming it."

94-Black's Law Dictionary defines sovereignty as follows: "By 'sovereignty,' in its largest sense is meant supreme, absolute, uncontrollable power, the absolute right to govern."

Here is a clear statement by the Supreme Court as to the extent of the meaning of "on an Equal Footing in all respects whatever."

DOMINION AND SOVEREIGNTY

It is in the case of Escanaba Co. v. Chicago, quoted immediately preceding, that we see for the first time, the words "dominion" and "sovereignty." Note the meaning of "dominion" and "sovereignty" as defined in the footnotes immediately following that quotation. However, it is important to understand what these two words meant to our founding fathers, for it is to them that we must turn to find their original intent with respect to the ownership and disposition of the land after statehood.

Blackstone's "***Commentaries on the Laws of England***," first published in 1765, was the law-book of the day. It was the only authoritative book on law that existed during the time of our founding fathers. In fact, it was used as the textbook for all law students even as late as the days of Abraham Lincoln; he became a lawyer by studying Blackstone prior to his apprenticeship as a budding lawyer. He wasn't alone; they all did. For law, meaning and structure, our founding fathers only had Blackstone to which to turn. Our founding fathers knew it reasonably well, therefore, what Blackstone said about dominion and sovereignty is important; it is pivotal.

Blackstone traces "dominion" in time back to the Bible: "the all-bountiful creator gave to man dominion over all the earth; and over the fish of the sea, and over the fowl of the air, and over every living thing that moveth upon the earth."[95] He then expands upon the origin of property, both real and personal and had the following to say about the vesting of this property:

> "The only question remaining is, how this property became actually vested; or what it is that gave a man an exclusive right to retain in a permanent manner that specific land, which before belonged generally to every body, but particularly to nobody."

Continuing,

> "...occupancy gave the right to the temporary use of the

95-Blackstone: "Commentaries on the Laws of England," Vol. II, "Of Things," p. 2.

soil, so it is agreed upon all hands that occupancy gave also the original right to the permanent property in the substance of the earth itself; which excludes every one else but the owner from the use of it."[96]

The following is what Blackstone had to say about the sale of this property:

> "...the proprietor declares his intention no longer to occupy the thing himself, but that his own right of occupancy shall be vested in the new acquirer. Or taken in the other light, if I agree to part with an acre of my land to Titius, the deed of intention, immediately steps in and fiefs[97] the vacant possession: thus the consent expressed by the conveyance gives Titius a good right against me; and possession, or occupancy, confirms that right against all the world besides."[98]

Clearly, "dominion" includes the ownership of land and the right of disposal.

Sovereignty has a different origin and a different meaning incorporated in that origin. Sovereignty is a derivative of the word "sovereign." The sovereign was the king. The king owned all the land, and it was all subject to his right of disposal. It was his alone. He could convey it to a subject as a reward for fighting for the king. Much of England was conveyed for exactly this reason to different subjects at different times. At times, the king even took the land back and conveyed it to another who pleased him more for one reason or another. This could be equated to the right of eminent domain.[99] The important point is that the king had the supreme right of ownership and of disposition. The king possessed eminent (a word that is founded upon the Latin word "eminens" meaning "peak" or "highest") domain. Eminent domain was an integral and inseparable part of sovereignty. In other words, you cannot have sovereignty if you do not also have the right of eminent domain. It is that basic. Today, we tend to consider the meaning of eminent domain as only a power to take back. It is far more than

---

97-The word "fief" is the origin of the term "fee," such as in "fee simple." They mean the same thing.

98-Blackstone: "Commentaries on the Laws of England," Vol. II, "Of Things," p. 10.

99-*Black's Law Dictionary* defines eminent domain as follows: "The power to take private property for public use by the state, municipalities, and private persons or corporations authorized to exercise functions of public character." Black adds: "...the right of the state...to reassert, either temporarily or permanently, its **dominion** over any portion of the soil of the state on account of public exigency and for the public good."

that. It is the highest form of title. It is the ultimate fee (title or ownership).

Sovereignty goes beyond dominion in that it constitutes absolute power over the land with the right to take it back—eminent domain. (Our Constitution limits the conditions for the exercise of eminent domain.)

This is what our founding fathers understood. This is the meaning to be extracted from the quotation from Escanaba Co. v. Chicago. These were integral parts of their meaning of what was to be included when a new state was to be admitted on an Equal Footing with the original states because this is exactly what the original colony-states possessed: complete and absolute title to the land within their borders—the ultimate fee.

The king's conveyance was often accompanied by the term "tenure."[100]

Tenure implies that perhaps occupancy or use and ownership wasn't permanent and could be revoked. And the king, at times, did exactly that. The important point here is not that tenure existed, but that sovereignty did, for it was this sovereignty that was possessed by the original state (colonies)—which included their right of eminent domain. The original states were given absolute sovereignty just like the king—absolute ownership and the unilateral right of disposition of the land within their borders to do with it as their separate constitutions dictated. With the fore-going in mind, read again the quotation from Escanaba Co. v. Chicago. Essentially, this same language will appear later a number of times in other cases: A newly admitted state was to have "all the rights of dominion and sovereignty which belonged to the original states."

At this point, a sense of perspective is necessary. Pollard v. Hagan was decided in 1845 and Coyle v. Smith was decided in 1911. I must refer the reader to Part One for the historical background surrounding conditions and the modus operandi of disposition of our public lands during the earlier years. In short, retention of title to the land seemed to be necessary until it could be conveyed to the ultimate land buyer: There was no survey; parts of the land were "a common fund" of the United States; land purchased by

---

100-Black's Law Dictionary defines "tenure" as follows: "Generally, tenure is a right, term, or mode of holding or occupying...especially with regard to time." Black's adds: "Tenure is the direct result of feudalism, which separated the dominium directum (the dominion of the soil), which is placed mediately or immediately in the crown, from the dominium utile (the possessory title), the right to the use and profits in the soil, designated by the term 'seisin,' [Possession of real property under claim of freehold estate.] which is the highest interest a subject can acquire."

funds from the United States, such as the Louisiana Purchase, certainly dictated a repayment prior to reconveyance: an interim conveyance of title to the state prior to the passage of title by patent from the United States to the buyer or homesteader could become a cloud on the title. The court knew all this at the time of the two decisions.

However, the question remains: Does the withholding of the title to the public land from a state, albeit in trust, constitute a condition of inequality between the states? Clearly, the court insists that the states must be equal. And it is true that the court does, without definition, insist that political equality is not the same as geographical or physical equality. The court has clearly indicated that economic equality is not a consideration. The states never were economically equal, nor was there any intent to make them so. But what does equality mean? What are its limits? How is it defined? Justice Lurton, in citing Escanaba Co. v. Chicago as quoted previously certainly indicates that equality means that the state is the owner of the land after admission into the Union.

This raises the issue of "Equal Footing" and entering the Union "on an Equal Footing in all respects whatever." Do these two phrases mean the same thing? Is one an extension of the other?

Before going directly into the issue of "Equal Footing," which is discussed later, it seems of considerable importance to first examine what our founding fathers had in mind?

THE FOUNDING FATHERS: LIMITS ON FEDERAL & STATE GOVERNMENT

The founding fathers never envisioned a federal government that would be a "land baron." In fact, the Articles of Confederation did not contain any provision for such ownership or control by the central government. If anything, it was limiting. They were deathly afraid of any such burgeoning development of a central government, but equally, if not more so, they were fearful of separate states or a combination of states acquiring too much power. Their interest was to limit. Madison, in the *Federalist Paper No. 44*, defends the seemingly simple and brief wording of Congressional Power, namely: Article I, Sec. 8, Clause 18:

...the power to make all laws which shall be necessary and proper for carrying into execution the foregoing powers, and all other powers vested by this Constitution in the government of the Unites States."

He almost says, "That's the best we can do in view of the alternatives." He does go into detail about those alternatives and finally concludes with the following as to any excesses, usurpation or abuse of power by Congress:

> "...the success of the usurpation will depend on the executive and judiciary departments, which are to expound and give effect to the legislative acts; and ***in the last resort***, a remedy must be obtained from the people, who can by the election of more faithful representatives, annul the acts of the usurpers." (Emphasis added)

Our founding fathers never envisioned the possibility of a federal establishment that would dwarf that of the states, and it is with some irony that I quote the following from Madison's *Federalist No. 45*:

> "The number of individuals employed under the Constitution of the United States, will be much smaller, than the number employed under the particular States."

To them, the central government would perform only those things that the states themselves could not perform. Dealing with foreign governments was, of course, one of these, and treaties were an integral part of this. Because all the states, as United States, had a huge war debt and the Northwest Territory as "a common fund" (a collective source of repayment), the federal government was called upon to handle its disposition and disposal. The federal government held the land in trust for the states that would be later created in the area. Our founding fathers envisioned that as soon as a new area—territory—became a state the people of the new state would be the title holder of all the land except that which would remain in federal ownership for "forts, magazines, arsenals, dock-yards, and other needful buildings"—and only then if the state legislature approved. That is what the U. S. Constitution says. In reality, the "if" is big and it has been ignored for many, many years.

CONSTITUTIONALITY OF THE NORTHWEST ORDINANCE OF 1787

Two elements of historic and constitutional importance come from the Northwest Ordinance of 1787, an ordinance enacted by the Confederation that was established in 1781, nearly six years before the Constitution was ratified.

The first element: Is the Northwest Ordinance of 1787 a part of the Constitution? Yes, it is, in an indirect manner. The Federal Union, known as the Confederation, operating as the head of the provisional government during the American Revolution, ratified "The Articles of Confederation and Perpetual Union." These were the fundamental operating regulations that would become provisions, in part or in whole, of what would be included in the U.S. Constitution. In fact, to insure that they **were** a part of the U.S. Constitution the framers of the Constitution included the following language: Article VI, Clause 1.

> "All debts, **contracts** and **engagements** entered into before the adoption of this Constitution shall be as valid against the United States under this Constitution as under the Confederation." (Emphasis added)

This clause ratified the inclusion of all of the provisions included in The Articles of Confederation and Perpetual Union, as well as the Northwest Ordinance of 1787, an act of the Confederation. There seemed some doubt that an act of the Continental Congress was binding—even by Article VI, Section 1 quoted above—so Congress re-enacted the Northwest Ordinance of 1787 in its exact words.

The second element has to do with the Equal Footing Doctrine.

THE ORIGIN OF THE "EQUAL FOOTING DOCTRINE" AND THE RIGHT OF SOVEREIGNTY UPON STATEHOOD

The term, "Equal Footing" finds its actual origin in the *Report of Government for the Western Territory*, April 23, 1784 which is quoted a little later. Following this earliest use of the term, the Northwest Ordinance of 1787 mentions it twice. Both citations bear directly upon the subject matter of Part Two. First in paragraph 13:

"...to provide also for the establishment of states, and permanent government therein, and for their admission to a share in the Federal Councils on an *Equal Footing with the original states*." (Emphasis added)

Succinctly, this says that each state shall *share equally* in the *federal councils*. Clearly, this is a political consideration. Secondly, in Article V:

"And, whenever any of the said states shall have sixty thousand free inhabitants therein, such state shall be admitted, by its delegates, into the Congress of the United States, *on an Equal Footing with the original States, in all respects whatever*...." (Emphasis added)

This statement says that each state shall be "*admitted...into the Congress*" on an Equal Footing with the original states. This begs the question as to the extent of the meaning of "Equal Footing." Does this mean that this includes more than just "their admission to a share in the federal councils...with the original states" and an admission "into the Congress of the United States?" How far does "in all respects whatever" go? Bluntly, does this mean that if the original thirteen colony-states did or did not possess something, such as sovereignty of their land, then the new state was to be put on the same basis? I believe that this was the intent and that the meaning of the words, "in all respects whatever," meant exactly that to the framers of the Constitution: Each new state was to be *exactly* (as much as possible with the exception of economic equality) equal in all respects to the original states. As mentioned earlier, the Supreme Court believed this as well and stated this in the case of Escanaba Co. v. Chicago.

Did this intent include land? Of course it did. A state was to have dominion and sovereignty over the land within its borders. Certainly, each of the original states possessed both dominion and sovereignty over the land within their borders. There, then, was the criteria of equality as it pertained to land. It was not limited to just jurisdiction or some form of half-way sovereignty; it included full dominion and sovereignty—the same as the original thirteen colony-states.

There are those that believe that this equality encompasses only a limited form of sovereignty which they claim, does not require ownership of the land by the state upon entering the Union, and that this equality is limited solely to political equality.

There is basis for refuting their line of reasoning.

The words, "equal rights, Equal Footing, same footing, footing of equality, equality," appear many times in the deliberations of the Federal Convention of 1787 in June and July of that year. It was obvious that the seeds of what we call the Equal Footing Doctrine were already implanted in all their minds. If I were to paraphrase their issues, they were endeavoring to lay a foundation that would keep everything equal in perpetuity. Certainly, dominion and sovereignty were a big part of this. Keep in mind that all of these separate colony-states already had their own dominion and sovereignty (ultimate fee ownership of the land) except that which they had voluntarily foregone when they joined together to form the Confederation.

Also a part of "equality" was the right of sovereignty. The earliest pronouncement on the subject of the right of sovereignty[101] that I have been able to find is contained in The Resolution of Congress on Public Lands, October 10, 1780:

> "RESOLVED, that the unappropriated lands that may be ceded or relinquished to the United States, by any particular States, pursuant to the recommendation of Congress on the 6 day of September last, shall be disposed of for the common benefit of the United States, and be settled and formed into distinct republican States, which shall become members of the Federal Union, *and shall have the same rights of sovereignty, freedom and independence, as the other States*;" (Emphasis added)

This resolution has a two-fold purpose for us. First, it tells us what is to become of the land so ceded: It "shall be *disposed* of for the common benefit of the United States." This indicates intent. It does not say that the land shall be held. Second, the resolution tells us that the states formed from this ceded land will have the same right of sovereignty (ultimate fee ownership) of its land as the other states—a statement of equality. This indicates the extent of the meaning of the phrase, "on an Equal Footing with the original states in all respects whatever." Keep in mind, however, that the prerogatives of Congress as defined by the Constitution, approved some

101-Note the definition of "sovereignty" in a preceding footnote as explained in *Black's Law Dictionary*. Some believe that this indicates political supremacy only and does not necessarily pertain to land. Not so. They overlook that sovereignty includes eminent domain—the highest form of ownership: ultimate fee. To our founding fathers, their knowledge of law and meaning of words came from Blackstone's *"Commentaries on the Laws of England,"* not from *Black's Law Dictionary*, first printed in 1891. This was discussed earlier.

seven years later, did not give to Congress any powers beyond those clearly defined by the Constitution. The definition of "Equal Footing" was never up to Congress to define. We therefore must look elsewhere to find what the original intent of the framers of the Constitution was as well as their meaning of the term "equal."

The right of sovereignty is an adjunct of dominion and sovereignty which was explained in a preceding section entitled DOMINION AND SOVEREIGNTY. The "same rights of sovereignty" that appears in the preceding resolution certainly included the ownership of the land. Suppose for the sake of argument that it did not include the land—any of the land. Could anyone successfully argue that this was the intent of our founding fathers, that none of the land was to be included in a new state? I think not. Then how about *some* of the land? Here we must look at the intent of the founding fathers. Their definition was clear: each new state must be "equal in all respects whatever" to the original states. The delegates to the Federal Convention of 1787, the convention that formulated our U.S. Constitution, sheds considerable authoritative light on this subject which is discussed later, and from that convention, we come to know the attitude and opinions of the delegates as a whole.

To the question, were the original states sovereign over their land and did they own the unappropriated land? Their answer was yes. And in that simple question and answer lies one of the cornerstones of one element to which other states were required to be equal: ownership of the land within their border. Each new state was to be sovereign over its land, have title to it and have the right to dispose of it, just like any one of the original thirteen colony-states. The Supreme Court says exactly that in Escanaba Co. v. Chicago, for after all, that is exactly what dominion and sovereignty mean.

There is additional reinforcement to this pronouncement of the right of sovereignty. It is repeated almost word for word in Virginia's *Cession of Western Lands to the United States*, December 20, 1783:

> "...and the States so formed shall be distinct republican States, and admitted members of the Federal Union, having the same **rights of sovereignty**, freedom, and independence as the other States." (Emphasis added)

Just a few months after the ***Virginia Cession of Western Lands to the United States, The Report of Government for the Western Territory*** on April 23, 1784 stated, with respect to new states formed from the ceded territory:

"...such State shall be admitted by it's delegates into the Congress of the United States on an Equal Footing with the said original states:" (Emphasis added)

I do not think that this is a diminution of the intent of the words contained in Virginia's cession quoted earlier, even though it uses the phrase "admitted...into the Congress of the United States." I believe that the term "Equal Footing," as it first appears here, was intended to include the right of dominion and sovereignty—ownership of the land—as an integral part of their equality with the original states.

However it may have been, the term "Equal Footing" was thereafter used almost exclusively.

Next in the chronology of actions contemplated by our founding fathers appears a most interesting intent in The Land Ordinance of May 20, 1785. It answers the question: Was there ever an intent to withhold land from the states by the federal government early on? No, there wasn't. Included in The Land Ordinance of 1785 is the following statement:

"The board of treasury [after the proper survey of the land] shall transmit a copy of the original plats...to the ***commissioners of the land-office of the several states***, who, after giving notice...shall proceed to sell the townships or fractional parts of townships, at public vendue [sale]," (Emphasis added)

Note that it was the state that was to sell the land, not the federal government. For this to be so, obviously, the right of dominion and sovereignty (ownership) had to be included. Otherwise, the state would have nothing to sell.

This, then, was the background and foundation of the Northwest Ordinance of 1787, in which the term "Equal Footing" was used, and by usage has become the basis for what we commonly call the Equal Footing Doctrine. The Equal Footing Doctrine, if taken from the Northwest Ordinance alone, with no background, as I have tried to point out here, limits the equality to a political basis alone. As you can see from the earlier ordinances quoted above, admission to statehood was not intended to be limited to just an equal admission to the Congress or the federal council—political equality. Admission to the Union had to be on an equal basis with the other original states— "in all respects whatever"—which, of course, would including the right of sovereignty and ownership of the land. To arbitrarily eliminate sovereignty (ultimate fee ownership of the land), denying the latter to future states, and still claim that this is "equal in all respects whatever" is a gross stretch of the original intent.

Nevertheless, there are those who believe a new state admitted to the Union has no right to demand that land within its borders be a part of its dominion and sovereignty (ownership of the land); that the federal government has every right to withhold land (in any quantity, in any location, for any length of time up to permanently) from becoming a part of the new state's dominion and sovereignty; that there is no requirement that the transfer from federal ownership at the time of territorial status to state ownership take place at the time of joining the Union; that the ultimate ownership of the land is not a part of the equation.

In other words, they believed that the Equal Footing Doctrine was not intended to extend to land; that it was to extend only to political equality. Their base and fundamental argument is that you cannot find the words "Equal Footing" anywhere in the Constitution. They are right. Those words are not there. And further, they argue, the Disclaimer Clause included in nearly all of the Enabling Acts was a limiting clause that literally precluded a new state from any and all claim, present or future, to the dominion and sovereignty of the land within its borders which the United States had set aside or reserved—even after statehood—into perpetuity. This is a powerful argument—even if it is wrong.

To rebut this argument one must look into the character of our founding fathers themselves and examine the term "intent;" first, as it pertained to their concept of what they thought was "equal," and next, as to what they thought with respect to dominion and sovereignty (ownership of land) after statehood. What was the intent of our founding fathers? Did they intend that the new federal government should establish states that were other than equal with the original colony-states? Should the new federal government have the power to withhold land from any given new state for any purpose whatsoever? If there were to be limits, what was their purpose, and how long would they withhold?

If our founding fathers were anything at all, they were fair-minded, and their ideas of equality were exactly that: All states were to be equal one to the other in all respects except economic equality. They knew that economic equality was already a product of whatever already existed in each of the separate states; some were wealthier than others. But aside from economic equality, they wanted nothing in any state that another did not have or would have access to. Their model for this level playing field existed in the original colony-states themselves, now "free and independent States of America"[102] and their dominion and sovereignty as it existed as a result of the Treaty of Paris with Great Britain. Further, as we discover later in the deliberations of the Federal Convention of 1787, they were not about to give it up.

An examination of the records of the Federal Convention of 1787 shows that the delegates to that convention labored hard to make sure that all states were "equal," and that no state, large or small, wealthy or otherwise, would be in a position of advantage over the other. The deliberation toward equality was never out of their minds. First, in the form of countless resolutions during the months of May and June of 1787 and later in August in the form of actual verbiage to be contained in the proposed new Constitution. They agreed and disagreed. Their record is filled with resolutions as well as numerous actual suggested wordings to be contained in the new Constitution that were voted down. Their finally accepted selection of wording was after much discussion, soul searching, and examination of multitudinous, varied, possible circumstances. They made every effort to be fair and treat every state and its inhabitants "equally."

The Record of the Federal Convention of 1787 reveals far more than what the meaning of "equally" was to them. It reveals the attitude of mind of each delegate had about what each state believed to be its own actual dominion and sovereignty. Keep in mind that their concept of dominion and sovereignty included the ownership of the land—the ultimate fee ownership. Clearly, the delegates did not go to the convention to give this up even though there were some delegates who thought that such an event might quite possibly be necessary in order to form an effective replacement for the Articles of Confederation—the very reason they were all assembled in Philadelphia for nearly six months. However, as you shall see later, this was an abhorrent idea to most states—a most unacceptable event and one that some felt they were simply not authorized to even consider. One delegate, Edmund Randolph, Governor of Virginia, wanted to literally sack all state law in preference to a new national government, admittedly an event that would require the approval on the part of the states themselves, an event no one really thought politically possible. In Madison's Journal he notes what Mr. John Lansing said on Wednesday, June 20.

> "It could not be expected that those possessing Sovereignty could ever voluntarily part with it. It was not to be expected from any State, much less from thirteen." [103]

102-*The Record of the Federal Convention of 1787*, edited by Max Farrand, Volume III, p. 595

Delegate Patterson opposed Randolph's Plan vehemently, as did delegate Martin. Madison, in his journal of June 16, 1787 makes this observation relative to what these two delegates said about the two different plans submitted for debate:

> "That of Mr. Patterson says he sustains the sovereignty of the respective States, [while] that of Mr. Randolph destroys it: the latter requires a negative on all the laws of the particular States; the former, only certain general powers for the general good."[104]

Madison continues in his journal of the same date:

> "N. York would never have concurred in sending deputies to the convention, if she had supposed the deliberations were to turn on a consolidation of the States, and a National Government."[105]

Meaning: New York was not about to give up its already-possessed dominion and sovereignty to a national government.

Further, Madison writes in his journal of the same date in reviewing Mr. Patterson's remarks:

> "If we argue the matter on the supposition that no Confederacy at present exists, in can not be denied that all the States stand on the footing of equal sovereignty."[106]

This statement reflects that prior to the Articles of Confederation, all the states possessed total dominion and sovereignty. Further, from the different views expressed, it is quite clear that most of the delegates were of the opinion that after the Articles of Confederation, they still retained all powers that they had not granted to the Confederacy. Dominion and sovereignty were not things any of the Confederated states gave up by joining the Confederacy.

However, they all knew that a compromise was necessary in order to form an effective national government. Madison, in his letter to W.C.

103-Ibid. Vol. I, p. 337.
104-Ibid. Vol. I, p. 249
105-Ibid. Vol I, p. 249
106-Ibid. Vol. I, p. 250

Rives (October 21-31, 1778), in clear concise words states the basic problem with the Articles of Confederation.

> "It must be kept in mind that the radical defect of the old confederation lay in the power of the States to comply with, to disregard, or to counteract the authorized requisitions & regulations of Congress..."[107]

The real crux of the argument or dilemma was the extent that state power was to give way to a new national government in order to make it effective. The final settlement of that issue is best gathered from the **Federalist Papers** themselves. In the section that follows shortly, THE FEDERAL GOVERNMENT AND THE RIGHT OF EMINENT DOMAIN (ULTIMATE FEE OWNERSHIP) this is taken up.

In the New Jersey Plan or Patterson Resolution presented to the Federal Convention on June 14-15, 1787, the following is noteworthy:

> "Resolved, That every State in the Union as a State possesses an **equal Right to**, and Share of, **Sovereignty**, Freedom, and Independence-"[108] (Emphasis added)

To Mr. Patterson of New Jersey and the other lessor states that assisted in the preparation of this offered resolution, "equal right to...Sovereignty" meant that sovereignty of the land was to be equal in all states, existing or in the future. Further, sovereignty, to them, meant ownership (the ultimate fee) of the land. The goose was to have it no differently than the gander.

After exploring what our founding fathers said or wrote about "equality," or its derivative, the Equal Footing Doctrine, it is extremely difficult for me to see where and how it can be claimed that the western land these delegates were talking about was to remain in federal ownership or control in perpetuity. There is simply no foundation for it.

Even though they did nothing of the kind, for the sake of argument, let me offer an example of what circumstances would dictate if the delegates to the Federal Convention of 1787 had resolved and approved amendments that did declare that dominion and sovereignty (ultimate fee ownership) of the western land were to remain federal in nature rather than state—a

107-Ibid. Vol. I, p. 250

108-Ibid. Vol. III, p. 613.

condition that would allow the federal government to do whatever it pleased, into perpetuity even, of any and all of the land within any of the new states that joined the Union.

Under those circumstances, we would find that the original thirteen colony-states had full dominion and sovereignty (ultimate fee ownership) of all the land within their borders. Those thirteen colony-states possess it from their start and they clearly did not forego this at any time. Next to this, we would find a wide strip of land extending to the Mississippi that was in a sort of quasi trust in which the federal government had a somewhat semi sovereign interest inasmuch as it had been ceded to the United States by seven of the original thirteen colony-states for a specific purpose. Further to the west, clear to the Pacific Ocean, we would find that the land in all the new state was within the dominion and sovereignty (ultimate fee owner-ship) of the United States exclusively. Why? Because the United States either purchased it or secured it as the spoils of war. Based upon that, and that alone, that land west of the Mississippi was to be treated differently. States from the Mississippi clear to the Pacific Ocean would be outside the loop of the exclusivity of the original thirteen colony states. What would those states have instead? They would have jurisdiction! That is a far cry from dominion and sovereignty. As I stated earlier, it is hard for me to believe that this can be termed to be "equal."

If I were able to line up Alexander Hamilton, Gouvereur Morris, Thomas Jefferson[109], James Madison, John Jay or any of the other founding fathers and ask them the following question: "Do you believe that a future state that is to enter the Union should be deprived, in perpetuity, of the land within its border? And, if so, under what circumstances and in what amount?" You would certainly not get an unconditional, "Yes." I think they would all answer somewhat along the following line:

"Our purpose was to treat all States equally and fairly

109-Thomas Jefferson is considered to be one of the founding fathers (he was a strong Antifederalist who did not want the Bill of Rights but he did have opinions relative to what later became parts of the Bill of Rights even though his participation in its formulation was very little more than what he relates in his journal). However, he also had little or nothing to do with the formulation of the Constitution. He was not a delegate to the Federal Convention of 1787 inasmuch as he was the ambassador to France. The following is a quotation that I believe is from his journal that reflects the contents of a letter he addressed to Madison that confirms this: "On receiving it [the Constitution while in France] I wrote strongly to Mr. Madison, urging the want of provision for the freedom of religion, freedom of the press, trial by jury, habeas corpus, the substitution of militia for a standing army, and an express reserva-tion to the State of all rights not specifically granted to the Union...This is all the hand I had in what related to the Constitution."

and insure that they would always remain so. No State was to be any different from any other State, either as to its dominion and sovereignty—land included—or to its rights or powers. You use the term, Equal Footing. We used it as well. It was one of our underpinnings. However, there were two areas in which this equality had to function, one on a national level and other on a state level. Even so, no state was to forego anything that was not expected and demanded of the original Colony-State.

"We tried to cover that very issue of delegated Power and I think that we did so by enumerating those powers that would be reserved to the Federal Government while all other powers would remain with the different States. While we did not grant power to the Federal Government to withhold land specifically, we did outline that the Federal Government did have the rights and powers that we did enumerate. To the extent that it is necessary to carry out those delegated Federal Powers, we surely would not have been agreeable to allow any State to negate that delegated power that we thought so important as to specifically delegate."

While this is a fictitious response, I do not think that it is not far from what you would hear from any one of the founding fathers.

In order to make an unequal treatment of land conform to what some think is equal, one must ignore what "equal" meant to our founding fathers—at least I think so.

There is little doubt in my mind that if our founding fathers could answer this question today, they would confirm that it was their intent that this equality extends to ownership by the state upon statehood of all the land within its border. This is not in conflict with what our founding fathers had in mind when they clearly wanted the exclusive right to dispose of western land—either that which composed the Northwest Territory or that land acquired as a result of the Louisiana Purchase. From these huge parcels, they sought and received the proceeds from the sale of that land for the repayment of the debt created by the American Revolution. Debt repayment was their intent. However that may be, in the case of Pollard v. Hagan the court did come as close as it could to indicating this very fact, but it was precluded from deciding it in that case; that was not the subject matter of the controversy before the court. The court did say, as best it could, that what the original states had the new states were to have also: Equality "in all respects whatever."

But what about the western land that was ceded by Great Britain? What was to become of it? How was it to be disposed of? This effectively brings up another issue.

THE FEDERAL CONVENTION OF 1787 AND ITS ANSWER TO THE QUESTION OF LAND FOR PAYMENT OF DEBT

Were it not for how this early treatment and thought with respect to this western land was to later affect the presumed ultimate fee ownership by the United States (by some adherents to that view) of the acquired land from France, Mexico and Russia, it would make no difference at all as to who really had dominion and sovereignty over this western land—the individual states or the United States. Because it does make a big difference we must examine it thoroughly. However, before getting into this subject too far, it is worth reviewing a timeline of events that preceded the Federal Convention of 1787 with respect to this land ceded by Great Britain.

1780: "The Resolution of Congress of October 10, 1780 and the attitude of Maryland toward ratification of the Articles of Confederation gave powerful impulse to the cession of the land claims of the States to the United States."[110]

1781: New York and Connecticut expressed their willingness to cede their claims.

1781: Virginia's first cession of their western land to the United States was refused by Congress.

1782: Congress accepted New York's cession.

1783: Virginia offers its second cession to Congress.

1784: Congress accepts Virginia's cession.

1787: The Federal Convention convenes to take up, among other things, what to do about the western lands that had already been ceded to the United States by the different states and had become, as a result of that cession, the property of the United States.

110-Federal and State Constitutions, edited by F. N. Thorpe, Vol. II, p. 955-6

1787: Congress enacts The Northwest Ordinance on July 13, 1787 at the very time when the disposition of the western land is being discussed by the Federal Convention.

Obviously, there was nothing sudden about considering the use of land as the means of paying off the debt incurred by the American Revolution.

In spite of what the Treaty of Paris said, there were still those delegates that thought that this land had been ceded to the Confederation—or perhaps they thought that it should have been. It doesn't make any real difference. During the debate as to how this land was to be used to pay off the debt incurred by the American Revolution, there were resolutions and amendments to the affect that this land had been ceded to the United States. Note the following:

> "...vacant land ceded to them [the United States] by the late 'treaty of Peace.'" [111]

Another amendment, later withdrawn, said almost the same thing:

> "...Provided nevertheless that nothing in this Constitution shall be construed to affect the claim of the United States 'to vacant lands ceded to them by the late Treaty of peace.'" [112]

Neither one of these amendments survived. What did survive was the confirmed view that the land had been ceded by Great Britain to the separate and independent colony-states and as a result thereof, it became the property of the separate states—a part of their dominion and sovereignty (ultimate fee ownership). The land was theirs; it was not the property of the Confederation of States (the United States) as it existed at that time. This is material in that it is an integral part of what was "equal" in the Equal Footing Doctrine; it was a part of the equation.

Conversely, if it had been determined by the delegates and agreed to by resolution or amendments that did survive, that the ceded land from Great Britain was in fact ceded to the Confederation of States, then, and only then, would there be any basis for the claim that the United States had anything other than a temporary claim to the public lands that came into existence as a result of the Louisiana Purchase, the Treaty of Guadalupe

---

111-The Record of Federal Convention of 1787, edited by Max Farrand, Vol. II,

112-Ibid. Vol. II, p. 458 p. 458

Hidalgo, or the Cession of Alaska from Russia. Under these converse conditions, the ultimate fee ownership—dominion and sovereignty—would have resided in the United States, and that in turn, would have found its inclusion as a part of the Equal Footing Doctrine. But that did not happen.

Debt and its repayment was a compelling problem to all of them. This spilled over into their discussions in August of 1787 when they were deliberating on what was known at that time as Article XVII: The admission of New States into the Union—how and under what circumstances. They knew that new states would be formed before long out of the western land, and they also knew that the debts of the United States, as a whole, would not have been paid off by that time. How then do we apportion this debt to the new states? That was one of their primary questions. See Article XVII [XVI] as it originally appeared:

> "New States lawfully constituted or established within the limits of the United States may be admitted, by the Legislature, into this Government; but to such admission the consent of two thirds of the members present in each House shall be necessary. If a new State shall arise within the limits of any of the present States, the consent of the Legislature of such States shall be also necessary to its admission. If the admission be consented to, the new States shall be admitted on the same terms with the original states. ***But the Legislature may make conditions with the new States, concerning the public debt which shall be then subsisting.***"[113] (Emphasis added)

In Madison's journal of June 25th, he attributes to Mr. George Read the following:

> "He brought into view the appropriation of the common interest in the Western lands, to the use of particular States. Let justice be done on this head; let the fund be applied fairly and equally to the discharge of the general debt."[114]

This links the sale of land to debt repayment. There was the tie-in connection: Land for debt.

The following amendment was proposed. Its importance is such

113-Ibid. Vol. II, p. 188

114-Ibid. Vol. I, p. 405.

that I am compelled to quote all of it inasmuch as it reflects the connection between debt and land and **the power given to Congress to make rules and regulations** (obviously) for the disposition of that same land they were all talking about at the same time.

"It was moved and seconded to agree to the following proposition.

"Nothing in this Constitution shall be construed to alter the claim of the United States or of the individual States to the western territory but all such claims may be examined into and decided upon by the supreme Court of the United States.

"It was moved and seconded to postpone the last proposition in order to take up the following.

"The Legislature shall have power to dispose of and make all needful rules and regulations respecting the territory or other property belonging to the United States: and nothing in this Constitution shall be so construed as to prejudice any claims either of the United States or of any particular State"
(Emphasis added)

This last emphasized amendment passed and is a part of the U.S. Constitution: Article IV, Section 3, paragraph 2.

In the final analysis, it had been debt that became the catalyst that finally resolved all differing opinions. Land had been ceded to the United States by the different states; it was to be sold in order to pay the total debts of all the federated states, and Congress was empowered to make rules and regulations to govern its disposition.

It is that simple.

There is no getting around it: Land for debt and the power given to Congress to make rules and regulations in order to dispose of it are all tied together.

A state's entry into the Union was to be conditioned upon the state's pledge of its assets (land) and/or its ability to assume its share of the national debt in some other way. As it turned out, a pledge of its land was the way it was to take place. Unappropriated western land and debt were interconnected. One could arguably question: If there had been no debt, would there have been a pledge of that land? I rather think not. There would have been no need. But there was a need, and this need was to be fulfilled by the pledge of the western unappropriated land. And it was.

As was pointed out in a previous section, entitled, MEANING AND LIMITATIONS OF "TERRITORY," the land the delegates were discussing was the western land ceded by Great Britain to the separate, sovereign, and independent thirteen original colony-states. That was the intent of our founding fathers.

What took place at the Federal Convention of 1787 gives immense credence to a previous section entitled, " TERRITORY" DEFINED: DRED SCOTT V. SANDFORD.

The question of what to do about the western land was the subject of extensive deliberation by the delegates to the Federal Convention of 1787. It was answered, as pointed out earlier, by the adoption of Article IV, Section 3, paragraph 2 of the U.S. Constitution. That section that grants to Congress

> "the power to dispose of and make all needful Rules and Regulations respecting the Territory or other Property belonging to the United States..."

The purpose of Article IV, Section 3, Paragraph 2 was to provide for the disposal of the western land that had been ceded to the United States by the several original states. There is nothing in the language or deliberation to lead anyone to believe that they were thinking about any other land than that which had already been ceded by the colony-states to the United States.

THE FEDERAL GOVERNMENT
AND THE RIGHT OF EMINENT DOMAIN
(ULTIMATE FEE OWNERSHIP)

This nagging question has plagued a number of people: Does the United States, as a Union of separate states, possess dominion, sovereignty, and the right of eminent domain, (ultimate fee ownership) of all land within these United States, or put slightly differently, have the ultimate fee owner-ship of the land and all the rights that go along with this ultimate fee ownership—namely, the right to take and the right of ultimate, final disposal belong to the United States?

This is an important question. If the Unites States does not possess this right, then what happens on and to the land that is within the border of any given state is not up to the United States as a Union of states, but up to the separate states who compose this Union.

As colonies of Great Britain, this right of eminent domain or ultimate fee resided in King George III, the King of England. But all of that changed in 1776 when the thirteen colonies each separately and collectively signed the Declaration of Independence. From that moment on, the separate colonies declared that they were free and independent.

Unquestionably, the Federal Union that was later to be known as the United States, had its embryonic origin in the Declaration of Independence. Here was the gauntlet laid down—we have had enough; we will not tolerate it any longer; we are no longer a part of you; we are now free; and here's why, with an expression of defined intransigence on the part of King George's government.

Our interest here, with respect to how this affected the sovereignty of the individual states, is to examine who signed the Declaration of Independence and in what capacity? It was signed by people representing individual colonies, later to become states. To be exact, the colony-states they were representing were named—whose very initial being was the result of a charter from the king they were now expunging. They declared themselves to be free and independent colony-states, whose identity—by definition and signature—was that of a colony-state. Their representative had signed on the colony-state's behalf. This is the very essence of a federal governmental act, not a national governmental act.

Why is it important to note that this was a federal governmental act rather than a national governmental act?

If this had been an act on the part of the collective people of all the colonies, acting together as a whole, this would have been a ***national*** governmental act. And if it had been, it would have created from that moment on an amalgamation—a oneness or union of all the people settled on all the land of all the colonies—into one new nation. Such an act would have been a ***national*** governmental act, and it would have established a new dominion, sovereignty and right of ultimate ownership of all the land— all of which would thereafter be subject to this new ***national*** government. This would have had to have been an act of the people who happened to reside in the thirteen colonies. This would have been an act of a national nature rather than a ***federal*** one.

But it was not an act of the ***people***, as such, but rather the act of the separate colonies acting in consort with one another for a common purpose represented by individual people. Each colony-state representative signed the Declaration of Independence on behalf of the colony from which he came. This was a ***federal*** act. He had no authority to do otherwise.

This gives rise to the question: What is the difference between a ***national*** government and a ***federal*** government as our founding fathers saw it? Madison, in the *Federalist Number 39* goes into a lot of detail to explain the difference between the two as he explains how the Constitution is a combination of the two in the structure of its being while all the while preserving its republican nature. To the men of that time, ***federalism*** was believed to be an act of concurrence or combined association or league of sovereign states. On the other hand, **nationalism** was an act of concurrence of the separate individual people, the majority of whom bound the minority. In both cases, or a combination of the two, as Madison points out, a republican form of government was to be preserved, and he defines in paragraph 4 of *Federalist Paper Number39* what a republic is:

> "...we may define a republic to be, or at least may bestow that name on, a government which derives all its powers directly or indirectly from the great body of the people, and is administered by persons holding their offices during pleasure, for a limited period, or during good behavior."

Of course, it was New York that was the pivotal colony-state that caused these *Federalist Papers* to be written. As New York went, so went the Constitution itself—down in flames or over the top—at least so they thought. New York was fearful that their separate sovereignty was to be abrogated and that a national government would be the result of the proposed Constitution. It was Madison's job in this paper to point out that this was not the case. It is this "pointing out" that also clearly states what sovereignty was to be given up and what sovereignty was to be retained. Madison's *Federalist Paper Number 39* is critical and clear in this regard. Note the following quotation:

> "...it appears, on one hand, that the Constitution is to be founded on the assent and ratification of the people of America, given by deputies elected for the special purpose; but, on the other, that this assent and ratification is to be given by the people, not as individuals composing one entire nation, but as composing the distinct and independent States to which they respectively belong. It is to be the assent and ratification of the

several States, derived from the supreme authority in each State,—the authority of the people themselves. ***The Act, therefore, establishing the Constitution, will not be a national, but a federal act.***" (Emphasis added)

> "***That it will be a federal and not a national act, as these terms are understood by the objectors; the act of the people, as forming so many independent States, not as forming one aggregate nation...***"
> (Emphasis added)

He goes on to say,

> "***Each State, in ratifying the Constitution, is considered as a sovereign body***, independent of all others, and only to be bound by its own voluntary act. In this relation, then, the new Constitution will, if established, be a federal, and not a national constitution." (Emphasis added)

This reconfirms that the act of ratification is done by a ***federal*** and not a ***national*** body.

In short, this means that no colony-state gave up its individualism or sovereignty in any other manner than that which was already done in the Article of Confederation—and they certainly did not "give it all away" by joining the Confederacy or by being under its control after joining. Further, to clarify the issue of state sovereignty, they were not being asked to give up their sovereignty in any other manner than that which was prescribed by the new Constitution.

This then calls upon a review of the meaning of the word "sovereignty": What was its meaning to the founding fathers? I refer you to the section that deals with DOMINION AND SOVEREIGNTY in Part Two. In short, "sovereignty" means the ultimate fee or ownership of the land; all other ownership rights—be they tenure, transfer of ownership rights, or even fee ownership as we use the term today—were and are all subject to the prior ultimate fee ownership of the sovereign or its successor—in this case, the state. If he (or the state) wanted to take it back, he (or the state) could do so—the very essence of eminent domain. The ultimate fee was his (or the state's). The federal union never did nor does it have any sovereignty of the land at all other than that which it is authorized by the Constitution to acquire—and even in that case, not without the approval of the legislature of the state in which this acquisition of sovereignty is sought. In other

Federalist Papers this is pointed out, and I do so later.

But how do we know that the founding fathers considered the new Constitution to be one in which sovereignty was to be retained by the individual states? Hamilton covers their views in his *Federalist Paper Number 32*. While this paper deals primarily with taxation, Hamilton expands on the limitations of sovereignty in his second paragraph:

> "An entire consolidation of the States into one complete national sovereignty would imply an entire subordination of the parts; and whatever powers might remain in them, would be altogether dependent on the general will. ***But as the plan of the convention aims only at a partial union or consolidation, the State government would clearly retain all the rights of sovereignty which they before had, and which were not, by the act, exclusively delegated to the United States. This exclusive delegation, or rather this alienation of State sovereignty, would only exist in three cases: where the Constitution in express terms granted an exclusive authority to the Union; where it granted in one instance an authority to the Union, and in another prohibited the States from exercising the like authority; and where it granted an authority to the Union, to which a similar authority in the States would be absolutely and totally contradictory and repugnant.***" (Emphasis added)

In other words, the states did not give up their sovereignty of the land: They had this sovereignty to start out with and they most certainly did not go to the Federal Convention of 1787 to give it up! They went there to form a replacement for the Articles of Confederation and that Confederation did not take away their sovereignty of the land. In fact, giving up sovereignty in any form was the very problem with New York. New York feared that they were giving it all up and they threatened to not ratify the Constitution if they, in fact, were required to do so. Hamilton's job was to let them know that they would be required to give up only that sovereignty as outlined and defined in the new Constitution. He goes on to give examples of what the Constitution required in the way of abrogation of sovereignty. Even his last reference to **contradiction** and **repugnance** is explained. Though his focus was upon taxation, he did dwell upon what he considered "a constitutional repugnance that can by implication alienate and extinguish a preexisting right of sovereignty." Then he proceeds to tell how:

> "The necessity of a concurrent jurisdiction in certain

cases results from the division of the sovereign power; and the rule that all authorities, of which the States are not explicitly divested in favor of the Union, **remain with them in full vigor**." (Emphasis added)

In other words, a state gives up only what the Constitution says it must give up in terms of its sovereignty, and conversely, the Union has jurisdiction and sovereignty only over what the Constitution defines.

Nothing eliminated the State's sovereignty of its land.

Even in Madison's *Federalist Paper Number 39*, he gives further back-up to this contention while he addresses the issue of a **national** government.

"In this relation, then the jurisdiction extends to certain enumerated objects only, **and leaves to the several States a residuary and inviolable sovereignty over all other objects**." (Emphasis added)

Note his emphasis on enumerated objects only, leaving all else to the several states. These enumerated objects are defined in Article I, Section 8 of the Constitution. This same thought is the basis for the 10th Amendment.

Madison's *Federalist Paper* No. 40 is worth noting on the collateral issue of initial sovereignty and retained sovereignty of the states as envisioned in the new Constitution. First, Madison asks the question, and then he promptly answers it.

"Do they require that in the establishment of the Constitution, the States should be regarded as distinct and independent sovereigns? **They are so regarded by the Constitution proposed**." (Emphasis added)

He goes on to point out where the new government operates directly upon the states and in other cases upon individuals. He is referring here to the enumerated powers of the Constitution, Article I, Section 8, and he points out that it is in these precisely defined areas that the new Constitution gives the federal government authority, jurisdiction and sovereignty. Then he sums it up by asking a question and then answering it:

"Do these principles, in fine, require that the powers of

the general government should be limited ,and that beyond this limit, the States should be left in possession of their sovereignty and independence? We have seen that in the new government, as in the old, the general powers are limited; and that ***the States, in all unenumerated cases, are left in the enjoyment of their sovereign and independent jurisdiction***." (Emphasis added)

Nothing in the **enumerated** cases in the Constitution relieves the state of its sovereignty of the land. However, as I point out later, the federal government has the right to take certain property by condemnation in order to perform the function of governance in the areas of these enumerated cases. This right of condemnation has been strictly limited to only the cases where the federal government has one or more of the enumerated rights or powers as set forth in Article I, Section 8, of the Constitution.

Much has been said about the Powers Section of the Constitution, and, in essence, that this gives the federal government the right to make rules and regulations regarding the public lands of the United State. This it does. However, see EXPANSION OF FEDERAL POWER: KLEPPE v. NEW MEXICO where this power has been expanded to reach far, far beyond the obvious intention of the framers of the Constitution. In Kleppe, the expansion of this power to Congress is " without limitation"—a grant of power derived from another case taken out of context which does no such thing in context. The limitation of the Powers Section of the Constitution and the very reason for its being was explained in the preceding section, THE FEDERAL CONVENTION OF 1787 AND ITS ANSWER TO THE QUESTION OF LAND FOR PAYMENT OF DEBT. While much maligned, the case of Dred Scott v. Sandford reiterates the same conclusion. (See "TERRITORY" DEFINED: DRED SCOTT V. SANDFORD.) Granted, the finding by the court in that case is despicable—by finding that a human being is private property. In spite of this, however, one cannot ignore what Chief Justice Taney said about the Property Clause of the Constitution—he took the very same information I point out in THE FEDERAL CONVENTION OF 1787 AND ITS ANSWER TO THE QUESTION OF LAND FOR PAYMENT OF DEBT and explained and limited it. It is pivotal. He had to define the Property Clause of the Constitution in order to explain anything at all. What he said about the Property Clause and its limitations bore directly upon the case—and it was not obiter dicta either. That part of his ancillary finding, incidentally, is not something any of us can ignore. If we do, we throw out the baby with the dirty water. The dirty water is the finding that Dred Scott was private property; the baby is the definition of what the Constitution means with relation to the Powers Clause and the rules and regulations it authorizes. Taney was a historian as well as a jurist—as most good judges should be—and he knew his history. In fact, I suspect he also read what I am about to recite that comes from Madison's *Federalist Number 43*.

In the minds of our founding fathers, what was the need for Article IV, Section 3, Par. 2 of the Constitution?[115] Obvious! The Union had a lot of land that had been ceded to it in order to pay off the debt of the American Revolution. It had to be sold. How? When? For how much? Beside land, there was, and would be in the future, other property that would have to be disposed of as well. After reciting, word for word, what the Constitution states in Article IV, last portion of Section 3, Madison defines its importance and then states why:

> "This is a power of very great importance, and required by consideration similar to those which show the propriety of the former [power]. The proviso annexed is proper in itself [Meaning that it was added to the above section as an add-on.], and was probably rendered absolutely necessary by jealousies and questions **concerning the Western territory** sufficiently know to the public." (Emphasis added)

Shortened it says: "The Proviso...was...necessary by...questions concerning the Western territory."

In short, this "annex" is there to provide for the sale of the western territorial land—nothing more.

It does not give ad-infinitum power to the federal government over land it does not own or acquired without the consent of the various state legislatures.

But what about that little clause in Article I, Section 8, Paragraph 17 that states that concurrence by the state legislature is required prior to any federal appropriation for the seat of government? Madison goes into this in some detail, again in *Federalist Paper 43*. He gets the point across:

> "The extent of this federal district is sufficiently circumscribed to satisfy every jealousy of an opposite nature. And as it to be appropriated to this use with the consent of the State ceding it; as the State will no doubt provide in the compact for

---

115- "The Congress shall have Power to dispose of and make all needful Rules and regulations respecting the Territory or other Property belonging to the United States; and nothing in this Constitution shall be so construed as to Prejudice any Claims of the United States, or of any particular State."

the right and the consent of the citizens inhabiting it; as the inhabitants will find sufficient inducements of interest to become willing parties to the cession; as they will have had their voice in the election of the government which is to exercise authority over them; as a municipal legislature for a local purpose, derived from their own suffrages, will of course be allowed them; and as the authority of the legislature of the State, and of the inhabitants of the ceded part of it, to concur in the cession."

In short, the government can appropriate it only with the concurrence of the state legislature.

He goes on to state that this is also true with respect to forts, magazines, etc. Why? He adds: Because public money is involved thus necessitating that it be "exempt from the authority of the particular state." Then he continues:

"All objections and scruples are here also obviated, by requiring **the concurrence of the States concerned, in every such establishment**." (Emphasis added)

Why, you may ask, has any of this other material to do with sovereignty of the land? Is it state land after statehood or is it federal land?

Quite a bit. If the federal government was the sovereign of the land after statehood, none of this bilateral conditional approval or concurrence by the state would be necessary at all; the ultimate fee would reside in the federal government and not the state. The state would be outside the loop and their conditional approval or concurrence would not be necessary nor would it be sought.

Based upon what our founding fathers had to say in the *Federalist Papers*, there is no foundation for the claim that the federal government possesses dominion, sovereignty, or ultimate fee of any land within the separate states except that which is acquired in conformance to Article I Section 8, Paragraph 17 of the Constitution—an act that would give the federal government dominion sovereignty, and ultimate fee of such land so acquired. Taken a step further, this, collaterally speaking, would mean that the states are the ones that are or should be in control of their own land—and it is their land; it is, after all, inside their borders.

After having examined what our founding fathers had to say on the subject, there is still another questioning addendum: Has any of this changed or been clarified, and if so how and why?

Certainly none of this has changed as a result of any constitutional amendment, but certain clarifying decisions by the Supreme Court have been made that define the extent of any federal rights of eminent domain (ultimate ownership) versus any state rights of eminent domain. There are a number of areas in which the Supreme Court has defined as those in which the United States does have this right. However, that area is reasonably narrow and it is well defined. It is defined in the Constitution itself in the form of the enumerated powers, Article I, Section 8. It is in this section that our founding fathers relegated to the United States, as a nation, those powers that the individual states were precluded from enjoying. The list is well defined and reasonably exact, such as lay and collect taxes, duties, pay debts, provide for the common defense, coin money, fix standards of weights and measures, establish post offices and roads, and a handful of other defined powers. In other words, the federal government had certain powers that would provide uniformity for and between all states and provide the federal government the necessary powers to act, and interact with foreign nations.

In re-examining what Madison wrote in the *Federalist 39* it is clear that the intent was to make it unmistakable that the act of ratifying the new Constitution was a *federal* act, not a *national* act. Hamilton, on the other hand, in *Federalist 32*, makes it clear that the United States, as a new Union, would have exclusive powers *only* in the areas defined in the new Constitution (Article I, Section 8). Note again the following:

> "...the State government would clearly retain all the rights of sovereignty which they before had, and which were not, by the act, [of agreeing to the provisions of the new Constitution] exclusively delegated to the United States [in Article I, Section 8]."

In other words, Article I, Section 8 defines the only area in which federal governance or sovereignty would or could exist.

The case of Kohl v. United States[116] is an important case to note. This was a case that involved a lot in Cincinnati, Ohio that was planned to become the cite of a federal custom-house and post office. The question was raised as to whether or not condemnation proceedings were within a Federal Court's jurisdiction. The owner did not wish to sell the lot to the federal government, thus giving rise to the issue of federal condemnation. Note the following extracts from that case:

116-Kohl v. United States: (1875) 91 U.S. 367

"That [Federal] Government is as sovereign within its sphere as the States are within theirs."

"If the right to acquire property for such uses may be made barren [void] by the unwillingness of property holders to sell,...[then] the constitutional grants of power may be rendered nugatory [of no cause or affect]...This cannot be."

"[the Federal Government's] sphere is limited. Certain subjects only are committed to it; but its power over those subjects is as full and complete as is the power of the States over the subjects to which their sovereignty extends."

In other words, the federal government does have the right of eminent domain in order to exercise its **enumerated** powers as set forth in Article I, Section 8, of the Constitution, but in that area only. All else belongs to the state.

Professor David E. Engdahl at the Seattle University School of Law says it clearly and succinctly:[117]

"The federal Government's prerogative of eminent domain, as recognized by the Court in Kohl, is thus inexorably connected with the principle of enumerated powers. Its basis, in fact, is the "necessary and proper" clause in the Constitution's Article I, Section 8."

There are a number of cases[118] that follow Kohl but they do not modify its original meaning; they merely expand upon what is "necessary and proper." These two words appear near the conclusion of Article I, Section 8 with respect to powers granted to Congress:

"To make all laws which shall be **necessary and proper** for carrying into Execution the foregoing Powers, and

---

117-Professor Engdahl's "Pilot Memo on Federal Eminent Domain," dated September 22, 1994, goes into considerably more detail that I do here, and I would recommend that any serious reader explore what he has to say on the subject. (Professor David E. Engdahl, Seattle University School of Law, 900 Broadway, Seattle, WA 98122-4340)

118-The Cherokee Nation v. The Southern Kansas Railway Company: (1890) 135 U.S. 641

Chappell v. United States: (1896) 160 U.S. 499

United States v. Gettysburg Electric Railway Company: (1896) 160 U.S. 668

United States v. Carmack: (1946) 329 U.S. 230

all other Powers vested by this Constitution in the Government
of the United States,..."

Kohl expands the federal right of eminent domain to that area of
delegated powers contained in Article I, Section 8 of the Constitution, thus
modifying the requirement that all federal acquisitions can only take place
with the concurrence of state legislatures. However, Kohl clearly and strictly
limits federal eminent domain to that area alone; it is not general by any
means. That fact is overlooked by a number of people.

Another fact that is overlooked is that there was a time when it
would not have been necessary to sell public land in order to pay the debts
incurred by the American Revolution—and even the purchase price of the
Louisiana Purchase. Why? Because this debt had been paid in full by 1835,
the subject matter of the next section. Keep in mind that the repayment of
these specific debts were the reason of the inclusion of Article IV, Section 3,
paragraph 2 of the U.S. Constitution:

"The Congress shall have Power to dispose of and make all
needful Rules and Regulations respecting the Territory or other
Property belonging to the United States...."

THE AMERICAN REVOLUTIONARY DEBT: PAID IN FULL

After the repayment of the American Revolution war debt in 1835
by the proceeds from the sale of the "Northwest Territory"[119] as well as land
from the sale of the Louisiana Purchase, the land inside the borders of the
original states that was formerly crown land was still held in federal ownership or control awaiting disposition—probably a hold-up occasioned by a
lack of proper survey. This is covered in Part One. As mentioned in Part
One, I can find no act of Congress that cedes this trust land back to the separate states, even though the purpose of the trust had been fulfilled; the
contract had been completed; the Northwest Territory as a "common fund"
no longer had a purpose. As a matter of interest and in support of the foregoing, The Resolution of Congress on Public Lands in 1780 recites the
reason and use of the Northwest Territory land that was later ceded to the
United States "for a common fund:"

119-We know that the debt was paid off by 1835, for in that year, for the first time,
there was no national debt at all.

"That the necessary and reasonable expenses which any particular State shall have incurred since the commencement of the present war, in subduing any of the British posts, or in maintaining forts or garrisons within and for the defence, or in acquiring any part of the territory that may be ceded or relinquished to the United States, shall be reimbursed."

However, there was a big difference. The Louisiana Purchase was finalized in 1803, and parts of that added land were being partially settled by 1835 by "squatters" who had been filing their claims to the land with the General Land Office in accordance with the laws and regulation of the United States. They had been doing that in the "Northwest Territory" as well, yet in the western part of the Louisiana Purchase no such nearly complete disposal or conveyance of the land occurred. Most of it was, ostensibly, retained. With benefit of hindsight, we see that it was retained permanently. My conjecture that this delay was possibly caused by a lack of proper survey may or may not be accurate. In any event, the time delay, for whatever cause, became a permanent delay. Most of it never did get into private ownership, and, as such, upon the tax rolls of the different states. Some accounts in records of Congressional action even suggest that some land that was auctioned off went begging; it simply was unsold—there were no buyers. This unsold land—how much of it, I do not know—became a part of an inventory of the public land. What to do with it and how to dispose of it were questions of that time. But the modus operandi was well established by that time—too well established to simply grant the land to the states. The land simply remained in de facto federal (assumed) ownership or control. In mind-set, first in trust for the state, then as an unsold inventory in trust, then as unsold inventory, and finally as federal land. Justice Frankfurter in a dissenting opinion in the case of U.S. v. California,[120] laments:

"...a sliding from absence of ownership by California to ownership by the United States."

The land retained was to become a "reserve." The subject of reserves is taken up later.

One need look no further than the map at the end of Part One to see that the eastern states have little or no withheld land or even public land under federal control, while the eleven western states plus Alaska, have, in toto, approximately sixty percent of their land under federal control (de facto ownership). Even in an Orwellian society, this is scarcely equal. This federal control (de facto ownership) of these land areas is a violation of

120-United States v. California, (1947), 332 U.S. 19; 91 L. Ed. (1898-1900)

Article V of the Articles of Confederation, the Equal Footing Doctrine, as I have explained its meaning to include the "Right of Sovereignty", and as such, a violation of the U.S. Constitution. By no stretch of the imagination is there equity—little or no federal land on the one hand with a majority of federal land on the other.

Some states in the west are more impacted than others. See the table on pages 27 and 28 of Part One for the approximate percentage of federally controlled land in each of the western states.

This intent, namely, that land ownership was to be that of the state upon statehood, is also reflected in Congressional action as late as 1845.

THE ANNEXATION OF TEXAS: CONGRESSIONAL INTENT FOR THE PUBLIC LAND

An examination of the annexation of Texas is quite revealing. Texas was admitted by treaty, but it wasn't a cut and dried process at all. It took many years to accomplish, and the treatment of the public lands of Texas was a critical element of Texas' admission; first it was to be ceded to the United States in exchange for the assumption of Texas' debt, then it was to be retained by Texas for the express purpose of paying off Texas' debt.

Briefly, the history of the annexation of Texas follows.

Texas was a sovereign, independent country and was recognized as such by the United States. Texas had its minister in Washington D. C. while the United States had its ambassador at the Texas capital, Washington on the Brazos. In 1836, Texans, by an overwhelming majority, voted to seek annexation to the United States. However, when the matter came before Congress, it was filibustered to death by John Quincy Adams. President Houston of Texas withdrew the offer of annexation. Six years went by during which time increasing concerns of British interests in Texas and elsewhere surfaced. Further, Texas had additional concerns regarding its Mexican neighbor to the south. Into this breach stepped President Tyler of the United States, a southern sympathizer. His additional concern involved the continuation or prevention of slavery in a possible state south of the Missouri compromise line.

After these six years, President Houston was willing to allow discussion on the subject to proceed cautiously, quietly, and unenthusiastically—fearful that any other approach would place him and

Texas in an awkward diplomatic position with other nations. One of his prerequisites was that the United States place its armed forces in a position to protect Texas.

After a different Secretary of State entered office, this condition was agreed to. As a result, The Treaty of Annexation of April 12, 1844[121] was signed by Texas and the United States. All that remained was that it be ratified by the United States Senate. The treaty was rejected by the United States Senate by a vote of 35 to 16.

Germane to our interest in Part Two is not that it was rejected, but what its conditions contained. Article I of that proposed treaty contained the following:

> "The Republic of Texas...cedes to the United States all it territories, to be held by them in full property and sovereignty, and to be annexed to the said United States as one of their Territories, subject to the same conditional provisions with their other Territories. ***This cession includes all public lots and squares, vacant lands, mines minerals, salt lakes and springs,*** public edifices, fortifications, barracks, ports and harbors, navy and navy yards, docks, magazines, arms, armaments, and accouterments, archives and public documents, public funds, *debts*, taxes and dues unpaid..." (Emphasis added)

Note, in particular, the cession of Texas land to the United States and the assumption by the United States of the Texas debt—which was substantial.

In Article IV., the following is noteworthy:

> "The public lands hereby ceded shall be subject to the laws regulating the public lands in other Territories of the United States,..."

Note that the land so acquired was to be subject to the laws regulating the public lands in other territories. Texas was to be a state, yet the laws of regulation of the public lands were to be similar to those of a territory—Federal Law, not state law. Why? Because the federal government was to retain titular ownership of the land in order that it could be sold and the funds so generated could be applied to the debt assumed by the United States.

121-From United States, 28th Congress, 1st Session, Senate Document, No. 341 (Washington, 1844), 10-13

In support of this, note the following in Article V wherein Texas agreed that the amount of its debt would not exceed ten million dollars and the United States agreed that the proceeds from the sale of the public land would apply to this debt.

> "The United States assumes and agrees to pay the public debts and liabilities of Texas....For the payment...of the debts and liabilities of Texas,...[which] shall not exceed ten millions of dollars, the public lands herein ceded, and the net revenue from the same, are hereby pledged."

Further support of this is found in Article VI where it addresses the specific payment of funds to a Frederick Dawson as follows:

> "...payable to him on order, **out of the net proceeds of the public lands hereby ceded**..."

In short, the public lands were intended to be sold in order to pay the Texas debt. Nothing is said about what happens to the title to the public land after the debt is paid.

However, none of this took place as specifically outlined above. What is clear is the intent that was present with respect to the proposed sale of the public land in Texas.

What finally led to the annexation of Texas as a state was a resolution passed by both the Senate and the House (at the insistence of President Tyler upon his re-election) entitled The Resolution Annexing Texas to the United States, dated March 1, 1845.[122]

The changes that this resolution made in the treaty were substantial. Texas would cede certain of its claimed northern land beyond its current border. Texas would not cede its public lands to the United States, but retain them; Texas would retain all of its debt; Texas would cede all of its public edifices, fortifications, barracks, ports and harbors, etc. to the United States; Texas would retain the right to divide itself into four additional states for a total of five states at its sole option.

With respect to its public lands, note the following from the resolution:

> "[the] Republic of Texas...shall also retain all the vacant

122-From United States Statutes at Large, V, 797-798.

and unappropriated lands lying within its limits, to be applied to the payment of the debts and liabilities of said Republic of Texas, **and the residue of said lands, after discharging said debts and liabilities, to be disposed of as said state may direct**." (Emphasis added)

There can be no mistake about what the public lands were to be used for, either from the language of the original Treaty of Annexation that was rejected or from The Resolution Annexing Texas To The United States.

There can be no mistake about what the public lands were to be used for, either from the language of the original Treaty of Annexation that was rejected or from The Resolution Annexing Texas To The United States.

The public land (territory) was to be sold in order to pay debt. That is consistent with the intent expressed all along. Here we see it expresses again in 1845 by the United States Congress.

Most important of all is the expression by Congress that after the debt is paid the land is subject to disposal by the state. The land started out being state land with certain strings attached (the debt had to be paid). This is an expression of what Congress thought was an extension of the Equal Footing Doctrine. To them, this was not an exception: this was an expression of what they perceived the meaning of that doctrine to be: After statehood, the public land within the state was to become state land and subject to the discretionary disposal by the state—not the federal government.

The statement with respect to admission on an Equal Footing was not overlooked. This statement appears in the last paragraph:

"...[The] Republic of Texas shall be admitted into the Union, by virtue of this act, on an Equal Footing with the existing States,..."

The Resolution Annexing Texas to the United States was approved by the Republic of Texas and Texas joined the Union officially on December 29, 1845—twelve years after the initial process of annexation commenced.

SEPARATION OF POWER AND THE 10TH AMENDMENT

Our founding fathers were also concerned about the separation of the powers between the states and the United States as a federal government. They went after this separation in a rather unique way. They gave all the power to the states *except* those that they **specifically** gave to the United States.

They said it first in the Articles of Confederation.

Article II:

"Each state retains its sovereignty, freedom and independence, and every power, jurisdiction and right, which is not by this Confederation expressly delegated to the United States in Congress assembled."[123]

Another important excerpt from the Articles of Confederation follows:

Article IX:

"provided also that no state shall be deprived of *territory* for the benefit of the United States."

Here are two clear statements of the separation of power. They cannot be ignored; they are provisions of limitation placed upon the United States with reference to land. The importance of this is dealt with later.

LAND ACQUIRED BY TREATY AND WAR

The issue of treaties is very important, inasmuch as the land composing all 50 states, as well as all present territorial possessions of the United States, are involved; their possession is the result of one treaty or another.

All of the land, even that acquired from Great Britain following the

123-The same meaning was later conveyed in the 10th Amendment to the U.S. Constitution.

Revolutionary War, was finalized by **treaty**. Even the land acquired as the spoils of war was finalized by **treaty**. So were all outright purchases of land finalized by **treaty**.

LAND ACQUIRED FIRST BY PURCHASE AND FINALIZED BY TREATY:

Louisiana Purchase in 1803:

> Purchased from France for $15,000,000, consisting of 7 states and parts of 6 other states: Louisiana, Arkansas, Missouri, Iowa, Nebraska, Kansas, Oklahoma, and parts of Minnesota, North Dakota, South Dakota, Colorado, Florida in 1819: Wyoming and Montana.

Florida in 1819:
> Purchased from Spain for $6,500,000.[124]

The Gadsden Purchase in 1853:
> Part of New Mexico was purchased from Mexico for $10,000,000.

Alaska in 1867:
> Purchased from Russia for $7,200,000.

LAND ACQUIRED BY TREATY[125]

Texas from the Republic of Texas in 1845

The "Oregon Compromise" in 1846

> Part of Minnesota and North Dakota; disputed land between Great Britain and the United States.

124-This land was somewhat disputed. Congress annexed this land to the Louisiana Purchase while Spain still claimed it. After the war of 1812, in 1819, both East and West Florida were purchased.

125-I have purposely omitted lands outside of the continental United States that were acquired by treaty.

LAND ACQUIRED AS THE SPOILS OF WAR AND FINALIZED BY TREATY[126]

The Mexican-American War in 1848:

> Consisting of 4 states and parts of 3 others: California, Arizona, Nevada, Utah; parts of New Mexico, Colorado and Wyoming (Treaty of Guadalupe Hidalgo)

TREATIES

This raises the issue of treatment of land as a result of treaties. Here again, the U.S. Constitution deals with the issue in Article VI, Section 1:

> "This Constitution, and the laws of the United States which shall be made in pursuance thereof; and **all treaties** made or which shall be made, under the authority of the United States, shall be the supreme law of the land; and the Judges in every state shall be bound thereby, any thing in the Constitution or laws of any state to the contrary notwithstanding."
> (Emphasis added)

Meaning: There would be no difference; land and property acquired by treaty or purchase were to be treated **exactly** in the same manner as other land or property of the other several states or territories. There is no difference other than the fact that this land belonged to—at least until it was disposed of in a similar manner as the Public Domain land of the other states—the federal government as "territory," in a defacto trust for the purpose of disposition. Land acquired by purchase was not directly covered by an article in the U.S. Constitution. Rather, it is covered by the prior Articles of Confederation and Perpetual Union[127] which in turn are covered by Article 6, Section 1 of the U.S. Constitution:

> "All debts, **contracts** and **engagements** entered into before adoption of this Constitution shall be as valid against the United States under this Constitution as under the Confederation." (Emphasis added)

There is a catch however. Note the following verbiage of the U.S. Constitution as quoted earlier:

> "...all **treaties made** or which shall be made, under the authority of the United States, shall be **the supreme law of the land**..." (Emphasis added)

126-There were other lands that were added to the United States, such as the Philippines, Guam, Haiti, etc that are, for the sake of brevity, being omitted here.

127-Organizing document of United States: 1781-1788.

That means that we must look at exactly what that treaty says. The verbiage in that treaty *is the supreme law of the land*. Note that the U.S. Constitution requires that Congress pass laws in "pursuance" of (in accordance with) the Constitution. On the other hand, treaties have no such direct requirement. The protection that they too be in pursuance to the Constitution is by secondary method; they must be *approved* by the Senate. And Senators—all of them—take an oath to uphold the Constitution. Meaning that they may do nothing that is *contrary* to the Constitution.

In the case of the Treaty of Guadalupe Hidalgo, the treaty that followed the Mexican-American war, which resulted in the acquisition of California, Arizona, Nevada, Utah, and parts of New Mexico, Colorado and Wyoming, the treaty itself envisions the incorporation of all such people (and their property) into the Union of the United States. That was the *purpose* of the acquisition of the land. Article IX of the Treaty of Guadalupe Hidalgo is quoted as follows:

> "Mexicans who, in the territories aforesaid, shall not preserve the character of citizens of the Mexican republic...shall be incorporated into the Union of the United States, and be admitted at the proper time the Union of the United States, and be admitted at the proper time...to the enjoyment of all the rights of citizens of the United States, according to the principles of the constitution..."

This declaration envisions the inclusion of this new land into the union as states. The land was not acquired as a source of future wealth for a nation in search of colonies. The Constitution precluded any such transaction. To do otherwise would have been a case of history repeating itself! Memories had not dimmed. The thirteen colonies under King George III were mute testimony in the not too distant past.

Nothing in this language leaves room for the United States to withhold one square inch of land from state ownership upon statehood that is not specifically authorized by the U.S. Constitution. To withhold any land beyond the boundary of the *purpose* of the treaty without the consent of the legislature of the separate states would be unlawful. The Constitution gives to the president, with the advice and consent of the Senate, the power to make treaties. The treaty then becomes the law of the land upon the concurrence of "two thirds of the Senators present."

In short, all the land acquired by the Treaty of Guadalupe Hidalgo was destined to become states and as such would become land of the state upon its acceptance into the Union—just like the land inside the boundary of the original thirteen colonies: an exercise of the "Equal Footing Doctrine."

Similarly, the land acquired from France in the Louisiana Purchase was intended for statehood. Note the following quote from Article III of the Cession of Louisiana, April 30, 1803:

> "The inhabitants of the ceded territory shall be incorporated in the Union of the Unites States and admitted as soon as possible according to the principles of the federal Constitution..."

The purchase of Alaska from Russia was not much different with respect to its future. Note the following quote from Article III of the Cession of Alaska, March 30, 1867:

> "The inhabitants of the ceded territory...shall be admitted to the enjoyment of all the rights, advantages and immunities of citizens of the United States..."

In other words, the United States cannot retain ownership of this territorial land in perpetuity by authority of the Treaty of Guadalupe Hidalgo, the Cession of Louisiana, the Cession of Alaska or the U.S. Constitution. All this land was destined and anticipated for statehood. There is no language authorizing any retention. It is simply not there. The land cannot be retained based upon a treaty. But it was anyway.

Why, you may ask. Note the language in each of these treaties. It says almost the same thing in each of them:

In the treaty with France that solemnized the Louisiana Purchase:

> "The **inhabitants**...shall be incorporated in the Union of the United States and admitted as soon as possible according to the principles of the federal Constitution..." (Emphasis added)

In the Treaty of Guadalupe Hidalgo:

> "**Mexicans**...shall be incorporated into the Union of the United States, and be admitted as the proper time...according to the principles of the constitution...." (Emphasis added)

In the Cession of Alaska from Russia:

> "The **Inhabitants**...shall be admitted to the enjoyment of all the rights, advantages and immunities of citizens of the United States...."

There are a number of people that believe that the language of all of these treaties does not address itself specifically to the land—only the people; that this leaves the issue of land ownership and its dispositions clear out as a condition of statehood; that this gives a free license to the federal government, and the federal legislature to do whatever it wishes with the land—set it aside, reserve it temporarily or permanently; that the Equal Footing Doctrine does not apply except as to political equality only; that this land is a part of the dominion and sovereignty (ultimate fee ownership) of the United States and as such, the states have no say except as to the enforcement of state law.

This is a gross departure from the intent of the founding fathers as I have pointed out earlier in that section entitled, THE ORIGIN OF THE "EQUAL FOOTING DOCTRINE" AND THE RIGHT OF SOVEREIGNTY UPON STATEHOOD. It is an insult to their concept of equity.

CALIFORNIA DECLARED OWNER OF LAND UPON STATEHOOD

In the case of Friedman v. Goodwin,[128] the history of ownership and its ultimate ownership by the state of California is traced:

> "On the cession of California [Mexican land] to the United States [Treaty of Guadalupe Hidalgo], all the public lands therein became the property of the United States. On her [California] admission into the Union, *she [California] became the owner of all the public land not disposed of by law of congress*." (Emphasis added)

Note the constitutional conformity: Mexico to the United States; United States to California. There was no withholding of land mentioned.

This 1856 case is a Federal Circuit Court decision and not a

128-Friedman v. Goodwin, (CC. 1856) Fed. Cas. No. 5, 119, 1 McAll. 142

Supreme Court decision. As a result thereof, it does not carry the same weight as a Supreme Court decision. However, the case was never appealed to a higher court. This means that this lower court decision stands with all its full force and effect, intact, as though it had in fact been decided by the Supreme Court.

The important point of this case is that it is a clear statement of what the court understood the delineation of title to the public land to be: namely, that upon their entry into the Union, each state "became the owner of the public land not disposed of by law of Congress." This remained the opinion of the court until 1903. The closest thing to a reversal can be seen in two cases that I shall deal with later: U.S. v. Mission Rock Co. (1903) and Scott v. Lattig (1913), nearly 50 years later. In all fairness, those cases have their limitations as well: Ownership was not argued; it was assumed.

Constitutionally, the only land Congress could dispose of would be that which would go to a third party, such as a foreign government or individual who had a preemptive or appropriated right consistent with the law (homestead, etc.).

FEDERAL OWNERSHIP OF LAND "LIKE ANY OTHER CITIZEN"

As a matter of interest, read the following from People, by McCullough, v Shearer: [129]

"The relation of the United States to the public land since the admission of California into the Union is simply proprietary, that of an owner of lands *like any other citizen who owns lands, and not of a municipal sovereign.*"[130] (Emphasis added)

This means, simply, that the land which the federal government owns is subject to the same conditions as that of any private citizen's land. It is subject to all the controls, planning and approval by state extensions—counties—as that imposed upon all citizens' land, except those lands that are for "Forts, Magazines, Arsenals, dock-Yards, and other needful Buildings."

129-People, by McCullough v. Shearer (1866) 30 C. 645, 1 P.L.M. pt. 2, 97.

130-This statement certainly assumes that the United States owns the public land after statehood. Important: The court assumes that the United States owns the public land; the court does not decide that the United States owns the public land. Assumption is not law.

SEPARATION OF POWERS

There is a distinct separation and definition of powers outlined in the Constitution: Each of the three branches of the federal government—executive, legislative and judicial—are separated from each other. Another, federal from state, is equally important.

During the time of ratification of the Constitution following the Revolutionary War, each of the colonies already had their separate sovereignty even though they were bound together by the Articles of Confederation. They had to give up their independent sovereignty to such extent as the new constitution required in order to form a union of states. It should be noted that they were not required to give up the sovereignty of any land other than that land which was to become a part of the Northwest Territory, and even that, only in trust. The original thirteen colonies possessed complete sovereignty of the land within their borders, and those states still possess it today. These new states did not, nor were they required to, give up the sovereignty of their land in order to form a union of states. There was nothing in the new constitution that required it.

There was much more than just land involved. As independent, sovereign states, they were about to form an irrevocable alliance as United States under a new constitution that was to supercede the Articles of Confederation. They all had agreed that the Articles of Confederation needed improvements and expansion. However, none of the colonies were willing to give unilateral power to the federal government except in a defined and limiting manner, and this defined and limited manner was specifically stated in the new constitution. Even so, the extent of this "limiting" was subject to question. According to some of its critics, the new constitution did not clearly define the separation of power between the new union of states and that of the thirteen colonies about to become separate states in that union. There were others, but the one with which we are most concerned is the defining words contained in the 10th Amendment to the new constitution. It was added because it wasn't quite clear enough in the new constitution where the power of the new constitution stopped. Could it be assumed that it went beyond the enumerated powers at some time in the future? Just maybe, they thought. This concern resulted in the adoption of the 10th Amendment to the U. S. Constitution. It is powerful, clear, concise and unmistakable. It is quoted in its entirety:

"The powers not delegated to the United States by the Constitution, nor prohibited by it to the States, are reserved to the States respectively, or to the people."

In other words, the federal government has no power other than those specifically granted to the federal government by the U.S. Constitution. If the power is not granted by the Constitution to the federal government, it does not exist. Who then does have the power? The individual state, in conformance with its own state constitution. It's that simple.

THE POWERS CLAUSE OF THE CONSTITUTION AND ITS LIMITATIONS

How far does the Constitution go as to powers granted to Congress, and exactly how does the Supremacy Clause of the Constitution fit in? One of these questions is plain enough: Doesn't the U.S. Constitution say that Congress can pass laws and that these laws are the law of the land? Read again the following quote from Article VI, Clause 2 of the U.S. Constitution:

"This Constitution, and **the laws of the United States which shall be made in pursuance thereof**...shall be the supreme law of the land..."
(Emphasis added with omission for the sake of clarity.)

The key word is "pursuance."[131]

In other words, Congress, the only body that can pass any laws of the United States, are *bound* by the provisions of the Constitution to pass laws **pursuant** (in accordance with) to the Constitution. And the Congress is limited to pass laws or exercise power in **only** those areas where this exercise of power is authorized by the Constitution. All other powers not so delegated to the United States by the Constitution are the express area of power reserved, exclusively, to the separate states. The powers of Congress are limited and restricted to the powers delegated to it by the Constitution. To pass laws that are outside of this limit is unconstitutional. And the laws they pass that are not pursuant to the provision of the U.S. Constitution are, to the extent, in whole or in part, that they are not pursuant thereto, are not constitutional or actually enforceable. In Pollard v. Hagan[132], the court put it in unmistakable and understandable language.

131-Webster's Dictionary: "Execution, as pursuance of a purpose; done in pursuit of a desired end; in accordance with."

132-Pollard v. Hagan: (1845) 44 U.S., (3 How), 212, 11 L. Ed. 565.

"1.That portion of sovereign power which is **vested in the United States by our Constitution and laws** is unlimited.

2. The exercise of power by any department or functionary of the government, as among and operating on ourselves, is limited.

3. The sovereign power as a nation in its **foreign intercourse** is subject to no constitutional restraint. (Emphasis added)

Meaning:

In 1. above: The United States has unlimited power where that power is specifically stated in the Constitution.

In 2. above: Departments of the government are limited by the Constitution, to wit: if that power is not specifically delegated to the United States, it is power reserved to the states—it is not federal power.

In 3. above: There is no constitutional restraint with respect to foreign affairs; this includes treaties which I will deal with in more detail later, for it is in the area of treaties that immense power has been acquired by the federal government in the past that has spilled over into the domestic arena.

One should be cautioned about believing that there is no limit to which a treaty can or cannot go with respect to its constitutionality. This is discussed later in the section entitled, TREATIES AS A SOURCE OF INCREASED POWER. In short, Justice Black says that a treaty must comply with the provisions of the Constitution and that they are limited to dealings, sovereign to sovereign. And, further, they may not arbitrarily negate or eliminate the protection provided by the Constitution. In the Dred Scott v. Sandford decision, the following quotation is noteworthy. It appears on page 451 of that decision.

"...there is no law of nations standing between the people of the United States and their government and inter- fering with their relation to each other. The powers of the government, and the rights of the a citizens under it are positive and practical regulations plainly written down....It [the govern- ment] **has no power over the person or property of a citizen but what the citizens of the United States have granted. And no laws or usages of other nations, or reasoning of statesmen or jurists...can enlarge the** *powers of the government, or take from the citizens the rights they have reserved.*" (Emphasis added)

In other words, there is no way Constitutional rights and privileges as outlined and guaranteed in the Constitution can be abridged, limited or modified.

In an important way, the Dred Scott case contained a defining of the limitations of the Powers Clause. Dred Scott cites American and Ocean Insurance Companies v. Cantor [133] to show that jurisdiction can be delegated from federal to state government (or to a territorial tribunal as was the case in American and Ocean Insurance Companies) by an act of Congress. More to the point, in a later case, Downes v. Bidwell,[134] note the following quotation.

"The Constitution does not extend to territories of its own force. Congress has power over territory it does not possess in the States."

Or, put in reverse, Congress ceases to have power it once had in a territory.

Or, put in a still different way, Congress has absolute power over a territory which it ceases to possess after statehood.

CONGRESSIONAL AUTHORITY TO PASS LAWS

Congress has the **authority** to pass whatever laws it wants to pass. That is not to say that all the laws they pass are constitutional or enforceable simply because they pass them: To be binding, the law must be in **pursuance** of the Constitution. If a law goes unchallenged it is enforceable until its legality is challenged by someone and finally decided by the U.S. Supreme Court.

One could surely ask, where does our federal government get the right to regulate, withhold or sell these public lands? Surely, it was not fabricated out of whole cloth. No, it wasn't and isn't. In a strict sense, the origin is in Article I, Section 8, Clause 18:

133-American and Ocean Insurance Companies v. Canter; 1 Pet. 511.

134-Downes v. Bidwell; (1901) 182 U.S. 244.

"The Congress shall have Power...To make all Laws which shall be necessary and proper for carrying into Execution the foregoing Powers, and all other Powers vested by this Constitution in the Government of the United States, or in any Department or Officer thereof."

This is called the Powers Clause of the Constitution.

There is Congress' right to make laws and regulations.

This Powers Clause gives Congress the power "....To make all Laws which shall be necessary and proper for carrying into Execution the *foregoing* Powers..." All the foregoing powers deal with taxes, money, commerce, naturalization, post offices—a whole host of different things, none of which has anything whatever to do with land.

Land (territory) and property are referred to in Article IV, Section 3, Clause 2.

"The Congress shall have Power to dispose of and make all needful Rules and Regulations respecting *Territory* or other Property belonging to the United States;" (Emphasis added)

The reference to "territory" and "property" is restricted wholly to that which was already in existence (see Dred Scott v. Sandford) at the time of the acceptance of the Constitution (1787). The federal government's power with respect to "territory" as referred to in the Constitution was extinguished when the purpose for which the "territory" was established in the first place had been fulfilled: namely, the repayment of the debts created by the Revolutionary War. That debt was paid in full by 1835, and such land as was then remaining unappropriated or preempted within the "Northwest Territory" eventually was purchased and became private property. I can find no act of Congress that directly ceded this unappropriated trust land back to the states. The land of the Northwest Territory eventually dissolved into private ownership by sale. In any event, it no longer was in federal ownership.

This clause (Art. IV. Sec. 3, Clause 2), quoted above, governs the "territorial" land at the time, in 1787. It does not cover land acquired later, and for the sake of identity or name consistency was called by the same name, "territory." (As explained in section, "TERRITORY" DEFINED: DRED SCOTT V. SANDFORD)

LIMIT OF HOLDING LAND "FOR A COMMON FUND"

The federal government continued to withhold land "for a common fund" even after the federal debt had been paid off. This is not in conformance with the Constitution. In the case of United States v. Hawthorne[135] collateral support for this contention is quoted:

"A regulation dies with the statute from which it gains its life."

With respect to "property" as identified in Article IV, Section 3, Clause 2 above, this has to do with the only real (land) property the **United States** can own as identified in Article I, Section 8, Clause 17:

"Forts, Magazines, Arsenals, dock-Yards and other needful Buildings;..."

The other kind of property, classified generally as "personal property," is covered as well by Article I, Section 8, Clause 17: desks, chairs and equipment—all the way to tanks, cannons, and warships.

Another issue is that of "places" (land) purchased by the federal government. With respect to "places" **purchased**, the U.S. Constitution deals with this as well in Article 1, Section 8, Clause 17:

"......and to exercise like authority over all places purchased, *by the consent of the legislature of the state in which the same shall* be, for erection of Forts, Magazines, Arsenals, dock-Yards, and other needful Buildings."
(Emphasis added)

Note the inclusion of "...consent of the legislature of the state..."

AUTHORIZED FEDERAL WITHHOLDING OF LAND

One could argue that the withholding of land by the federal government from the state for the sake of its proper regulation or management by the federal government is not, in and of itself, a regulation; but rather, it is simply a reservation from a grant of title to land—a withholding. If this is so,

135-United States v. Hawthorne: (1940) 31 F. Sup. 827, 829 (N.D. Tex.).

one could surely (and should) ask, where in the Constitution is such a with-holding authorized? If it is withheld, is this not a violation of the Equal Footing Doctrine, as well as a violation of the 10th Amendment? Certainly, it would "prejudice a[ny] claim......of a[ny] state."

Here again, the U.S. Constitution deals with that in Article 1 Section 8, Clause 17:

> "...and to exercise like Authority over all Places purchased by *the Consent of the Legislatures of the State* in which the same shall be, for the Erection of Forts, Magazines, Arsenals, dock-Yards, and other needful Buildings:"
> (Emphasis added)

In the case U.S. v. Gratiot[136] the Court observes the following:

> "...Congress practiced and sanctioned the plan of reserving from sale certain portions of the Public Domain; that they held them during an indefinite period for *future disposition*; and that this disposition consisted either in selling them when *no further reason* for reserving them existed, or in ceding them to the states on certain conditions;"
> (Emphasis added)

The last part of this quotation seems to imply that it was a general practice of the federal government to cede certain withheld land to the state(s). I am unaware of any such ceding of land other than that land which was designated for support of public education.

Further, this quotation does not define "indefinite period." The case cited refers to leases or contracts, the longest of which was seven years. Therefore, it would be erroneous to conclude that this "indefinite period" is limitless.

It is clear that the federal government did withhold portions of the Public Domain; they withheld the conveyance of the title to the land to the States pending the acquisition of the land by homesteaders in the earlier years. It took a lot of time to survey the land and this had to be done before it could be conveyed by patent. In those earlier years there never was any attempt or intent to withhold such lands permanently. That came later.

The term "indefinite" is not synonymous with "forever," particu-

136-U.S. v. Gratiot: (1840) 39 U.S. (14 Pet) 526 10 L. Ed. 573.

larly where there was an anticipated use or purpose. And there was. The treaties stated it. The land was to become separate states.

U.S. v. Gratiot deals with a war material, lead, and as such the land would fall within the purview of "Magazines, Arsenals"—a constitutionally authorized federal ownership. Nonetheless, it is important to know how the court dealt with this issue and what was concluded.

STATE AGREEMENT REQUIRED TO WITHHOLD LAND

Nowhere in the Constitution is the federal government granted enumerated, or even implied, power to exercise sovereignty, dominion, jurisdiction and authority over lands within the border of these western states *unless it has been granted that right by the legislature of the state*. This the states have not done. And in accordance with the Constitution, even then, only for "Forts, Magazines, Arsenals, dock-Yards, and other needful buildings."

Can the federal government simply take the land owned by the separate states? No. The federal government's power is limited by the Constitution. In a strict sense, the federal government cannot simply "take" land for any purpose other than that which is outlined in the Constitution *without the agreement and consent of the state legislature*. And even then, unless the land is a gift by the state, the federal government is compelled to pay for it.

Clearly, the United States can acquire land with "Consent of the Legislatures of the State...." Without this express "Consent of the Legislature of the States...," there is no authority to withhold or even unilaterally manage one square inch of land that is inside the border of an individual state. There is, however, one exception and that case is easy to take out of context and lead to a wrong conclusion. The case: Kleppe v. New Mexico.

EXPANSION OF FEDERAL POWER: KLEPPE V. NEW MEXICO

See appendix A for an expanded summary of this case. The courts have been less than consistent about limiting or defining the power conveyed to Congress by the Constitution. In a whole host of earlier cases, the court has slowly enlarged these powers. It almost would appear as though the watch-words were, "Congress shall have whatever powers as are necessary to get the job done!" And there is nothing consistent about that definition. In short, it has been dynamically expanding. In the case of Kleppe v. New Mexico[137], the following excerpts are most interesting, for they would appear to expand the Property Clause well beyond the literal:

> "...while courts must eventually pass upon them, determinations under the Property Clause are entrusted primarily to the judgment of Congress."

> "...the power granted by the Property Clause is broad enough to reach beyond territorial limits."

> " the [Property] Clause, in broad terms, gives Congress the power to determine what are "needful" rules "respecting" public lands."

> "...we have repeatedly observed that '[t]he power over the public lands thus entrusted to Congress is without limitations.'..."

Note, in the immediately above quotation, that a period appears following the word "limitations." This is not as it appears in U.S. v. Gratiot.

In arriving at the above observations, the court cites U.S. v. San Francisco, Light v. U.S. and U.S. v. Gratiot. All three cases are summarized in the Appendix. Noteworthy, however, is that the first two of the cases refer to U.S. v. Gratiot. It is from this case the last quotation comes—the one that would seem to deliver to Congress very nearly unlimited power. Read this case in the appendix. It is pivotal. The quotation is out of context. Its original meaning is limited to territorial government. Its full quotation is as follows:

> "...this power is vested in Congress without limitation, ***and has been considered the foundation upon which the territorial government rest***." (Emphasis added)

The only limiting statement in Kleppe v New Mexico is as follows:

> "...where Congress does not purport to override state

137-Kleppe v. New Mexico: (1976) 426 U.S. 529, 49 L. Ed. 2d 34.

power over public lands under the Property Clause and **where there has been no cession**, a federal official lacks power to regulate contrary to state law." (Emphasis added)

Note the underlined words "where there has been no cession." The court is stating directly that where a state has not ceded jurisdiction to the federal government, no jurisdiction or federal regulatory power exists contrary to state law.

Note further, in the above quotations, that where the court is referring to "public lands" it does not refer to these public lands as federally owned. Note the word, "purport." As used, this implies a notice of intent. This notice of intent "made very clear" is discussed later.

Further, this last quote implies, conversely, that if Congress does purport to override state power over public lands by making such intent "made very clear," it does have power to regulate. In the absence of the above, there would be an instant constitutional question involving the 10th Amendment of usurpation of federal over state power. In this case, by stipulation, ownership was not decided; it was assumed inasmuch as New Mexico agreed that the land was in federal ownership. (See the appendix for a more detailed analysis of this case.) The question of ownership was not a subject of the case. But, not surprisingly, the power to regulate federal land was confirmed. There has never been a question of power granted to the federal government to regulate its federal property where cession by the state has occurred. This case simply does not confirm that the public land of New Mexico is federal property.

As broad as Kleppe v. New Mexico is, the court did limit its decision:

> "While it is clear that regulation under the Property Clause may have some effect on private lands not otherwise under federal control, we do not think it appropriate in this declaratory judgment proceeding to determine the extent, if any, to which the Property Clause empowers Congress to protect animals on private lands *or the extent to which such regulation is attempted by the Act* [Wild Free-roaming Horses and Burros Act]....We...leave open the question of the permissible reach of the Act over private lands under the Property Clause.)" (Emphasis added)

Paraphrased: "Try us later on some specific issue, and we'll tell you."

Kleppe v. New Mexico is one of the cornerstones of the proponents that claim federal ownership of the public land. This simply cannot be done. Ownership of the land was not an issue to be decided by the court. As pointed out, New Mexico agreed by stipulation that the land was in federal ownership thus permitting the court to **assume** that it was. And the court did just that; the court did not *decide* that it was in federal ownership.

Please re-read carefully the earlier section dealing with dicta. In short, the observation of the court in this case is dicta and must not be used as the basis for law. Regardless of this fact, many lawyers do.

JURISDICTION: FEDERAL OR STATE?

The term "jurisdiction"[138] was impliedly raised in the Kleppe case and as an immediate result thereof, some explanation at this juncture is in order. Who has jurisdiction (authority or control), the federal government or the state government of the public land within a given state?

This is one area in which the Supreme Court has been crystal clear with numerous cases defining that clarity.

It all goes back to what the Constitution says in Article I, Section 8, Paragraph 17. And in the interest of ready reference and clarity it is quoted again in its entirety:

> "To exercise exclusive legislation in all Cases whatsoever, over such District (not exceeding ten Miles square) as may, **by Cession of particular States**, and the Acceptance of Congress, become the Seat of the Government of the United States, and to exercise like Authority over all Places purchased by the **Consent of the Legislature of the state** in which the Same shall be, for the Erection of Forts, Magazines, Arsenals, dock-Yards, and other needful Buildings;" (Emphasis added)

Note the emphasized portions. Bluntly, according to this, the federal government cannot commandeer, arbitrarily take, or assume jurisdiction (authority or control) of even one square inch of land without the concurrence of the legislature of the state involved. And it is this jurisdiction, authority and control as it applies to all public lands, that Kleppe

---

138-Webster: "1. The right and power to interpret and apply the law. 2. Authority or control."

impacts. However, I must remind the reader that federal jurisdiction, authority and control of the public land was stipulated to by New Mexico, the defendant. Most readers of this case overlook this stipulation and treat this case as definitely final.

However that may be, Kleppe is not the case of origin setting forth that our public land within a given state are under federal jurisdiction, authority and control. That issue goes a long way back. The earliest case that defines the two jurisdictions, state or federal, that I am aware of, is United States v. Bevans.[139] This case had to do with a murder committed on a U.S. Naval vessel in Boston harbor. Who had jurisdiction, the federal govern-ment or the state of Massachusetts? With respect to the state, Chief Justice Marshall first asks the question and then promptly answers it.

"What then is the extent of jurisdiction which a state possesses?...the jurisdiction of a state is co-extensive with its terri-tory [state boundary]; coextensive with it legislative power."

Then with respect to federal jurisdiction he goes on to say:

"Congress has power to exercise exclusive jurisdiction over...all places purchased by the consent of the legislature of the state in which the same shall be, for the erection of forts, maga-zines, arsenals, dock-yards, and other needful buildings....the power of *exclusive legislation [jurisdiction] is united with cession of territory*, which is the free act of the states." (Emphasis added)

In other words, the exclusive jurisdiction which the United States have in "Forts, Magazines, Arsenals, dock-Yards, and other needful Buildings" passes to the United States only when that jurisdiction is ceded to the United States by an act of the legislature of a given state. Bluntly put, the federal government has no jurisdiction within a state with respect to land unless the state legislature gave it to them. This jurisdiction includes, not just the defined area of "Forts, Magazines, Arsenals, dock-Yards, and other needful Buildings," but all other land within a state after statehood. federal jurisdiction can be derived in no other manner. It cannot be simply assumed.

The court then states that the "framers of our constitution" did not have in mind any kind of general jurisdiction that was to be reserved to the federal government when they described the judicial powers in Article III of

139-United States v. Bevans, 16 U.S. (3 Wheat.) 336 (1818).

the Constitution. This is certainly true. A reading of Madison's *Federalist, Number 43* with respect to this matter confirms this.

> The indispensable necessity of complete authority at the seat of government carries its own evidence with it. It is a power exercised by every legislature of the Union, I might say of the world, by virtue of its general supremacy. Without it not only the public authority might be insulated and its proceedings interrupted with impunity, but a dependence of the members of the general government on the state comprehending the seat of the government for protection in the exercise of their duty might bring on the national councils an imputation of awe or influence equally dishonorable to the government and dissatisfactory to the members of the Confederacy. This consideration has the more weight as the gradual accumulation of public improvements at the stationary residence of the government would be both too great a public pledge to be left in the hands of a single state, and would create so many obstacles to a removal of the government, as still further to abridge its necessary independence. The extent of this federal district is sufficiently circumscribed to satisfy every jealousy of an opposite nature. ***And as it is to be appropriated to this use with the consent of the State ceding it***; as the state will no doubt provide in the compact for the rights and consent of the citizens inhabiting it; as the inhabitants will find sufficient inducements of interest to become willing parties to the cession; as they will have had their voice in the election of the government which is to exercise authority over them; ***as a municipal legislature for a local purposes***, derived from their own suffrages, will of course be allowed them; and as the authority of the legislature of the state, and of the inhabitants of the ceded part of it, to concur in the cession will be derived from the whole people of the state in their adoption of the Constitution, every imaginable objection seems to be obviated.

> "The necessity of a like authority over forts, magazines, etc., established by the general government, is not less evident. The public money expended on such places, and the pubic property deposited in them, require that they should be exempt from the authority of the particular State. Nor would it be proper for the places on which the security of the entire Union may depend to be in any degree dependent on a particular member of it. All objections and scruples are here also obviated by requiring the concurrence of the States concerned in every such establishment. (Emphasis added)

United States v. Bevans was the foundation of a large number of cases that followed that consistently said, in short: if the state has ceded territory (land) to the United States by an act of their state legislature, jurisdiction (authority and control) becomes federal. On the other hand, if the state has not ceded the territory by an act of their state legislature, the jurisdiction remains in the state. There are a number of cases wherein the federal government has occupied or is in control of state land but does not have such occupancy or control approved by the state legislature. In these instances, the court has held that jurisdiction (authority and control) remains with the state.

The consistent principal is as follows: Absent cession by the state, jurisdiction remains with the state; with cession by the state legislature to the federal government, jurisdiction is transferred to the federal government.

Another important case with respect to jurisdiction is Benner v. Porter.[140] This 1850 case was only about jurisdiction, and it is worth noting inasmuch as it reinforces the position taken in United States v. Bevans in that it reaches beyond just court jurisdiction.

This case had to do with a claim for money owed for supplies furnished to a vessel while it was in the port of Key West, Florida. The case was filed on March 24, 1846 in the Federal Court. The question brought before the Supreme Court was simply a matter of jurisdiction. Was it state or federal jurisdiction?

In its opening summary of the case, the court had this to say:

> "Whilst Florida was a Territory, Congress established courts there [in the Territory of Florida], in which cases appropriate to federal and State jurisdiction were tried indiscriminately."

> "Florida was admitted into the Union as a State on the 3rd of March, 1845."

> "The constitution of the state provided that all officers, civil and military, then holding their offices under the authority of the United States should continue to hold them until superseded under the state constitution."

140-Benner v. Porter, thirteen L. Ed. 119 (1850)

"But this article [State constitution] did not continue the existence of courts which had been created, as part of the territorial [Federal] government, by Congress."

"In 1845, the Legislature of the State passed an act for the transfer from the territorial [federal] to the State courts of all cases except those cognizable by the Federal Courts; and, in 1847, Congress provided for the transfer of these to the Federal Courts."

"Therefore, where the territorial [Federal] court took cognizance, in 1846, of a case of libel [as use here, it means a claim for money owed], it acted without any jurisdiction.'"

Justice Nelson delivered the opinion of the court. The following statement in his opinion is of particular note inasmuch as it sheds light on what starts and stops at the moment a state enters the Union. Certainly territorial [federal] court jurisdiction did cease with respect to state matters, but, as he notes in his opinion, so did all other federal powers—one of those powers being the power to own state land.

"...we are satisfied that...the act of Congress admitting the Territory of Florida, as a State, into the Union with her constitutional and organized government under it, alone or in connection with the establishment of a Federal Court, within her limits, her admission immediately, and by constitutional necessity, **displaced the territorial government, and abrogated all its powers** and jurisdiction." (Emphasis added)

Earlier in his opinion, Justice Nelson clearly pointed out the differences between a federal and a state court.

While this does not necessarily influence or determine ownership of our public lands, it certainly determines who has the legal jurisdiction with respect to any dispute arising out of the use or occupancy of our public land. And because of this factor alone, it is included in this text.

"After the unconditional admission of the territory into the Union as a state, on the 3d of March, 1845, with her constitution, and complete organization of the government under it, by which the authority of the state was established throughout her limits, it is difficult to set upon what ground it can be maintained that any portion of the territorial government [federal] or jurisdiction [federal] remained in force.

"The distinction between the federal and State jurisdictions, under the Constitution of the United States, has no foundation in these territorial [federal] governments....They are legislative governments, and their courts [are] legislative courts,"

He goes on to say:

"[These Federal courts] are not organized under the Constitution, nor subject to its complex distribution of powers of government, as the organic law, but are the creations, exclusively, of the Legislative Department [Congress], and subject to its supervision and control....

"We think it clear, therefore, that on the unconditional admission of Florida into the Union as a State, on the 3d of March 1845, the territorial government was displaced, abrogated, *every part of it*; and that no power of jurisdiction existed within her limits, except that derived from the State authority [an act of the State Legislature]." (Emphasis added)

In the quotation above, note that the underlined portion, *every part of it*, is not tied to "power of jurisdiction," but to "the territorial government." Does this mean that everything is transferred from the territorial (federal) government, including authority and control (sovereignty and dominion) of the public land to the state upon statehood? I think that it does.

The following list of cases also support the doctrine that jurisdiction from federal to state takes place immediately upon entry into the Union of a given state and that federal jurisdiction can only occur with the concurrence of the legislature of the state:[141]

United States v. Cornell, 25 Fed. Cas. 646, No. 14, 867 (C.C.D.R.I., 1819)
Pollard v. Hagan, 44 U.S. (3 How.) 212 (1845)
Fort Leavenworth R. Co. v. Lowe, 114 U.S. 525 5 S. Ct. 995 (1885)
Champaign County, Illinois v. United States Law Enforcement Ass. Administration, 611 F. 2nd 1200 (7th Cir. 1979)

141-This list is only partial. I would refer the interested reader to the treatise on this subject by Lowell Becraft, Federal Jurisdiction. His address is 209 Lincoln Ave. Huntsville, AL 35801.

Hoppe v. King County, 95 Wash. 2nd 332, 622 P. 2nd 845 (1980)
Lavin v. Marsh, 644 F. 2nd 1378 (9th Cir., 1981)
Bollow v. Federal Reserve Bank of San Francisco, 650 F. 2nd 1093
(9th Cir., 1981)
Railroad Yardmasters of America v. Harris, 7221 F 2nd 1332,
(D.C. Cir., 1983)

A number of State Supreme Court cases say the same thing:
Commonwealth v. Young, Brightly, N.P. 302 (Pa., 1818)
People v. Godfrey, 17 Johns. 225 (N.Y., 1819)
American Federation of State, County, and Municipal
Employees v. Olson, 338 N.W. 2nd 97 (N.D., 1983)
Umpleby, by and through Umpleby v. State, 347 N.W. 2nd 156,
(N.D., 1984)

The findings in these cases seem to put it rather plainly: There is no federal jurisdiction if no grant of cession by the state to the federal government has occurred. Moreover, state cession can be limited to what the state determines shall be included in the cession. In general terms, jurisdiction goes with land title.

There would be no argument if there were not a catch to it: What if the federal government lays claim to the ownership of the land within the border of a given state where cession by the state has not occurred, such as Forest Service and BLM land? As a landowner, is the federal government not entitled to the same rights and privileges with respect to its land as an ordinary proprietor? The answer, yes, is precisely stated in Camfield v. United States. This case is summarized in the appendix. However, in order for Camfield to be effective, the ownership or title to the land must be established to be federal rather than state. Quite obviously this points up the importance of establishing unquestioned federal ownership or title to the land within the borders of the state if jurisdiction is to remain federal. (Keep in mind that as territory, prior to statehood, the land was under federal jurisdiction—hence the use of the term "remain federal.")

Germane to the immediate issue, then, is this: if land ownership can be proved or even assumed, with acceptance of that assumption,[142]

142-I have read many cases wherein the state or individual has agreed by either stipulation or in the body of their pleadings that the title to the public land within the state is federal and not state. By so doing, the court need not nor is required to rule on the ownership of the land; that has already been agreed to by the litigants. If I have referred to any of these cases, I have simply pointed out that federal ownership of the land has been assumed, not decided—which is true.

jurisdiction is federal and the rights to enter into contracts or other agreements such as Use Permits are permissible and quite legal. Obviously, this places a whole new emphasis upon the necessity of possessing title to the land. Until just recently, the federal government has been forced to rely upon the assumption of their ownership of the public lands within a given state. The two cases that give them ownership of the public lands are United States v. Gardner and United States v. Bradshaw. Both of these cases are summarized in the section entitled, SUMMARY AND CONCLUSION.

The reach of these two cases settles, for the time being, title to the public land, and correspondingly, until limited by some new case, the jurisdiction of this same public land. Be that as it may, this is not all, for federal jurisdiction can be and is asserted as a result of one or more of the hundreds upon hundreds of treaties entered into by the United States. And, most alarming to some, a number of these treaties impact the utilization of private land and property as well as the public land. However, before assuming that treaties are above the U.S. Constitution in all respects whatsoever, read that section entitled TREATIES AS A SOURCE OF INCREASED "POWER." Pay particular attention to what Justice Black said in Reid v. Covert. Treaties do have their limits as to their constitutionality, but if they go unchallenged, they are constitutional until ruled otherwise.

The impact of the now established federal jurisdiction of the public lands within the state resulting from Gardner and Bradshaw raised the question, "So what? How can that make any difference?"

Simply stated, the difference is that with jurisdiction goes the application of either Federal Law or state law. In the area of our interest here, the effective law results from the ownership or title to the land. It makes quite a difference if the land is subject to federal or state law. It makes quite a difference if the land is subject to federal or state law. State law is founded in the Constitutions of the states while Federal Law is the result of the United States Code[143] and the Code of Federal Regulations, neither one of which is subject to all the protections most of us assume go along with the U.S. Constitution. The U.S. Constitution authorizes the establishment of a Federal Judicial System of Federal Courts. It does no address itself to state courts other than to declare that "the supreme Court shall have appellate jurisdiction." However, the Constitution does declare, separately, that federal jurisdiction ("judicial power") extends to all cases in law and equity, laws of the United States and to cases of admiralty and maritime Jurisdiction. (There are others that I have omitted in the interest of focus.)

143-For a brief history of the United States Code, Revised Statutes, Statutes at Large and United States Code Annotated, see *Black's Law Dictionary*.

The important distinction between the two is this: state law derives its power and authority from the constitution of the different states, while Federal Law derives its power and authority from the Congress of the United States and what it may unilaterally declare, not necessarily inclusive of all other provisions of the Constitution. The United States Code Annotated (U.S.C.A.) is a derivative of Congressional power and was compiled and published by the authority of Congress. It isn't the fact that Congress has certain powers with respect to the formulation of federal law that concerns us here, but the changes that occur in the United States Code, ostensibly done with Congressional approval, that impact and even change the Constitutional guarantees themselves or enlarge federal authority and control (jurisdiction) authorized by the Constitution itself. Some claim that this comes dangerously close to the ability to preclude the states from the exercise of a republican form of government[144]—a provision guaranteed to the states by the Constitution itself. They point out that all the representatives from all of the states— Congress, not the inhabitants of the state, would then have the authority to dictate to the people of a given state what their choices shall be.[145]

However that may be, the following is reasonably axiomatic: Where the jurisdiction is federal, the law is governed by the U.S.C.A. Conversely, where jurisdiction is state, the law is governed by the laws of the given state.

Obviously, the establishment of title to the land within a state's borders is of the utmost importance to both the state and the federal government. Until Gardner and Bradshaw, there was some question: federal ownership was assumed, not decided. No state has objected to the usurpation of their ownership rights of the land. Perhaps that will, one day, occur.

But let us look as the situation as it existed prior to both Gardner and Bradshaw.

1   All the land came into the territorial limits of the United States by various treaties.

144-Black's Law Dictionary: "Republican government: A government of the people; a government by representatives chosen by the people."

145-The constitutional guarantee contained in the Constitution is that each separate state shall have a republican form of government. After accepting the state's separate constitution, which it must do prior to the state's joining the Union, Congress has no power to change the state's constitution. The section, THE SUPREMACY CLAUSE AND THE "SUPREME LAW OF THE LAND" deals with Congressional limitations.

2. Each treaty established a trust for the holding of these lands until they could be established as states. In the case of the establishment of the Northwest Territory as "a common fund," this trust was formal. In the case of land acquired later by treaty, the trust is implied by the verbiage in the treaty.

3. If there was debt to pay off, the de facto (or otherwise) land trust established by the treaty, provided the funds for the payment of this debt upon the sale of the land.

4. The land was to be held "temporarily" until it could be sold or disposed of.

5. There is no provision in the Constitution for the permanent with-holding of land other than that contained in Article I, Section 8, Clause 18. ["Forts, Magazines Arsenals..."]

6. Each state shall enter the Union on a Equal Footing with the original thirteen colonies, "equal in all respect whatever."

With this as a background we can now ask: If the jurisdiction of the Public Domain was conveyed to the State at the time of admission to the Union, are the Public Domain lands of the former Territory still public after their jurisdiction is transferred to the State? And if so, can their use be mandated by the federal government? "Yes" to the first question and "No" to the second. The land would still be public lands, but the ownership of that same land would have been transferred from the federal government to the state. Its mandated use cannot be thrust upon the state by the federal government without the approval of the legislature of the state.[146] To do otherwise would be usurpation of a right or power that was the state's and a violation of the 10th Amendment. Further, this use could be determined by the state and whatever its state constitution said about the public land. State constitutions, as a rule, give the state the right to own, convey, encumber, etc.—almost anything they want to do with their property; land is simply a form of property. The state has a relatively free hand and has the right to do what it deems appropriate with its land.

Obviously, the impact of Gardner and Bradshaw has changed all this. The federal government is now the recognized owner of the land; by refusing to hear either Gardner or Bradshaw, the Supreme Court has confirmed that the land never became state land, in trust or in any other

---

146-Note the discussion and quotes from Kleppe v. New Mexico, U.S. v. New York, and Utah v. U.S.

way. It simply remains as federal land. [My immediate reaction to this is a question: How is Nevada, whose federal land encompass approximately 86 percent of the entire state, going to react to this? Or even Alaska, whose federal land, if superimposed upon the lower United States would cover nearly half of the 11 western states?]

But what about the jurisdiction of that land? Is it federal or state? Or is it some hybrid kind of jurisdiction such as "concurrent jurisdiction" (words that appear in Title 18, Section 7, paragraph 3 of the U.S. Code which is discussed next)? In any event, Gardner and Bradshaw have made immense inroads in the plan our founding fathers had for the public land. They had no other plan than to sell the land to private individuals. The nagging question is there: Is there any constitutional authority for the permanent retention of what now appears to be federal land within the borders of a given state without the approval of the legislature of that state? I don't think that there is and others concur with this belief.

A brief aside is necessary at this point. Jurisdiction can be a slippery thing to the keep in its rightful place.

Suppose for the moment that push has come to shove with respect to some disagreement with the federal government over an issue that involves the public land. Suppose that a Summons and Complaint has been filed in Federal Court. Suppose, further, that your attorney believes that the issue is unquestionably one that involves federally owned land, and as such there is no doubt in your attorney's mind that the proper jurisdiction is in Federal Court. In other words, he is unaware of the impact of United States v. Bevans or the supporting argument presented in Benner v. Porter that declare that jurisdiction remains with the state unless an act of the state legislature shifts that jurisdiction to the federal government. Keep in mind that no states have done this on any wholesale basis. I really cannot blame the attorney for drawing this erroneous conclusion. After all, this is what his law-school days taught him! See p. 14 of *Federal Public Land and Resource Law*, the textbook most law-students study. However all of this may be, the attorney, believing that the jurisdiction is unquestionably federal, answers the complaint as a general appearance and not as a *specific* appearance. Colossal mistake! He has just agreed to federal jurisdiction automatically. The issue is now a matter of Federal Law solely and completely. Excerpts from *Black's Law Dictionary* explain the difference and the error rather clearly:

Appearance: "The voluntary ***submission to a court's jurisdiction***."

Carefully note the emphasized words. Black's continues:

"An appearance may be either *general* or *special*; the former is a simple and unqualified or unrestricted submission to the jurisdiction of the court, the latter a submission to the jurisdiction for some specific purpose only, not for the purposes of the suit."

In other words, if you are unaware that federal jurisdiction is subject to doubt and answer the complaint as a general appearance, you are now subject to Federal and not State Law automatically. This compels the next questions: what are the Federal Laws governing these public (now federal) lands? What are they and how are they applied? What is the federal law that governs the public lands if they are indeed federally owned?

FEDERAL LAW ON OUR PUBLIC (FEDERAL) LAND:
UNITED STATES CODE &
CODE OF FEDERAL REGULATIONS

The actual United States Code came into being in 1926. Prior to that time the statutes—laws passed by the federal legislature—Congress—were printed in a single volume of the Revised Statutes of 1875 and each subsequent volume of the Statutes at Large. In 1926 a Revisor of Statutes was appointed by Congress. His efforts resulted in the rearrangement of all the statutes into 50 titles and the printing of all of the statutes: the United States Code, 1926. Every six years a new edition of the United States Code is published.

The United States Code Annotated is the same United States Code, but in this series of volumes the code is cross referenced to other related sections, historical notes and library references as well as court cases that apply, give rise to, or define the law. In short, the United States Code is supposed to represent the applicable **Federal Law** of the land. It is the law that is applicable where federal jurisdiction exists. I emphasize the word "federal" because state law may be somewhat different. (It is state law that is applicable where state jurisdiction exists.)

Our interest in the U.S.C.A. (United States Code Annotated) is largely confined to the section that deal with its applicability to federal lands, Title 18, U.S. Code, Sec. 7, entitled, "Special maritime and territorial jurisdiction of the United States defined."[147] This section is sometimes referred to as Admiralty Law and I do so later on. Paragraph 3 of Section 7 is quoted:

> "*The term 'special maritime and territorial jurisdiction of the United States', as used in this title, includes*:...(3)Any land reserved or acquired for the use of the United States, and under the exclusive or concurrent jurisdiction thereof, or any place purchased or otherwise acquired by the United States by consent of the legislature of the State in which the same shall be, for the erection of a fort, magazine, arsenal, dockyard, or other needful building." (Emphasis added)

This defines where federal jurisdiction takes place.

Somewhere along the line (probably around 1940) there was a substitution of wording. The emphasized wording above that tells us this is where maritime and territorial jurisdiction of the United States can and does occur was substituted for wording that defined where crimes and offenses were a federal concern. The original words before the substitution of the underlined words in the quotation above were:

> "The crimes and offenses defined in sections 451-468 of this title shall be punished as herein prescribed."

For ready comparison, paragraph 3 used to read as follows before the substitution:

> "The crimes and offenses defined in sections 451-468 of this title shall be punished as herein prescribed....[When committed on] (3) Any land reserved or acquired for the use of the United States, and under the exclusive or concurrent jurisdiction thereof, or any place purchased or otherwise acquired by the United States by consent of the legislature of the State in which the same shall be, for the erection of a fort, magazine, arsenal, dockyard, or other needful building."

Obviously, there is no similarity of meaning between the original, immediately above, and the amended code quoted earlier. "Territorial jurisdiction" is the new, compelling additive. It appears to me that this sub-

---

147-This section is often referred to as Admiralty Law inasmuch as it deals with waters and places outside the limits of the United States. A territory is not a part of the United States; it has not joined the Union of States.

stitution of words enlarges and even changes the meaning and/or scope of federal jurisdiction altogether.

The foundation for this appears in the U.S. Constitution in Article I, Sec. 8, Cl. 17. For ready reference it is quoted once again here.

> "To exercise exclusive legislation in all cases whatsoever over such district (not exceeding ten square mile) as may, by cession of particular states and the acceptance of Congress, become the seat of government of the United States and to exercise like authority over all places purchased, by the consent of the legislature of the state in which the same shall be, for the erection of Forts, Magazines, Arsenals, dock-Yards, and other needful Buildings."

The federal jurisdiction as defined in the U.S.C.A. is a sizable stretch of authority as defined in the Constitution. Clearly, the Constitution limits the "exclusive legislation" of the federal government to only the following: the seat of government and to places purchased for the erection of "Forts, Magazines, Arsenals, dock-Yards, and other needful buildings." And in all of those cases, the legislature of the state involved must consent.

Now, go back and re-read paragraph 3, Section 7 of Title 18 quoted a little earlier. This says that special maritime and territorial jurisdiction of the United States extends to "Any land reserved or acquired for the use of the United States, and under *exclusive or concurrent jurisdiction*..."

Where in the Constitution does such authority come from? I don't think that it does. Further, where did the term "concurrent jurisdiction" come from?[148] What is it and where is it applicable? How can you have two jurisdictions at the same time—state and federal? It seems to me that that is like having two captains on the same ship at the same time—and they don't take turns!

The remainder of paragraph 3 goes on to nearly quote from the

---

148-The only case in which I find that concurrent jurisdiction occurred or was a possibility was the case of O'Donnell v. Great Lakes Dredge & Dock Co., 318 U.S. 36; 63 S.Ct. 488; 87 L. Ed. 596. This had to do with admiralty or maritime jurisdiction—law that is related to marine commerce and navigation outside the confines of a state. Obviously, along the border of a state adjacent to the Great Lakes that are also an international border, some doubt could occur as to jurisdiction inasmuch as the controversy that occasioned the suit could have taken place in either or both the state as well as the federal waters—and probably did.

Constitution where this same exclusive legislation exists. Exclusive Federal legislation does exist wherein state legislatures have consented to federal acquisition in accordance with the Constitution.

Nonetheless, the U.S.C.A. goes well beyond the explicit language of the Constitution and gives the federal government jurisdiction of "Any lands reserved or acquired for the use of the United States, and under exclusive or concurrent jurisdiction"—all without the consent of the separate states involved. That is a stretch!

An application of this concurrent jurisdiction can be seen in Title 18, Section 13.

> "(a) Whoever within or upon any of the places now existing or hereafter reserved or acquired as provided in section 7 of this title, is guilty of any act or omission which, although not made punishable by any enactment of Congress, would be punishable if committed or omitted within the jurisdiction of the **State**, Territory, Possession, or District in which such place is situated, by the laws thereof in force at the time of such act or omission, shall be guilty of a like offense and subject to a like punishment." (Emphasis added)

Keep in mind that all National Forest land is reserved land as authorized by Congress in 1891 (The Forest Reserve Act of 1891), while BLM land is the residual Public Domain lands that were never homesteaded.

Note that this paragraph gives the federal government the authority to enforce state law even if a given crime is not a violation of Federal Law. This, too, is a stretch!

Coupled with the United States Code is the Code of Federal Regulations, which in some ways has a far more profound effect upon the laws governing our public land than does the U.S.C.A. The difference between the two is rather extreme. The U.S.C.A. at least has congressional origin. The Code of Federal Regulation has nothing of the kind. While it is true that its authority for being is a direct result of Congressional delegation of authority, the rules and regulations that find their way into the Code of Federal Regulation come first from the different bureaus or agencies of the federal government, such as The Forest Service, the Bureau of Land Management, Alcohol, Tobacco and Firearms Agency, the IRS, etc. *After it becomes law*, Congress can get involved. This is exactly backwards to the U.S.C.A. Facetiously, I call the Code of Federal Regulations "law by publication!"[149]

Simply put, an agency may see that for their purposes, whatever those may be, there is a need for additional rules or regulations. The bureau or agency then develops the rule or regulation and prints it in the Federal Register. If no objection to the new rule or regulation is forthcoming from Congress for a period of 60 days, the rule or regulation becomes law. And make no mistake about it: That which was just printed in the federal register and to which no objection was raised for 60 days becomes the law of the land and is just as enforceable as any other Federal Law. That is not to say that it cannot be changed, but the change is now up to Congress—or up to the individual to question the constitutionality of the rule or regulation and proceed through the courts—at his own expense—to have the issue adjudicated. In other words, for the most part, Congress is in the position to "second guess" the appropriateness, effect and scope of the new law; Congress is not the prime mover, but the secondary mover. In effect, Congress is on the bench while the game is going on!

But what is the long term impact of all of this?

STATE SOVEREIGNTY ON ITS WAY OUT

State sovereignty is indeed on its way out. Gardner and Bradshaw insure this. Simply put, these two cases lay an additional layer of groundwork for the diminishment of the sovereignty of the state and its replacement by the institution of federal sovereignty. In short, Congress now has the authority to govern the federal land—which in the instance of the West, is a huge amount of real estate—without state input or concurrence! Further, Congress now has the power to modify or even destroy the constitutional structure of these United States. Will this power or resultant change take place immediately? Probably not, but the ground-work is there in full force and effect so that it *can* take place—eventually.

It is paramount to keep in mind that Congress has already delegated an immense amount of their power to the different administrative agencies such as the Forest Service and Bureau of Land Management—the two main agencies that are the focus of our interest here. Congress has given those agencies the power to make their own organic acts—rules and regulations—as they independently may and do see fit. Congressional oversight is secondary—after the fact. Further, in essence, the Equal Footing Doctrine that was so precious to our founding fathers has been emasculated.

149-During 1997, the IRS alone issued 271 new regulations.

The impact of this federal incursion upon state's rights, sovereignty and jurisdiction is succinctly addressed in the Petition for a Writ of Certiorari in the case of Barry Bradshaw v. United States. The following quotation is an extract of the entire section dealing with this subject matter from that writ: Section II, of Reasons for Granting the Writ.

"The claimed ownership and assertion since the Kleppe case, of jurisdiction pursuant to the Article IV, Sec. 3, Clause 2,[150] violates a structural component of the U.S. Constitution. Such claimed ownership and jurisdiction deny to the people of the State or Nevada [or any State] essential elements of sovereignty. Such claimed ownership and jurisdiction violate the prohibition of any involuntary reduction of a State's territory under Article IV, Section 3.

"In years prior to Kleppe, decision assertions of jurisdiction to enforce federal regulations on the public lands within the State of Nevada [or any other state] were based on 18 U.S.C. 7 (Special Maritime and Territorial Jurisdiction of the United States Defined). Since this Court's opinion in Kleppe v. New Mexico, 426 U.S. 529 (1976), that jurisdiction is claimed to rest on ownership of the public lands. No act of Congress conferring such jurisdiction on the Federal Courts is relied on. Jurisdiction is claimed "without limitation" under Article IV, Section 3, Clause 2.

"The Kleppe opinion has been severely criticized in the scholarly writings [of] Professor David E. Engdahl in his treatise, *Constitutional Federalism in a Nutshell*, Second edition, West Publishing Co. (1987). [He] writes of the opinion as follows:

"In 1976, with an opinion that displays darkest ignorance of what had been established for two centuries before, the Supreme Court unanimously (albeit unawares) revolutionized its doctrine under that clause. (Article sdIV, Section 3, Cl. 2) Kleppe v. New Mexico, 426 U.S. 529 (1976). The briefing on behalf of New Mexico was inept; and for its part, the Court conspicuously failed to deal with many of the relevant cases and demonstrably misunderstood others. Kleppe held that "Congress exercises the power both of a proprietor and of a legislature over the public domain."...On this view, Congress can make rules

150-"The Congress shall have Power to dispose of and make all needful Rules and Regulations respecting the Territory or other Property belonging to the United States;"

for federal property which have no relation whatever to any matter otherwise of legitimate federal concern, and any such rule, being legislative in character, "necessarily overrides conflicting state laws under the Supremacy Clause."...as to property located within the boundaries of states, that is a profoundly novel proposition which makes a mockery of the basic purpose of enumerated powers doctrine....What Kleppe really means is that over all the vast federal Public Domain within states, the United States has plenary, general governmental jurisdiction, and is not confined to those enumerated powers which it may exercise elsewhere in the country. It means that as to the east and the middle west, enumerated powers doctrine remains the foundation of constitutional power analysis, but as to the roughly half of the country from the Rocky Mountains states westward it has absolutely no significance at all."

"Bradshaw submits that Kleppe, as interpreted and applied by the Ninth Circuit in this case, means that they are surrounded by lands governed as territorial or colonial holdings "without limitation" by a government whose seat of power is further away from them than the colonists were from England."

These are rather alarming words, and one could surely ask: Are these concerns I should have now, or is this just something I should be aware of, about which I need not do anything inasmuch as it does not affect my life or my lifestyle today?

Let me give you a scenario of what you might possibly expect over the next number of years.

More and more often, the different federal agencies have requested that they be granted police power by the different counties of the western states—police power that can only be granted by the local county commissioners or supervisors. That is what they used to do, and they may continue to do so, until the agency decides, unilaterally, that such grant of authority by the local county officials is not really necessary or required. The hard fact is that it isn't necessary any longer. The court decisions in Gardner and Bradshaw no longer make that necessary; those decisions granted "concurrent jurisdiction"—in truth, an application of Special Maritime and Territorial Jurisdiction as defined in Title 18 U.S.C., Section 7. Those exact words are used in Section 7. The federal agencies now have police power. Will they exercise that authority immediately? I don't think so. I think they will continue to seek county or state grants of authority for the exercise of police power. I believe there will be an exercise of restraint—for now. But as time goes on, I believe there will be a increased feeling that seeking county and state grants of authority are no longer necessary or needed. Some day, the federal agencies will probably act unilaterally to enforce all of the then-applicable rules and regulations that their agencies have developed for the governing of "their" now clearly federal land. These vast areas will be governed in a similar manner as a federal enclave—like Washington D.C. The state and county governments will be outside the loop. That is the power that Congress has given the different governmental agencies, and that is the same power that the courts have, through Gardner and Bradshaw, authorized.

Is all or any of this in accordance with the Constitution? Not in any way that I am able to identify. When that happens—if it happens—that will surely affect all of our lives, no matter where we live, and it will surely affect our lifestyle. Will it be too late to reverse at that late date? I really don't know!

It is timely that some discussion take place at this point with respect to territory, which, of course means any land that at one time was called by the name "territory."

"TERRITORY" DEPRIVED FOR THE BENEFIT OF THE UNITED STATES

Article IX of the Articles of Confederation, quoted earlier, says,

> "...no state shall be deprived of **territory** for the benefit of the Unites States." (Emphasis added)

It would be a difficult argument to claim that the states have not been deprived of territory for the benefit of the United States where land has been withheld. The states have been deprived of land over which they have had little or no control; they have been precluded from the collection of the revenue that land has produced (partial collection is not the same by any means); they have been outside the loop as to its management; their say has been minimal and in the final analysis can be totally overridden.

What does it really mean to a state to not be in control of its own land? First, the federal government pays no property tax. Second, the state is outside the loop as to its use. Who feels this pinch directly? The various counties of these states. It is these counties that must build the infrastructure, maintain it and improve it. Grants may come from the State or the federal government, but it is not quite the same by any means. The axiom, "He who puts up the money controls how it shall be spent," comes into play here. The county becomes the pawn in an overpowering game of chess. The county simply cannot compete. Bluntly, their resources have been impinged upon.

There never has been an argument that the federal government doesn't have a clear right to regulate that which it *owns*; namely, "Forts, Magazines, Arsenals, dock-Yards and other needful Buildings." It has no authority to regulate land which is not so named except when the land was still territorial in nature prior to statehood. No such land exists today. Treaties can give immense power and authority, but this did not happen either. All such land acquired via treaty was for a purpose the treaty either directly or by implication envisioned; it was destined to become a state.

USURPATION OF POWER BY THE FEDERAL OVER THE STATE

With respect to the usurpation of power by the federal over the State Government, Madison in the *Federalist No. 46* almost dismisses this as preposterous but then he does go on to suppose a conclusion:

> "...should an unwarrantable measure of the federal government be unpopular...the means of opposition to it are powerful and at hand. The disquietude of the people, their repugnance and perhaps ***refusal to cooperate*** with the officer of the Union, the frowns of the executive magistracy of the state, the embarrassments created by legislative devices,...would oppose in any state difficulties not to be despised; would form in a large state very serious impediments, and where the sentiment of several adjoining states happened to be in unison, would present obstructions which the federal government would hardly be willing to encounter." (Emphasis added)

However, it has happened: The federal government has encroached upon that of the states, and in an early decision Chief Justice Fuller had this to say in the case of U.S. v. Knight Co.:[151]

151-U.S. v. Knight Co. 156 U.S. 11.

"It cannot be denied that the power of the state to protect the lives, health and property of its citizens and to preserve good order and the public morals, the power to govern ***men and things*** within the limits of its dominion, is a power originally and always belonging to the state, ***not surrendered*** to the general government, nor directly restrained by the Constitution of the United States, and essentially exclusive." (Emphasis added)

RULES AND REGULATIONS AND THE 10TH AMENDMENT

What about the regulatory provision of Art. IV, Sec. 3, Clause 2 of the Constitution quoted earlier? Doesn't Congress have the right to regulate as a provision of the Constitution? Yes, but not as an unlimited regulation. It can regulate all that it owns. See Article 1, Section 8, Clause 17 quoted earlier. Unless the state or states have given consent, the United States cannot regulate land it does not own. That ownership and management belongs to the State.

The federal government can regulate the people; it cannot regulate the state. This is succinctly stated in New York v. United States:[152]

"The Federal Constitution confers upon Congress the power to regulate individuals, not states."

That is the prerogative reserved and given to the states. That is what the 10th Amendment of the U.S. Constitution is all about. This, in short, is a definition of the states' rights. You will notice that it says, in slightly different form, the same thing as that which appeared in The Articles of Confederation. The 10th Amendment to the U.S. Constitution follows and defines States' Rights:

"The powers not delegated to the United States by the Constitution nor prohibited by it to the States are reserved to the States respectively, or to the people."

How about the last 4 words of this paragraph, "or to the people"? Isn't that enough authority for the federal government to claim that all the land so set-aside or retained is in truth public land—property of the people

---

152-New York v United States (1992) 505 US 144; 120 L Ed 2d 120

and, as such, under the managerial authority of the United States? Here again, no. To arbitrarily retain this land, as was the case with all the Enabling Acts of the West, and not relinquish ownership to these lands to the respective states, would be a violation of the "Equal Footing Doctrine," a violation of Article V of the Articles of Confederation, and thus a violation of the U.S. Constitution. Further, also at issue would be Article IX of the Articles of Confederation quoted earlier, namely:

> "...no state shall be deprived of territory for the benefit of the United States."

FEDERAL USURPATION OF STATES' RIGHTS: NEW YORK V. U.S.

A recent Supreme Court case, New York v. United States (1992), is of primary importance. It is a plethora of statements defining the separation of powers between the sovereigns—federal and state. In fact, it is more than that; it is a historical recitation of the origin, purpose, and intent of the separation of powers. It is the reflection of the highest court's view—and recently at that—of those separate powers. It is clear. It is well written. It is long. And it is important. The following quotations are particularly noteworthy with reference to the subject matter of Part Two:

> "Where Congress exceeds its authority relative to states, the departure from the plan of the Federal Constitution cannot be ratified by the consent of state officials because the Constitution divides authority between federal and state governments for the protection of individuals and not for the benefit of states or state officials,"

This raises the dilemma: How far can one go in avoiding the rubber stamp syndrome of automatic approval of a perceived departure from "the plan of the Federal Constitution"? As is threateningly indicated in a letter later quoted from the Forest Service, not much, or else!

Continuing:

> "The Federal Constitution's division of power among the three branches of government is violated where one branch invades the territory of another, ***regardless of whether the encroached-upon branch approves the encroachment.***"
> (Emphasis added)

"If a power is delegated to Congress in the Constitution, the Tenth Amendment expressly disclaims any reservation of that power to the States; if a power is an attribute of state sovereignty reserved by the Tenth Amendment, it is necessarily a power the Constitution has **not** conferred on Congress." (Emphasis added)

Justice Story, appointed by one of our founding fathers, Madison, probably reflecting similar views to those of Madison, bluntly said in Commentaries on the Constitution of the United States (1833) on page 752 the following:

"Being an instrument of limited and enumerated powers, it follows irresistibly, that what is not conferred, is withheld, and belongs to the state authorities."

The foregoing is recited in New York v. United States.
Also recited is the following from United States v. Butler:[153]

"The question is not what power the Federal Government ought to have but what powers in fact have been given by the people."

Continuing:

"...this Court never has sanctioned explicitly a federal command to the States to promulgate and enforce laws and regulations."

This is certainly a smack at the permanent withholding of land from the States as commanded in the Enabling Acts and in fact enforced in the West.

"...the Constitution has never been understood to confer upon Congress the ability to require the States to govern according to Congress' instructions [Coyle v. Smith[154]]"

"The constitutional authority of Congress cannot be expanded by the 'consent' of the governmental unit whose domain is thereby narrowed, whether that unit is the Executive Branch or the States."

153-United States v. Butler: (1936) 297 U.S. 1, 63; 80 L Ed. 477; 56 S Ct 312, 102 ALR 914.

154-Coyle v. Smith: (1911) 221 U.S. 559

"State officials thus cannot consent to the enlargement of the powers of Congress beyond those enumerated in the Constitution."

Put another way, no state official, consistent with his oath of office to uphold the Constitution, may allow the enlargement of the powers or controls of any bureau or department beyond that which is provided for in the Constitution.

The horns of the dilemma are sharpened.

A summation follows:

"...the Constitution protects us from our own best intentions: It divides power among sovereigns and among branches of government precisely so that we may resist the temptation to concentrate power in one location as an expedient solution to the crisis of the day."

CONGRESS MAY NOT COMMANDEER STATE LEGISLATURE PROCESS

Can Congress simply tell the legislature of a state what to do? No. In Hodel v. Virginia Surface Mining & Reclamation Assn., Inc.[155] the following is quoted:

".... Congress may not simply commandeer the legislative processes of the States by directly compelling them to enact and enforce a federal regulatory program."

Further reinforcement of this same issue is contained in FERC v. Mississippi:[156]

".....this Court never has sanctioned explicitly a federal command to States to promulgate and enforce laws and regulations."

155-Hodel v. Virginia Surface Mining & Reclamation Assn., Inc.. 452 US 264, 288, 69 L Ed 2nd 1, 101 S. Ct 2352 (1981)

156-FERC v Mississippi, at 761-762, 72 L Ed 2nd 532, 102 S Ct 2126.

In New York v. United States,[157] Sandra Day O'Connor observes for the Court the following excerpts:

"...no Member of the Court has ever suggested that such a federal interest would enable Congress to command a state government to enact state regulation. No matter how powerful the federal interest involved, the Constitution simply does not give Congress the authority to require States to regulate....Where a federal interest is sufficiently strong to cause Congress to legislate, it must do so directly; *it may not conscript state government as its agents*." (Emphasis added)

"Where Congress exceeds its authority relative to the States, therefore, the departure from the constitutional plan cannot be ratified by the "consent" of the state officials."

"State officials thus cannot consent to the enlargement of the powers of Congress beyond those enumerated in the Constitution."

"...the Constitution protects us from our own best intentions: It divides power among sovereigns and among branches of government precisely so that we may resist the temptation to concentrate power in one location as an expedient solution to the crisis of the day." (Emphasis added)

What the court is saying, repeatedly: there is a division between the federal authority and that of the state and one cannot encroach upon the sphere of the other. In other words, the 10th Amendment defining this separation is not extinct and cannot be ignored. And most important of all, Congress has **no authority** to take from the state that which is theirs and demand it for the federal establishment. They have no such power. To do otherwise would be a direct violation of Article IV, Section 3, of the Constitution which is footnoted earlier. Note the last part of that footnote quoted on page 67:

"...and nothing in this Constitution shall be so construed as to Prejudice any Claim of the United States, or of any particular State."

To do otherwise would certainly "prejudice" a claim of a State.

157-New York v. United States: 505 US, 144; 120 L Ed 120

CONGRESS PASSES LAWS TO RESERVE OR SET ASIDE LAND

The first mention of "reserve" occurred in an Act of Congress in 1830.[158] It authorized the pre-emption of Public Domain land by settlers who had been streaming west into the ceded territory created by the Northwest Ordinance, the ceded land from Georgia and the Louisiana Purchase. However, the settler had some restrictions with respect to the land upon which he could settle: He could not appropriate or preempt land that had been reserved. This act allowed this pre-emption subject to the *pre-existing* reservations. The Act of 1830 had absolutely nothing to do with land that was to be settled after 1830 other than to recognize preemption.

> "be it enacted...That every settler or occupant of the public lands, *prior to the passage of this act*, who is *now* in possession, and cultivated any part thereof, in the year one thousand eight hundred and twenty-nine, shall be and is hereby authorized to enter, with the register of the land office...Provided however, That no entry or sale of any land shall be made, under the provisions of this act, which shall have been reserved for the use of the United States, or either of the several states, in which any of the public lands may be situated."
> (Emphasis added)

This act was directed toward land that had already been occupied—not land that was to be occupied in the future. This act was later to be cited, erroneously, in Grisar v. McDowell. It was taken out of context; this is discussed later.

Earlier, Congress had reserved West Point, on the Hudson River, and other land for the "Erection of Forts, Magazines, Arsenals..." There is nothing in the above quotation from that act that would lead anyone to presuppose that this possible reservation would be for any other purpose than "Forts, Magazines, Arsenals,..."

Later, in 1841, the reservation of land is mentioned again. This time it is in connection with land that is to be conveyed to territories or states for "internal improvements." With respect to reservation, the Act of 1841[159] has this to say:

158-Act of 1830: 21st Congress, Sess. I. Ch. 208, May 29, 1830.
159-Act of 1841: 27th Congress, Sess. I. Ch. 16, September 4, 1841.

"...such land [to be conveyed shall be] subject to the following limitations and exceptions:...no lands included in any reservation, by any treaty, law or proclamation of the President of the United States, or reserved for saline, or for other purposes...;"

Almost as a rider on this act, the right of preemption by settlers is again recognized.

Note in the quotation above: "for other purposes." This was to have a profound effect for it was to give the president a nearly carte blanche right to reserve land by executive order. In the case of United States v. Midwest Oil,[160] the court enumerated the times Presidential Executive Orders were mentioned in public documents through 1910 that affected land use: 99 times with respect to Indian reservations; 100 times with respect to military reservations "and setting apart land for water, timber, fuel, hay, signal stations, target ranges, and rights of way for use in connection with military reservations;" and 44 times for bird reserves. Just recently, president Clinton set aside 1,600,000 additional acres in Utah by Executive Order citing the *Antiquities Act of 1906* as his authority. See the section that follows, titled, THE ANTIQUITIES ACT OF 1906 for an explanation of theat act. In short, no such sweeping authority can be derived from that act. Specifically, the act states the following with respect to the scope of any set aside for a National Monument.

"and may reserve as part thereof [for National Monument] parcels of land, the limits of which in all cases shall by confined to the smallest area compatible with the proper care and management of the objects to be protected."

The act addressing itself to, "...historic landmarks, historic and prehistoric structures, and other objects of historic or scientific interest..." 1,600,000 acres is a wildly overstated necessary area of land that has literally no substantial foundation in fact for the protection of a site such as is described in the act. Many believe that this is an illegal land-grab on the part of the Clinton Administration.

With the compounding use of Executive Orders, the Federal government was not precluded from acting on and in behalf of the people of these United States to set aside lands for purposes of conservation or preservation even though the original use of the Executive Order was, for the most part, directed toward military installations or supplies for the military. The

160-United States v. Midwest Oil Co. (1914): 236 US 459; 59 L.Ed. 673.

case of United States v. Midwest Oil centered around the reservation of oil-bearing land for naval ships.

Congress could and did enact laws that did precisely the same thing. However, strictly speaking, with respect to the Constitution, after statehood all such set-aside or withholding from settlement was supposed to occur only with the approval of the legislature of the involved state. This the different states have never done!

Presidential Executive Orders are another matter. These orders look directly to Congress for their approval, tacit, implied or otherwise. Of course, their scope and extent is also governed by the provisions of the Constitution. However, these orders do not seem to draw nearly the attention an act of Congress would that is enacted to accomplish the same result.

THE IMPACT OF PRESIDENTIAL EXECUTIVE ORDERS

Presidential Executive Orders have been used for a long time, and it would be wrong to say that their use is contrary to the provisions of the Constitution. The right to issue an order certainly is authorized, even though the content of the order may not be.

The first line of control or oversight of any Executive Order is Congress itself. If the order is not challenged there, it can and usually is construed to be in conformance with Congressional desire.

With respect to presidential reservations of public land, the frequently quoted confirmation of the existence of this presidential power are derived from a statement of Secretary Teller, made in 1881:

> "That the power resides in the Executive from an early period in history of the country to make reservations has never been denied either legislatively or judicially, but on the contrary, has been recognized. It constitutes in fact a part of the Land Office law, exists ex necessitate rei, as indispensable to the public weal, and in that light, by different laws enacted as herein indicated, has been referred to as an existing undisputed power too well settled ever to be disputed."

Government law officers have issued opinions on the subject as

171

well. Note the following in 1889 (19 Ops. Atty. Gen. 370):

> "...a long established and long-recognized power in the President to withhold from sale or settlement at discretion, portions of the Public Domain."

And from 1881 (17 Ops. Atty. Gen. 163):

> "the power of the President was recognized by Congress, and that such recognition was equivalent to a grant."

The actual cornerstone of the extent of power attributed to Executive Orders with respect to public lands comes from an often cited case, Grisar v. McDowell.[161] (This case is reviewed in the appendix.) In turn, Grisar derives its authority from the Act of 1830. Grisar takes the Act of 1830 out of context and applies it to all public lands *after* 1830. That is clearly not what the act says at all, as was pointed out in that section entitled, CONGRESS PASSES LAWS TO RESERVE OR SET ASIDE LAND.

The large problem with respect to Executive Orders is the acquiescence to such action by Congress. Executive Orders can come with little or no Congressional or public input; they can come on short notice. This is not all bad. In short, the Executive Order is in reality an administrative tool. The continued permanence of the order is the danger. Their impact can last a long time—even well beyond the exigency of the moment.[162] The case of United States v. Midwest Oil deals extensively with this subject and is very interesting reading.

The extent and impact of acquiescence is dealt with in that section entitled, PRESCRIPTIVE LAW AND THE "CLAIM OF RIGHT."

Acquiescence can have the implied force of law, and it has not been limited to Congress. States have been and are involved.

With respect to the public land, states have ***acquiesced*** to the act that specifically provides for the set aside reserves: the Forest Reserve Act of

---

161-Grisar v. McDowell, (1867): 73 US 363; 18 L.Ed. 863.

162-One such Executive Order was issued by President Roosevelt in connection with war powers that Congress gave him during a time of peace—in 1932. He used it to close all banks. It is that same war powers grant to the President that accounts for many of the presidential actions that seemingly are taken unilaterally. To this writer, the extension of war powers to any president for peace-time activity is more than stupid; it is dangerous. Worst of all, it has neither been withdrawn nor limited by Congress

1891. This is not to say that they did not object, for they did so vociferously.

However, to my knowledge, they did not do so judicially. Their acquiescence, as it turned out, cannot be construed to mean legal acceptance. There is no statute of limitation for constitutionality. Even at this late date, that issue is still open. And because of its importance, this act becomes the next topic for discussion.

FOREST RESERVE ACT OF 1891

In 1891 Congress passed a critical and pivotal law: The Forest Reserve Act of 1891. Among other things, Yellowstone National Park was expanded. The Forest Reserve Act of 1891 and Clause 24 of that Act is the corner-stone that eventually led to the set aside of approximately sixty percent of all western lands that are under federal control today. This is discussed at length in Part I. Clause 24 of the Forest Reserve Act of 1891 is again quoted:

> "Sec. 24. That the President of the United States may, from time to time, set apart and reserve, in any State or Territory having public land bearing forests, in any part of the public lands wholly or in part covered with timber or undergrowth, whether of commercial value or not, as public reservations; and the President shall, by public proclamation, declare the establishment of such reservations and the limits thereof."

This act sets into motion a violation of the Equal Footing Doctrine when the territory became a state. The disclaimer of title that was intended for one purpose in 1812 would now be interpreted differently: The Public Domain land *inside* the boundary of a new state was to be retained in federal ownership in perpetuity—not for "future disposition".[163] There is no other legal justification for this act other than the fact that it sets aside land for the preservation of the forest reserves of the United States so that these forests would not become depleted. There are numerous cases cited in Part One that recognize the authority of the federal government to regulate the use of this land, but not its ownership. So far as I have been able to discover, the courts have not ruled on the constitutionality of withholding of this land without approval of the legislature of the states. (They have, however, ducked the issue when it was raised in one of the cases cited later, Light v. United States.)

163-U. S. v. Gratiot: (1840) 39 U.S. 14 (Pet) 526

Two violations are involved. First, a violation of the Equal Footing Doctrine and the second, a violation of Article I, Section 8, Clause 17 of the Constitution, quoted earlier. In the case of Light v. United States,[164] the right to make rules and regulations regarding its use either directly or through the Secretaries of the Interior or Agriculture is upheld.

In the case of Light v. United States, all the proper arguments were brought up by Light and also by the United States regarding the basic issue of trespass. Light claimed that the Forest Reserve Act of 1891 was unconstitutional. The court ducked this issue entirely as follows:

> "This makes it unnecessary to consider how far the Unites States is required to fence its property, or the *other constitutional questions involved*."[165] (Emphasis added)

THE RIGHT TO REGULATE REINFORCED: SHANNON V. U.S.

A brief analysis of the case of Shannon v. United States[166] brings up a number of collateral issues. This case in general is about trespass onto Forest Reserve Land adjacent to private fenced land by sheep. The fence was cut. The sheep roamed. There was no water on the private land; water was on the Forest Reserve land. (I don't know if the water had been filed upon with the state. There was no mention of that in the case.) What sheep there were could not be sustained on the private land without grazing on the Forest Reserve land. This Forest Reserve land had been used for many years for grazing. A regulation by the federal government declared that no further grazing would take place on that same Forest Reserve land. The owner of the sheep ignored this prohibition.

I must digress for a moment. Cattle, in accordance with common law (common law from England, the basis of our laws), were free to roam as "free commoners."[167] Not so with sheep in those early days. Sheep were herded by a *person*; they were under a *person's* control and direction. Thus cattle were treated, legally, differently from sheep. If other control was required, it was necessary to fence the sheep *in*. Cattle were considered to be commoners, and as such, if one is to restrict their movement, fences were

---

164-Light v. United States: (1911) 220 US 523; 55 L Ed 570; 31 Sup. Ct. Rep. 485

165-Siler v. Louisville & Nashville R.R., 213 U.S. 175.

166-Shannon v. United States, 160 F 870 (9th Cir. 1908), 172, 180n., 181.

167-The Legal Aspects of Grazing Problems, Judge Ethelbert Ward, p. 4

required on the part of the person who owns the land to fence the cattle *out*. The control of sheep, being in the hands of a person provides both the federal government as well as the owner of the sheep, full remedy both at law and in equity. Cattle were different; they were commoners in their own right.

Back to the issue at hand. The federal government, as a land owner, if that is what he is, has been held to be nothing more than...

"an ordinary proprietor.....[and] is subject to the legislative authority and control of the states, equally with the property of the private individuals."168

This same observation was held in Woodruff v. North Bloomfield Gravel Mining Co.169 Regardless of these cases, in Shannon v. United States the court overturned the state fencing law in Montana that required the federal government to fence its land like "an ordinary proprietor" and put the burden of trespass onto its federal, unfenced land directly upon the owner of the livestock. In other words, inasmuch as sheep were involved, it became the responsibility of the sheep herder or the land owner to fence his sheep in. However, it was not just sheep that the fencing law in Montana was addressing: cattle were the subject matter as well, and as commoners, they must be fenced out by the land owner, in this case, the federal government. It is interesting to note that the two were lumped together and the burden of control was placed entirely on the owner of the privately owned land. I mention Shannon v. U.S. to point out that there are divergent cases. However that may be, the preponderance of cases **consistent with the Constitution** do not favor Shannon v. U.S.

Judge Ward,170 as well as Judge Georgetta,171 believe that, in this regard, Shannon v. U.S. is in error and in conflict with other decisions of the Supreme Court as well as the Constitution. Ward cites the following cases to support his contention:

N.W. Fertilizing Co. v. Hyde Park Co. 97 U.S. 667
Escanaba v. Chicago, 107 U.S. 689
U.S. v. Knight Co. 156 U.S. 11

168-Fort Leavenworth R. Co. v. Lowe, 114 U.S. 525

169-Woodruff v. North Bloomfield Gravel Mining Co. 18 Fed. Rept. 753

170-The Legal Aspects of The Grazing Problem, Judge Ethelbert Ward: p.5

171-*Golden Fleece in Nevada*, Judge CLel Georgetta, p. 161.

OTHER CASES SUPPORTING THE RIGHT TO REGULATE

In the case of Gibson v. Chouteau,[172] where two parties claimed the same land by U.S. Patent, one prevailed because the State Court claimed that the statute of limitation barred the other party from the exercise of his title issued by a U.S. Patent. In overturning the State Court decision the U.S. Supreme Court said the following:

> "...the statutes of a state prescribing periods within which rights must be prosecuted are not held to embrace the state itself [in this case the United States],"

> "With respect to the Public Domain, the Constitution vests in Congress the power of disposition and of making all needful rules and regulations. That power is subject to no limitation.[173] Congress has the absolute right to prescribe the times, the conditions and the mode of transferring this property or any part of it, and to designate the persons to whom the transfer shall be made. No state legislature can interfere with this right or embarrass its exercise;"

This was said in connection with the right of the federal government to sell the public land within a state. It implies but does not grant the right of eminent domain; that is granted to the state upon statehood, in accordance with the Equal Footing Doctrine. Simply put, the federal government has the right to sell the public land—an exclusive sales contract. This was discussed in THE DISCLAIMER CLAUSE: AN EXCLUSIVE SALES CONTRACT. Many attorneys and judges interpret the above quotation as entitlement to eminent domain. To do so, they must not take into consideration nor address the question of the Equal Footing Doctrine. They must ignore it. Judge Clel Georgetta says this in strong language. He calls it a breach of trust.[174] Lower Federal Courts have followed the lead of the Supreme Court, and more inconsistencies have been added.

In the case of Camfield v. United States,[175] the court was more circumspect and limited the powers granted:

172-Gibson v. Chouteau, thirteen Wall. 92, 99, 20 L. Ed. 534

173-Note the language, "subject to no limitation." Quite obviously this is taken from U.S. v. Gratiot—out of context. No such authority, in context, is granted.

174-*Golden Fleece in Nevada*, Clel Georgetta, p. 161

175-Camfield v. United States, 167 U.S. 519 525, 17 Sup. Ct. 864 867, 42 L. Ed. 260.

"...we do not think the admission of a territory as a state deprives [the United States] of the power of legislating for the protection of the public lands...***so long as such power is directed to its own protection***." [The protection of the land.] (Emphasis added and shortened for clarity)

Here no mention of ownership of the land was made, just its use.

For the moment, let us assume that The Forest Reserve Act of 1891 is, in all respects, lawful. As a matter of fact, all federal departments and bureaus that have any present, acting, managerial authority over these lands assume that it is lawful, irrespective of the fact that it was a territorial convention that disclaimed title to the land before the state joined the Union—an act only the legislature of the given state can perform—irrespective of the fact that it is a violation of the intent of the Resolution of Congress in 1780,[176] "...lands...shall be...formed into distinct republican States, which shall become members of the Federal Union, and shall have the same rights of ***sovereignty***, freedom and independence, as the other States;" irrespective of the broad intent of the "Equal Footing Doctrine," which was discussed earlier;[177] and irrespective of the fact that the disclaimer of title to the land contained in the Enabling Acts of the various states is not constitutional as proclaimed in the case of Pollard v. Hagan. That case is discussed later.

Suppose for the sake of argument that under the Powers Clause, Congress does have power to withhold land from transfer to the states, irrespective of the Equal Footing Doctrine. Arguably, that right to withhold could be more effective prior to statehood—a time when the land was clearly under federal ownership as territory, in trust and also, arguably, less effective after statehood.

The following table is supplied as a point of reference as to the dates of statehood for the western states as that date bears upon the Forest Reserve Act of 1891.

STATE	DATE ADMITTED TO UNION
California	1850
Oregon	1859
Nevada	1864
Colorado	1876

176-Resolution of Congress on Public Lands, October 10, 1780. (JOURNALS OF THE CONTINENTAL CONGRESS, ed. by G. Hunt, Vol. XVIII, p. 915)

177-See ORIGIN OF THE "EQUAL FOOTING DOCTRINE" section for details.

Washington	1889
Montana	1889
Idaho	1890
Wyoming	1890

Forest Reserve Act of 1891-	
Utah	1896
Arizona	1912
New Mexico	1912
Alaska	1959

Note that, of this list, Utah, Arizona, New Mexico and Alaska are the only states that were admitted to the Union after 1891. [Hawaii was another. It has not been included in the focus of this review.]

REVERSAL OF FEDERAL OWNERSHIP OF LAND: UTAH V. U.S.

The case of Utah v. United States[178] reverses a finding that land, while still in territorial condition (federally owned), could be reserved and by so reserving preclude the passage of title to the state upon its entry into the Union. In reversing, the court held that *title to the land passed to the state when it became a state consistent with the Equal Footing Doctrine*.

This recent court decision is of the utmost importance, for it redefines land ownership and the limits of federal ownership of Public Domain after a state is accepted into the Union. This case is clear and understandable. It is lengthy, but it accurately traces the history of the land from acquisition to disposition, citing intent and purpose. It should be read in its entirety; it is that important. In short, it says that the land that was under federal titular ownership and control while a part of a territory becomes state-owned land when that state is accepted into the Union.

This waters down the absolute finding of the court in Shannon v. United States and Gibson v. Chouteau quoted earlier.

Just recently, the Federal District Court in Las Vegas cited Scott v. Lattig[179] as its authority to rule in favor of the United States with respect to

---

178-Utah Division of State Lands v. United States: (1987) 482 U.S. 193, 96 L Ed 2nd 162, 107 S Ct 2318

179-Scott v. Lattig, (1913), 227 U.S. 229.

two summary judgment requests by the United States in a pending case, U.S. v. Nye County.[180] (Scott v. Lattig is summarized in the appendix.) Titular ownership of the land after statehood is an issue in U.S. v. Nye County. It should be noted that Utah v. U.S. post-dates Scott v. Lattig and as such takes precedents.

Further, states do have rights, and the right to be equal to other states, and in particular to the original thirteen states, is one of them. The important point here is that the court is saying that the withholding of land title upon the entry into the Union is a condition of inequality. This is a shift in the singular focus of "equality" from political equality to equality in another sense: possessory equality of land title similar to that possessed by the original thirteen colonies. There is some limitation, however. The subject-matter of Utah v. U.S. was about land under navigable waters as well as a strip of dry (fast) land two miles in width beyond the water's edge. It is this strip of dry (fast) land about which we are concerned here. Pollarad v. Hagan was about water under navigable water. In dicta, Pollard v. Hagan addressed itself to dry (fast) land and thereby set the stage for what I believe the Justices in that case wanted to be understood: The Equal Footing Doctrine dictates that upon entry into the Union, all land within the border of a state became the property of the state. In this case, Utah v. United States, we see this interpretation confirmed.

TO WITHHOLD TITLE, IT MUST BE MADE "VERY PLAIN"

Utah v. United States[181] is an interesting case that deals with the issue of "intent:"

"We simply cannot infer that Congress intended to defeat a future State's title to land.... 'unless the intention was definitely declared or otherwise made very plain.'"

In other words, "what for" and "why" they—Congress—were preempting the Constitution. Neither of these questions are answered. The intention was not declared nor made "very plain." It then follows that it must not have been the intent of Congress to circumvent the Constitution, and, as a result thereof, the language in the Enabling Act was a referral to

---

180-U.S. v. Nye Co.: 920 F. Supp. 1108 (D. Nev. 1996).

181-Utah Division of State Lands v. United States.

"Forts, Magazines, Arsenals, dock-Yards, and other needful buildings," and a clearing of title.

One might simply draw the conclusion that since Utah came into the Union after the Forest Reserve Act of 1891, it came into the Union and was subject to this prior act. Not so. In Utah v. United States, the court places considerable emphasis on the Equal Footing Doctrine and in effect is saying that the Enabling Acts do not give the federal government the right to defeat this doctrine. Moreover, of equal importance in this case, the words "definitely made very plain" surface; the Court points out that in the case of the U. S. v. Holt State Bank,[182] a necessary notice of an intention by Congress to defeat a state's claim to title to territorial land within its borders under the Equal Footing Doctrine upon entry into statehood is required. In the absence of such a notice "made very plain," it is inferred that no such withholding could occur. With respect to the disclaimer clause, other Enabling Acts of the states that were formerly a part of the Northwest Territory as well as the Louisiana Purchase, contain much the same language—except Louisiana. Irrespective of this disclaimer, the title to the Northwest Territory and most of the Louisiana Purchase ultimately resulted in either a transfer of title to the states for specific purposes such as education, or was transferred by sale into private hands. In the absence of such a notice "made very plain," it can rightfully be assumed that the transfer of title from the federal government to the state upon statehood would and should take place. And so it was assumed. However, the retention of title did not happen by any direct, formal Act of Congress "made very plain." It happened in a different way: the federal government, via their bureaus,asserted their assumed management and control of the public land to delay or prevent the sale of the public land. Any adherence to the dictates of the Equal Footing Doctrine that dominion and sovereignty of the land passed to the state upon statehood was overlooked or ignored. Further, the disclaimer clause in each of the Enabling Acts was evidence to these same bureaus that ownership of the public land did not pass to the state upon statehood. Of course, to make this claim, they had to completely ignored the fact that these same disclaimer clauses were declared unconstitutional in both Pollard v. Hagan and Coyle v. Smith. In short, the position of the different Bureaus was clear: the land would remain theirs—title included—until it was formally announced otherwise or relinquished by some specific act of Congress. In a way you might even say that these same bureaus "hung around" in this semi-state of limbo until the passage of the Taylor Grazing Act. That act was their legal authority to "stay."

While the subject-matter of Utah v. United States revolved around

182-U.S. v. Holt State Bank: (1926) 270 U.S. 49, 55, 70 l Ed 465, 46 S Ct 197.

land under navigable water and its transfer of title or the withholding of such transfer to the state, the case did at the same time deal with a strip of dry (fast)[183] land, as mentioned before, not under navigable water at all: 2 miles in width around the lake. The court applied the same principle to both the fast land as well as the land covered by navigable water: That which occurred for the thirteen colonies was the expectation and mandatory occurrence for a future state—an application, in fact, of the Equal Footing Doctrine.

Recited in Utah v. United States is the following:

"In Pollard's Lessee [Pollard v. Hagan] this court announced the principle that the United States held the lands under navigable waters in the Territories "in trust" for the future States that would be created, and in dicta even suggested that *the Equal Footing Doctrine absolutely prohibited the United States from taking any steps to defeat passing title to land underneath navigable water to the States*. Half a century later, however, the Court disavowed the dicta in Pollard's Lessee, and held that the federal government had the power, under the Property Clause, to convey such land to third parties:

"Thus under the Constitution, the Federal Government could defeat a prospective State's title to land under navigable water by a pre-statehood conveyance of the land to a private party for a public purpose appropriate to the Territory."

It was noted that Congress had never done this (convey any land to third parties) and under those circumstances....

"...we have consistently acknowledged congressional policy to dispose of sovereign lands only in the most unusual circumstances. In recognition of this policy, we do not lightly infer a congressional intent to *defeat a State's title* to land under navigable waters:" (Emphasis added)

The court goes on to quote Montana v. United States[184] with respect to the conveyance of title to another (In this case, title to the bed of the Big Horn River to the Crow Indian Tribe:

"...conveyance by the United States, and must not infer

183-The court uses the term "fast" land. Fast land is simply dry land.

184-Montana v. United States: (1981) 450 U.S. 544, 552; 67 L Ed 2d 493; 101 S Ct 1245.

such a conveyance unless the intention was ***definitely declared*** or otherwise ***made very plain***, or was rendered in ***clear and especial words***,"[185] (Emphasis added)

In addition, the court quotes U.S. v. Holt State Bank:

"disposal by the United States during territorial periods are not lightly to be inferred, and should not be regarded as intended unless the intention was ***definitely declared or otherwise made very plain***." (Emphasis added)

Congress passed the 1888 Act,[186] that set aside and reserved land. Utah was admitted to the Union in 1894 "on an Equal Footing with the original States." The court said:

"...the strong presumption is against finding an intent to defeat the State's title....we simply cannot infer that Congress intended to defeat a future State's title to land under navigable waters '***unless the intention was definitely declared or otherwise made very plain***.'"
(Emphasis added)

"...we would not infer an intent to defeat a State's Equal Footing entitlement from a mere act of reservation itself. Assuming arguendo that a reservation of land could be effective to overcome the strong presumption against the defeat of state title, the United States would not merely be required to establish

---

185-The wording "clear and especial words" comes from Martin v. Waddell, while "made very plain" comes from U.S. v. Holt State Bank, both of which relate to an automatic passage of title to another (a state) *unless a withholding* of title is done in "clear and especial words" or "made very plain" that there is an intent to withhold. In the case of Montana v. United States we see this verbiage in reverse: Title will not pass unless such passage is done in "clear and especial words" or "made very plain." The Equal Footing Doctrine is involved as defined in Pollard v. Hagan. With respect to the Equal Footing Doctrine, the court said "...the Federal Government holds such lands in trust for *future States*, to be granted to such States when they enter the Union and assume sovereignty on an 'Equal Footing' with the established States." Aside from the twist of verbiage, in a footnote on page 501 of 67 L Ed 2d (493) title to upland, even though small, is acknowledged: "...if the bed of the river passed to Montana upon its admission to the Union, the State at the same time acquired ownership of the *banks of the river* as well."

186-The 1888 Act had the practical effect of reserving all of the public lands in the West from public settlement and was repealed in 1890 by Congress. However, in doing so, Congress provided "that reservoir sites heretofore located or selected shall remain segregated and reserved from entry or settlement as provided by [the 1888 Act]."

that Congress clearly intended to include land under navigable waters within the federal reservation; the United States **would additionally have to establish that Congress affirmatively intended to defeat the future State's title to such land**." (Emphasis added)

The court is saying, by indirection, that regardless of the reservation of the land, the Equal Footing Doctrine dictates that the state's claim to title is valid. The court would seem to make allowances for "unusual circumstances" not defined, for example, that international affairs could influence the disposition of federal lands. Short of this, to defeat a state's claim to title, Congress would have to make "very plain" an intent to circumnavigate the Constitutional right under the Equal Footing Doctrine to withhold title.

DISCLAIMER IS UNCONSTITUTIONAL: POLLARD V. HAGAN

The case of Pollard v. Hagan[187] is pivotal. It is clear, succinct and compelling. In that case the court observed that the Enabling Act by which Alabama became a state contained a disclaimer to all right or title to the waste or unappropriated lands lying within the state, and that this land would remain at the sole disposal of the United States. The court held that that provision was in violation of the Constitution and therefore void. Justice McKinley had this to say:

"We think the proper examination of the subject will show that the United States never held any municipal sovereignty, jurisdiction, or right of soil in and to the territory of which Alabama or any of the new states were formed; **except for temporary purposes to execute the trusts** created by the act of Virginia and Georgia legislatures, and the deeds of cession executed by them to the United States, and the trust created by the treaty with the French Republic of the 30th of April 1803 ceding Louisiana." (Emphasis added)

With respect to the disclaimer, Justice McKinley continued:

"...Such stipulation would have been void and inoperative; because the United States **have no constitutional capacity to exercise municipal jurisdiction, sovereignty,**

187-Pollard v. Hagan, 223, 11 L. Ed. 565, 180n.

or eminent domain, within the limits of a state, or else-
where, except in cases in which it is expressly
granted." [Article 1, Section 8, Clause 18, "Forts, Magazines,
Arsenals,.."] (Emphasis added)

Note that Justice McKinley states emphatically that the United
States has no jurisdiction, sovereignty or eminent domain within the limits
of a state except in cases where it is expressly granted. By whom? The legislature of the state.

He states the reason for withholding in the first place:

"The object of all the parties to these contracts of cession
was to convert the land into money for the payment of the debt,
and to erect new States over the territory thus ceded; and *as*
soon as these purposes could be accomplished, the
power of the United States over these lands, as prop-
erty, was to cease. (Emphasis added)

Justice McKinley makes an interesting point:

"The argument so much relied on by the counsel for the
plaintiffs [Federal], that the agreement of the people inhabiting
the new States, 'that they forever disclaim all right and title to
the waste or unappropriated land lying within the said territory;
and that the same shall be and remain at the sole and entire
disposition of the United States,' *cannot operate as a*
contract between the parties, but is binding as a law."
(Emphasis added)

In other words, the disclaimer was a law and not a contract. As law,
this raises the question of intent and objective. This Justice McKinley stated
earlier above. Quite obviously, this objective had a termination point in
time:[188] when all the land had been disposed of by sale and a state had been
formed. To arbitrarily cease to sell the land would be a violation of the intent

---

188-The cession by Virginia of its "waste and unappropriated lands in the western
country" to the United States is quoted herewith: "That all the lands so ceded to the United
States...shall be considered as a common fund for the use and benefit of...the United
States...and shall be faithfully and bona fide disposed of for that purpose, and for no other use
or purpose whatsoever..." The purpose of the trust is outlined in the cession in considerable
detail and refers specifically to Resolution of Congress On Public Lands (October 10, 1780)
which states that the proceeds from the common fund shall be used to repay "...the necessary
and reasonable expenses which any particular State shall have incurred since the commencement of the present war...."

or objective of a trust agreement. This was never done with regard to the ceded land of the seven colonies; that land was eventually all sold or ceded to the states for a specific purpose. Not so with the land acquired later by purchase or as the spoils of war.

Continuing:

"The right of Alabama and every other new state to exercise all the powers of government, which belong to and may be exercised by the original states of the Union, must be admitted; and remain unquestioned except so far as they are temporarily deprived of control over the public lands."

This commands the question: What is "temporarily deprived?"

In spite of all this, The Forest Reserve Act of 1891 was passed. It was far reaching. A new interpretation of the disclaimer in the Enabling Acts was in force. Pollard v. Hagan was ignored, or, to suit the situation, it was bent; what was really meant, according to the "benders," was that this case referred only to land under navigable waters. The new precedent established by the Forest Reserve Act of 1891: Land inside the boundary of a state—after it ceased to be territory of the federal government—could be set aside by federal edict. And it was. States were affected. Land that had little or no timber was immediately withdrawn from settlement. It was a set-aside of major proportions even though it was not set aside all at once. It was done in a piece-meal fashion—some here, some there. In the meantime, open lands were still being used by ranchers to graze their sheep or cattle. Most of these ranchers already held valid water rights on this open rangeland. Suddenly, one day, that open range land was declared to be a Forest Reserve. The rancher could no longer use the land without complying with the rules and regulations for its use developed by the Secretary of Interior or the Secretary of Agriculture. The cases referred to later as authority to regulate were the obvious result. The rancher had his use of the land restricted or even eliminated. He didn't like that. And his objections went all the way to the Supreme Court. He lost. It is true that Forest Reserve boundaries were established without any consultation with the counties; they seemed to be arbitrarily set—suddenly. Further, and most distressing, a lot of the land so set aside was not forested land at all. While I do not know for sure, I would hazard a guess that the set-aside land was covered by merchantable timber to the extent of no more that perhaps 60 percent. However, once set aside, this land stayed that way, even over the voluble protest of its residents. It was set in concrete.

GRADUAL INCREASE OF FEDERAL "POWERS" CLAUSE

Federal power has not come from any sudden discovery of a new source. It has been gradual and certainly pervasive; it has been in dynamic growth. The most obvious source of this increased Federal power has been that which Congress has, little by little, added as a result of the ever expanding interpretation of the Powers Section of the Constitution. Repeating Justice Frankfurter in the case of U.S. v. California: "...sliding from absence of ownership by California to ownership by the United States." The same "sliding" has occurred with respect to increased Federal powers as well.

TREATIES AS A SOURCE OF INCREASED "POWER"

While we have mentioned treaties as they relate to the land of the United States, this by no means is the totality of treaties. Unmentioned are the related powers this bestows upon Congress. This is the least balanced of all the bestowed powers granted to the federal government by the Constitution. By definition, the founding fathers left the freest hand to the central government in this area. The reason for so doing was that the Articles of Confederation made it almost impossible for the Federation, with respect to the Treaty of Paris, to effectuate a provision of that treaty: Namely, to protect the property rights of British creditors of American citizens. Seven of the thirteen colonies—then sovereign nation-states— respected the provision; the other six ignored it. The result: The President, with the advice and consent of the Senate, can execute a treaty. The Constitution declares a treaty to be the law of the land. Treaties were intended by our founding fathers to be related to national defense and international agreements relative to trade and commerce (not domestic issues) and, as such, a concern of a central government, to which they gave a freer hand in order to deal with other sovereign, foreign governments. *The Federalist No. 75* is quoted on that subject:

> "Its objects are CONTRACTS with foreign nations, which have the force of law, but derive it from the obligations of good faith. They are not rules prescribed by the sovereign to the subject, but agreements between sovereign and sovereign."

Treaties are not limited to a narrow view—and they have not been. Today, treaties can cover migratory birds along with a whole host of other things—and they do. The question to ask is simple enough: Can and do these treaties enlarge the scope of the Constitution to include flora and fauna and thereby grant them the same privileges and protection heretofore provided to the citizens of the United States? In other words, are flora and fauna to be treated as equals to Homo sapiens?

The courts have both explained and limited the scope of treaties as differing issues have come up.

In the case of Ware v. Hylton,[189] a very broad power was pictured:

> "It is the declared will of the **people** of the **United States** that every treaty made, by the authority of the **United States** shall be superior to the **Constitution**..."
> (Emphasis added)

This case, and a general fear of a superior authority to that of the Constitution, led to an effort in the 1950s to seek a constitutional amendment to preclude such an interpretation. This proposed amendment was called the Bricker Amendment. The amendment effort failed. A later court decision, modifying this interpretation, was the probable cause of the failed amendment attempt.

Not all treaties are self-executing; they may require Congressional implementation. In other words, the treaty may be legislative in one sense and executive in the other. As Jay observed in *The Federalist No. 75,*

> "...though it does not seem strictly to fall within the definition of either."

And as Marshall stated in Foster v. Nielsen,[190]

> [a treaty is] "to be regarded in courts of justice as equivalent to an act of the legislature, whenever it operates of itself, without the aid of any legislative provision."

In other words, if the treaty does not require implementation by Congress, the treaty can be the equivalent of an act, and conversely, when its implementation by Congress is required, the federal government cannot do

189-Ware v. Hylton: 3 Dall. (3 U.S.) 199 (1796).

190-Foster v. Nielsen: 2 Pet. (27 U.S.) 253, 314 (1829).

so alone. Congress can implement only those things that are provided by its *limit* of power established by the Constitution.

What happens, then, when a treaty provision and an act of Congress conflict? Neither has any intrinsic superiority over the other. In general, the one of the later date will prevail. "In short, the treaty commitments of the United States do not diminish Congress' constitutional powers."[191]

In Head Money Cases,[192] the following quotation is noteworthy:

"Its infraction becomes the subject of international negotiations and reclamations,...which may in the end be enforced by actual war....the judicial courts have nothing to do and can give no redress."

Chief Justice Marshall, in Foster v. Nielsen stated,

"When the terms of the stipulation import a contract— when either of the parties engages to perform a particular act, the treaty addresses itself to the political, not the judicial department; and the legislature must execute the contract, before it can become a rule for the court."

In other words, the treaty itself may, by its terms, require implementation by Congress.

Justice Holmes, in Missouri v. Holland[193] observed,

[By supremacy clause, both statues and treaties] "are declared...to be the supreme law of the land, and no superior efficacy is given to either over the other."

He did differentiate the two in another way:

"Acts of Congress are the supreme law of the land only when made in pursuance to the Constitution, while treaties are declared to be so when made under the authority of the United States. It is open to question whether the authority of the United States means more than the formal acts prescribed to make the convention."

191-The Constitution of the United States, Analysis and Interpretation (1972), prepared by the Congressional Research Service Library of Congress, p 490.

192-Head Money Cases: 112 U.S. 580, 598-599 (1884)

193-Missouri v. Holland: 252 U.S. 416, 432 (1920)

He cautions:

> "we do not mean to imply that there are no qualifications to the treaty-making power."

It's pretty hard to get a definitive line from the foregoing with respect to the limits that *might* be placed upon treaty-making.

However, in the case of Reid v. Covert,[194] Justice Black limited treaty-making powers with the following statement:

> "There is nothing in this language which intimates that treaties do not have to comply with the provisions of the Constitution. Nor is there anything in the debates which accompanied the drafting and ratification of the Constitution which even suggest such a result."

There you have it: Finally, a definitive statement about the limitations to treaty-making powers. Treaties must comply with the provisions of the Constitution.

He goes on to tell why such was true in the first place: Namely,

> [so] "that agreements made by the United States under the Articles of Confederation, including the important treaties which concluded the Revolutionary War, would remain in effect."

Their purpose: Sovereign to sovereign.

Justice Black adds:

> "the United States possesses all the powers of a constitutionally centralized sovereign State; and therefore, that when the necessity from the international standpoint arises the treaty power may be exercised, even though thereby the rights ordinarily reserved to the States are invaded."[195]

In other words, it is not the treaty power which enlarges either the federal power or the congressional power, but the international character of

194-Reid v. Covert: 354 U.S. 1 (1957).

195-The Constitutional Laws of The United States, by W. Willoughby (New York: 2d ed. 1929), p. 569

the interest concerned which might be acted upon.

In spite of all of the above, the concept of international concern is elastic and has constantly expanded over the years. This expansion has allowed Congress, by virtue of a given treaty, to expand legislation in a manner that it would be precluded from so doing were it not for the treaty. Most of these areas of expansion of authority and power have to do with environmental issues.

It does affect domestic affairs. One owner of land in southern California was told that he could not clear brush from his private land because his private land was the habitat of the kangaroo rat, an endangered species. His house burned to the ground in a fire started on public land.

FEDERAL GOVERNMENT RIGHT TO MAKE RULES AND REGULATIONS UPHELD

There is no doubt that the federal government does have the authority to make rules and regulations governing the use of its land. But what is the limit of the words "its land?" Is it limited to "Forts, Magazines, Arsenals," as defined in the Constitution?" Regardless of the answers to these questions, rules and regulations were made to regulate the use of the public land both outside and inside the boundaries of states.

RULES AND REGULATIONS

Can the federal government own land indefinitely without the concurrence of the legislatures of the states? Does the Powers Clause of the Constitution allow ownership? Does constitutional authority given to Congress to make Rules and Regulations allow Congress, acting alone, to authorize the ownership of any land by the federal government?

As pointed out in Part One, the care and protection of the land itself from overuse, erosion, etc. was the basis of rules and regulations regarding the use of that land. A number of cases have been cited that support the right of the federal government to regulate the use of public lands. The following list of cases support this claim and are cited by the different bureaus and departments as their authority to regulate:

United States v. Tygh Valley Co.: (1896) 76 F 693
Dastervignes v. United States: (1903) 122 F 30
Dent v. United States: (1904) 76 P 455
Shannon v. United States: (1908) 160 F 870
United States v. Grimaud: (1911) 220 U.S. 506
Light v. United States: (1911) 220 U.S. 523

These cases have to do with grazing or trespass onto federal land and the right to delegate the authority of regulation and rule-making to the Secretary of Interior or the Secretary of Agriculture. Further, in each of these cases, no mention was made at all about the possible existence of water rights and the preemptive use of the land that went with those water rights. The constitutionality of the 1891 act was challenged, as stated earlier, and that question was ducked in Light v. United States. Further, the question of ownership was not raised, and, as such, it was not answered that these same lands were privatized and under the sovereignty of the states upon admission to the Union. Nor, for that matter, was the question raised that the land was held "temporarily" in trust by the federal government, in accordance with trusts of ownership created by treaties (Louisiana Purchase from France, the West from Mexico, etc.). However, in each of the above cited cases, ownership of the land by the United States was assumed by the court, even though the land in question was inside the boundary of a given state. These cases are all **assumptions** of federal ownership of the land and not **decisions** that the land is owned by the federal government. Ownership of the land was not an issue in any of these cases; the ownership of the land was not challenged. As far as the court was concerned, both the plaintiff and defendant assumed federal ownership of the land. This made it an easy transition and assumption to make: no one objected or argued otherwise! Thus the validity of the various rules and regulations regarding the land were authenticated.

THE EQUAL FOOTING DOCTRINE AND RECENT CASES

The foundation for the claim of perpetual federal ownership goes back to Section 24 of the Forest Reserve Act of 1891. In a way, this forced a new meaning for the Equal Footing Doctrine: political equality was all that was necessary in order to be "equal." State dominion and sovereignty of the public land were no longer a part of the equation comprising the Equal Footing Doctrine. However that may be, without dominion and sovereignty, political equality is not, in totality, equality "in all respects whatever." It is only a part of "equality." Economic equality was never claimed or required, and the courts have clearly indicated this. Economic equality never existed in the original colonies. However, ownership and control of the land within the border of the original states did exist; the thirteen colony-states owned their own land as the sovereign thus making state dominion and sovereignty of all future states an essential part of the Equal Footing Doctrine.

There are two cases that appear to be at opposite ends of the spectrum: Namely Kleppe v. New Mexico,[196] which was discussed earlier, and Utah v. United States. They seem to overlap in a big way. Kleppe deals with Congressional Power to make Rules and Regulations respecting public land and animals on the land, while Utah deals with land ownership as a result of the Equal Footing Doctrine. In assuming without deciding federal ownership of the land, Kleppe emasculates the 10th Amendment and gives immense power to Congress by virtue of the Property Clause. In addition, Kleppe gives an enlarged meaning to the Powers Clause of the Constitution respecting public land, and implies, by assumption, that the land is Federally owned after statehood. This was not hard to do. New Mexico agreed by stipulation, that the public land in New Mexico was federally owned. On the other hand, in the Utah case, where the ownership of the public land was not agreed by stipulation to be federal, the court says that the land belongs to the states upon their entry into the Union.

With regard to the Property Clause, read the following from Kleppe v. United States:

> "And while the furthest reaches of the power granted by the Property Clause have not yet been definitely resolved, we have repeatedly observed that 'the power over the public land thus entrusted to Congress is without limitations.'" [The court cites U.S. v. San Francisco.[197]]

As pointed out earlier in that section, EXPANSION OF FEDERAL POWER: KLEPPE V. NEW MEXICO, this quotation is out of context. See the review of this case in the appendix. This quotation originated in U.S. v. Gratiot and was picked up in United States v. San Francisco. In truth, the power so granted to Congress was limited to the territory, not the state. Here in Kleppe v. New Mexico we see it without this restraint.

Does this failure on the part of the court to recognize this restraint

---

196-Kleppe v. New Mexico (1976) 426 U.S. 529

197-U.S. v. San Francisco (1939) 310 U.S., at 29-30.

weaken the extent of the powers delegated to Congress by the Property Clause? I think that it does.

With the foregoing in mind, read the additional quotations that follow.

With respect to wildlife:

"In our view, the 'complete power' that Congress has over public lands necessarily includes the power to regulate and protect the wildlife living there."

"We hold today that the Property Clause also gives Congress the power to protect wildlife on the public lands, state law notwithstanding."

With respect to state consent to Federal legislative jurisdiction:

"The argument...that Congress could obtain exclusive legislative jurisdiction over the public lands in the State only by state consent, and that in the absence of such consent Congress lacks power to act contrary to state law...is without merit."

This last statement flies in the face of a whole host of previous Supreme Court decisions that start with U.S. v. Bevans. See the section, JURISDICTION: FEDERAL OR STATE? Further, the Kleppe case tends to overturn Coyle v. Smith inasmuch as Kleppe v. New Mexico is a later case. On the other side of the coin, U.S. v. New York and U.S. v. Utah are later than Kleppe. Besides, all of this is dicta. Kleppe is a determination as to whether or not Congress can regulate animals on federal land. In short, the court here says that it can. Land ownership was not decided; it was assumed by stipulation. Moreover, New Mexico agreed that the land was federally owned. Further, they stated that the animals in question were "taken upon federal land."

The statements made by the court in Kleppe are strong indeed— giving federal authority over public land within the boundary of a state.

With respect to private property, Kleppe observes Camfield v. United States and quotes the following:

"...the power granted by the Property Clause is broad enough to reach beyond territorial limits."

With respect to treaties:

> "...the Treaty Clause, U.S. Const., Art. II, Section 2, permits Congress to enter into and enforce a treaty to protect migratory birds despite state objections."

Note the international implication, "migratory birds." However, free-roaming horses and burros are scarcely international in scope.

Having said all of the above, the court did some limiting:

> "We find that, **as applied to this case**, the Act [Wild Free-roaming Horses and Burros Act] is a constitutional exercise of congressional power under the Property Clause. We need not, and do not, decide whether the Property Clause would sustain the Act in all of it conceivable applications." (Emphasis added)

Continuing:

> "We...leave open the question of the permissible reach of the Act [Wild Free-roaming Horses and Burros Act] over private lands under the Property Clause."

The above would appear to set a "no-limit" game. Were it not for the fact that the quotation above regarding state consent to Federal legal jurisdiction is not required, is dicta, this would be the end of the line. It isn't! Ownership of the land was not a subject to be determined by the court. New Mexico, by stipulation, agreed that the land was in federal ownership. After that, the court need not, and did not, do anything but direct its attention to the controversy between the plaintiff and the defendant. This case clearly assumes federal ownership of the land; it does not decide it.

This case was heard in 1976. Utah v. United States came at a later date—1988—thus giving the latter case precedence. Are the two cases in conflict? They surely set up a conflict. If the land passes to the state upon statehood as a result of the Equal Footing Doctrine, the federal government then ceases to have exclusive jurisdiction, and for that matter, dominion and sovereignty as well, when the state joins the Union. Further, the ability of the federal government to make rules and regulations with respect to the land within the state would be impaired or prohibited by the 10th Amendment. See New York v. United States regarding state's rights versus federal rights that was discussed earlier. Further, it could be argued that there is a breach of Article IV, Section 3 of the Constitution:

"...The Congress shall have Power to dispose of and make all needful Rules and Regulations respecting Territory or other Property belonging to the United States; and nothing in this Constitution shall be so construed as to Prejudice any Claim of the United States, *or of any particular state*."
(Emphasis added)

The Forest Reserve Act of 1891 is still operative. To my knowledge, the only challenge to the Forest Reserve Act of 1891 was done in the case of Light v. United States. The court did not decide the validity of the Forest Reserve Act of 1891 in this case. They left it open for future challenge. Or, more bluntly, the court ducked the issue entirely.

EXPLANATION OF NEVADA V. U.S. & CONFLICT WITH UTAH V. U.S.

Nevada v. United States[198] has been cited as proof that the public land belongs to the federal government rather than the states after the state has joined the Union. This case is no such authority for such a finding. However, it is important to review its findings and limitations so that this lack of authority is clear. Further, the Supreme Court touched on the same subject in a different way in Utah v. United States at a later date, and it is noteworthy that this case was not cited by the Supreme Court in their findings in Utah v. United States.

Any research on the subject of the "Equal Footing" Doctrine and state ownership of land upon entry into the Union is eventually going to lead to the case of Nevada v. United States. This case is referred to consistently by advocates of federal ownership of the land after statehood. This is a mistake.

Now, as to why.

First, an examination of this case is in order. In brief, this case is as follows:

It was brought in the first place to stop the Federal Land Policy Management Act of 1976 (FLPMA) from placing a moratorium—which had been done—on the disposal of public land within the state of Nevada. Nevada alleged that the Land Policy Management Act of 1976 was unconsti-

---

198-Nevada v. United States: (1981) 512 FS 2nd 1665; (1983) 699 FS 2nd 486.

tutional and further, that the act infringed on Nevada's 10th Amendment and "Equal Footing" rights. Declaratory relief was sought.

It should be noted, early on, that at no time did Nevada claim ownership of the land. That was not what the suit was all about. ***The suit was about constitutionality*** of the Federal Land Policy Management Act (FLPMA) of 1976. Nevada **assumed** federal ownership of the land and accepted this as a given. This was a mistake.

In the United States Ninth Circuit Appellate Court to which the District Court decision was appealed, Justice Schroeder observed that Nevada agreed that 88 percent of the land within the borders of Nevada was federally owned. Ownership was, therefore, not an issue. It should have been. Schroeder observed:

"...this action did not claim title to any land; it challenged only the moratorium."

Continuing:

"...the amended complaint sought no additional or alternative relief to that sought in the original complaint."

The court had asked the plaintiff to amend their complaint if they wished to do so, inasmuch as the FLPMA had dropped the moratorium.

And:

"Nevada agrees that this case does not involve a claim of title to land."

Inasmuch as Nevada expressed no further concern that a new moratorium would be instituted, because the one that had been placed upon the land had been lifted, Schroeder observed:

"...all cases illustrative of the general rule that when action complained of have been completed or terminated, declaratory judgment and injunctive actions are precluded by the doctrine of mootness."

In other words, there was nothing the court could do under these circumstances but affirm the District Court's dismissal of the action. This the court did.

But that was not all. Schroeder adds this in concluding:

> "Any future challenges to actual or anticipated federal action with respect to ***federally held*** lands will arise in a different legal and historical context from that surrounding the 1964 moratorium which prompted this suit." (Emphasis added)

This is about as close as the court could come to saying that the decision might have been different if a different question had been asked.

Earlier, in the District Court, Nevada had raised the issue that the United States did hold the public land in trust and, secondly, that new states were to be admitted on an "Equal Footing," and on that score said the following in their argument:

> "...that Equal Footing is a constitutional condition of all states of the Union."

Of Course! That was a wrong way of putting it. There was no argument! "Equal Footing" is a constitutional condition and the court could easily agree. At no time did the state of Nevada argue that the land was state land as a result of the "Equal Footing" Doctrine. This is a classic example of asking the wrong question. Later, the District Court observed by citing Alabama v. Texas,[199]:

> "The Equal Footing Doctrine does not affect Congress' power to dispose of federal property."

Quite true. Federal property would include "Forts, Magazines, Arsenals..." as well as tanks, ships, etc.

The court went on to say:

> "Federal Regulation which is otherwise valid is not a violation of the "Equal Footing" doctrine merely because its impact may differ between various states because of geographic or economic reasons."

And citing Unites States v. Texas[200]:

> "The doctrine applies only to political rights and sover-

199-Alabama v. Texas: (1954) 347 U.S. 272; 74 S. Ct. 481; 98 L.Ed. 689.

200-United States v. Texas: (1950) 339 U.S. 707; 70 S. Ct. 918; 94 L. Ed. 1221.

eignty; it does not cover economic matters, for there never has been equality among the states in that sense."

The court seems to be drifting away from land as a part of the "Equal Footing" Doctrine and implying that land is an economic issue and as such not a part of the consideration of "Equal Footing." And it is this "drifting" that has become, in part, what the proponents of federal ownership of the land after statehood are basing their conclusions upon. There is a catch to their argument: The meaning of the word "sovereignty" includes the right of ownership of the land and the right to its disposal. However, what the court is saying is no basis for law or for finding that the land is federal in ownership. That was not an issue in this case at all. The court is simply *assuming without deciding* that the federal government owns the land after statehood. In another sense, this is all dicta.

For a more complete summary of this case, please refer to the summary in the appendix.

Now for Utah v. United States (1987).

This that follows is somewhat repetitions to that which was discussed with reference to this case in the previous section entitled, REVERSAL OF FEDERAL OWNERSHIP OF LAND: UTAH v. U.S.

Utah v. U.S. deals with the ownership of land under navigable water as well as a strip of dry land passing to the state of Utah upon its entry into the Union in conformance to the Equal Footing Doctrine. Much history was traced, and the court observed that land—upland as well as land under navigable water—did indeed pass to the state at the time of statehood. The case deals with the Equal Footing Doctrine and its application.

This is a pivotal case, for it does recognize the transposition of ownership from federal to state lacking an intention to withhold the land "made very plain."

In other words, if Congress does not "make it very plain," the land does in fact become the property of the state upon statehood. This case does not deal with land not under navigable waters, but arguendo, the principle is the same. The question was not asked, so therefore, it was not answered by the court. That simply was not an issue to be decided by the court.

If, however, the principle is the same, the date of this case, 1987, takes precedence over the case of Nevada v. United States, which was decided in 1981 and appealed in 1983. Utah v. United States does impact the meaning of the dicta observations in Nevada v. United States. It clarifies it.

Nevada v. United States reaffirms Congressional power to make rules and regulations affecting our public land. Nevada v. United States assumes the ownership is federal without deciding it. But what is the outcome of the public land? If it becomes the land of the state upon state-hood as Utah suggests, then it is not subject to federal regulation. If we were talking about land under navigable water, there would be no argument at all. That was decided in Pollard v. Hagan and has since been reaffirmed time after time. Pollard did, in dicta, trace the history of ownership and drew no distinction in that tracing between land above or below navigable water. The only difference: Pollard did not decide that part of the historical passage of title. Here in Utah, we see much the same observation—again in dicta but with one exception: To defeat a state's Equal Footing right of dominion and sovereignty, "...the intention [must be] definitely declared or otherwise made very plain."

You can't have it both ways however you want to look at it. On the surface, there does appear to be a conflict between these two cases with regard to ownership, assumed ownership, congressional power affecting ownership and constitutional provisions to admit states "upon an Equal Footing in all respects whatever." But that is not quite accurate.

Ownership of the land *was* asked in Utah v. United States and it was not asked in Nevada v. United States. For a more detailed summary of Utah v. United States, please refer to the appendix.

COYLE V. SMITH: EQUAL FOOTING & STATE DISCLAIMER OF LAND

Of all the Supreme Court cases, there is probably none other than Coyle v. Smith that deals directly with the Equal Footing Doctrine and a state's disclaimer of title to public lands, included in nearly all Enabling Acts. It clearly, unequivocally confirms that a state may not be deprived of its Equal Footing rights with the original thirteen states upon joining the Union; it sets aside any contractual agreement made, voluntarily or other-wise, by the state as a condition of entering the Union. This would include the disclaimer by the state to title to public lands.

In this case, the issue revolved around the extent to which Congress could, by command or edict, "bargain" with a territory to become a state as a condition of entry into the union. The extent and limitation of this "command" or "edict" is discussed at length in this case. The definition of "Equal Footing in all respects whatever" is discussed, as well as is the power of Congress with respect to admission of states into "this Union."[201]

Congressional authority respecting statehood comes from Article 4, Section 3 of the Constitution.

"new States may be admitted by the Congress into this Union."

The court goes into considerable detail to explain this and points out the limitation in the Constitution respecting Congressional authority in this regard:

"The only expressed restriction upon this power is that no new State shall be formed within the jurisdiction of any other State, nor by the junction of two or more States, or parts of States, without the consent of such States, as well as the Congress."

And continuing, the court points out the variety of language used to admit new states—even where no terms or conditions were exacted from states upon entry into the Union. Significant is the following quotation:

"...admission in 1796 of Tennessee, as the third new State, it being declared to be 'one of the United States of America,' 'on an Equal Footing with the original States in all respects whatsoever,' phraseology which has ever since been substantially followed in admission acts..."

And:

"The power is to admit 'new States into *this* Union.' 'This Union' was and is a union of States, equal in power, dignity and authority, each competent to exert that residuum of sovereignty not delegated to the United States by the Constitution itself. To maintain otherwise would be to say that the Union, through the power of Congress to admit new States, might come to be a union of States unequal in power, as including States whose powers were restricted only by the Constitution, with others whose

201-Extracted from Art. 4, Sec. 3 of the Constitution.

powers had been further restricted by an act of Congress accepted as a condition of admission." (The court's emphasis)

The court says that this cannot be:

> "The argument that Congress derives from the duty of 'guaranteeing to each State in this Union a republican form of government,' [additional] ***power to impose restrictions upon a new State which deprives it of equality with other members of the Union, has no merit***."
> (Emphasis added)

In restrictive language, the court observes that Congress has the duty of seeing that a state's form of government is not changed to one that is anti-republican and goes on to say:

> "...it obviously does not confer [upon Congress the] power to admit a new State which shall be any less a State than those which compose the Union."

With respect to the provisions in the Enabling Acts disclaiming title to public lands, the court lays this foundation and observes:

> "...quite common in enabling acts, by which the new State disclaimed title to the public lands, and stipulated that such land should remain subject to the sole disposition of the United States,......[the United States] can derive no force from the consent of the State."

In other words, the state cannot give away its right to be "equal." The disclaimer to ownership of the land by the state, by itself, has no force and effect. The court continues:

> "...there is to be found no sanction for the contention that any State may be deprived of any of the power constitution-ally possessed by other States, as States, by reason of the terms in which the acts admitting them to the Union have been framed."

The court cites Pollard's Lessee v. Hagan and makes the following observation:

> "The plain deduction from this case [Pollard's Lessee] is

that when a new State is admitted into the Union, it is so admitted with all of the powers of **sovereignty** and **jurisdiction** which pertain to the original States, and that such powers **may not be constitutionally diminished, impaired or shorn away by any conditions, compacts or stipulations embraced in the act under which the new State came into the Union, which would not be valid and effectual if [it became] the subject of congressional legislation after admission.**" (Emphasis added)

Note the words, sovereignty and jurisdiction: How could this not include land inside the border of a state after statehood? I think that it does.

The court cites Escanaba Co. v. Chicago[202]:

"Whatever the limitation upon her powers as a government whilst in a territorial condition, whether from the ordinance of 1787 or the legislation of Congress, **it ceased** to have any operative force, except as **voluntarily adopted by her**, after she became a State of the Union. On her admission she **at once** became entitled to and possessed of all **rights** and **dominion** and **sovereignty** which belonged to the original States. **She was admitted, and could be admitted only on the same footing with them**.... 'on an Equal Footing with the original States in all respects whatever.'" (Emphasis added)

Note again, the words, "rights and dominion and sovereignty." Dominion means ownership and title. For that matter, so does sovereignty, inasmuch as eminent domain is a part of sovereignty. Its reappearance again in this case as a reference cements the extent of the meaning of the Equal Footing Doctrine; it includes the intended passage of the title to the land from the federal government to the state upon statehood.

To reinforce this statement, the Court cites Bolln v. Nebraska:[203]

"...this court has held in many cases that, whatever be the limitations upon the power of a territorial government, **they cease** to have any operative force, except as voluntarily adopted after such territory has become a State of the Union. Upon admission of a State it becomes **entitled to and possesses all the rights of dominion and sovereignty which belonged to**

202-Escanaba Co. v. Chicago, 107 U.S. 678, 683.
203-Bolln v. Nebraska, 176 U.S. 83, 89.

202

the original States...'upon an Equal Footing with the original States in all respects whatever.'"
(Emphasis added)

Here, for the third time, appear the words, "rights of dominion and sovereignty."

In concluding, the court makes this statement and warning:

"...the constitutional equality of the States is essential to the harmonious operation of the scheme upon which the Republic was organized. When that equality disappears we may remain free people, but the Union will not be the Union of the Constitution."

These are chilling words of warning.

In this case the court has almost in so many words said that the Enabling Act cannot force a state to forego its title to land after statehood. The court does say that Congress does not have this derivative power from Article 4, Section 3, referred to above. And, clearly, the court defines that the Equal Footing Doctrine means exactly what it says: Equal..."in all respects whatever."

While it does not say so in words, such as "title to the land," the statement is clear; title to the land passes to the state—so that they will be exactly like the thirteen original states—each of whom had title to their land before they voluntarily allowed their so-called "waste" land to be used for a "common fund" (in trust) to pay for the debts of the American Revolution.

EARLIER, THE COURT ASSUMED FEDERAL OWNERSHIP OF LAND

By this time, it cannot be a surprise to anyone that the different bureaus of the federal government have assumed ownership of all so-called public land and have designated them as federal land or national land. This is axiomatic. But in the past the court as well has done it.

In all the cases I have cited on page 191 that give the federal government the right to make rules and regulations regarding land that is inside the boundaries of states, whether it was National Forest land, Bureau of of Land Management land, or whatever—other than that land used for "Forts, Magazines..." etc., the courts have assumed this same federal ownership. Note that I said, "within the boundaries of states." Territorial land is not included. That is land before it became a state during which time federal ownership and jurisdiction has not been questioned.

EFFECT OF UTAH V. UNITED STATES & EQUAL FOOTING DOCTRINE

Utah v. United States bluntly declares that the land—fast (dry) land, not just land under navigable waters—belongs to the states after they join the Union. This has a far-reaching effect even though the finding of the court was restricted to land under navigable waters: That was all that was brought before the court to decide.

In addition to this momentous declaration, consider the following quotation from New York v. United States:[204]

> "In providing for a stronger central government, therefore, the Framers explicitly chose a Constitution that confers upon Congress *the power to regulate individuals, not states*. As we have seen, the Court has consistently respected this choice." (Emphasis added)

In other words, in a broad sense, the federal government may regulate people, not the state, nor by implication, the land (after statehood). Why? Because it is not theirs! It is an integral part of a state.

Until Utah v. United State in 1988, the Court *had also assumed* federal ownership of the land in these earlier cases or it could not have approved the right to make rules and regulations on land that was not federally owned!

In an important respect, this case is a reversal of sorts for "rules and regulations" as well. No longer can the rules and regulations developed and laid down by Congress and picked up by the different federal agencies be applicable to land that is not federal. This undercuts and may even overturn the host of cited cases on page 204 that establish, reinforce and unequivocally allow the federal government authoritative control over federal (public) lands to make rules and regulations affecting these lands.

204-New York v. United States: 120 L. Ed. 2nd, p. 144.

Simply put, as state land, the rules and regulations placed upon them by the federal government no longer apply. That function is up to the state.

This case is a "clarifier." It sets the course of Constitutional behavior back on track and begs the quotation from United States v. Butler cited on page 61:

> "The question is not what power the Federal Government ought to have but what powers in fact have been given by the people."

There is one catch, however. Those who adhere to the belief that federal lands are exactly that until ceded by the federal government to the separate states point out that the case of United States v. Utah is a case about land under navigable water and not land above the water. They are right. That is what the case was all about, and that is the limit of the actual finding of the court. In fact, the reference to Pollard v. Hagan is clear. That was the basis of the finding in that case too. Read the summary of Pollard v. Hagan in the appendix. That case was about land under navigable waters. As has happened in much of the tidelands of the United States, it was reclaimed, so to speak "from the sea," hence the question, who owned it: The United States or the separate state? In Pollard v. Hagan, the history is traced from the original colony from which the land originally came—Georgia, which makes it doubly important; it was original and not clouded by any extenuating circumstances such as purchase or spoils of war.

FUNCTION OF THE SUPREME COURT

Certainly, at this point it would be appropriate to outline briefly exactly what it is that the Supreme Court deals with. The Supreme Court does not deal with fact-finding other than the questions laid before it. However, in dicta, the court more often than not will give its understanding and the historical background upon which it draws its opinion. The court is not an independent, expeditionary force that strikes out into the legislative arena on its own to take up a matter that has not been brought before it by an aggrieved party. An action must be filed by someone or some government agency in a lower court (except state cases in conflict with the United States) in order to be heard by the Supreme Court. Even then, if you don't ask the court the right question, you will not get the right answer. Sometimes the court may not elect to hear a case. However, the Supreme Court has no choice other than to hear a case if a matter of constitutionality has been raised. The court ducked the constitutional issue raised in Light v. United States. In that case they were able to rule on the basic issue brought before the court—trespass—without determining the constitutionality of the Forest Reserve Act of 1891. And that is what they did.

The Court tries as best it can to **narrow** its findings. It will never use a shotgun when a rifle will do. In other words, it does not deal with peripheral vision at all—only the focal spot, and the smaller the better. Obviously, it is of the utmost importance to ask the right question. I have read many cases in doing the research for this book wherein I have felt that the right question was not asked at all; I have wondered if the issue as I understood it to be had been asked more directly, or differently the finding of the Court would have been different. Perhaps.

When given the proper question about ownership and control of the land, the courts have no problem determining its ownership. They had no problem on that issue in Utah v. United States.

Some will say that they need a Supreme Court decision that says, in general, that federally controlled lands are really owned by the separate states. Bluntly, again, the Supreme Court is not about to remind you that you really have rights that you did not realize you had. The point is, you already have the rights; the fact that you did not or do not know it or about it does not in and of itself negate that right or title. Doing nothing about the foregoing assumption of power by the federal government is an available option to all the aggrieved, as well as doing something. But even this has its risks: the longer the status quo remains intact and unchallenged the greater the possibility of a prescriptive law of sorts becoming acceptable. And, of course, if unchallenged, this power could become more and more and more pervasive and controlling.

THE SUPREMACY CLAUSE AND THE "SUPREME LAW OF THE LAND"

Many suppose that the Supremacy Clause of the Constitution gives to Congressional laws or acts the force and effect of the supreme law of the land.

Not at all. There are limitations and qualifications.

The powers of Congress are limited to pass **only** those laws that are in **conformance** to the Constitution. Read the quotations from *The Federalist 44* and *46* which follow. They spell out the intent of the Supremacy Clause. The Constitution is a reflection of that intent and that intent only. Laws that depart from that intent and the Constitution are **not enforceable**. And, more sobering, all officials, no matter at what level, are duty-bound, by oath, to uphold the Constitution of the United States.

Simply stated, the Supremacy Clause deals with the fact that the **U.S. Constitution** is supreme over any and all **state** laws—not just any law Congress may decide to pass. The Supremacy Clause of the Constitution does not allow Congress latitude to make unlawful laws, and as such, claim that those laws are protected by the Supremacy Clause. An unlawful act or law is **never** protected or **enforceable**.

The "Supremacy Clause" is Article VI, Section 2 of the U.S. Constitution:

> "This Constitution, and the laws of the United States which shall be made in pursuance thereof; and all treaties made or which shall be made, under the authority of the United States, shall be the supreme law of the land; and Judges in every state shall be bound thereby, any thing in the Constitution or laws of any State to the contrary notwithstanding."

Again, the word "pursuance" appears; the **laws** of the United States shall be made in **pursuance** thereof—not just any law that Congress passes.

This Supremacy Clause is bilateral, too. It limits state government as well as the federal government. Each is bound by the Constitution.

W. Cleon Skousen says it far more eloquently and succinctly than can I:

> "The word, SUPREME, means no more than this—that the Constitution and laws made pursuant thereof, **cannot** be controlled or defeated by any other law...the State, as well as individuals, are bound by these laws; but the laws of Congress are restricted to a certain sphere, and when they depart from this sphere, they are no longer supreme or binding."[205]

205-*The Making of America*, by W. Cleon Skousen; pages 657-658.

It should be clear that nothing in this "Supremacy Clause" grants to Congress any sole, supreme power. Congress has only that power that the Constitution conveys to Congress and no more. Put another way, Congress does not have a supreme power over powers not granted by the Constitution. The primary reason for the Supremacy Clause can best be summed up by reading Madison, in *The Federalist No. 44*:

> "...as the Constitutions of the States differ much from each other, it might happen that a treaty or national law of great and equal importance to the States, would interfere with some and not with other Constitutions, and would consequently be valid in some of the States at the same time that it would have no effect in others."

In other words, conformity to one supreme law was essential in order to effectuate a treaty or national law of great importance. They envisioned two sovereign governments operating in two areas. Note that Madison relates his comments to international and not domestic events. Madison, in *The Federalist No. 46*, describes those two areas:

> "The powers delegated by the proposed Constitution to the Federal Government, are ***few and defined***. Those which are to remain in the State Government are ***numerous and indefinite***. The former will be exercised principally on external objects, as war, peace, negotiation, and foreign commerce;.... The powers reserved to the several States will extend to all the objects, which, in the ordinary course of affairs, concern the lives liberties and properties of the people; and the internal order, improvement, and prosperity of the State." (Emphasis added)

Note again the international limitation and scope he places upon the Supremacy Clause of the federal government as well as the power he envisions for that of the "several States."

The original intent was distinct indeed: The federal government generally international in scope; the state government generally domestic.

PRESCRIPTIVE LAW AND THE "CLAIM OF RIGHT"

As far as prescriptive law is concerned, in an over-simplified manner, prescriptive law simply reaffirms that if something has been going on for a protracted period of time, it becomes binding, enforceable and legal. There is a limit however, in the case of the federal government and the constitutionality of this issue. There are some things that *never* become legal regardless of how long they have been going on. It is like a statute of limitations that cannot be invoked. In other words, if something is found to be in conflict with the Constitution, it can never become legal simply because that's-the-way-we-have-been-doing-it. This is not in pursuance (in accordance) to the U.S. Constitution.

But that's-the-way-we-have-been-doing-it is a factor to contend with; it was as early as 1789 when that very issue was raised, in the case of Stuart v. Laird (1 Cranch, 299, 309; L. Ed. 115, 118). Even though that case had to do with circuit powers to judges of the Supreme Court, it recognized that there was some credence and force in such a behavior.

> "...practice and acquiescence under it for a period of several years, commencing with the organization for the judicial system, affords an irresistible answer, and has indeed, fixed the construction. It is a contemporary interpretation of the most forcible nature. This practical exposition is too strong and obstinate to be shaken or controlled."

In 1914, this same factor is given even more weight, in the case of United States v. Midwest Oil Co.[206]

> "But government is a practical affair, intended for practical men. Both officers, lawmakers, and citizens naturally adjust themselves to any long-continued action of the Executive Department, on the presumption that unauthorized acts would not have been allowed to be so often repeated as to crystallize into a regular practice. That presumption is not reasoning in a circle, but the basis of a wise and quieting rule that, on determining the meaning of a statute or the existence of a power. weight shall be given to the usage itself,—even when the validity of the practice is the subject of investigation."

The "claim of right" is an ancillary matter. And one could and should expect the federal government to raise this issue with respect to our public land. In a substantial way, this tends to reinforce prescriptive law and implies the time-worn expression, "possession is nine-tenths of the law."

Black's Law Dictionary defines "Claim of ownership, right and title" in the following manner:

206-United States v. Midwest Oil Co. (1914) 236 US 459; 59 L.Ed. 673.

"As regards adverse possession, claim of land as one's own to hold it for oneself. ***Claim of right, claim of title and claim of ownership are synonymous. Claimant's intention to claim in hostility to real owner.***"
(Emphasis added)

Black's defines the Claim of Right doctrine as follows:

"As contemplated under doctrine of adverse possession is simply that claimant is in possession as ***owner, with intent to claim the land as his own, and not in recognition of [the] record title owner.***"[207] (Emphasis added)

It should not be inferred that constitutionality is that easily circum-navigated. It isn't. Claim of Right was raised and questioned in the case of U.S. v. California[208] and is discussed later as it bears to the final disposition of title to the submerged land off the coast of California.

Our founding fathers were very, very wary about allowing a Federal Government to encroach upon the rights of the state. The 10th Amendment spelled out that separation. This was the safe-guard.

The Forest Reserve Act of 1891 keeps returning as a pivotal issue. How does this affect public land after 1891? This act does give the federal government the right to set aside *state* lands. The language in Section 24 of the act says exactly that. However, as already pointed out, in the absence of approval by the legislature of the state, no such sweeping authority exists. On the other hand, the federal government does have the right to set aside whatever it pleases of such lands that it may properly own that is consistent with the Constitution; namely, "Forts, Magazines, Arsenals, dock-Yards..." However, even here, state approval is required.

With respect to public lands, the federal government is simply precluded by the U.S. Constitution from acting unilaterally after a territory becomes a state.

Bluntly, the federal government has no unilateral jurisdiction or powers over lands other than those which are defined by the Constitution; again, "Forts, Magazines, Arsenals, dock-Yards...." That is what the Constitution says. In other words, a conflict does exist between the Act of 1891 setting aside state land without the approval of the legislature of the

207-*Black's Law Dictionary* relies upon Sisson v. Koelle, 10 Wash, App. 746, 520 P.2d 1380, at 1384 for this definition.

208-U.S. v. State of California, (1978) 436 US 32, 56 L Ed 2d 94, 98 S Ct 1662.

states and the provisions of the Constitution. To "take" this land and place it under the umbrella of federal control and jurisdiction and hold it in perpetuity is a clear violation of the Equal Footing Doctrine, and a violation of what our founding fathers envisioned in the first place, as well as a violation of the intent and specificity of the 10th Amendment!

The public lands outside of those defined by the Constitution belong to the states and are outside federal jurisdiction.

Of course it could be argued that this land is simply being withheld for "an indefinite" time. But in this context is it still an "indefinite" period of time after one hundred years? I think not, and many others agree with me; it is a permanent retention. Even in the law school textbook, *Federal Public Land and Resource Law* by Coggins, Wilkinson and Leshy (third edition), that conclusion is recited:

> "Because the federal government now intends to retain ownership of almost all its lands, the basic public land legal conflicts are over use, not disposition, of the public resources." (p. 14)

It is no wonder that almost all attorneys assume federal ownership of the public land: That is what they are taught in law school. What happened to the Equal Footing Doctrine and the trustor-trustee relationship or even the intent to retain the land after that intention to do so must be "made very plain?" That question is not raised in the textbook. federal ownership of the land is simply assumed.

PRESUMPTION OF POWER

Is it possible that the federal government may have the stewardship of this public land that is, in reality, state owned? Certainly, it must be agreed that the federal government has been managing the forest reserves and Public Domain land ever since 1891. Can it be that this is an effective, de facto, unalterable, management agreement with the several states? It could be *if* the various states want it that way and so indicate such agreement by the approval of their legislature. Some may argue that time has made it a fact. In Buford v. Houtz,[209] the U.S. Supreme Court found that the federal government had, in effect, acquiesced to a system and practice of disposition of and by preemption and/or appropriation; that this acquiescence, inasmuch as the federal government had known for almost 100 years

---

209-Buford v. Houtz, (1890) 133 U.S. 618.

that it had been going on and had encouraged it, indicated, through continuous acceptance, that the disposition of the land was legal, proper and acceptable. Here it is as turn-about. The states have "allowed" the federal government to manage *their* state-owned land for just about the same length of time. In a way, this begs the prescriptive law issue in favor of the federal government, to wit: "We've been doing it all this time. You have said nothing about it. You can't change now. You have accepted it!" A good argument, but it does not conform to the Constitution. That's an issue you *cannot* get around by application of prescriptive law. Further, the question of prior or continuous knowledge would be an issue. If you did not know that it was your land, would this be acquiescence? Prior knowledge and consent were the issues in Buford v. Houtz. With respect to the states, ***most state officials simply do not know that the land is theirs***. They seem to be waiting for someone (else) to tell them!

THE END TO PRIVATIZING THE LAND: THE TAYLOR GRAZING ACT

To a large extent, the issue of federal control of these lands "in perpetuity" has literally prevented the privatizing of the land altogether. In all the reading I have done, the total objective—all the way from the time of our founding fathers—has been to privatize the land.

The Taylor Grazing Act and the Multiple Use Act, which are discussed at length in Part One, were essentially the coup de grace to privatizing the land. Those acts more or less—mostly more—placed land that was destined to become state land, (and as such private property and an addition onto the tax rolls of the state,) into a quasi-permanent status of federal land exempt forever from privatization. Unequivocally, Judge Georgetta states that both of these acts are unconstitutional.

> "...we now have a government within a government in each of the public land states.... This is a clear violation of the intent, the expressed purpose and explicit provisions of the treaties, the ordinances, state compacts and also the Constitution of the United States. ***The Taylor Grazing Act is clearly an unconstitutional act.***"[210]
>
> (His emphasis)

210-*Golden Fleece in Nevada*, by Judge Clel Georgetta; p. 228, 229

The short scenario goes thus: Acquire the land; hold it (in trust) until it can be settled by enough (60,000) people, all the while encouraging settlement; form a state; continue to sell such land that remained unsold at the time of acceptance by the state into the Union or transfer its ownership to the state. The last item never occurred on any measurable scale.

There is one phrase that says it all: Privatize the land.

To our founding fathers, this was the sole objective of the entire process. To them, there was no other.

CASES OFFERED AS BASIS FOR FEDERAL OWNERSHIP OF LAND

In the course of my research, the following cases have been brought to my attention as authority for the proposition that the federal government owns all the public land today, including, of course, National Forests and Bureau of Land Management land—the bulk of our public land.

> Alabama v. Texas: (1954) 347 US 272;
> Arizona v. California: (1963) 373 U.S. 546
> Camfield v. United States: (1897) 167 U.S. 518
> Coyle v. Smith: (1911) 221 US 559
> Irvine v. Marshall: (1858) 61 U.S. 558
> Kleppe v. New Mexico: (1976) 426 U.S. 529
> Light v. United States: (1911) 220 U.S. 523
> Nevada v. United States: (1983) 699 FS 2nd 486
> Scott v. Lattig: (1913) 227 U.S. 229
> Stearns v. Minnesota: (1900) 179 US 223
> U.S. v. California: (1947) 332 U.S. 19
> U.S. v. Gratiot: 1840 39 U.S. (14 PET) 526
> U.S. v. Mission Rock Co., 189 U.S. 391
> U.S. v. San Francisco: (1939) 84 L.Ed. 1450
> U.S. v. Texas: (1950) 339 US 707
> Utah Div. of State Lands v. U.S.: (1987) 482 US 193
> Utah Power & Light v. United States: (1917) 243 U.S. 389
> Wilcox v. Jackson: (1839) thirteen PET 498

Some of these cases offer bits of information on both sides of the issue and may be relevant in both arguments, for and against, in different ways. Therefore, it would be a mistake to assume that because they appear in the list above they have no bearing on the issue of federal ownership of the public land after statehood or the lack of such ownership.

It is vital that one know what the case was about and analyze the court's observation **relative to the subject matter** of the case. It is very easy to get sidetracked and draw a hasty conclusion that, upon a second look, is really not what you at first thought it to be. The key: keep track of the subject matter.

I have summarized each of these cases in the appendix, along with a number of others that are not named directly above. Each is important in its own way, for it tends to shed light upon the subject matter of Part Two— either for or against the proposition that the federal government owns all existing public lands today.

I must say that in all of the cases listed above, except Scott v. Lattig and U.S. v. Mission Rock, I have found none that **decide** that the ownership is federal. Even in these two cases, the ownership of the land is not a subject of the decision; rather, the decision is based upon the finding by the Court that the land is or was in federal, titular ownership. For the most part, all of them **assume** that the ownership is federal, but **not one** of them **decides** that issue. Where there is an assumption of federal ownership expressed by the court—the statement upon which many attorneys rely as proof that the ownership is indeed federal—I have found that the "proof" is, in reality, dicta. And as pointed out in the previous section, dicta is no basis for law for the reasons outlined therein. A little later for comments regarding Scott v. Lattig and U.S. v. Mission Rock. (Each of these cases are summarized in greater detail in the appendix.)

Other cases summarized in the appendix that are not listed in the previous list of CASES OFFERED AS BASIS FOR FEDERAL OWNERSHIP OF LAND are the following:

Pollard v. Hagan: (1845) 44 U.S. (3 How) 212
Dred Scott v. Sandford: (1856) 60 U.S. (19 How) 383
New York v. United States: (1992) 505 U.S. 144; 120 L.Ed. 120.

I place these on a separate list because they are not heard from in the context of authenticating federal ownership of land as often. Certainly, Pollard v. Hagan is referred to often by both sides of the issue, but it doesn't tend to authenticate federal ownership of land after statehood; hence, it is not on the first list. Careful reading of Pollard v. Hagan shows it to be evidence of the opposite conclusion. Dred Scott v. Sandford is mentioned often as well by proponents of federal ownership, but what is heard mostly about Scott v. Sandford, is revulsion with or vilification of the racial, slavery aspects of the finding of the court, not the other part of the decision in that case: The definition and limiting of the Property Clause of the Constitution. It is this other part of that case that is germane to us in Part Two. And lastly, New York v. United States is really a legal history lesson on the limits of powers granted to Congress by the Constitution. Of course, it is more than that too, for it covers the 10th Amendment in detail as a further limitation of federal power over the states. This lesson and explanation of the limits of power were important background for the finding in that case.

THE TIDELANDS OF CALIFORNIA:
A STORY OF REPATRIATION

The story of the tidelands that are a part of the Channel Islands National Monument, now a National Park, is most interesting—and telling. In its totality, from the time it was the land of Mexico to the final Supreme Court decision, U.S. v. California (1978), declaring the submerged land to be, indeed, owned by the state of California, this story is ironic and probably prophetic.

But first, the history of what took place and why. The implications of this story go well beyond the oil under the sea and the harvesting of kelp that prompted the two cases: U.S. v. California (1947) and U.S. v. California (1978). Both the state of California and United States wanted and ownership and sovereignty. It took two Supreme Court decisions and an act of Congress to settle the issue.

The initial issue was who owned the land between the mean low-water mark to 3 miles offshore of the California coast, the state of California or the United States? This was settled in the first case of U.S. v. California (1947).[211] The court held that this submerged land belonged to the United States. The court's argument was that the original colonies had not claimed the land off their coast and as a result, California could not claim ownership of its off-shore land either—an extrapolation of the Equal Footing Doctrine. See the appendix for a more detailed explanation of this case. Furthermore, with respect to disposal of land, the court reaffirmed Congress' power "without limitation"[212] in this regard. Congress disagreed with this finding

211-U.S. v. California (1947): 332 U.S. 19; 91, L. Ed. 1889; 67 S. Ct. 1658.

212-The authority attributed to Congress by the Supreme Court "to make all needful Rules and Regulations respecting the Territory and other Property belonging to the United

by the Court that the submerged land belonged to the United States and corrected this by passing the Submerged Lands Act of 1953 which granted this submerged land to California.

The time-line of this story is as follows:

1848: The land is ceded to the United States by Mexico (Treaty of Guadalupe Hidalgo.

1849: California decrees itself to be an independent nation and adopts its state constitution.[213]

1850: California joins the Union on an "Equal Footing."

1906: The Antiquities Act of 1906 permits the President to set aside certain *federal lands* of special interest.

1938: President Roosevelt sets aside the Channel Islands National Monument.

1940's: Oil, having been discovered under the submerged lands, is extracted within the 3-mile limit off California.

(212- continued) -States." comes directly from the U.S. Constitution. This power with respect to territory, however, is restricted solely to territory in existence in 1789—The Northwest Territory. (See Dred Scott v. Sandford in the appendix for a more detailed explanation.) The "power over the public land thus intrusted to Congress is without limitation," attributed to Congress by the Supreme Court is a quotation from U.S. v. City and County of San Francisco, which the Court cites in this case. (See U.S. v. San Francisco in the appendix for a more detailed explanation.) In turn, this quotation from U.S. v. San Francisco is referenced to U.S. v. Gratiot. (See U.S. v. Gratiot in the appendix for a more detailed explanation.) It is improperly taken out of context in Gratiot. In Gratiot, the power so attributed to Congress is limited to territory—not land after statehood.

213-Some authorities point out the salient fact that California became an independent nation (by it own choosing) and then joined the Union a year later. If this was actually and legally so, then California's admission into the Union would be much like that of Texas which retained ownership of *all* its land. In California's Enabling Act of admission, California disclaimed its ownership to its public land whereupon this land became federal. The question they raise is: Did California become a territory prior to its becoming a nation? (Probably, yes.) If it became a nation and was recognized as such, did it thereby become the sovereign of *all* its land? If it did, then the land it disclaimed in its Enabling Act had to be approved by its state legislature. Was it so approved? I don't think so. If not, it would appear that the ruling in Pollard v. Hagan and Coyle v. Smith precluding a state from disclaiming any land without the approval of its legislature would render the passage of title from state to federal null and void. These are interesting questions.

1947:   U.S. v. California:[214] United States declared to be the owner of the submerged land.

1949:   President Truman adds to the Channel Islands National Monument.

1953:   Submerged Land Act of 1953 grants title of submerged land to the state of California.

1978:   U.S. v. California:[215] State of California is declared the owner of the submerged land to the 3 mile limit off shore as well as being declared the owner of the tidelands (between mean high and low water) ever since statehood in 1850.

President Roosevelt, by presidential proclamation in accordance with the authority he at that time presumed he had (provided by the Antiquities Act of 1906), established the Channel Islands National Monument—most of Anacapa and Santa Barbara Islands. In 1949, President Truman issued another proclamation enlarging the monument to encompass "the areas within one nautical mile of the shoreline of Anacapa and Santa Barbara Islands...."[216]

[I have, while doing the research for this book, wondered why the different states have acquiesced to federal unilateral determination by proclamation effecting the public land within their borders without so much as a whimper or a word of consent or dissent. This would include, among others, wilderness areas, wild and scenic river additions and even national monuments.]

This proclamation, brought about the second case of U.S. v. California (1978),[217] which was prompted by California's difficulty in executing contracts for the harvesting of kelp within the one-mile extension in the sea of the Channel Islands National Monument. The finding in the case, in essence, said that the submerged land covered by this proclamation had been conveyed to the state of California by the Submerged Land Act of 1953 and, further, that the tidelands had been conveyed to the state of California upon its entry into the Union—a time predating both President Roosevelt's and Truman's proclamations setting aside the Channel Island National Monument. As such, the submerged land was not subject to the

214-U.S. v. California (1947) 332 U.S. 19

215-U.S. v. California (1978) 436 US 32l; 56 L. Ed. 2nd 94; 98 S. Ct. 1662

216-See page 97 of U.S. v. California, 56 L. Ed. 2d 94.

217-U.S. v. California (1978): 436 U.S. 32; 56 L. Ed. 2d 94; 98 S. Ct. 1662.

Federal Channel Island National Monument. The federal government's power over or claim to land was limited to land that the federal government legitimately owned—not state of California land.

There are rocks and small islands off the coast of these Channel Islands that are never submerged. Who then owns them? The Court clarified this.

Two footnotes from this case are of particular note. The first is footnote number 3:

> "Federal title to the islands can be traced to the 1848 Treaty of Guadalupe Hidalgo, 9 Stat 922, by which Mexico ceded to the United States the islands lying off the coast of California, along with the adjacent mainland. See Bowman, The Question of Sovereignty over California's Off-Shore Islands, 31 Pac Hist Rev 291 (1962). While the Treaty obligated the United States to respect private property rights derived from Mexican land grants, all non-granted lands previously held by the Government of Mexico passed into the federal Public Domain. When California was admitted to the Union in 1850, the United States retained ownership of these public lands. See An Act for the Admission of the State of California into the Union, 9 Stat 452."

[I have referred to this Act of Admission as the California Enabling Act: They are one and the same.]

The court is relying upon the disclaimer of ownership in the California Enabling Act and at the same time ignoring what the Court had previously said in Pollard v. Hagan and Coyle v. Smith with respect to a state's disclaimer of ownership of this same land, namely; that the disclaimer has no validity unless it is approved by the legislature of the state. No state has ever done this.[218]

The second is footnote number 7, which traces the ownership of the tidelands off the immediate coast of California, as well as the Channel Islands and their surrounding islets and rocks.

> "The term 'tidelands' is 'defined as the shore of the mainland and of islands, between the line of mean high water and the

---

218-The state of California through its legislature did convey its title to Yosemite to the United States. Other states also conveyed National Parks within their borders to the United States.

line of mean lower low water...' U.S. v. California, 382 U.S. at 452; 15 L. Ed 2d 517; 86 S. Ct. 607. Those tidelands in California that had not been subject to Mexican land grants entered the federal Public Domain in 1848, where they remained in trust *until California gained statehood in 1850. At that time, they passed to the state under the 'Equal Footing' doctrine*. See Borax, Ltd. v. Los Angeles, 296 U.S. 10; 80 L. Ed. 9; 56 S. Ct. 23; United States v. California, 382 U.S. 448; 15 L. Ed. 2d 517; 86 S. Ct. 607. Because the tidelands within the monument were not 'owned or controlled' by the United States in 1938 or in 1949, Presidents Roosevelt and Truman could not have reserved them by simply issuing proclamations pursuant to the Antiquities Act." (Emphasis added)

The tidelands of U.S. v. California (1978) are not all submerged—some of it is dry land, small offshore islets and rocks, which are not below mean high water at any time. The court confirmed that title to those islets and rock was indeed federal and at the same time confirmed that the tidelands around those islets and rocks belonged to California.

This restatement of title passage from federal to state upon statehood was limiting: Automatic title passage from one to the other in accordance with the Court's finding in Pollard v. Hagan occurred only for the tidelands. As pointed out earlier, any other automatic transfer of title of uplands (fast-land) from the federal government to the different states as Pollard v. Hagan indicated should happen was not law; that statement was the opinion of the court, and, as such, it is dicta. Title passage of the upland upon statehood as Pollard, in dicta, would indicate, was not and has not been recognized.

This case turns the focus back to Pollard v. Hagan and begs the question: How clearly did the Court indicate their feeling about the uplands in Pollard? (See this case in the appendix for a more detailed examination.) In their examination and tracing of jurisdiction, sovereignty and ownership, the Court drew no distinction between uplands and lowlands. Both were to be transferred from federal to state jurisdiction, sovereignty and ownership. This was a primary ingredient of the Equal Footing Doctrine—and still is. Problem: The Pollard case was about lowland and not uplands, leaving the door open until title to the uplands was challenged. That door has been held open by the federal government with what I believe to be malice of forethought, and it has only been challenged obliquely in such form and fashion that it was never decided by the Court. That shoe is yet to drop.

There is another facet of this case that is worth noting inasmuch as it may well be prophetic. In presenting their argument that title to the tidelands should be vested in the United States, the federal government raised the Claim of Right doctrine.[219] The basis? The federal government occupied the land! The Court ducked this issue completely. The important point to remember is that the federal government raised it as a valid argument to title. Under similar circumstances in the future, should their occupancy of land be challenged, one should expect to see this same Claim of Right doctrine or adverse possession raised: Its mine, and I own it because I am big enough and strong enough to keep and hold it.

THE ANTIQUITIES ACT OF 1906

Inasmuch as the Antiquities Act of 1906 has been referred to in the preceding section and that it has recently been used by the Federal Government as their authority to set aside additional public land, this Act requires some explanation and examination at this juncture. This Act is specific in nature and has been and is being misused in order to assume broad authority which is simply not there.

The title of what is commonly called the Antiquities Act of 1906 is actually titled, *An Act For the Preservation of American antiquities*.[220] In the opening paragraph it details penalties for anyone...

> "who shall appropriate, excavate, injure, or destroy any ***historic or prehistoric ruin or monument, or any object of antiquity***, situated on lands owned or controlled by the Government of the United States without permission..." (Emphasis added)

This is an obvious reference to American Indian, a prehistoric ruin or site as well as the intent to keep it intact and safe from desecration. No ruin or site is very extensive or very large.

Next, in Section 2. of the Act, it authorizes the President, in his discretion,

---

219-Black's Law Dictionary defines the claim of right doctrine as follows: "As contemplated under doctrine of adverse possession is simply that claimant is in possession as owner, with intent to claim the land as his or her own, and not in recognition of or subordination to record title owner."

220- *An Act For the Preservation of American antiquities:* (1906) Ch 3060, 34 Stat 225.

"to declare by public proclamation historic land-marks, *historic and prehistoric structures, and other objects of historic or scientific interest* that are situated upon the lands owned or controlled by the Government of the United States to be national monuments, and may reserve as a part thereof parcels of land, the limits of which in all cases shall by confined to the smallest area compatible with the proper care and management of the objects to be protected..." (Emphasis added)

This is simply a grant of authority to the president detailing what he may do about preserving these same American antiquities—the subject of the Act itself.

There is nothing in this act that authorizes the establishment of any national monument that is not directly connected with "any historic or prehistoric ruin or monument, or any object of antiquity."

However that may be, President Truman extended the Channel Islands National Monument to encompass "...the area within one nautical mile of the shoreline of Anacapa and Santa Barbara Islands..." Congress reversed this proclamation. (See the section entitled, THE TIDELANDS OF CALIFORNIA: A STORY OF REPATRIATION.)

In the not too distant past, President Clinton set aside approximately 1,600,000 acres of public land in Utah as a National Monument. Nothing has been heard from either Congress or State of Utah about this obvious misuse and probable unconstitutional use of this Act as the authority for such a proclamation. Where is the ruin, historic, prehistoric structure, or object of historic or scientific interest within this 1,600,000 acres? Is there one there that qualifies? How big is it if it indeed exists at all? How much adjacent land is necessary for its reasonable preservation? The use of this Act to set aside such a vast area of land by presidential proclamation is such a stretch that it is ludicrous. Some believe that President Clinton has acted well beyond his granted authority. And I agree.

Just recently, again, President Clinton set aside all the off-shore rocks along the coast of California as a national preserve. Again, misuse and probably unconstitutional use of this Act as the authority for such a proclamation. Can it by that he simply "took" the authority for such a set aside of coastal offshore rocks because nothing was heard from either the State of Utah or Congress with respect to the set aside of 1,600,000 acres in Utah? The set aside of these coastal offshore rocks is an even bigger stretch than the Utah land. Can we expect California or Congress to negate this procla-mation?

What does it take to wake up a state that their sovereignty is being plowed under? Will Utah ever act? Will California do so now that Federal control and authority has been imposed upon their off shore rocks? Will Congress reign in the acts of a president who has acted beyond his delegated authority?

THE EFFECT OF U.S. v. MISSION ROCK AND SCOTT v. LATTIG UPON THE QUESTION OF FEDERAL OWNERSHIP OF PUBLIC LANDS

These two cases are important in the tracing of the chronology of the court's findings as to the ownership of the public lands after statehood.

The oldest of these two cases is U.S. v. Mission Rock, which was decided in 1903. See the summary of this case in the appendix for a detailed examination of this case.

In short, the decision of the court in this case upheld the finding of the United States Circuit Court of Appeals, Ninth Circuit (Mission Rock Co. v. U.S. (1901), 109, Fed. 763.), to wit: the title to the two very small rock islands in San Francisco bay remained in federal ownership after admission to the Union by the state of California. The United States had claimed filled land in addition to the rock-islands. Further, the United States demanded rental or compensation payments for the occupancy of that filled land which was, by then, covered by a number of buildings and other improvements. The claim for compensation was denied, and the court declared that the filled-land (formerly, submerged tidelands) was, indeed, the property of the state of California as per Pollard v. Hagan and subject to California law. In other words, the land was state land and subject to the state's right of disposal. In a way, one could say that this was a kind of land-grab by the federal government, though unsuccessful. The court saw it this way and said so in almost so many words.

The important point, however, is not that the court denied the United States claim to the filled-land or compensation for its use, but its finding that the title to the rocks (5,900 square feet and 420 square feet respectively) remained in federal ownership after the state of California joined the Union in 1850. This is a reversal, of sorts, of Friedman v. Goodwin (1856).[221]

In reaching this finding the court relied upon the disclaimer of ownership of the public land contained in the California Enabling Act (1850) admitting California into the Union "on an Equal Footing with the original states in all respects whatever," and quotes from the California Enabling Act that section dealing with the disclaimer of state ownership or disposal rights to the public lands:

> "[Admission of California into the Union is subject to the] express condition that the people of said state shall never interfere with the primary disposal of the public lands within its limits, and shall pass no law and do no act whereby the ***title of the United States to, and right to dispose of, the same shall be impaired or questioned***." (Emphasis added)

As already pointed out, this is contrary to what was stated in Pollard v. Hagan as well as Coyle v. Smith as to the force and effect of such a disclaimer. The court ignored these two cases as though they did not exist.

I found it rather interesting that the court was not irrevocably positive in its statement of United States ownership of the public land after statehood of California.

Note the following:

> "...title thereto [land] is still in the United States, ***unless the same passed to the state of California by virtue of the admission of that state into the Union under the act of congress of September 9, 1850*** [California Enabling Act]." (Emphasis added)

My question: Which is it? It can't be both ways. The court says one thing and then decides another!

The case of Scott v. Lattig (1913) is a case of a not-too-dissimilar situation. This case centered around the ownership of an island in the middle of a navigable river, the Snake River, that divides Idaho from Oregon in that location. Who owned the land at the time of the suit, who had the right to convey title to the land, the federal government or the state of Idaho? Under whose laws did the title pass, state or federal?

221-See CALIFORNIA DECLARED OWNER OF LAND UPON STATEHOOD, on page 141 for the quotation from that case.

The island (Poole Island) was not small by any means; it was over a mile in length and from 500 to 1,200 feet wide. At the time (1894) Lattig gained title to land he had purchased on the bank of the Snake River (not Poole island), the island in question had not been surveyed by the Surveyor General's office—a fact the court found to be an oversight. Scott settled upon the island in the early part of 1904 and requested that it be surveyed by the General Land Office so that he could claim it as authorized by the homestead law. It was surveyed in 1906, and Scott's application to enter the island as a homestead by virtue of his prior settlement was accepted by the federal government.

It is important to note that Idaho entered the Union in 1890, a date that predated all purchases and or occupancy by the parties involved. This focuses the question as to whether state or Federal Law is paramount. Does the island fall under the disposal rights of the federal government, or does the claim by Lattig of the island fall under state of Idaho law (extending ownership past the bank of the river to its thread [main channel]?

Lattig claimed the northern part of the island by reason of his ownership of the land on the east bank and the southern part of the island by adverse possession (its-mine-because-I-got-there-first and I'm-strong-enough-to-keep-it doctrine). [I think it would be fair to say that courts do not, as a rule, look upon adverse possession favorably.]

The court found that title to Poole Island did not pass to the state upon entry into the Union, but remained subject to disposal by the federal government. Scott's homestead rights were upheld.

In reaching this decision, the court cited U.S. v. Mission Rock as their referenced authority.

These two cases completed the shift from the earlier view expressed in Friedman v. Goodwin.

I would be remiss if I did not point out the limitations of both U.S. v. Mission Rock Co. and Scott v. Lattig. In both cases, state ownership of the land at the time of joining the Union was not argued. Ownership of the uplands was assumed to be federal. As a result, neither of these cases decide federal ownership of the land after statehood. Both of them simply assume it to be so.

Again, I must repeat the truism: Assumption is not law.

SUMMARY AND CONCLUSION

Based upon the forgoing, consistent with the U.S. Constitution and cases that adhere to the provision of the Constitution, I can come to no other conclusion than this: The public lands within the United States, including what we call our National Forests, the Bureau of Land Management land, the land set aside by and for the Fish and Wildlife Agency, even wild and scenic rivers, all belongs to the respective states.

However, this is not to say that this same land should not be set aside as a preserves of one sort or another. That is not the question. The question is this: Consistent with the provisions of the Constitution, and in conformance therewith, who should be making the decisions about the public lands: the federal or state government? Who really owns it?

This question has been answered in a wrenching way by the federal government. The different branches of the federal government have simply said, "The land is mine, and I'm strong enough and powerful enough to take and keep it." And they have. The claim of ownership and the act of control have accompanied this self-directed mandate. The legally minded reader will call this adverse possession. And it is. However that may be, our Constitution precludes any action on the part of the federal or state government that is outside of the confines and provisions of the Constitution itself.

Why and how is this federal claim of ownership and control of the public lands outside the provisions and confines of the Constitution?

Follow along with this summary.

Up through 1856, the date of Friedman v. Goodwin, the following quotation from that court decision expresses the court's view:

> "On her [California] admission into the Union, she [California] became the owner of all the public land not disposed of by law of congress."

There was really no question about who owned the land upon statehood. Even Congress had no question: The annexation of Texas reveals congressional intention. However, in the years that followed there was an inexorable shift, changing this earlier intent of state ownership of its public lands to a retention in fact by the federal government of this same land.

The nagging question I raise is this: Has this shift from state ownership to federal ownership been in conformance to the provisions of the Constitution? I don't think that it has been.

The federal government, time after time, demanded the right to administer and manage the public land. In 1856, most of the West was in a territorial state of being. As territory, there was no doubt as to who owned the land or as to who had the right to manage it: The federal government. That was a given. However, repeatedly, the Enabling Acts of each successive state declared that the states would not interfere with the federal government's disposal rights of this same public land after statehood. Based upon these various Enabling Acts, the federal government demanded the right to manage these same lands after statehood. The states never objected. What Pollard v. Hagan and Coyle v. Smith said with respect to the nullification of these disclaimers was ignored.

As an aside, the federal government cannot take or accept and the state governments cannot give that which the Constitution defines as not theirs to give. Conversely, the federal government cannot give nor can the states accept that which the Constitution defines as not theirs to give or accept.

Back to the issue: The courts went along with the demand of the federal government to manage the public land after statehood. There are numerous cases that deal with the court's agreeing with this contention. Important to note, however, is the fact that in agreeing that the federal government had the right to manage the public lands, the courts **never** decided that this same public land was federally owned—that is, up until U.S. v. Gardner and U.S. v. Bradshaw, both in 1997. Until these two cases, the court **assumed** that ownership to be federal.

Prior to Gardner and Bradshaw, one might successfully argue that this became a decision of the court without being a decision in fact.

This assumption of retained federal ownership of the public lands after statehood was a slow process. It took a number of Congressional acts and a number of court decisions following Friedman v. Goodwin over the next 50 years to complete the change. But it did take place.

The court finalized its changed view as we have just seen in U.S. v. Mission Rock and Scott v. Lattig. Congress changed its view as well: The Forest Reserve Act of 1891 truly began to cast this changing view into law.

However it may be, this question nags: Is it really the basis for law? I don't believe that it was until the Gardner and Bradshaw cases. Is it now? Yes, but read on. As Justice Frankfurter said in a dissenting opinion in the case of U.S. v. California (1947) quoted earlier:

> "...a sliding from absence of ownership by California to ownership by the United States."

Wayne Hage put it in another way: "Nature and politics abhor vacuums." By failing to express their views and by doing nothing, the states literally either backed off or welcomed the federal government to take over titular ownership and managerial rights of state land. The federal government "slid" into a proprietary position.

This "sliding" has been gradual, profound, and even inexorable. This "sliding" is certainly contrary to what our founding fathers had in mind. To them, I believe, it would be unquestionably considered an erosion of the Equal Footing Doctrine and a massive expansion of federal power, the very thing they tried to limit in the framing of the Constitution, for after all is said and done, the Constitution is a document limiting federal power. This expansion of federal power is a blunting of the meaning and purpose of the 10th Amendment, not to mention the obfuscation of the Guarantee Clause of the Constitution (Art. IV, Section 4): "The United States shall guarantee to every State in this Union a Republican Form of Government."

The obvious next question begs to be asked: Is this in conformance to the provisions of the Constitution? I do not think that it is, and others share my view as well. However, I am also mindful that there are numbers of people who believe that the Constitution is or should be a "living" document; subject to interpretation to meet today's needs—or at least, their interpretation of what those needs may be.

I cannot help but call back to mind what Justice Sandra Day O'Connor said so well in New York v. U.S.:

> "...the Constitution protects us from our own best intentions: It divides the power among sovereigns and among

branches of government precisely so that we may resist the temptation to concentrate power in one location as an expedient solution to the crisis of the day."

Throughout the forgoing from a Constitutional point of view, it is rather clear that the federal government has been operating outside of its prescribed constitutional limits. It makes little difference that this has or has not been done to protect perceived individual rights, the natural resources, flora or fauna. Even in good faith, one could surely declare that the federal government should have the right to do all of these things— protect or preserve our personal rights, the common good, a dwindling resource, be that resource timber, grasses, birds or animals.

The real question underlying all of the above is: Are these the concerns the responsibility of the federal government or that of the different states? Over the past 100 years, increasingly, Congress has thought it was the responsibility of the federal government. They thought so in 1891 when they passed Forest Reserve Act of 1891, and they have been thinking the same thing about snail darters, spotted owls, old growth timber, whales, porpoises, kangaroo rats, and a whole host of other animals. (As of this date, over eight hundred are on the endangered species list and several thousand more are on the "to be considered" list.) They even thought so way back in 1864 and 1872, when Yosemite and Yellowstone were first set aside. The difference is immense, however. Yosemite was set aside with the concurrence of the state involved. That was the last time the federal government "asked." 1891 was the beginning of being "told," and the "telling" has been going on ever since. The "telling" has become a redundancy with a suspect motive: If said often enough, an untrue statement can become accepted as fact.

Irrespective of the constitutionality of the Forest Reserve Act of 1891 the ownership of the land was intended to be vested in the states unless the legislature of the state has given its consent to federal ownership or control. This the states did not do. None of them did.

Note what was said regarding the Enabling Act in Coyle v. Smith. Note the limiting in Pollard v. Hagan of the term "territory;" ceded territory by the original colonies only. Note the definition of the Powers Clause in the Constitution and specifically, the meaning of the term "territory" as found in Dred Scott v. Sandford. All of this substantiates the basis that the public lands of the west were not intended to be federal at all.

I must point out, however, that if one were to ask if Congress had the power under the Constitution to enact the Forest Reserve Act of 1891, the answer would be "*YES*." Congress has the authority to pass whatever law and regulation it wishes. If, on the other hand, one were to ask if the act or law is enforceable you may get an entirely different answer. To be enforceable, it must be within the scope of the Constitution—not just a law passed by Congress.

However, at this point a word of caution is necessary: Anyone who wishes to oppose the federal establishment had better be prepared to expend upward of two million dollars (a conservative estimate of the legal cost to carry a grievance to the Supreme Court). Even then, there is no assurance that the Supreme Court will choose to hear it. In short, to take on the federal establishment is about like battling King Kong; he can crush you with his thumb!

I do not believe that the Forest Reserve Act of 1891 was a constitutional act. That act has turned out to be a sort of loophole in order to circumnavigate the constitutional requirement of a state's concurrence and approval of federal appropriation of state land. An interesting point supporting this contention is the tracing of Yosemite National Park in its course toward becoming a National Park. It actually became a national park only a few months after the Forest Reserve Act of 1891. My guess is that the full impact of Section 24 of that act was not fully realized. For ready reference, Section 24 is repeated:

> "That the president of the United States may from time to time, set apart and reserve, in any state or territory having public land bearing forest, in any part of the public lands wholly or in part covered with timber or undergrowth, whether of commercial value or not, as public reservations; and the president shall, by public proclamation, declare the establishment of such reservation and limits thereof."

Prior to that act, the federal government did pursue the course of state approval prior to federal appropriation, but not always.

Yellowstone National Park is an example of land set aside of another kind: A set aside without state approval. But then, in a broad sense, it was not necessary. Wyoming became a state in 1890 whereas Yellowstone was set aside in 1872, when Wyoming was still a territory. In a strict sense, in accordance with the Constitution, the approval by the legislature of the state of Wyoming should have been obtained after statehood. Approval was sought and received from California in the case of Yosemite National Park after California joined the Union.

After the Forest Reserve Act of 1891, the federal government never asked again. They simply took. They assumed that Congress had the constitutional power to make rules and regulations broad enough to circumnavigate the rather specific provisions of another section of the Constitution: Art. I, Sec. 8, cl. 17 (The clause that requires a state legislature to approve a federal appropriation of land for "Forts, Magazines, Arsenals,...", etc.). The court ducked this very issue of constitutionality that was raised in Light v. U.S. This ducking has provided a kind of support for the contention that Congressional power does go that far. Until just recently, I had found no other case in which the issue of federal ownership of the public lands within the boundaries of a state was raised. Two new cases have emerged within the past several years; namely, U.S. v. Gardner[222] and U.S. v. Bradshaw[223]. Both have challenged federal ownership of the public lands, and both of them lost. The ramifications of these two cases are dealt with shortly, for, on the surface, this would appear to be the end of the line. Such is not the case.

With respect to Congressional power, a critical part of the U.S. v. Gratiot case is taken out of context that entirely distorts its meaning, and, in turn by such distortion, grants Congress limitless powers it simply does not have with respect to our public land. (The impact of this quotation taken out of context was addressed in that section entitled, EXPANSION OF FEDERAL POWER: KLEPPE V. NEW MEXICO. Further, U.S. v. Gratiot is examined in the appendix.) This "limitless" power, as defined by this quotation out of context, is the basis of the finding in the case of Kleppe v. New Mexico. Taken in context, the decision in Kleppe v. New Mexico is outside of the parameters of the Constitution.

Of equal importance is the meaning of the term "territory," as it is referred to in the Constitution. This, too, has been discussed and is also repeated in the appendix in the review of Dred Scott v. Sandford. To repeat: Territory, as defined in the constitution, is only that land *in existence* at the time of the acceptance by the states of the Constitution (1789)—the Northwest Territory only. That means that none of the land west of the Mississippi River was governed by this provision of the Constitution, regardless of its commonly used name, territory. It was territory of a different sort.

Further, I must conclude that the language in the Enabling Acts of

222-United States v. Gardner (1997) 107 F. 3rd. 1314 (9th Cir.)

223-United States v. Bradshaw (1997) Case No. 96-2680111 (9th Cir.)

the western states contains no such notice that there was an intent "made very plain" to **defeat** the transfer of title of territorial land to the state. The court doesn't think so either. See Utah v. United States wherein the issue of "made very plain" is stressed. While it is true that Utah v. United States deals with land under navigable water, its application to fast land (land not under navigable water) gains strength because a strip of land two miles in width was also involved in that case. Further, Pollard v. Hagan is referenced. In dicta, that case does cover land above water. In fact, in dicta, Pollard v. Hagan draws no distinction between the land under navigable water and dry land not under navigable water in its tracing of history from whence it came: Confirming that title to the land passed to the states upon statehood—at least in the opinion (dicta) of the Supreme Court in 1856.

And, as a matter of interest, in Utah v. United States, the court drew no distinction as to whether the Forest Reserve Act of 1891 occurred before or after the state entered the Union. It made no difference. The Equal Footing Doctrine was involved—not an act of Congress reserving land. However that may be, the Equal Footing Doctrine is involved, and it was emasculated to a large extent in a recent finding in the case of U.S. v. Gardner. In this case, the court found that there was a difference in the origin of the land that was later to become a state. Alabama was to be on an Equal Footing with the other states with respect to ownership of its land after statehood because its land came from Georgia, an original state. On the other hand, Nevada's land was to remain in federal ownership after statehood because its land originated from land acquired by war with Mexico. In other words, it was federal land prior to its becoming a state and not land from one of the original states! I find this kind of reasoning absurd and a gross distortion of the Equal Footing Doctrine as laid down by our founding fathers. What is most disappointing about the case of U.S. v. Gardner is that the U.S. Supreme Court refused to hear the case upon appeal. They let the lower court finding stand.

One could ask, "What about the land ceded to the U.S. for the purpose of payment of debt that literally became territorial land?" This land was ceded **in trust** by six of the original thirteen separate colonies (states) for a specific purpose.

There is no question that a trustor/trustee relationship existed between the states that ceded their western land to the United States (the Northwest Territory and the ceded land from Georgia) for the specific payment of debts incurred during the Revolutionary War. In "Virginia's Cession of the Western Lands to the United States", December 20, 1783, it says so in so many words. Also, it is true that the land of the Louisiana

233

Purchase and the western land taken from Mexico as the spoils of war were in a quasi-trust as well; the treaties in both instances say as much: both land areas were to become states on a Equal Footing with the original thirteen states.

After the purpose for which they were established in the first place ceased to exist, these trusts themselves no longer existed. And they did cease to exist in 1832. Why? Because the Revolutionary War debt, as well as the acquisition cost of the Louisiana Purchase, were paid off in full by 1832. How do we know this? Because there was no federal debt at all at the close of 1835. Following that date, all of the land eventually became a number of separate states. However, the public land was never released back to the states by the trustee. Ownership of the public land was never acknowledged by the trustee, the federal government.

To not recognize state ownership of the public land upon statehood after all the conditions of a trust agreement had been fulfilled would be exactly as if the average home buyer, after he had paid off the loan on his home, found that the trustee (the trust company) refused to convey the title of his home to him.

This last condition was not a condition of the trustor/trustee relationship in the first place. It would be a new condition arbitrarily placed thereon by the trustee. That is exactly what the federal government has been doing for a long, long time with respect to state ownership of the public land upon statehood. The federal government refuses to recognize that any state ownership exists or, for that matter, ever existed.

The federal government has simply violated the condition of the original trust by unilateral, arbitrary action. There is no foundation for the retention of the public land by the federal government after a state joins the Union when the debt was paid off by 1835. As homebuyers, none of us would stand for such action by a trustee (trust company), yet the states have and do.

Is it possible to make a case for the existence of the Disclaimer Clauses[224] that with rare exception each Enabling Act contained? I think there is. The sale of the public lands—no matter what their origin: trust, treaty or spoils of war—was a considerable source of revenue to the federal government. The Disclaimer Clauses insured that this source of revenue would continue to flow into the federal coffer and not that of the state. In

---

224-Upon entry into the Union, the state will not interfere with the federal disposition of the public land.

an important way, these Disclaimer Clauses amounted to what most of us today would consider to be an exclusive sales contract of land belonging to another. The only difference was that in this specific case the proceeds went to the seller and not to the owner of the land, even after payment in full of an implied or de facto mortgage. However this may be, this, in and of itself, is not authority to retain federal ownership in perpetuity and to arbitrarily decide for the owner [the state] when and how or even if the owner should dispose of his land. There simply is no constitutional authority to do so. Further, I cannot make the case for the existence of the Disclaimer Clause without ignoring the findings in both Pollard v. Hagan and Coyle v. Smith, which declared that the Disclaimer Clauses were unconstitutional.

The Forest Reserve Act of 1891 was the real beginning of Congressional expansion of power of the federal government over that of the states. It gave enormous power to the president, clearly beyond the confines of the Constitution. It effectively sacked the 10th Amendment. Note the first part of Section 24 which is quoted again in part for ready reference:

> "That the president of the United States may from time to time, set apart and reserve, in any **state** or territory having public land..." (Emphasis added)

The Equal Footing Doctrine precludes Congress from granting power to the president of the United States to effectively take away or place restriction upon land that became the property of the individual state upon the state's admission to the Union. Upon statehood, that became the area of responsibility of the state and not the federal government.

The odd thing about the Forest Reserve Act that granted this extra-ordinary power to the president, is that it was never challenged. It was complained about bitterly by the different states, but never challenged by the states themselves. It was challenged in the case of Light v. U.S., but the court ducked the issue altogether.

In a strict constitutional sense, this act is contrary to the Constitution and should be unenforceable for several reasons: First, it is a violation of the "Equal Footing Doctrine." Why? Because it deprives a state of "being equal in all respects whatever" with the original thirteen nation-states with respect to the land within its borders. Each nation-state had sovereignty of its vacant or unappropriated land.[225] Second, it is a violation of the 10th Amendment. Why? Because it takes away from the state a right and power over its own land in a way that is not provided for in the Constitution.

225-Following the American Revolutionary War, the state of New York established

Third, it violates Article IX of the Articles of Confederation and, as such, the Constitution.[226] Fourth, it lays the foundation for the implementation of a 2nd tier of law (Admiralty Law: Title 18, U.S. Code, Sec. 7), to wit:

> "(3) Any lands reserved or acquired for the use of the United States, and under the exclusive or **concurrent jurisdiction** thereof, or any place purchased or otherwise acquired by the United States by consent of the legislature of the State in which the same shall be, for the erection of a fort, magazine, arsenal, dockyard, or other needful building." (Emphasis added: Remember these two words; they surface later.)

Note the expansion from the meaning contained in Art. I, Sec 8, Cl. 17 of the U.S. Constitution, which is quoted again for ready comparison:

> "To exercise exclusive legislation in all cases whatsoever over such district (not exceeding ten square miles) as may, by cession of particular states and the acceptance of Congress, become the seat of government of the United States and to exercise like authority over all places purchased, by the consent of the legislature of the state in which the same shall be, for the erection of Forts, Magazines, Arsenals, dock-Yards, and other needful Buildings."

Note that there is no mention of the words "concurrent jurisdiction" in the Constitution. That was fabricated out of whole cloth later to serve a different purpose for Federal Admiralty Law, a derivative power extended to the Federal judicial system by Congress.

The expansion of Admiralty law into a state after statehood is a violation of the intent and letter of the constitution. In short, without the finding of the Court in Gardner and Bradshaw, the federal government, simply does not have the jurisdiction. The Court said as much in United States v. Bevans, Benner v. Porter, and American Insurance v. 365 Bales of Cotton:[227] Federal governance ceases immediately upon statehood. Again,

---

(225 continued) (around 1784—prior to the Union) the Commission of Forfeiture to exercise the right of eminent domain (the ultimate fee) and sell land of those settlers who sided with the British and fled to Canada. In other words, the state of New York confiscated the land and sold it. The state of New York had eminent domain of its land and exercised it.

226-Article IX: "...no state shall be deprived of territory for the benefit of the United States."

227-American Insurance v. 365 Bales of Cotton; (1828) 26 U.S. 511.

much later in 1901, in the case of Downes v. Bidwell[228] the Court said the same thing in a little different manner:

> "The Constitution does not extend to territories of it own force. Congress has power over territory it does not possess in the States." (Emphasis added)

The expansive meaning of Title 18, Section 7, quoted earlier, does not require the consent of the legislature of the state. It is wide open. It can and does include,

> "any land reserved or acquired for use of the United States, and under the exclusive or ***concurrent jurisdiction*** thereof..." (Emphasis added)

End of statement! The phrase after the "or" quoted above in Title 18, U.S. Code, Sec. 7. is a second thought or condition altogether different from the first. The two statements are not interrelated or restrictive one to the other. They are separate.

The case of Utah v. United States raises more than the issue of just ownership of land. It raises the constitutional issue of rules and regulations laid down by the federal government regarding the use of land now owned by the state. Are those rules and regulations still binding? If they were passed before the territory became a state, would the state "inherit" those rules and regulations? If the rules and regulations postdate the date of acceptance into the Union of the state, can they be binding upon a state? The Constitution and the supportive cases say "No" to all of these questions.

Dicta plays an important part in all of this. While it is certainly true that Dred Scott v. Sandford is a despicable finding,[229] it is not the initial finding of the court with which we are concerned. It is the definition and limitations this case places upon the Property Clause (Article IV.) of the Constitution—a clause many believe, in error, to be dicta, in which we are interested. Even assuming that it were dicta, the historical background that is recited in this case is compelling. Certainly, in 1845, the date of the Dred

---

228-Downes v. Bidwell; (1901) 182 U.S. 244

229-This case was about whether or not a slave was personal property under the Constitution of the United States. And in finding that he was, the Justices each wrote their own opinion explaining their abhorrence to the idea, but in the majority, agreeing that he was.

Scott decision, the court was in an excellent position to relate history and its conclusions with reference to that history; most of the court was composed of justices who grew up with the history they were relating.

I must conclude that the Constitution refers to the ceded territory only and not the land acquired later by either purchase or the spoils of war and called by the same name, "territory."

Those who claim the public lands of the West are federally owned have, until the Gardner and Bradshaw cases emerged, had to rely upon assumption or dicta for this authority. But in order for them to make their claim complete, they have had to throw out dicta in one important case and consider another to be dicta so that they can throw it out. The first is Pollard v. Hagan, and the other is the Dred Scott v. Sandford case just referred to above. In Pollard v. Hagan, they rely and agree totally with the finding of the court: Tidelands, land below high water is indeed state land. That is exactly what the court found. However, the dicta in that same case traces history in a manner that is unmistakable. If the question before the court had been about land above high water, based upon the historical dicta in that case, the court would have found that that land, too, was state Land (after entry into the Union).

While it is pure conjecture, after relating all the history in the case of Pollard v. Hagan, if the court had added six little words just before stating their finding in that case, it is just possible that most of this seemingly meta-morphic change over the past 100 years from state ownership of the public lands within the borders of the state to that of federal ownership might not have occurred at all. The six little words: "As a result of the foregoing." I believe it *was* the court's intention that the reader of Pollard v. Hagan would know, without their saying it in clear unmistakable words, that their finding was the result of the foregoing recitation of history. But the words are not there, and the basis for law has been strictly limited by the propo-nents of federal ownership to mean only tidelands below high water. After all, that was what the case was about.

With respect to Dred Scott v. Sandford, these same proponents for federal ownership of land must claim that the definition and limitations this case places upon the Property Clause of the Constitution is dicta—which it is not—and can be ignored totally. Or, perhaps, they think that such a despi-cable finding—declaring that a slave is personal property—warrants the entire finding in the case to be ignored. Even if that case were to be accepted as simple, pure history alone, it cannot be ignored. Accurate history, regard-less of from whom it comes, is still accurate history. I certainly am not going to say that justices of the Supreme Court are incapable of relating or reciting history accurately!

Another very important point is the inappropriate and fallacious reliance by the proponents of federal ownership upon the case of U.S. v. Gratiot. The pertinent quotation from Gratiot that is cited and quoted is as follows:

> "And Congress has the same power over it [land] as over any other property belonging to the United States; and this power is vested in Congress without limitation."

This gives Congress unlimited power.

This quotation is out of context. There is no period following "limitation." The complete quotation is as follows:

> "And the Constitution of the United States (article four, section 3) provides, 'That Congress shall have power to dispose of and make all needful rules and regulations respecting the territory or other property, belonging to the United States.' The term 'territory' as here used, is merely descriptive of one kind of property, and is equivalent to the word 'land.' And Congress has the same power over it as over any other property belonging to the United State; **and this power is vested in Congress without limitation, and has been considered the foundation upon which the territorial government rests.**" (Emphasis added)

Taken in its full context, above, the meaning is limited. The limitation? Territorial government! Or put another way, while in a territorial condition, Congress had unlimited power. And it did only while the land was in a territorial condition. That power ceased after statehood. It no longer applied. The territory ceased to exist.

To claim that this case gives Congress unlimited power over the state land is grossly wrong. It simply does not. In order to give Congress unlimited power over state land, Gratiot *must be* quoted out of context! To say that this quotation out of context is the basis for law is preposterous.

Further, U.S. v. Gratiot was decided in 1840, a time when much of the land was in a territorial condition. This reinforces my contention that the court was, indeed, referring to Congressional powers without limitation with respect to territorial land only.

Another important pivotal case is Grisar v. McDowell. This case would not exist at all if the Act of 1830 had not been taken out of context. The tragic irony is that it was taken out of context, and in so doing it gave the president vast power to set aside, by Executive Order, vast land area— federal or state. The only way state land could possible be included was to forcefully claim that the public lands never passed to the state. This flies in the face of The Equal Footing Doctrine, the trustor/trustee relationship between the United States and future states, and Article I, Section 8, Clause 17 of the Constitution.

It is inconceivable to me to stretch Article I, Section 8, paragraph 1, to include the withholding of approximately 1,600,000,000 acres from the various states under the general guise of "general welfare." That is not to say that all of this land is ineligible for inclusion, for some of it could or should be. But that inclusion is not an arbitrary federal decision. The 10th Amendment mandates that this is a matter for the states to decide.

In light of the above, I cannot conclude anything other than this: The states are the owners of the public lands after joining the Union. If there is a limitation, and I believe that it is consistent to believe so, that limitation extends to the withholding of titular ownership **until the purchase price of the land has been repaid by the sale of their public land**. That was done long ago.

Now, a word about the impact of U.S. v. Gardner and U.S. v. Bradshaw. They are both reviewed a little later. Both cases were found for the United States: Title to the public lands within the boundaries of the separate states is, indeed, federal. But is that the end? I don't think so.

Why not? The Supreme Court did not hear the case. A lower court decision was allowed to stand. This is not the same as having the judgment come after deliberation by the Supreme Court. Will the issue arise again? I think that it will, but next time I think that it will be brought up by one or more separate states. States can go directly to the Supreme Court for a legal determination.

I should like to point out a rather glaring finding that in fact sets up Admiralty Law as a 2nd tier of law for each of the public (now federal) land states.

Note the finding quoted later in Gardner. I quote it here for its importance of the moment:

"The state government and the federal government exercise ***concurrent jurisdiction*** over the land."
(Emphasis added)

Here are the two words underlined earlier, "concurrent jurisdiction." They are exactly the words that are used in Title 18, U.S. Code. Sec. 7 (known as Admiralty Law) previously quoted.

What does all this mean? What will this mean to the Public Land states in which there are vast stretches of public (now federal) land? Not that it will happen, but it is rather apt to happen. The Federal agencies, the Forest Service, the BLM, the Fish and Wild Life Service, the Army Corp of Engineers, will all have police power to arrest and prosecute any infraction of the law, be it a Federal Law or a state law.

What's wrong with that, you may ask?

Federal judges are not *elected* representatives of the people. They are not responsible to the public at large. They are all appointed and they cannot be removed like a civil court judge. Further, the fines and or penalties they mete out are often arbitrary and capricious.

There are far too many fines and incarceration episodes that go well beyond the test of reasonableness. The fines and incarceration are designed to be so punitive and severe as to compel instant acquiescence. Fear is a bludgeoning instrument, and it certainly gets everyone's attention. But unlike a civil procedure, an appeal of a Federal District Court decision is not easy, rapid or inexpensive. This produces a rather natural penchant to settle the matter or accept the finding. Compromise, regardless of equity, is often achieved.

One could ask, "How can I combat that kind of force?" In most cases, you simply cannot.

Fines have been levied, so much a day or month, that in some cases far exceed the value of the land involve. The fine can become an instrument of confiscation.

Compromises have been reached wherein the alleged offender has been "let off the hook" by deeding to one federal agency or another a part of the land or personal property involved. Just recently one large corporation was fined one million dollars a day until it complied with a ruling of a federal bureau, agency or judge. Where do they get that kind of power? From the exercise of Admiralty Law!

In most cases, these fines are arbitrary. These are things that stretch the element of fairness to an extreme.

The tragic part of this kind of ferocious enforcement of the law, rule or regulation is that it does insult our sense of justice and fairness.

It should not be necessary, but I must point out that it was an issue not too dissimilar to this that, as nearly the last straw, catapulted the original thirteen colonies into a state of war for independence with Great Britain. The issue: The Stamp Act. Why? Taxation without representation.

Why am I pointing out such a calamitous possibility? Because that is exactly what one might now expect from the federal establishment with respect to the "concurrent jurisdiction" they now possess as a result of the Gardner and the Bradshaw cases: Police power.

Will it happen? Perhaps, yes; perhaps, not. In any event some changes will surely take place. I rather doubt that less federal government control or supervision is a viable alternative!

WHAT CAN BE DONE ABOUT IT?

First of all, one should realize that by now there simply is no way that authority and power will be willingly relinquished by the different bureaus and departments of the federal government. To them, prescriptive rights of "ownership" are already cast in concrete. The limiting factors of the Constitution will be bent by them to conform to their preexisting conclusion: That public land (federal land as we commonly refer to it) is owned by the federal government and is under their exclusive management and control. I might, ironically, suggest that these same people read the Constitution, but such advice, I fear, would fall upon deaf ears. Their minds are made up. They honestly believe federal ownership is legal. The Justice Department of the executive branch of our federal government has recently made that direct claim in three suits: United States v. Nye County,[229] United States v. Gardner,[231] and United States v. Bradshaw.[232] In all three,

---

229-U.S. v. Nye County: 920 F. Supp. 1108 (D. Nev. 1996).

231-U.S. v. Gardner: 107 F. 3rd 1314 (9th Cir. 1997).

232-U.S. v. Bradshaw: Case No. 96-16801 (9th Cir. 1997).

the federal government claim that the public land is in federal ownership. These cases are reviewed later.

LETTER FROM THE FOREST SERVICE

Any endeavor to secure the rights of ownership or even managerial control will not be for the fainthearted. Nevada has already drawn the "growl" that foreruns the "bite." The following letter addressed to NACO (Nevada Association of Counties Organization), dated December 17, 1993, from Toiyabe National Forest Supervisor R. M. "Jim" Nelson, is an example:

"We are in receipt of numerous memoranda, ordinances, resolutions and plans that all call for basically the same item. That is that county governments are requiring federal authorities to relinquish or submit to county demands of ownership of public lands.

"These memoranda, ordinances, resolutions and plans are null and void as applied to the administration of any federal lands by any officer or official of the Forest Service. These counties are embarking on a very perilous path of illegal conduct if they believe these documents have any legal standing...

"We have instructed our employees that any memoranda, ordinances, resolutions and plans that purport to assume ownership or management of public lands are without legal effect. All employees, officers and agents for Nevada Counties are hereby on notice that any attempt to enforce these documents against any officer or agent of the Forest Service or other federal official could constitute unlawful interference with a federal officer. In this regard, we call your attention to the felony provisions of Title 18, Section 111 of the United States Code.

"We are fully aware of numerous other counties in other states which have enacted similar actions in an attempt to constrain Federal Land management prerogatives. All are similarly void and unlawful; they are also unnecessary. There are ample provisions in existing laws which afford state and local government numerous opportunities to participate in Federal Land management. We encourage NACO to advise their member counties to seek out these legal processes. We believe that, in the long run, such cooperation and consultation will be the more effective way to coordinate and reconcile the mutual interest of NACO and the Forest Service."

I must call attention to one missing item in the letter above: In no place does the Forest Service claim that they own the land! This is just the point. Until Gardner and Bradshaw, they wanted everyone to **assume** that the land is owned by the federal government. That is also why they never allowed a case that questioned the ownership of the land to reach the Supreme Court. This is the Achilles' heel. And the Forest Reserve Act of 1891 is right in the middle of it.

MEMORANDUM OF UNDERSTANDING

The Forest Service has already acted to head off the confrontation the above letter would indicate is in the offing. On February 15, 1994, the Forest Service signed a Memorandum of Understanding with Catron County, New Mexico, the leader in the Catron County type ordinance movement. Quoted below is language from that Memorandum:

> "to establish a mutual harmonious and productive planning relationship between the County and the Forest. This MOU addresses how and when each agency participates in Forest and County planning process. The parties hope that successful implementation of this MOU encourages positive intergovernmental relationships."

Memorandums of Understanding are really nothing more than palliatives; they may make you feel good, but they are by no means compulsory. See the excerpt from California Coastal Commission v. Granite Rock Company, contained in the section entitled COUNTY ORDINANCES. In the final analysis, the federal government can do as they please, all the verbiage and conversation to the contrary notwithstanding.

The crux of the issue is that of accommodation. Short of accommodation, a close examination of the U.S. Constitution reveals that the land **should not** belong to the federal government.

When enough of us—primarily in the West—know the history of our own land and become concerned enough to do something about it, a change will take place.

FREEDOM OF INFORMATION ACT

The Freedom of Information Act has proven to be an excellent tool to combat such a claim of ownership. ***When properly asked***,[233] how do you suppose the Forest Service is going to respond where in the Constitution ***ownership*** of the land is authorized? And where in the Constitution their authority is authorized? ***Without proof of ownership and authority, one has no standing in any court***. This has an interesting effect. If no authority can be produced, any federal officer may be shown to be acting outside of his authority.

ASK THE RIGHT QUESTION

One is *compelled* to ask the right question (or rely upon the right law). In the Case of Bell v. Hood[234] this is pointed out:

"...the party who brings a suit is master to decide what law he will rely upon."

What happens when these two forces collide—and they will? Will the forces of the federal establishment, which are admittedly more than considerable, overrun the opposition?

Not necessarily.

WHERE FEDERAL IMMUNITY DOES NOT EXIST

In the case of Bell v. Hood, cited above, another clause is more apropos to the issue of federal agents acting ***within their authority***:

233-Ed Presley, in Reno, Nevada, is an expert on the Freedom of Information Act. He stresses that the proper question must be asked. Further, he points out that understanding the answer that is received is important as well; it may have nothing whatever to do with the question as a proper response *consistent with the Constitution*.

234-Bell v. Hood: 71 F. Sup. 813.

"The immunity of the Federal Government from suit extends to all federal officers and agents acting *within* the scope of their duties as such." (Emphasis added)

Read on:

"Whenever a federal officer or agent *exceeds* his authority, in so doing *he no longer represents the Government and hence loses the protection of sovereign immunity from suit*." (Emphasis added)

It is not enough to simply "think" you are within your authority.

Put bluntly: If a federal officer operates outside the limits of his authority—whether he knows it or not—he becomes, just like any other citizen of these United States, *personally* liable and responsible for his acts or actions.

This has happened. One federal official was told, summarily, that the federal government would not, and could not, defend him in court; the expense was his, personally. His house and car were in jeopardy. There are real teeth in this procedure. Some of the federal officials know it, too! They are not sure the rest of us know it as well.

EXPANSION OF THE "POWERS" SECTION OF THE CONSTITUTION

How do these powers get returned from the federal to the state? "Returned" is the wrong word; they were never granted away in the first place!

Review first where the source of growing power has emanated; clearly, it is from the "Powers" section of the Constitution. In a changing world, the Congress, and even the Supreme Court, is going to be hard-pressed to do much limiting of these powers. At best, the Court may do what I think they did in Kleppe v. New Mexico (At issue there was constitutionality of the Wild Free-roaming Horses and Burros Act): "Try us again on a specific issue and we'll tell you." Even so, as I expressed earlier, I believe that the court expanded the powers of Congress beyond the parameter of the Constitution. On the other hand, they may, when confronted with the proper question, define specifically what the Constitution says—not what some say it ought to say. Sandra Day O'Connor said it so well in New York v. U.S.:

> "...the Constitution protects us from our own best intentions: It divides the power among sovereigns and among branches of government precisely so that we may resist the temptation to concentrate power in one location as an expedient solution to the crisis of the day."

TREATIES AS A SOURCE OF ADDED "POWER"

A second source of growing power is from the treaty Powers Section of the Constitution. This is not supposed to be an area for domestic issues. Our founding fathers meant for treaties to be international in scope and to spill over into the domestic area on an urgent *international* need basis only. This "urgent need" has not been tested with respect to this spillage. For that matter, neither has the priority, if any, of Homo sapiens over animals, birds or fish.

THE ACHILLES' HEEL: THE FOREST RESERVE ACT OF 1891

Certainly, the Forest Reserve Act of 1891 is an Achilles' heel to the federal government. I'm sure they realize that too. Were that not so, many, many grievances against the Forest Service and the Bureau of Land Management would not have been settled short of the Supreme Court.

That should tell you something.

COUNTY ORDINANCES

Many county governments are either adopting Catron County type ordinances or are seriously considering them. Catron County, New Mexico, was the first county of the West to implement an ordinance, a Land Use Policy Plan, that requires their concurrence—at least advice and consent—to rules and regulations of federally controlled land within their county promulgated by the federal land management agencies. The purpose:

> "...to ensure self-determination by local communities and individuals..."

The method:

> "...to develop and implement land use planning mechanisms that focus on federal and state land uses and activities."

In order to make these ordinances enforceable, they have been honed and modified in degrees while still, hopefully, retaining the purpose. Because these ordinances are not all exactly the same, the term "Catron County type" is used as a collective."

These ordinances have a major flaw which has nothing whatever to do with how they are worded or employed or what they want to achieve. ***All of them accept federal ownership of the land as a fact***. This is simply not supportable by the Constitution. In the final analysis, whenever that is to be, the constitutionality of the issue of land ownership must and will be determined. When that happens, being on the ***right*** side of the Constitution will be of the utmost importance. As originally written, the Catron County type of ordinance has been ruled to be inconsistent with the Constitution. However, other ordinances have emerged that require county participation in any federal planning or rule-making that affects land within the county. To forestall the acceleration of this kind of county ordinance-making, the federal government has instituted a program of seeking and getting Memorandums of Understanding and a non-confrontational attitude. While these memorandums reflect a cooperative spirit—which they do—they still leave the last word of any controversy up to the dictum of the federal government. In other words, if push comes to shove, the federal government can do just as it pleases. There is absolutely no compulsion to abide by any other desire espoused by the county. In reality, they are unilateral documents—federal. Aside from making you feel good, they do nothing.

In the case of California Coastal Commission v. Granite Rock Company,[235] this contention is illuminated. The following quotation is noteworthy:

> "The FLPMA [Federal Land Policy and Management Act of 1976] directs that land use plans developed by the Secretary of

---

235-California Coastal Commission v. Granite Rock Company (1987): 480 U.S. 572; 94 L. Ed. 2d 577; 107 S. Ct. 1419.

Interior 'shall be consistent with State and local plans to the maximum extent [the Secretary]*finds consistent* with Federal law,' and calls for the Secretary, 'to the extent *he finds practical,* to keep apprised of state land use plans, and 'assist in resolving, '*to the extent practical*, inconsistencies between Federal and non-Federal Government plans." (Emphasis added)

Nothing in that language indicates that a mandatory bilateral agreement is necessary.

CLEARLY DISCLAIM ANY FEDERAL OWNERSHIP OF LAND

One authority suggested that whenever a Catron County type ordinance is employed, wording along the following line be used in the ordinance itself, so that by its inclusion, acceptance cannot later be claimed that the ordinance in any way recognized the ownership of the land to be federal:

"Nothing in the content of this ordinance shall in any way, shape or form be construed to indicate that the title to what is commonly called Federal Land, Federally controlled lands, or Public Land is recognized or accepted by _____ county, in the State of _____, to be Federally owned by the United States."

PLACING FEDERAL OFFICIALS UNDER OATH

Another authority on the subject of delegated authority suggests the following when dealing with a federal agent:

1. Require that the federal agent be put under oath prior to hearing any testimony he may give on a given subject under discussion or review by a county.

2. Require proof of delegated authority—in writing. He should be asked to bring copies of his delegated authority from the U.S. Government.

3. Where Federal lands are under discussion, proof of ownership should be required.

4. Failing any part of the above, the person simply does not have what is required prior to acceptance of his testimony.

There is no doubt that federal encroachment upon authority of state governments in the western states is a pressing and serious problem.

ACTIONS TAKEN

HAGE V. UNITED STATES

United States Court of Federal Claims
Case Number: 91-1470L

This case was filed by Nevada ranchers Wayne and Jean Hage against the United States in the United States Court of Federal Claims in Washington D.C. It is a landmark property rights case, and it would be hard to overemphasize its importance.

The Hage's Pine Creek Ranch, constituting approximately 7,000 acres of fee land and an associated 752,000 acres of permitted land [public (federal) Lands upon which federal grazing rights exist in their name], has been in existence in whole or in part for over 150 years. At this juncture, it is important to point out that the two parcels, one fee and the other permitted, are inseparable; what occurs on one part impacts the other: Take away or impinge one part and the other is adversely affected.

The first catalyst for a confrontation between the Forest Service and the Hages was centered around a spring the Hages owned. The spring was on the public land (National Forest land), to which the Hages had water rights. Aside from its location within the National Forest, the water rights to this spring had been filed upon long, long before the Hages purchased their ranch with either the territory or state of Nevada; the spring was the private property right of the Hages.[236] Arbitrarily and without permission, the Forest Service decided they would pipe the water from the spring for their own use. Wayne Hage objected. At this juncture, the important point was that the Forest Service refused to acknowledge that the water was the private property of the Hages even after being shown two court decrees saying that the water was his, as well as a similar statement of this fact from the state water engineer. The Forest Service fenced the spring so that cattle and wildlife could not drink—all this while still piping the water for their own use.

236-Keep in mind that water rights have always been under territorial or state authority or control and as such fall exclusively under state law. This is recognized by the federal government albeit, it would appear, not lately.

The Hages considered this act an outright invasion of their personal property rights, even a confiscation. Normal, congenial relations deteriorated between the two parties. Neither one gave in to the other. The Hages were firm in their belief that a wrong had been committed. To the Hages, this was an illegal confiscation, to which they vociferously objected. This generated considerable animosity, as one might expect.

The U.S. Forest Service was just as determined and began applying pressure upon the Hages in a number of ways that affected the operation of the ranch and the use of Forest Service permitted land, an integral part of the overall ranch operation. In the course of 105 days, Hage was sent 40 certified letters of corrections or infractions of regulations, and he was visited 70 times by the Forest Service in connection therewith, citing him for these violations. Included in these charges were 45 accounts of trespass—Hage's cattle were allegedly found on un-permitted land. On a ranch the size of Pine Creek, this meant sending riders as far as 20 miles to locate, if possible, the stray cattle and drive them back. Hage claims that on several occasions, eye witnesses watched Forest Service employees move Hage's cattle into trespass areas, and then immediately cite him for the violation.

Hage states that even under what some would consider harassment, he complied with every one of their requests or demand. He even had the Forest Service personnel over to his ranch house when the day's work was done.

Ultimately, over the course of the next eight years, Hage filed three administrative appeals and won all three. The cost: over $150,000. New regulations were developed by the Forest Service. Hage stated that he complied with all of them. However that may be, in un-fenced open range land, cattle will and do roam. This roaming would lead to additional trespass of Hage's cattle on range land that was not a part of Hages permitted area. Hage was in the process of rounding up all of his cattle when the actions of the Forest Service took on a finalizing phase. Time: July 1991. 30 Forest Service riders armed with semiautomatic weapons, wearing bullet-proof vests, confiscated 100 head of Hage's cattle.

Was the Forest Service trying to run Hage out of business? Hage claims so. Quite obviously, these adverse actions made for difficult times, and staying in business was certainly not facilitated, to say the very least. This act of confiscation of Hages remaining herd was to be a memorable occasion. ABC, NBC and CBS had been invited beforehand to view the affair. It would appear that a western style shoot-out was anticipated, but none took place. Hage was there, however, armed only with his camera and several rolls of film. The invited television networks did not show up.

The confiscation of Hage's cattle was the last straw, and on September 26, 1991, Hages filed a law suit for an unlawful "taking" and demanded payment of 28 million dollars for compensation and damages. They were not demanding that their private property be returned; they demanded payment for its confiscation.

But things got worse.

In the arid west, water is where you find it, and its use on unappropriated public lands was yours as long as you used it for beneficial use. It need not be on your own fee land; it could—and often was—on adjacent public land. You could develop a seep, improve a spring and even ditch the water to a location for irrigation of a meadow that was a part of your fee land. This latter case was to be cataclysmic for Wayne Hage; his predecessor and he had been transporting water by ditch from springs on their appropriated public land for over 100 years. No ditch anywhere is without its stimuli to vegetative growth. Hage's White Sage ditch, as it was called, was no different. The very act of clearing this ditch right-of-way of pinion and juniper in the spring of 1991 finalized the Forest Service's adverse action. Hage was cited for this clearing; his right-of-way was confiscated and canceled, and Hage was charged with a felony—destruction of federal property. It took years, but Hage was finally absolved of any felonious action. But this absolution took a great deal of time and money. Moreover, the felony charge stood in the way of the proper prosecution of their case, Hage v. United States.

Finally, the judge was to hear their case, and as is usually routine, one side or the other will request a summary judgment in their favor. The federal government did so. The case could have been closed right there, but the request for summary judgment was denied and in denying, the Court clearly indicated that if the Hages could provide evidence that their water rights were valid and predated the claim of this same water by the federal government by **state of Nevada law**, then the Hages could proceed with the trial. Note the underlined words; we are talking about state law, not Federal Law. This was a new, potentially strong finding.

The Court's order filed February 1, 1996, is as follows:

"Pursuant to this court's forthcoming opinion granting in part and denying in part defendant's motion for summary judgment, the court will hold a limited evidentiary hearing addressing plaintiffs' property interest as defined by ***Nevada law in water rights, ditch rights of way and forage rights*** in the Toiyabe National Forest.

"The Court concludes that a limited evidentiary hearing is necessary to the court's analysis of plaintiffs' taking claims. Plaintiffs [Hage] claim vested water rights, encompassing vested ditch rights of way and forage rights, from the mid-1800s. Defendant [Federal Government] claims the same water rights beginning in the 1900s. If plaintiffs can prove that their rights vested before defendant claimed its water rights, plaintiffs' water rights predate defendant's water rights. Therefore, under the prior-appropriation doctrine, plaintiffs would have the priority water right. If plaintiffs prove prior vested rights in the water, encompassing forage rights and vested ditch rights of way, plaintiffs are entitle to proceed with their taking claim.

"Defendant [Federal Government] claims that plaintiffs do not have conclusive water rights until completion of the state adjudication procedure. Furthermore, even if plaintiffs do have water rights, defendant claims that those rights would not permit ingress and egress of the livestock to the water. Following defendant's theory through to its logical conclusion, defendant believes the court should rule that even if plaintiffs owned property rights dating from the 1800s, such water and ditch rights have no relevance today because of state administrative proceedings and the application of Federal Law."
(Emphasis added)

In mid November, 1998, the evidentiary hearing called for above was held by Chief Justice Loren Smith in Reno, Nevada. The results of that hearing came about rather swiftly with the issuance of a preliminary opinion by Justice Smith. While not final, the preliminary opinion would lead one to believe that a landmark decision is about to be made with respect to property rights: Water rights on the public land and appurtenant forage rights concomitant with the water rights. Stewards of the Range,[237] in a newsletter to its members, issued a summary of the evidentiary hearing as well as Chief Justice Smith's preliminary opinion. Extracts from that letter to its members dated November 20, 1998 follows:

237-Stewards of the Range, P.O. Box 1189, Boise, Idaho 83701, is a non-profit organization dedicated to restoring private property rights.

"There are three important rulings in this preliminary opinion that if incorporated in his final opinion will change the national landscape:

"1. The court has adopted the Nevada State Water Engineer's Determination Order that Hage is the senior water rights holder of the waters within Hage's allotments in Monitor Valley. [The court left open an opinion with respect to Hage's Ralston and McKinney allotments]. In this decision the court upholds the prior appropriation water doctrine, historical and cultural use, and the principles of beneficial use. The court bolsters western water law and throws out the government's arguments of reserved water rights and ownership through the control of the federal lands. The Forest Service had filed claims over the top of Hage's water rights [An act the Forest Service and the Bureau of Land Management have been doing all across the West for a number of years on hundreds of water rights for the altogether too transparent purpose of gaining complete control of the land when and if the grazing permit is canceled. And cancellation of these permits seems to be an underlying objective of some people within these bureaus.], and argued because they held the land upon which the waters were located, that they were the rightful owners. The State Water Engineer disagreed as did Judge Smith.

"2. Hage owns 1866 Act ditch rights of ways, and has a 50 foot easement on each side of the ditch. The court also concluded that he owns the forage within the easement. The Forest Service had argued that Hage was required to have a special Use Permit in order to maintain his ditches. They even filed felony charges against him in 1991 because he did not have the permit. In this ruling the court decides contrary to the government's position. Much of the West is covered by 1866 Act rights of ways, and the agencies have been aggressively requiring private landowners, counties and even states to have special Use Permits before they can do routine maintenance. Smith's decision clearly states the right of way is a property right. The agency's actions to require permits might well result in takings across the West.

"3. As holder of vested water rights, Hage owns the forage adjacent to those waters. [The court left open the issue of ownership of surface-estate (forage rights) which Hage claims on 752,000 acres of grazing land on federal allotments.] The court's ruling indicates it understands the historical settlement practices and the laws and court decisions that protect the western landowner's right to use the forage. The court's preliminary ruling describes the relationship between the water and forage and how if a rancher has a vested water right for which the beneficial use of livestock grazing, then he must also own the use of the forage. This decision alone reverses the agencies' practice of treating livestock grazing on the federal lands as a privilege."

In short, what does all of this mean?

In 1. above, this means that state law has a valid priority over certain Federal proclamations and Congressional acts. In this case, that priority has to do with prior-appropriation of water, and it even implies the extension of that doctrine to forage rights on public (federal) land. This begs the question: When did the state secure this priority? It could not have come while a territorial state of being existed. It could have been started in some cases as territorial law, but as state law, it had to have come at the moment of statehood. That was when state law was operative, not before: State jurisdiction and authority commenced and federal jurisdiction and authority ceased upon statehood.

In 2. above, pending the final opinion of the court, this may preclude the requirement that a Use Permit is necessary prior to doing routine maintenance or perhaps other ancillary acts connected with a private property right on "federally managed lands." This quotation comes directly from Justice Smith's preliminary opinion. Noteworthy is the fact that Justice Smith refers to the "federally managed lands." He carefully avoids using the term, "federally owned lands." Can it be that Justice Smith has some of the same reservations that I have expressed in this book with reference to federal ownership of our public lands? I hope so.

In 3. above, this clearly indicates that forage rights are connected to water rights, at least so far as ditch rights are concerned. We must await Justice Smith's final opinion with respect to the extent that water rights filed on public (federal) land also include forage rights. I think that it does.

Already this is a landmark decision: The judicial system, at its ancillary highest recognizes that states and their laws have a priority with respect to public lands. Exactly how far this priority extends has yet to be determined or confirmed by the court. Further, one must wonder how this will affect Title 18, U.S. Code, Sec. 7 that speaks to "concurrent jurisdiction."

This has been a deadly battle for the Hages. It has already killed Jean Hage, with strain, anxiety, worry, and perhaps a host of other problems.

The final curtain has not come down for Wayne Hage. The trial is well underway, but this trial is not just one that has pitted the Hages against the federal government, for it includes a whole host of unnamed people across the West whose private property rights have been impinged or erased by actions taken by powerful federal bureaus. This case will have a profound effect upon the public lands of the West.

UNITED STATES V. NYE COUNTY
920 F. Supp. 1108 (D. Nev. 1996)

Here, too, is a landmark case, but this one is not a case of compensation for a "taking." This one strikes at the core of the growing concern about federal encroachment upon state's rights. More basically than even this, it raises the question of the right of sovereignty and dominion of the land. Is the public land within a state federal land or does it belong to the state? Nye County claimed that the title to the land passed to the state upon statehood, while the federal government claims otherwise.[238] But first, the background.

On July 4th, 1994, Nye County, Nevada reopened a road with a bulldozer. They declared the road to be on state land even though it was clearly within the boundary of the Toiyabe National Forest and had been washed out since 1983. The Forest Service was there in force—armed. The road was reopened. An official of the Forest Service was cited personally for interfering with the duties and function of a public official. (To this date he has not been prosecuted.) This action by Nye County brought about a response from the federal government; in February, 1995, the Justice Department filed a suit against Nye County. In the words of Lois Schiffer, Assistant Attorney General for Environment and Natural Resources:

238-The state of Nevada in an amicus curiae filing in this case stated that the land was not owned by the state of Nevada, but rather was in federal ownership. That statement, alone, forced Nye County to abandon their claim that the land was, indeed, state of Nevada land. If Nevada did not claim ownership, then how could Nye County do so? Certainly, not easily!

257

"Today's action is firm but restrained. It should send a message, loud and clear, *that the United States does indeed own and manage federal lands*. We expect the court to quickly affirm that the Federal Government has sovereignty over Federal Lands and that federal employees must be allowed to do their jobs without interference." (Emphasis added)

The above statement sums up the position taken by the federal government.

On the other side, Nye County claims that this land is not federal land at all, citing as their principal defense that title to this land passed to the state of Nevada upon its entry into the Union on an Equal Footing with the original states. On a subordinate level, Nye County claims that the county has at least a joint responsibility for the management of the land. Or, put another way, the federal government may not do whatever it pleases without taking Nye County into consideration and embarking upon a plan of action that is not compatible with Nye County.

The ramifications of this case are truly profound. In short, the real question being asked is a matter of power and control. Should that power and control be in a central government located in Washington D. C., or should it be local? Our founding fathers would hardly agree that that control should be in the hands of the federal government. They were in favor of state control except where national defense and international matters were concerned. How, now to get that power back to the level envisioned by our founding fathers? That won't be easy, nor will this case be as strong as it might otherwise be: The attorney general of the state of Nevada filed an amicus (friend of the court) declaring that the federal government did indeed own the land—not the state of Nevada!

Surprisingly, Nye County did not ask that the amicus be thrown out basing their request upon the statement of the court in Coyle v. Smith:

"The constitutional authority of Congress cannot be expanded by the 'consent' of the governmental unit whose domain is thereby narrowed, whether that unit is the Executive Branch or the States. State officials cannot consent to the enlargement of the powers of Congress beyond those enumerated in the Constitution."

And, repeated in a slightly different form in New York v. United States with the same meaning:

"Where Congress exceeds its authority relative to the States, therefore, the departure from the constitutional plan cannot be ratified by the 'consent' of the state officials."

Upon request for a summary judgment in the case of Nye County, the district Federal court in Las Vegas declared:

"...the United States owns and has the power and authority to manage and administer the unappropriated public lands and National Forest System lands within Nye County, Nevada."

The district Federal court cites Scott v. Lattig for this finding. In Scott v. Lattig, the court cites Mission Rock Co. v. United States. Scott v. Lattig and the follow-on case of U.S. v. Mission Rock are discussed and summarized in the appendix. As pointed out earlier, both of these cases are a rather shallow base for the establishment of federal ownership of the public lands after statehood; that issue was not argued in either of the two cases. It is clear, however, that in both of these cases it was assumed that the ownership of that land was federal rather than state after statehood.

Nye County claims that the United States lacks Constitutional authority or power to own lands.

Disappointingly, the district Federal court falls into the abyss that has been widened and deepened by repeated misquotation: U.S. v. Gratiot is again taken out of context:

"[t]he term territory, as here used, is merely descriptive of one kind of property; and is equivalent to the word lands. And Congress has the same power over it as over any other property belonging to the United States; and this power is vested in Congress without limitation...."

This statement, taken out of context has been discussed. The case is reviewed in the appendix.

The District Court continues from Gratiot:

"[t]he disposal must be left to the discretion of Congress."

What the District Court fails to recognize in this quotation is the fact that the case is about territorial land—land before statehood when it was an unquestioned fact that all territorial land was federally owned and as such subject to disposal or disposition by Congress.

All federal action with respect to U.S. v. Nye County has been limited to the summary judgments above discussed. At the time of this writing, the case is not closed at the District Court level, and when closed after trial, it is subject to appeal, whenever that may be.

What could happen if Nye County is eventually successful, and the ownership of what we call federal land in each state today, becomes, in fact, state land?

The ownership of this land would shift to the state. It would then be subject to state law, power and control. To say the very least, a shift of this kind would make a lot of people uneasy and unsure of themselves. The spotted owl, snail darter, kangaroo rat and other endangered species would become state problems and the land they occupy a state dilemma. The problem may be the same, but the solution is closer to home and subject to local input and, as Nye County would put it, a county by county problem under state guidance to solve. If this shift means anything at all, it means a strong place for local control. Local county government would be the vehicle for local input and where desired by the state, control.

Nye County's Dick Carver puts it best: County government is the highest form of government, because it is the closest to the people them-selves. He goes on to point out that the federal level of government only has what power there is left after the states have assumed all power upon state-hood, and, after having done so, given the United States (federal government) such power and only such power as is allowed and specified by the U.S. Constitution, no more. The fact that the federal government has assumed more power and even wrenched it from the states is the core problem itself, he adds.

UNITED STATES V. GARDNER
107 F. 3rd 1314 (9th Cir. 1997)

This case is of particular interest inasmuch as it directly challenges the federal ownership of the public lands. The issues are clearly stated on both sides, and by reading it one can see the differences as stated by the opposing counsels.

For the Gardners, this case is in reality the last scene of the last act; an act born out of an accumulation of residual actions. Shakespeare might have referred to them as the "slings and arrows of outrageous fortune." The Gardners have wondered if these "slings and arrows" weren't the product of malice of forethought—actions that were designed to run them off of their permitted rangeland.

But, first, a short synopsis of what the case is all about.

The Gardners have been ranchers for four generations on their ranch, which consists of approximately 6,000 acres of fee land, as well as about 9,000 of Forest Service and BLM land upon which they possessed grazing permits. Their relationship with the federal agencies had always been cooperative and amiable until the late 1980s or early 1990s. Even though the Gardners trace the beginning of conflict to much earlier times, it was this later date that marks the beginning of the legal conflict that has been brought to the courts for resolution.

In the mid-1970s, Congress passed the Federal Land Policy and Management Act and the National Forest Management Act. These acts, separately and individually, require that Forest Service, as well as the BLM, prepare management plans for the administration of the public lands. You may have already noted that the wording included in both of these acts is palliative; it requires that all effort be made to cooperate with the permittees, but if no agreement can be reached that is mutual, then the Federal government agency can act unilaterally. In general, that is what happened. Changes were made with respect to the management of the permitted land upon which the Gardners possessed grazing permits. (The Gardners would hasten to state that these grazing permits are not just permits to graze, but grazing rights, that these rights are personal property, that they were issued in the first place by the right of prior appropriation to those that had been grazing upon the land before the institution of the Taylor Grazing Act who additionally owned ranch land nearby. And they would be right.)

These management acts resulted in considerable reductions in the number of livestock permitted at any one time; reductions in the times of the year that grazing would or could be commenced as well as when it must be vacated. In other words, a rather complete control of the use of the land by the governmental agency. This exacting control took the form of numerous rules and regulations developed by the local governmental agency involved. The Gardners considered these rules and regulations to be arbitrary and capricious, unrealistic, confiscatory, and, more important to them, not in the best interest of the land itself—the land under their care and custody that constitutes a part of their ranch. In fact, the Gardners were and are convinced that the governmental agencies, for reasons of their own, want the land to be returned to its natural state with little or no human intrusion or that of any livestock; to wit, the less, the better.

A devastating forest and range fire in 1992 solidified this opinion and finally moved the Gardners to resist. The fire burned portions of their grazing allotments. In keeping with the management plan for these allotments, the Forest Service reseeded the burned area, and, in accordance with their management plan, required that no grazing take place upon these allotments for a period of 24 months.

Now comes the problem: Included in this allotment was their fenced right-of-way that paralleled their private land and effectively divided Forest Service land from their private land—including their ranch house. This right-of-way was approximately 100 feet in width—an effective fire break: It was a roadway to their ranch house.

Unusual as it happened to be, rain came in abundance during those two winters, producing an abundance of grass along this roadway. Thinking ahead, the Gardners knew that this now heavy growth of grass would be highly combustible in midsummer. Further, it was their firm belief that this same roadway had saved their home during the range fire of 1992. The difference? It had been grazed prior to the fire in 1992, and it had acted as a fire-brake: the flames did not jump the road.

Acting unilaterally, the Gardners announced to the Forest Service that they would allow their cattle to graze the fenced roadway. The Forest Service told them that they would not allow such grazing in May when the 24-month period would not expire until October and that if they grazed their cattle without permission to do so, their permits were subject to cancellation. In short, the Gardners grazed their cattle and the Forest Service canceled their permit.

I'm sure it was before this time that the Gardners, much like myself, had wondered and finally doubted that the federal government possessed the sovereignty over these public lands and that there was no real constitutional authority for their retention as federal land.

This case was brought by the Forest Service for trespass upon federal land. In general, it resembles Light v. United States, but the resemblance is only paper thin. The United States, in their pleadings, brings up all the arguments for federal ownership of the land, relying most heavily upon the case of Kleppe v. New Mexico, while the Gardners bring up all the reasons—most of which I have already pointed out—as to why the federal government lacks actual dominion and sovereignty, and, as a result, possesses no residual ownership or managerial control. Why? Because ownership and managerial control passed automatically to the state upon statehood.

As matters stood in early summer of 1997, the 9th Circuit Court agreed with the finding of district Federal court:

> "...there can be no reasonable doubt that the National Forests, reserved from the Public Domain, are the property of the United States...."

A Petition for a Writ of Certiorari[239] was filed by the Gardners; however, the Supreme Court elected to not hear the case, thus leaving the finding of the lower court to stand.

While this is not quite the same as if the Supreme Court had heard the case and had come to the same finding, it is almost the same. Its force as the basis of law is not impaired.

Inasmuch as this case is catapulted to a high level of importance, I would strongly recommend that any interested party read the complete Opinion of the United States Court of Appeals for the Ninth Circuit (U.S. v. Gardner; Fed. R. App. P. 34(a); 9th Cir. R. 34-4). It is clear; it is understandable; it is an expression of why the federal government believes it retains ownership of the public lands. The following, although condensed, is noteworthy:

With respect to title to federal land in Nevada, the court stated that title to the land was acquired by the United States from Mexico by the Treaty of Guadalupe Hidalgo in 1848. The court states that the United States owned the land ever after that date—even after the statehood of Nevada—and summarily dismissed Gardner's claim that the United States was obligated to hold the public land in trust for the formation of future states.

239-A Petition for a Writ of Certiorari is, in essence, an appeal to the U.S. Supreme Court to hear the case. The Supreme Court may elect to hear the case or it may simply refuse to hear it and by refusing, it allows the finding of the lower court to stand. When this occurs, the case permits the full force of law that may thereafter be based upon the finding of the lower court.

This is not what the Treaty of Guadalupe Hidalgo says. Article V of the treaty defines the boundary between Mexico and the newly acquired territory of the United States. Articles VIII and IX define what is to happen within this new territory—and the term "territory" is exactly what these articles call this new land. In addition, Article IX anticipates that citizens of this territory shall be "incorporated into the Union of the United States...according to the principles of the constitution."

The opening paragraph of Article XI of the treaty states what is anticipated to happen to this newly acquired territory. Note the following quotation from Article XI:

> "Considering that a great part of the territories which, by the present treaty, are to be comprehended for the future within the limits of the United States,..."

Literally, there is nothing in the Treaty of Guadalupe Hidalgo that grants any power to the United States to treat the land acquired by this treaty in any manner other than territorial land acquired by other treaties. Yet, the court seems to summarily dismiss this, and, by dismissal, grants the implied right of retention in perpetuity to the United States.

Continuing: Thus by establishing a continuing ownership (dominion and sovereignty) of the land after statehood, the court could and did state that the Powers Clause of the Constitution applied as outlined in the case of Kleppe v. New Mexico, to wit, "the power over the public land thus entrusted to Congress is without limitations."

Note: Here is the coup de grace: A case taken out of context and given meaning it never was intended to possess—Gratiot. Congressional power as defined in that case is unlimited only when the land was in a territorial state of being. Further, we see that the court ignores the finding of the court in Dred Scott v. Sandford, to wit: the Powers Clause does not apply to land after statehood.

What the court does say with respect to the chain of ownership is worth quoting here inasmuch as it draws a telling distinction between state land formed from pre-existing states and land acquired by treaty from a foreign nation. And in this regard, the court states:

> "Before becoming a state, however, Nevada had no independent claim to sovereignty, **unlike the original thirteen states**. Therefore, the same reasoning is not applicable to

this case, in which the federal government was the initial owner of the land from which the stated of Nevada was later carved." (Emphasis added)

This flies in the face of an earlier opinions of the Supreme Court: Mayor and Aldermen of the City of Mobile v. Eslava:[240]

> "...the original states acquired by the revolution the entire rights of soil, and of sovereignty, is most certain. *And if it be true, that Alabama was admitted on an Equal Footing in regards to the rights of soil with the original states, she can hold the high land equally with the land covered by navigable water,* and so can nine other states equally hold, to the utter destruction of all claim to the lands heretofore indisputably recognized as belonging to the United States, as being a common fund of the Union." (Emphasis added)

Note: This clearly ties the ownership of the high lands and the Equal Footing Doctrine together.

Continuing: From Pollard v. Hagan (1845) on page 196:

> "*We think a proper examination of this subject will show, that the United States never held any municipal sovereignty, jurisdiction, or rights of soil in and to the territory,* of which Alabama, or any of the new states were formed except for the temporary purposes, and to execute the trusts created by the acts of Virginia and Georgia legislatures, and deeds of cession executed by them to the United States, and the trust *created by the treaty with the French republic, of the 30th of April, 1803, ceding Louisiana [The Louisiana Purchase]...*"
> (Emphasis added)

Read this again carefully. Now read just the underlined words. This is not an act of taking something out of context; this is the boiled down meaning as it affects the states later formed from the Louisiana Purchase. Note that there is no municipal sovereignty or jurisdiction possessed by the United States over state land, only over territorial land, and that this limitation is not restricted to just land originating from the ceded land in trust from Virginia and Georgia.

240-Mayor and Aldermen of the City of Mobile v. Eslava; (1842) 41 U.S. 234.

The Gardners claim, additionally, that the Equal Footing Doctrine applies and that as a result thereof Nevada acquired "paramount title and eminent domain of all lands within its boundaries" upon statehood. The court summarily rejects this claim and in doing so, falls back upon the specific finding (and not the ancillary observation) contained in the case of Pollard v. Hagan: The Equal Footing Doctrine grants title to the submerged tidelands to the state upon statehood.

This has been the repeated opinion of the court, but after careful reading of that case, I do not believe that this would have been the opinion of the court that decided Pollard v. Hagan if the issue before the court in that case had been uplands rather than tidelands. They practically say as much. [Note the quotation above from that case. Further, read Pollard v. Hagan in the appendix.]

Regardless of the above, the court unequivocally states:

> "The Equal Footing Doctrine...does not operate to reserve title to fast dry lands to individual states."

With respect to the Tenth Amendment ("The powers not delegated to the United States by the Constitution, nor prohibited by it to the States, are reserved to the States respectively, or to the people."), the court did not strip the state of all power and said the following:

> "Federal ownership of the public lands within a state does not completely divest the state from the ability to exercise its own sovereignty over that land. ***The state government and the federal government exercise concurrent jurisdiction over the land***." (Emphasis added)

Note, specifically, the emphasized words above: "concurrent jurisdiction." These are the exact words contained in Title 18 U.S. Code, Sec. 7—Admiralty Law. Is this just happenstance? I am inclined to think not. I think the justice looked first at Title 18 and made his decision conform to it! I wish he had done what he is suppose to do: Look at Art. I, Sec. 8, Cl. 17 of the U.S. Constitution and conform to the Constitution rather than Title 18 of the U.S. Code. But he did not, and the impact is huge.

Among other things, the court in effect gives police power to enforce federal rules and regulations ***as well as state law***. Even though it has been requested by federal agents or bureau employees, I know of no county where police power has been granted to the federal government to enforce state law by local county governments in the West. It would appear as though the Gardner case now grants this sweeping authority.

Finally, with respect to the Guarantee Clause ("The United States shall guarantee to every State in this Union a Republican Form of Government,") which the Gardners claim is violated by the retention of the unappropriated public lands by the United States, the courts ducked the issue by stating that this issue had not been raised before the District Court.

This is untrue. The issue had been raised in the District Court.

On the other side of this same coin is the opinion of the Gardners, expressed by their attorney, Glade L. Hall.[241] It, too, is clear and understandable. Much of what I have related in this book that challenges federal ownership of the public land is succinctly brought out.

U.S. V. BRADSHAW
CASE NO. 96-1680111 (9TH Cir. 1997)

This case is similar to that of U.S. v. Gardner; trespass was alleged by the federal government.

The Bradshaw ranch was purchase by Barry Bradshaw's parents in 1952, and it has been a cattle ranch operated by the Bradshaws ever since. The ranch consists of approximately 1,000 acres of fee land as well as a large area of public land on which they have (or had, prior to their cancellation— an integral part of this suit) grazing permits. Their ranch is located in the dry, arid, eastern part of Nevada. Water is scarce. Even so, the Bradshaws possess valid, vested water rights on all of it inasmuch as, consistent with Nevada state law, the ranch dates back to the 1880's, and prior use can and has been shown by the Bradshaws. Further, the Bradshaws have developed the water by installing reservoirs, ponds and ditches for their cattle. However, there is another species that enjoys the water that would not be there for their use at all were in not for what the rancher has done to develop it: The free roaming wild horses.

At this juncture, it should be noted that these same free roaming wild horses are not native to or indigenous to North America. They are not the same as bears or buffalo in that respect. They were introduced largely by the Spaniards, and most of all, the wild horses today are really nothing more

241-Glade L. Hall, Counsel of Record, Attorney for Petitioners, 105 Mt. Rose, Reno, Nv 89509.

than part of some former rancher's herd of horses that were never rounded up from pasture on the open range. They reproduced, went wild, and are still wild. Mustangs, as we might like to call them today, are not an indigenous species to North America. They are a combination of all sorts of horse breeds that the rancher may have bred or developed for his own use. The same situation of domestic animals gone wild exists today in many places: cats on Catalina Island and goats on Poaha Island in the middle of Mono Lake. However, the difference is immense: Congress passed a law—the Wild Free Roaming Horses and Burros Protection Act. They didn't with respect to cats or goats!

In order to accommodate the increased use of the range by "wild" horses and for other reasons, the federal agencies have, in accordance with their management plans, continually added rules and regulations for the use of the rangeland—reduced the number of livestock permitted to graze, set definitive dates when cattle may be permitted onto the range as well as dates after which cattle may no longer graze—dates that reduce the number of days grazing is permitted.

Under these circumstance, a confrontation was probably inevitable, and 1995 was the pivotal year. It was at that time when the Forest Service told the Bradshaws that they must sign a new grazing permit that called for an 84 percent cut in their allotment. (Bradshaw arrived at this figure by calculating the reduced number of head permitted to graze at one time minus the number of days the cows would be permitted on the range.) This is an enormous reduction in use and as a result thereof, Bradshaw refused to sign the permit, stating in passing that this would reduce the economic effectiveness of his ranch to a less than marginal operation. Bradshaw was told that he could not be forced to sign the permit, but that if he did not, the Forest Service would issue an order for him to vacate the grazing allotments—an order that would take no more than a week to ten days to issue. Bradshaw considered this to be coercion—a sign it or else demand...and there wasn't much in the way of "else." He refused to sign the agreement. In the course of time, he was issued a cease and desist order by the Forest Service. As is customary, he was told that he could appeal the decision. As pointed out in Part Two of this book, the appeal process is akin to asking the fox how he likes to run the henhouse.

This was not the first of a number of new or modified rules and regulations that the BLM or Forest Service had instituted with reference to the Bradshaw's grazing permits. But this was the last.

Underlying this case is the use of this range by a burgeoning herd of wild horses. Just how many wild horses? In that same pivotal year, the federal government rounded up 2,000 head of wild horses in that area—and they did not get all of them! The Bradshaws claim the wild horses consume the feed to such an extent that there is little or none of it left for his cattle to use by the time he is allowed to graze upon the permitted land in accordance with his grazing permits

Bradshaw is no novice at understanding Constitutional law and Supreme Court cases that support that law. It was this knowledge and the ever increasing rules and regulations that he was forced to live with that finally forced him to declare that enough is enough. Bradshaw believes that there is no end to the seemingly continual increase in the rules and regulations that impact the very economic viability of his ranch and ranching in general. He believes, earnestly, that it is just a matter of time before these rules and regulations force him off of his private land as well. Bradshaw has drawn his line in the sand.

His research, as well as that of his attorney, Glade Hall, has produced an interesting array of constitutional issues, which have been ably set forth in their answer to the government's complaint. While space does not allow a complete analysis of their constitutional reasoning, I can summarize some of their salient points:

1. The United States possesses no municipal sovereignty or jurisdiction after statehood. Bradshaw and Hall quote the findings of the Court in Mayor and Aldermen of the City of Mobile v. Eslava as well as the excerpt from Pollard v. Hagan that I quoted earlier in U.S. v. Gardner.

Why? Because that sovereignty ceased to exist when the land was no longer in a territorial state of being—in keeping with the trustor-trustee relationship that existed between the United States and the future state. The Court recognizes that a trustor-trustee relationship does exist and says so.

2. The Enabling Act for Nevada, slightly different from that of other states, was for the "Inhabitants of the Territory of Nevada." As such, that places the "Inhabitants of the Territory of Nevada" under the laws developed for Federal Enclaves—"Forts, Magazines, and other needful buildings...," Federal Law and not under state of Nevada civil law. This, they argue, is a violation of the Guarantee Clause of the Constitution. And it is! In order to be "equal in all respects whatever" with the other states, you cannot have a two tiered law, state as well as federal, and have a Republican form of government, one of the guarantees provided by the U.S. Constitution. This has nothing to do with the Supremacy Clause of the

Constitution. The Supremacy Clause deals with Federal Law as the supreme law of the land respecting those powers that have been delegated to United States by the Constitution and not retained by the state.

3. The Property Clause of the Constitution does not extend to land within a state after statehood. They cite Dred Scott v. Sanford, in which the Court clearly states that the Property Clause applies only to "Territory of the United States." It is no longer applicable after statehood.

Why is this of particular importance? Because it is the Property Clause that the federal government claims gives them sovereignty of Nevada land after statehood in accordance with Kleppe v. New Mexico. (See this case in the appendix. I point out that Kleppe v. New Mexico grants unlimited power to Congress over the public land. For this authority, Kleppe cites United States v. San Francisco and in turn, United States v. San Francisco cites U.S. v. Gratiot as their authority. Gratiot is taken out of context. Taken in context, no such power exists.) Further, Bradshaw and Hall point out that the statement made in Dred Scott v. Sanford is not dicta, but a decision— and they are right. They point out the following quotations from Dred Scott:

> "Whether, therefore, we take the particular clause in question [the Property Clause], by itself, or in connection with the other provisions of the Constitution, we think it clear, that it applies only to the particular territory of which we have spoken [the territory ceded by the original states to the United States for a common fund], and cannot, by any just rule of interpretation, be extend to a territory which the new government might afterwards obtain from a foreign nation. Consequently, the power which Congress may have lawfully exercised in this territory, while it remained under a territorial government...can furnish no justification and no argument to support a similar exercise of power over territory afterwards acquired by the Federal Government."

The Court goes on to say that there is "no conflict between **the opinion now given** and the one referred to." (Emphasis added)

The Court in Dred Scott is referring to the findings in the case of The American and Ocean Insurance Companies v. Canter.[242] And to make their point clearer, the Court cites that case as follows:

> "Perhaps the power of governing a territory belongs to

242-American and Ocean Insurance Companies v. Canter, 1 Pet., 511.

the United States, which has not by becoming a State, acquired the means of self-government, may result necessarily from the fact that it is not within the jurisdiction of any particular State, and is within the power and jurisdiction of the United States. The right to govern may be the inevitable consequence of the right to acquire territory."

What we are talking about here is jurisdiction: Who has the jurisdiction, the federal government or the separate state (or as the case actually was in The American and Ocean Insurance Companies v. Canter, a duly constituted territorial government and court)? With that in mind please re-read the above.

Restated in simple terms, the power to govern belongs to the United States only when self-government by a state has not been achieved. Further, stated in reverse, acquiring territory (by treaty or conquest) and the right to govern go hand in hand.

Later, in observing this same case, the Court had the following to say about the decision rendered by the District Court—which the Supreme Court upheld:

"His opinion at the Circuit...and in that opinion he states, in explicit terms, that the clause of the Constitution [contained in Article IV of the Constitution—the Power to dispose of and make needful rules and regulations respecting Territory] applies only to the territory then within the limits of the United States and not in Florida,"

This statement clearly shows that Article IV powers (the Powers Clause), that the federal government relies upon for their authority to retain sovereignty and jurisdiction, can and does not operate after a state joins the union. Instead, it belongs to the state.

As an important aside, the next question that should be asked is this: Is this finding a decision of the court or is it dicta? The answer is contained in the underlined quotation that appeared earlier on page 79. Its importance commands that it be repeated:

"There is, however, not the slightest conflict between *the opinion now given*..." (Emphasis added)

There it is: "the opinion now given." The court renders an opinion about the meaning and limitations of the Property Clause of the Constitution—specifically the meaning of the word "territory" as used in the Constitution: It is limited to land ceded for a common fund by the original states only. ***It does not apply to land acquired late by treaty or conquest***. The Court says as much—specifically.

That is not all. Bradshaw and his attorney, Glade Hall, present a compelling, clear, logical and direct defense. It is easy to understand. In essence, they point out that dominion and sovereignty passes to the state upon statehood. (See the section: DOMINION AND SOVEREIGNTY in Part Two for a review of their exact meaning.) Further, they point out that the federal government has no sovereignty over the land after it was included within a state upon statehood; that Congress can only act with respect to land in areas where federal sovereignty does exist.

The status of this case is as follows: The Federal District Court ruled in favor of the federal government (The public lands within the state of Nevada belong to the federal government.). The case was appealed to the 9th Circuit Court of Appeals and the finding of the District Court was affirmed. Just recently a Petition for a Writ of Certiorari was refused by the Supreme Court. This leaves the finding of the Court of Appeals intact as the law of the land.

Inasmuch as the Court of Appeals simply affirmed the Federal District Court and the Supreme Court elected to not hear the case, we therefore must look to the language in the Federal District Court for specifics. Salient points are listed as follows:

> "Plaintiff [United States] owns and through the United
> States Department of Agriculture's Forest Service administers
> and manages the Humboldt National Forest:"

In presenting their analysis for this finding, the court simply states that the defendant offered nothing other than "argument" as required by F.R. Civ. P.56(e) "to show the existence of a genuine issue of material fact..."

This is simply preposterous. Reread, if you will, the issues I have summarized above that Bradshaw, through his attorney, Glade Hall presented rather clear evidence that the land, upon statehood, no longer belonged to the federal government. While it is true that they did not present The Equal Footing Doctrine as a basis for state ownership after statehood—perhaps they should have—they did present compelling constitutional issues: The Treaty of Guadalupe Hidalgo, which states what is to become of the land acquired by that treaty; the issues of dominion and sovereignty as an adjunctive attribute upon statehood; and, perhaps the most important issue of all, the real threat to the sovereignty of the state government itself: A duality of law, federal as well as state, at the expense of state civil law—an erosion of the Constitutional guarantee by the United States (the Guarantee Clause) to each state of a Republican form of government. These are, indeed, constitutional issues. To brush them aside as irrelevant is more than a little presumptuous. It is ludicrous.

However, having summarily dismissed all claims that title to the land passed to the State of Nevada upon statehood, the court then had no difficulty in drawing upon the statement contained in Kleppe v. New Mexico—taken out of context from Gratiot by U.S. v. San Francisco—"power over the public lands thus entrusted to Congress in without limitation." No such power exists, as I have repeatedly pointed out.

The court restated the findings of United States v. Gardner, which have been covered in detail in the preceding examination of that case.

This case and United States v. Gardner are two of the most important cases to come before the Court in recent years. Having finally been decided, the residual effect will be felt before very long with respect to the treatment of the public lands within the United States. Judicially, it may even set in concrete—at least for a time—the question I have raised: Who really owns these public lands?

I recommend that all interested parties to the issues raised in this book read the entire cases of U.S. v. Bradshaw and U.S. v. Gardner. They are compelling.

In a large sense, Part Two of this book is a lengthy examination of both sides of this issue. And, as pointed out in my summary and conclusion in Part Two, I must agree with both Gardner and Bradshaw: the land does pass to the state upon statehood and the federal government does not possess any rights of sovereignty or jurisdiction of state land.

However, this is not what the court now states.

As a person who believes that the U.S. Constitution is a document that must be adhered to and one that cannot be flaunted, distorted, modified or ignored, it is my belief that the only claim the federal government has to the public lands within a state, if any at all, is similar to that of an exclusive sales contract to sell state land!

I would like to think that I have shown how this is true.

OTHER ACTIONS

The Nevada Association of County Government has declared that Nevada owns all public lands within the state of Nevada.

Alaska has filed a 29 billion dollar law suit in the United States Court of Claims for what amounts to a breach of contract. Their claim is that the United States is precluding Alaska from developing their natural resources.

New Mexico counties, for the most part, have adopted Catron County type ordinances.

Some Arizona counties have also adopted Catron County type ordinances. Nye County hopes that counties in other states will consider doing so as well.

Some Utah counties have adopted Catron County type ordinances.

Some California counties have adopted Catron County type ordinances.

Some Counties in Colorado, Washington, Oregon, Idaho, Arkansas and Missouri have adopted Catron County type ordinances. Others are in the process at this writing, in Tennessee and North Carolina.

At one time, Wyoming considered the establishment of a State Land Trust, the ramifications of which are too numerous to spell out here. Further, some counties in Wyoming have adopted Catron County type ordinances.

The Utah Cattlemen's Association passed a resolution and asked that the state of Utah adopt such a resolution as well. It would be momentous, even though it would have no force of law. It clearly indicates their concerns and displeasure with respect to federal governmental actions. Quoted in its entirety:

"RESOLUTION REGARDING THE GUARANTEE CLAUSE OF THE U.S. CONSTITUTION

WHEREAS, Article 4, Section 4 of the U.S. Constitution requires: The United States, shall guarantee to every state in this union a Republican Form of government...

WHEREAS, A Republican Form of government is one in which the people control their rulers. All political power is inherent in the people. Each state has the right to Dominion and Sovereignty over the land within its boundaries, with the exception of Article 1, Section 8, Clause 17 enclaves.

WHEREAS, The Federal Government has ignored the clear language of the Constitution as the Supreme Law of America, remarks of the founders and early Supreme Court rulings, resulting in the usurpation and reversal of such, that today our control government has stripped the people of their guarantee of self governance.

WHEREAS, *Federalist Paper* Number 46, written by James Madison, addresses the subject: The State governments are to protect the nation from encroachments of power by the Federal Government.

WHEREAS, *Federalist Paper* Number 33, written by Alexander Hamilton, provides in Paragraph 6 that: If the Federal Government should make a tyrannical use of the its powers, the American people must redress the injury to the Constitution.

WHEREAS, *Federalist Paper* Number 39, also written by Madison, provides in Paragraph 8 that: The new Constitution guarantees a Republican Form of government to every state.

THEREFORE, BE IT RESOLVED, that the State Legislature of Utah exercise their Power of Redress of injury and require the Federal Government to honor the State of Utah's Constitutional guarantee of a Republican Form of government."

Utah rejected the suggested resolution.

Along with the suggested resolution to the Utah State Legislature was a suggested change to the Utah Revised Statute: Article 68-3-2a: Statutory Presumptions. The Utah Revised Statute is underlined in the following quotation as it would appear after the proposed changes:

> "Unless clearly indicated to the contrary in the text of a statute, *because of governmental duties to protect the rights and responsibilities guaranteed pursuant to Article ISS 1,2,,3,25 and 27 of the Utah Constitution and Article IV S 4 and the Tenth Amendment of the United States Constitution*, it shall be presumed that the statutes adopted by the Legislature of the state of Utah are intended to protect the exercise of inherent and inalienable rights of all residents under the Utah Constitution, fulfill the Federally mandated guarantee for a republican form of government, and strengthen families in the States,"

This seems like such a small thing, but it really isn't. In essence, the changes proposed are a reassertion of a state's authority over that of a federal mandate, law or some federal regulatory agency's rule or regulation. And, in light of a rash of cases decided in early summer of 1997, the Supreme Court agrees:[243] State laws and regulations are not overridden by just any Federal law or federal regulatory agency. In other words, the Supremacy Clause of the Constitution has its limits. In one of those cases, Justice Antonin Scalia said:

> "...risk of tyranny [is best avoided by preserving] a healthy balance of power between the states and the federal government."

It would appear as though the current court thinks the balance between state and federal government can be best preserved by putting its weight on the side of the state. If this is true, then why did the Supreme Court elect to not hear the appeals of the Gardner and Bradshaw cases?

There are two plausible answers, the first of which seems more compelling.

The Supreme Court has well over a thousand cases presented to it for review each year. These are honed down to one hundred of so. Who does the honing? A staff of reviewers. In short, in order to be heard by the Supreme Court you have first to get "past" the reviewers. It was not long ago that the Supreme Court instructed their staff of reviewers to reduce the

---

243-Kansas v. Hendricks, 117 S. Ct. 2072; Washington v. Glucksberg, 117 S. Ct. 2258; Blessing v. Freestone, 117 S. Ct. 1353.

number of cases to be submitted to the Court. It is possible that both Gardner and Bradshaw were eliminated in that process.

The second answer is thought-provoking.

This shift from state ownership to federal ownership of land within a state after statehood has been going on for a long, long time. It has been gradual, but it has taken place irrespective of the constraints contained in the U.S. Constitution and certain Supreme Court decisions. It goes back far enough to make most people wonder about the consequences of a decision of this magnitude. How do we suddenly right a wrong? Who will be affected? How will we settle the fallout of such a decision? How would we shift, suddenly, ownership and all that goes with it back to the states? How would they manage the land? What about the resources on and under that land? How could we trust the states to do what is "right?" This has crossed the minds of the justices, and I'm sure it still does. Could it be that this is one sleeping dog they would rather not awaken? Perhaps.

The names of the different states above makes one thing quite clear: Concern about expanding federal control is no longer just limited to the western states. It is all over.

Will Madison's prognostication be correct?

"...where the sentiment of several adjoining States happen to be in unison, [such an occurrence] would present obstructions which the Federal Government would hardly be willing to encounter."

I wonder. But we shall surely see.

APPENDIX

SUMMARY OF SUPREME COURT CASES

In the following summaries, it has not been my desire to try to do what has so ably been done in the Lawyers' Edition of the cataloging of Supreme Court decisions, wherein a review is contained of what each case is all about, as well as a condensation of the salient points contained in the case—all this in addition to the complete case itself. In the Lawyers' Edition, one will usually find the arguments presented by the plaintiff and defendant. Sometimes this is more revealing than you would suppose.

I have tried to concentrate upon and extract the pertinent passages that bear upon the subject matter of this book. My summary is by no means complete, but it is my best effort to reduce and review the cases to less than a lifetime of research and review. My summary is by no means a substitute for reading the original case, and I most certainly recommend that any interested reader secure the original cases from his law library and read them completely.

William C. Hayward

ALABAMA v. TEXAS (1954)

347 US 272; 98 L Ed. 689

This case is about the constitutionality of the Submerged Lands Act of 1953. The plaintiff claimed that this act was in violation of Art. IV, Sec. 3, Cl. 2 of the U.S. Constitution (the Powers Clause). That article is quoted below:

> "The Congress shall have power to dispose of and make all needful rules and regulations respecting the territory or other property belonging to the United States; nothing in this Constitution shall be so construed as to prejudice any claims of the United States, or of any particular State."

The court held that this act was not unconstitutional and disallowed the challenge [Motion for Leave to File Bill of Complaint].

The following quotations are noteworthy from the denial:

> "The power of Congress to dispose of any kind of property belonging to the United States 'is vested in Congress without limitation.' [U.S. v. Gratiot, 14 Pet. 526, 537]"

Note the reference to U.S. v. Gratiot. The decision of the court rests heavily on that case. But, here too, the quotation from Gratiot is taken out of context as it has been in a number of other critical cases. In context, Congress' unlimited power is restricted to the time prior to statehood when the area was a territory. However, with respect to property belonging to the United States, there is no argument: But what is it exactly that belongs to the United States? If that definition is according to the Constitution, it must be limited to "Forts, Magazines, Arsenals,..." etc.

> "For it must be borne in mind that congress not only has a legislative power over the Public Domain, but it also exercises the power of the proprietor therein. Congress 'may deal with such lands precisely as a private individual may deal with his farming property. It may sell or withhold them from sale.' [U.S. v. Midwest Oil Company, 236 U.S. 459, 474]"

Again, no argument: Congress has a right to govern the Public Domain while it is territory or that which is a part of "Forts, Magazines, Arsenals..." etc. According to the case of Dred Scott v. Sanford, "territory," as used in the Constitution, is limited to that land ceded to the U.S. by the original colonies. And this is not dicta. The land in question came into the U.S. by treaty and as such became a matter of being held in trust for the establishment of a future state.

The court continues:

> "Article 4, Sec. 3, Cl 2 of the Constitution provides that 'The Congress shall have Power to dispose of and make needful Rules and Regulations respecting the Territory and other Property belonging to the United States.' The power over the public land thus entrusted to Congress is without limitations. 'And it is not for the courts to say how that trust shall be administered. That is for Congress to determine.'" [Camfield v. U.S., 167 US 524; Light v. U.S., 220 US 536; U.S. v. San Francisco, 310 US 16, 29-30]

This quotation is referenced as having come from the cases noted. Originally it came from U.S. v. Gratiot and it is important to note that it is taken out of context. Please refer to that case in the appendix. The remaining part of the quotation limits the meaning of the entire quotation to land while it is in a territorial condition. No such broad power is given to Congress in Gratiot, and, inasmuch as it is out of context, this limits the power given to Congress in the above quotation. It is simply not "without limitation" after statehood.

With regard to territorial land there is no argument: Public land is entrusted to Congress while it is a part of a territory. As to the reference to a trust, after the acquisition of the land by treaty, the force and effect of the treaty which established the purpose of the acquisition of the land is governing. The treaty says that the acquired land shall become a state. In essence, a de facto trust is established which, while not formal, is similar in nature to that which was established by the original colonies when they ceded their land to the United States for payment of the debts of the American Revolution: The land was to be sold, and when enough people occupied the land, it was to become a state. See Massie v. Watts [6th vol. of Cranch, p. 148] as quoted in Irvine v. Marshall [61 US 558; 15 L Ed. 994] which sets forth a defined limit of a trustee. In short, the trustee cannot take title for himself. Regardless of this fact, after statehood, the U.S. retained title and has ignored the trustee relationship altogether.

> "We have said that the constitutional powers of Congress [under Article IV, Sec. 3 Cl. 2] is without limitation.

U.S. v. San Francisco, 310 US 16, 29-30"

As noted earlier, this quotation is out of context from Gratiot. In a strict sense, there is no argument. This article is restrictive to "Property belonging to the United States." If the property does not belong to the United States, but instead is owned by the various states for reasons already stated, this article does not apply. ***Art. I, Sec 8, Cl. 17 of the U.S. Constitution outlines the powers of Congress respecting "places purchased."*** The Louisiana Purchase falls into this category. The land from Mexico falls into land acquired by treaty.

Justice Reed, in concurring, has more to say:

> "If...the marginal lands were not declared by those cases [U.S. v. Texas; U.S. v. Wyoming; U.S. v. Louisiana; U.S. v. California; Coyle v. Oklahoma] to belong to the United States, ***title to them remained in the respective states.*** Either by original ownership or by the cession of the Act [Submerged Lands Act of 1953], the lands are now the property of the respective states." (Emphasis added)

This clearly recognizes the existence of prior state ownership of these lands. The cases cited in this quotation rely heavily upon Pollard v. Hagan; each separate case so states this reliance. Pollard v. Hagan is pivotal.

He goes on:

> "The responsibility of Congress is to utilize the assets that come into it hands as sovereign in the way that it decides is best for the future of the Nation. That is what it has done here. Such constitutional determination as the legislation here in question is not subject to judicial review."

This statement is rather limitless and flies in the face of the Constitution. Fortunately, it is not law! It is an opinion in support of what the court had already determined. It is dicta, and only that.

ARIZONA v. CALIFORNIA, et al (1963)

373 US 546; 83 S Ct 1468; 10 L Ed. 2nd 542

This case is about the apportionment of the water from the Colorado River to the different states. It mentions and supports the right of prior appropriation. Even though only 2 percent of the total bank of the Colorado was adjacent to California, California had appropriated most of the water from the river.

This case does not convey any title of land or decide any such title—federal or state. It does, however, make some observations regarding it; it *assumes* title. It does not decide it.

With respect to federal influence, control, and/or legislation regarding ownership, trusteeship, or related issues the following quotations from this case are noteworthy:

With respect to state fear of securing its fair share of the water:

"These fears were not without foundation, since the law of prior appropriation prevailed in most of the Western States. Under that law the one who first appropriates water and puts it to beneficial use thereby acquires a vested right to continue to divert and use that quantity of water against all claimants junior to him in point of time." (p. 555)

Further:

"Wyoming v. Colorado, 259 US 419, held that the doctrine of prior appropriation could be given interstate effect" (pp. 555, 556).

With respect to federal land:

"In these proceedings, the United States has asserted claims to waters in the main river and in some of the tributaries for use on Indian Reservations, National Forests, Recreational and Wildlife Areas and other government lands and works." (p. 595)

"Here, as before the Master [appointed by the court to investigate, recommend and propose settlement of the dispute],

Arizona argues that the United States had no power to make a reservation of navigable waters after Arizona became a State (p. 596).

"Arizona's contention that the Federal Government had no power, after Arizona became a State, to reserve waters for the use and benefit of Federally reserved lands rest largely upon statements in Pollard's Lessee v. Hagan, 3 How. 212 (1845), and Shively v. Bowlby, 152 US 1 (1894). Those cases and others that followed them [U.S. v. California and U.S. v. Holt State Bank] gave rise to the doctrine that lands underlying navigable waters within territory acquired by the Government are held in trust for future States and that title to such lands is automatically vested in the States upon admission to the Union." (p. 597)

The court clearly recognizes the trustee relationship of the United States and that "title to such lands is automatically vested in the States upon admission to the Union."

The court narrows this down in the following manner:

"But those cases involved only the shores of lands beneath navigable waters. They do not determine the problem before us and cannot be accepted as limiting the broad powers of the United States to regulate navigable waters under the Commerce Clause and to regulate government lands under Art. IV, Sec. 3, of the Constitution. We have no doubt about the power of the United States under these clauses to reserve water rights for its **reservations and its property**." (p. 597, 598)
(Emphasis added)

The court assumes the title of the land to be federal.

Art. IV, Sec. 3 Cl 2 of the Constitution:

"The Congress shall have power to dispose of and make all needful rules and regulations respecting the territory or other property belonging to the United States; and nothing in this Constitution shall be so construed as to prejudice any claims of the United States, or of any particular State."

Observation: "Territory" as used in this clause was defined in Dred Scott v. Sanford; "territory," as used in this clause of the Constitution was limited to the ceded land of the original colonies.

The court recognizes that Pollard's Lessee v. Hagan does grant title to the land under the shores of navigable water to the states upon statehood. But that is not all of what Pollard v. Hagan said in the background information upon which the decision was based. The background information directed its attention to all land—not just land under navigable waters. The court's finding in Pollard's Lessee v. Hagan was based upon that background and related it only to navigable waters inasmuch as that was all that was asked in the case. A narrow slice of the whole.

Again, this gives rise to the importance of Pollard v. Hagan.

In the instance of Arizona v. California, the court rejects Arizona's claim that the United States lacks the power to regulate *after* Arizona became a state except as it relates to shore lands. The court gives the power to regulate to the federal government under the Commerce Clause—"rules and regulations." (p. 598)

The court seems to recognize the existence of a Federal Trust for lands under the shore-land of navigable waters, resulting from Pollard v. Hagan. If Pollard v. Hagan is too narrowly interpreted—and I think that it is—a broader interpretation (what I believe the court really said in Pollard v. Hagan in the first instance) is that all land prior to statehood is held in trust for the state and becomes the property of the state upon statehood.

CALIFORNIA COASTAL COMMISSION v. GRANITE ROCK COMPANY (1987)

480 U.S. 572; 94 L. Ed. 2d 577; 107 S Ct 1419

This case is about jurisdiction and control. Do Forest Service regulations, federal land use statutes and regulations, or the Costal Zone Management Act of 1972 preempt the California Coastal Commission's requirement for a permit to operate an un-patented mining claim in a National Forest? In other words, does the federal government have the final jurisdiction over National Forest land or does the state? If there is an overlap of jurisdiction by the state, where does it begin and where does it end? How far does the planning process have to go in order to accommodate state or local concerns?

The first part of these questions goes to the core issue of ownership of the land. In this case, this was not questioned by either part: Ownership was assumed by both parties to be federal; it was not a question before the court. The question of ownership of the land was not asked. This left the remaining questions before the court, and it was to these that the court addressed its attention.

Granite Rock secured rights to the mining claims on National Forest land, claims to which had been duly acquired, originally, as a result of the Mining Act of 1872. After securing the proper authorization from the Forest Service, mining commenced.

There was no challenge as to state or federal ownership of the land. Ownership of the land was assumed by both the plaintiff and defendant to be federal in nature. The court assumed the same inasmuch as this was not a part of any conflict between the parties.

Two years later the Coastal Commission demanded that a permit was required from them for the mining operation to continue. This demand instituted the commencement of this suit. Granite Rock contended that jurisdiction remained with the federal government and that the Coastal Commission's possible regulations, whatever they might be, would be preempted by the federal government. The court stated that the only issue in this case is the purely facial challenge to the Coastal Commission's permit requirement.

The court said the following to establish jurisdiction for the federal government:

"The Property Clause provides that 'Congress shall have Power to dispose of and make all needful Rules and Regulations respecting the Territory or other Property belonging to the United States'"

Continuing:

"This court has 'repeatedly observed' that 'the power over the public land thus entrusted to Congress is without limitation.'" [citing Kleppe v. New Mexico]

See the appendix summary of Kleppe v. New Mexico. Kleppe makes this statement by relying on United States v. San Francisco which in turn relies upon United States v. Gratiot. Gratiot is taken out of context. In context, "the power over the public land thus entrusted to Congress is without limitation" only when that public land is part of a territory prior to statehood. (See United States v. Gratiot in the appendix.)

Continuing, the court observes:

"The Property Clause itself does not automatically conflict with all state regulation of federal land. Rather, as we explained in Kleppe: 'Absent consent or cession a State undoubtedly retains jurisdiction over federal lands within its territory, but Congress equally surely retains the power **to enact legislation** respecting those lands pursuant to the Property Clause. **And when Congress so acts**, the federal legislation necessarily overrides conflicting state laws under [the] Supremacy Clause."
(The court's emphasis)

In 1955, Congress passed the Multiple Use Mining Act, in order to give the Secretary of Agriculture authority to make "rules and regulations" to "regulate [the] occupancy and use" of National Forests for mining. The Forest Service, in turn, developed such rules for "use of the surface of National Forest System lands" by un-patented mining claims as authorized in the Mining Act of 1872 as follows:

"...shall be conducted so as to minimize adverse environmental impacts on National Forest System surface resources."

One of the purposes of the Multiple Use Mining Act was to gain more control over possible adverse use of natural resources. Environmental impact was one of the factors to be considered. The California Coastal Commission had a major concern in this exact area too. And the Commission's permit process was their way of regulating and controlling the negative environmental impact.

Duplication was the issue. Who was in charge? Could one pre-empt the other? If so, which one? Who had jurisdiction, the State of California or the federal government?

As I mentioned earlier, ownership of the land was not raised nor argued; it was assumed to be federal. This case boils down to cooperation between different governmental agencies. How complete should this cooperation be? How do you equate differences? And in the final analysis, who is paramount over the other if no compromise is possible?

With this in mind the following is noteworthy:

"...it is appropriate to expect an administrative regulation to declare any intention to pre-empt state law with some specificity."

The court then draws the following quotation from Hillsborough County v. Automated Medical Laboratories, Inc.:[244]

"Because agencies normally address problems in a detailed manner and can speak through a variety of means,...we can expect that they will make their intentions clear if they intend for their regulations to be exclusive. Thus if an agency does not speak to the question of pre-emption, we will pause before saying that the mere volume and complexity of its regulations indicate that the agency did in fact intend to pre-empt."

In other words, if the intent is to preempt, it must be "made very plain."

The Decision Notice and Finding by the Forest Service said the following:

"The claimant [Granite Rock Co.], in exercising his rights granted by the Mining Law of 1872, shall comply with the regulations of the Departments of Agriculture and Interior. The claimant

244-Hillsborough County v. Automated Medical Laboratories, Inc. (1985): 471 U.S. 707, p. 718; 85 L. Ed. 714; 105 S. Ct. 2371.

is further responsible for obtaining any necessary permits required by the State and/or county laws."

With respect to coordination with state and local plans, the court observed the following:

> "The FLPMA [Federal Land Policy and Management Act of 1976] directs that land use plans developed by the Secretary of the Interior 'shall be consistent with State and local plans to the maximum extent [the Secretary] *finds consistent* with Federal law' and calls for the Secretary 'to the extent he finds practical, to keep apprised of state land use plans,' and to 'assist in resolving, *to the extent practical*, inconsistencies between Federal and non-Federal Government plans.'" (Emphasis added)

Note the emphasized words and wording; if push comes to shove, the federal government can do as they singularly please.

The court assumed, and without deciding, clearly stated the assumption that the National Forest Management Act and the federal land Policy and Management Act preempt the extension of state land use plans onto unpatented mining claims in National Forest lands.

However, the court did not preclude the Coastal Commission from exercising environmental constraints on their own through the permit process. Granite Rock was concerned that this permit process would for all practical purposes be so restrictive as to preclude them from any mining—hence their desire and argument to have the federal government pre-empt state regulations.

The court said, so to speak, "If you did not get a permit and did not apply for one, how do you know you would have been precluded from mining?"

In the oral argument footnoted at page 595, the following is note-worthy:

> "We're dealing with the second type of permitting, which is by the Coastal Commission itself, not a local government....The Coastal Commission issues permits based upon compliance with the environmental criteria in the Coastal Act itself."

This is at major variance with the actual printed purpose in the

Californian Coastal Act.

In the dissenting opinion, Justices Scalia and White picked this up too and quoted from parts of the act. Their quotation is lengthy. The act covers a whole host of compliances and priorities with which to deal. A mining operation such as Granite Rock could expect to be rather far down on the list of priorities listed. I think this was Granite Rock's concern: They would be so far down the list that their mining operation could in fact be precluded from its operation altogether. They did not want to take the chance.

Because the extent of the restrictions the Coastal Commission Agency might place upon Granite Rock Co. were unknown and ostensibly limited to environmental concerns, as evidenced by the oral argument outlined above, the court found that the federal rules and regulations did not preempt or preclude a necessary permit from the Coastal Commission.

The important finding in this case has to do with the extent of federal cooperation or amelioration that are required in order to conform to local government concerns or plans.

Paraphrased it is this: Work out your differences as best you can and give opposing views every consideration possible, but if in the end you do not agree, the federal will and decree is final.

CAMFIELD v. UNITED STATES (1897)

167 US 518; 42 L ed. 260; 17 S Ct 864

This case is about the constitutionality of the Act of February 25, 1885, known as the Anti Fencing Act of 1885.

The case itself is about the placement of a series of fences on private land, where, by so doing, public land is within those fences, thus effectively precluding others from settling or using the enclosed public land. In effect, as the court said, "...inclose(d) them for private use."

The court observed that the reason why the 1885 anti-fencing law was passed by Congress in the first place was to preclude settlers from fencing off public land for their own private use. Camfield had done the fencing on his private land, but in so placing the fence on his own land, he effectively fenced off the public land as well. An entire township (36 square sections) was involved. Camfield placed a fence on his private property just inside the property line where he owned every other section in a zigzag manner at the outside property line, allowing insufficient room at each corner for the passage of cattle or wagons.

The following quotations are noteworthy:

> "...the government has, with respect to its own lands, the right of an ordinary proprietor, to maintain its possession and to prosecute trespassers. It may deal with such lands precisely as a private individual may deal with his farming property. It may sell or withhold them from sale. It may grant them in aid of railways or other public enterprises. It may open them to pre-emption or homestead settlement; but it would be recreant to its duties as *trustee* for the people of the United States to permit any individual or private corporation to monopolize them for private gain, and thereby practically drive ***intending settlers from the market***." (Emphasis added)

The land in question was in the state of Colorado. The court assumes the ownership of the public land inside the border of the state to be federal in nature even though it recognizes a trustee relationship and mentions the reason for such trusteeship: "intended settlers." It is important to note that in this case the court does not decide that the land is federal in ownership, it simply assumes it.

In reaching its finding, the court relies on early English law regarding a nuisance and says:

> While we do not undertake to say that Congress has the unlimited power to legislate against nuisances within a state, which it would have within a territory, **we do not think the admission of a territory as a state deprives it of the power of legislating for the protection of the Public Lands, though it may thereby involve the exercise of what is ordinarily known as the police power, so long as such power is directed SOLELY to its own protection. A different rule would place the Public Domain of the United States completely at the mercy of state legislation.** (Emphasis added)

The finding of the court is brief:

> "We are of opinion that in passing the act in question, Congress exercised its constitutional right of protecting the public lands from nuisances erected upon adjoining property; that the act is valid,..."

This is the finding of the court. That act is lawful. All of the other observations of the court included above are dicta, even though they clearly indicate the assumed ownership of the public land to be federal.

One could surely ask why the strong statement of the court quoted above is not a clear, unmistakable indication that the public lands within a state are federal in ownership. Quite simply, ownership of the land was not the question. That question was not asked. It was not argued, and because it was not argued it cannot be used as the basis of law.

Further, dicta is not law and cannot be used as the basis for law. Only the finding of the court can be the basis for law.

COYLE v. SMITH (OKLAHOMA) (1911)

221 U.S. 559

This case has to do with the question of power granted to a state to locate or change its seat of government when the Enabling Act relative to the admission of that state declares where the seat of government shall be. In other words, to what extent does the Enabling Act dictate to a new state its right to determine state affairs.

In reaching the finding that the state may decide for itself the location of its seat of government or change it at will, the court observed a number of things that defined the limitations of the Enabling Acts:

1. They may not impose restrictions that would create an unequal condition between states.

2. They may not limit any attribute of power essential to its equality with the other states.

3. Congress may place conditions in an Enabling Act that relate to defined powers granted to Congress by the Constitution, such as inter-state commerce, Indian affairs, and disposition of public lands.

In a collateral area, the court defined the responsibility of Congress with respect to admitting new states:

1. Congress has the power to admit new states....only. And only then when they are "equal in all respects whatsoever."

2. Congress has the duty to guarantee a republican form of government within the new state.

Of particular note are the following quotations that bear upon the subject-matter of this case:

What is "a state?"

"The definition of 'a state' is found in the powers possessed by the original States which adopted the Constitution,...."

297

The power of Congress is to admit "new States into this Union." (The court's emphasis.)

"'This Union' was and is a union of States, equal in power, dignity and authority, each competent to exert that residuum of sovereignty not delegated to the United States by the Constitution itself."

With respect to Congressional power to deprive a state of its equality with other states:

"The argument that Congress derives from the duty of 'guaranteeing to each State in this Union a republican form of government,' power to impose restrictions upon a new State which deprives it of equality with other members of the Union, has no merit."

Further:

"...it obviously does not confer power to admit a new State which shall be any less a State than those which compose the Union."

The court cites at length from Permoli v. First Municipality,[245] in which Justice Catron states that which is contained in Enabling Acts are terms and conditions...

"....quite common in enabling acts, by which the new State disclaimed title to the public lands, and stipulated that such lands should remain subject to the sole disposition of the United States, and for their exemption from taxation..."

"Whatever force such provisions have *after* the admission of the State may be attributed to the power of Congress over the subjects, derive[d] from other provisions of the Constitution, rather than from any consent by the compact with the State."
(Emphasis added)

In other words, the power of Congress, if any, to dispose of the public lands after a state enters the Union does not come from the disclaimer in the Enabling Act, but from the powers of Congress if any such power exists as all. The court does not say that Congress possess such power.

245-Permoli v. First Municipality, 3 How. 589.

Quoting further from Coyle v. Smith:

> "...there is to be found no sanction for the contention that any State may be deprived of any of the powers constitutionally possessed by other States, as States, by reason of the terms in which the acts admitting them to the Union have been framed."

Quite to the point, the court cites Escanaba Co. v. Chicago,[246] and in that case Justice Field said:

> "Whatever the limitation upon her powers as a government whilst in a territorial condition, whether from the ordinance of 1787 or the legislation of Congress, *it ceased to have any operative force, except as voluntarily adopted by her, after she became a State of the Union.*" (Emphasis added)

Caution: The subject matter referred to above was navigable waters, and it derived its basic authority from Pollard v. Hagan which the court referred to as "most instructive and controlling."

This case, as well as others, places a great deal of pivotal importance upon Pollard v. Hagan.

The following lengthy quotation is important in that it seems to go beyond Pollard v. Hagan in some respects and define additional meaning:

> "The court held [in Pollard v. Hagan] that the stipulation in the act under which Alabama was admitted to the Union, that the people of the proposed State 'forever disclaim all rights and title to the waste or unappropriated lands lying within the said territory, and that the same shall be and remain at the sole and entire disposition of the United States," cannot operate as a contract between the parties, but is binding as law. As to this the court said [in Pollard v. Hagan]: 'Full power is given to Congress 'to make all needful rules and regulations respecting the territory or other property of the United States.' This authorized the passage of all laws necessary to secure the rights of the United States to the public lands, and to provide for their sale, and to protect them from taxation."

246-Escanaba Co. v. Chicago, 107 U.S. 678.

The court is saying that the reason this cannot operate as a contract between the parties, but is binding as law, is because Congress has the power to make rules and regulations to secure the rights of the United States to the public lands, and to provide for their sale as well as protect them from taxation.

Nothing in the forgoing can be implied to give the United States the right to retain the public lands in perpetuity. To the contrary, it mentions "provide for their sale." Protection from taxation was only an interim measure.

With respect to the imposition of more restrictive measures than those that are effective upon other states, the court had this to say:

> "...this court has held in many cases that, whatever be the limitations upon the power of a territorial government, they cease to have any operative force, except as voluntarily adopted after such territory has become a State of the Union. Upon the admission of a State it becomes entitled to and possesses all the rights of dominion and sovereignty which belonged to the original States..."

Does this mean that the states then possess the dominion and sovereignty of its land? Many think that it does, and I agree.

But all of this is dicta except the actual finding of the court, which was that the location of the seat of the state government was a prerogative of the state, not the federal government, regardless of what the Enabling Act stated.

With one last admonition, the court had this to say in concluding:

> "To this we may add that the constitutional equality of the States is essential to the harmonious operation of the scheme upon which the Republic was organized. When that equality disappears we may remain a free people, but the Union will not be the Union of the Constitution."

This case was decided in 1911. Have we been traveling on the road to becoming a Union not of the Constitution? Many argue that we have and that the retention by the federal government of public lands in federal ownership is a big step in that process.

DRED SCOTT v. SANDFORD (1856)

60 U.S. (19 HOW) 393

This case had to do with a slave who traveled north of the Mason-Dixon Line into a "free" state. The question was asked of the court: Was the slave personal property and as such still the property of his "owner," or was he now "free" inasmuch as he was then living in the North—a free state?

The court labored over this decision to such an extent that all the justices wrote their own opinions. In its totality, it is probably the longest decision ever printed. (It is certainly the longest one I ever read.) It was left to Chief Justice Taney to write the collective opinion of the court—which he did.

The fact that Dred Scott was found to be still the personal property of his "owner" under the constitution makes this one of the darkest days of the Supreme Court. It was a tragic finding, and this case is looked upon as despicable—which in my opinion it is—and in the eyes of Sandra Day O'Connor as well, who expressed her opinion in that regard not long ago on television.

However bad this decision was with respect to the fate of Dred Scott, it is not his fate that is important to the subject matter of this book. Rather, it is the historical review and finding of the court with respect to the use and meaning of the term "territory". For in order to render a decision with respect to the disposition of a slave as private property in a different state from which he had been taken, the court was compelled to examine Article IV of the Constitution, the Powers Clause, which it did in detail. The court examined it and explained it piece by piece, sentence by sentence. A part of this examination was directed toward the definition of "territory" as used in Article IV. That part of the examination and decision of the court is germane to the subject matter of this book.

It is important to point out that the different Supreme Court Justices all understood the history that this case reviews, for after all, all of them grew up in the embryonic stages of the Union. They remembered the history; they lived it; it was, for the most part, a part of their early upbringing and personal memory.

The criticism this case has drawn has been based upon humanitarian reasons—one human being owning another as private property. And it should, however, that criticism has spilled over onto all of the finding of this case. There is a natural compulsion to ignore the entire case. That we cannot do. In the historical timeframe in which this case was decided, there was little else the court could do. Slavery, the possession of a human being by another was accepted—not completely, but nonetheless accepted. What the court had to say as to why and how they came to their decision included the examination of Article IV, the Powers Clause of the Constitution. That examination is a part of their decision.

This last statement flies in the face of those jurists and lawyers that claim that this examination of the Powers Clause can and should be ignored because it is dicta. ***That examination of the Powers Clause is not dicta*** for reasons I shall explain later.

The following quotations are important, for they lay the foundation of all the justices' different observations and collective findings as written by Chief Justice J. Taney:

> "The counsel for the plaintiff has laid much stress upon that article in the Constitution which confers on Congress the Power 'to dispose of and make all needful rules and regulations respecting the territory or other property belonging to the United States;' but in the judgment of the court, that provision has no bearing on the present controversy, and the power there given, whatever it may be, ***is confined, and was intended to be confined, to the territory which at that time belonged to, or was claimed by, the United States, and was within their boundaries as settled by the Treaty with Great Britain, and can have no influence upon a territory afterwards acquired from a foreign government.*** It was a special provision for a known and particular Territory, and to meet a present emergency, *and nothing more.*"
> (Emphasis added)

This that follows was history as they knew it. This was the meaning of the word "territory" as it was used in Article IV of the Constitution. It defined its limitations.

The court recites the background for the "territory:"

> "Every state at that time, felt severely the pressure of its war debt; but in Virginia, and some other States there were large territories of unsettled lands, the sale of which would enable them to discharge their obligations without much inconvenience;

while other States which had no such resource, saw before them many years of heavy and burdensome taxation, and the latter insisted, for the reasons before stated, that these unsettled lands should be treated as the common property of the States, and the proceeds applied to their common benefit."

Continuing:

"[The war debt] was the disturbing element of the time, and fears were entertained that it might dissolve the Confederation by which the States were then united. These fears and dangers were, however, at once removed, when the State of Virginia, in 1784, voluntarily ceded to the United States the immense tract of country lying northwest of the River Ohio, and which was within the acknowledged limits of the State. The only object of the State, in making this cession, was to put an end to the threatening and exciting controversy, and to enable the Congress of that time to dispose of the lands, and appropriate the proceeds as a common fund for the common benefit of the States. It was not ceded because it was inconvenient to the State to hold and govern it, nor from any expectation that it could be better or more conveniently governed by the United States."

Continuing:

"It was necessary that the lands should be sold to pay the war debt; that a government and system of jurisprudence should be maintained in it, to protect the citizens of the United States, who should migrate to the Territory, in their rights of person and of property."

Now for the reason the clause was inserted in the Constitution:

"And, moreover, there were many articles of value besides this property in land, such as arms, military stores, munitions, and ships of war, which were the common property of the States, when acting in their independent characters as confederates, which neither the new government nor anyone else would have a right to take possession of, or control, without authority from them; and it was to place these things under the guardianship and protection of the new government, and to clothe it with the necessary powers, that the clause was inserted in the Constitution which gives Congress the power to 'dispose of and make all needful rules and regulations respecting the territory or other property belonging to the Unites States.' It was intended for a specific purpose to provide for the things we have mentioned. It was to transfer to the new government the property then held in common by the States, and to give to that government power to apply it to the objects for which it had been destined by mutual agreement among the States before their league was dissolved. *It applied only to the property which the States held in common at that time, and has no reference whatever to any territory or other property which the new sovereignty might afterwards itself acquire*. The language used in the clause, the arrangement and combination of the powers, and the somewhat unusual phraseology it uses, when it speaks of the political powers to be exercised in the government of the territory, all indicate the design and meaning of the clause to be such as we have mentioned. *It does not speak of any Territory, nor of Territories, but uses language which, according to its legitimate meaning, points to a particular thing. The power is given in relation only to the territory of the United States—that is, to a Territory then in existence, and then known or claimed as the territory of the United States*.... It then gives the power which was necessarily associated with the disposition and sale of the lands—that is, the power to make rules and regulations respecting the Territory. And whatever construction may now be given to these words, everyone, we think, must admit that they are not the words usually employed by statesmen in giving supreme power of legislation. They are certainly very unlike the words used in the power granted to legislate over territory which the new government might afterwards itself obtain by cession from a state, either from its seat of government, or for forts, magazines, arsenals, dockyards, and other needful buildings.

"And the same power of making needful rules respecting the Territory is, in precisely the same language, applied to the other property belonging to the United States—associating the power over the Territory in this respect with the power over movable or personal property—that is, the ships, arms and munitions of war, which then belonged in common to the State sovereignties. And it will hardly be said, that this power, in relation to the last mentioned objects, was deemed necessary to be thus specially given to the new government, in order to authorize it to make needful rules and regulations respecting the ships it might itself build, or arms and munitions of war it might itself manufacture or provide for the public service.

"No one, it is believed, would think a moment of deriving the power of Congress to make needful rules and regulations in relation to property of this kind from this clause of the Constitution. Nor can it, upon any fair construction be applied to any property but that which the new government was about to receive from the confederated States. And if this be true as to this property, *it must be equally true and limited as to the territory, which is so carefully and precisely coupled with it—and like it referred to as property in the power granted*. The concluding words of the clause appear to render this construction irresistible: for, after the provisions we have mentioned, it proceeds to say, 'that nothing in the Constitution shall be so construed as to prejudice any claims of the United States, or of any particular State.'

"[The purpose of this clause] was to exclude the conclusion that either party, by adopting the Constitution, would surrender what they deemed their rights. And when the latter provision relates so obviously to the unappropriated lands not yet ceded by the States, and the first clause makes provision for those then actually ceded, it is impossible, by any just rule of construction, to make the first provision general, and extend to all territories, which the federal government might in any way afterwards acquire, *when the latter is plainly and unequivocally confined to a particular territory*; which was a part of the same controversy, and involved in the same dispute, and depended upon the same principles. The union of the two provisions in the same clause shows that they were kindred subjects, and that the whole clause is local, and relates only to lands, within the limits of the United States; *and that no other Territory was in the mind of the framers of the Constitution, or intended to be embraced in it*." (Emphasis added)

Much has been said about the power of Congress to make rules and regulations. Taney, on page 440, had this to say about "rules and regulations" as those words appear in Article IV.:

"The words, "rules and regulations" are usually employed in the Constitution in speaking of some particular specific power which it means to confer on the government, and not, as we have seen, when ***granting general powers*** of legislation. And to construe the words of which we are speaking as a general and unlimited grant of sovereignty over territories which the government might afterwards acquire, is to use them in a sense and for a purpose for which they were not used in any other part of the instrument [the U.S. Constitution]. But if confined to a particular territory in which a government and laws had already been established, but which would require some alterations to adapt it to the new government, the words are peculiarly applicable and appropriate for that purpose." (Emphasis added)

Bluntly put, the court is saying that "rules and regulations" as used here are *not* for the granting of a general power to Congress, but are restricted to making rules and regulations with respect to the territory granted to the United States for the payment of their debt, as well as rules and regulations to effect the disposal of other property owned by the United States.

Why was it necessary to grant to Congress such rights to make rules and regulations? Taney explains that on page 441.

"Assembled together, special provisions were indispensable to transfer to the new government the property and rights which at that time they held in common;...and this power could only be given to it by special provisions in the Constitution.

"The clause in relation to the territory and other property of the United States provide for the first, and the clause last quoted provided for the other. They have no connection with the general powers and rights of sovereignty delegated to the new government, and can neither enlarge nor diminish them. They were inserted to meet a present emergency, and not to regulate its powers as a government."

In light of the above, there is no way to assume that the territory acquired later by treaty or by war was or is "territory" as that term appears in Article IV of the U.S. Constitution.

Now, as to why these statements are not dicta.

The ultimate test as to whether or not a statement of the court is dicta lies in the simple question: Is it material to the case? Taney thought that it was and so stated it three times in different ways. (This is covered in detail in that section in Part Two: "TERRITORY" DEFINED: DRED SCOTT V. SANFORD.)

The case of The American and Ocean Insurance Companies v. Canter (1 Pet. 511) plays an important part in this determination. Note the following quotation:

> "...the case of The American and Ocean Insurance Companies v. Canter, 1 Pet. 511, has been quoted as establishing a different construction of this clause of the Constitution. ***There is, however not the slightest conflict between this opinion now given and the one referred to***; and it is only by taking a single sentence out of the other and separating it from the context, that even an appearance of conflict can be shown. We need not comment on such a mode of expounding an opinion of the court. Indeed it most commonly misrepresents instead of expounding it. And this is fully exemplified in the case referred to, where, if one sentence is taken by itself, the opinion would appear to be in direct conflict ***with that now given;***"
> (Emphasis added)

Clearly, Taney considered his statement about the lack of conflict between "this opinion now given" (said twice) and that of the opinion that appeared in the case of The American Ocean Insurance Companies v. Canter to be an opinion of the court.

There is still a third reference, which also appears on page 442:

> "It is thus clear, from the whole opinion on this point, that the court did not mean to decide whether the power was derived from the clause in the Constitution or was the necessary consequence of the right to acquire. They do decide that the power in Congress is unquestionable, and in this we entirely concur, ***and nothing will be found in this opinion to the contrary***." (Emphasis added)

In spite of the forgoing, I am reasonably certain that there will still be those that seriously doubt the necessity of paying any attention to this case. The argument I have heard is that reliance upon such a so-called antiquated case is passe', poor law, or simply not compelling; implying thereby that a case has no real merit unless it is recent. Dred Scott v. Sandford was decided in 1856. Eighty years earlier, in 1776, our founding fathers wrote a momentous document, the Declaration of Independence, which in turn spawned many, many others. I cannot disregard any of those, and I question the wisdom of disregarding something simply because of its age. The reasons have to be better than that.

This case simply cannot be ignored.

GRISAR v. McDOWELL (1867)

73 US 363; 18 L Ed. 863

This is a case arising out of the history of California prior to the war with Mexico, when the laws of Mexico prevailed. The extent and protection of property rights extended to Mexican pueblos (towns, cities, etc.) by the Treaty of Guadalupe Hidalgo (Mexico's cession of land to the United States) came into question; does the United States, in conformity with the Constitution, have the right to preempt or reserve land for a military installation? The term "reserve" is important in this case inasmuch as this case is cited in several other cases as authority for the set aside of reserve land. Please keep in mind that in this case the reserve land is for a military installation of the United States—one of the provisions allowed by the Constitution (Art. I, Sec. 8, par. 17).

The basic question in this case with respect to what we know today as the Presidio of San Francisco was this: Did the city of San Francisco or the United States have the right of possession in the year 1867?

Briefly, the chain of land title was as follows: Mexico to the United States, the United States to the State of California, with such variances that the Treaty with Mexico and the provisions of the Constitution allowed.

Mexican law allowed a rather indefinite and at times inconsistent provision with respect to land which a town could claim as "city land" (common land); at most, 4 square leagues. A single league equals 3 miles.

The time-line of this case is important and is listed below for clarity:

July 4, 1848:   Guadalupe Hidalgo Treaty (Cession from Mexico to United States).

September 9, 1850:   California admitted to the Union.

November 5, 1850:   President Fillmore's order to exempt and reserve "certain parcels on the Bay of San Francisco...from sale..."

March 3, 1851:   Mexican Claims Act: The establishment of the Board of Land Commissions to decide land claims.

December 31, 1851:   President Fillmore precisely defines the reserved land to be withheld from sale—which included the Presidio of San Francisco, site for a military installation.

June 20, 1855:   Van Ness Ordinance passed by the city of San Francisco and ratified by the legislature of the state of California.

The city of San Francisco presented their claim to the land in question to the Board of Land Commissions in July, 1852, to establish their claim to the land in question (as a part of the total land claimed by the city). The city's claim was affirmed in part, but not in total, by the board in December 1854. The decision of the board was appealable, and such was done by both parties; the city of San Francisco for not having been granted their total claim and by the United States, who in turn wanted title and control of more land than that which had been granted to them. The United States' major basis was reliance upon the reservation of the land by President Fillmore.

With respect to that portion of land that we now know as the Presidio of San Francisco, Grisar lived on the land and had already "acquired whatever right or title [to the land that] the city possessed..." In 1855, Grisar was ousted by the War Department of the United States. The land was to become a fort, and the justification of his ousting was based upon the earlier reservation of the land by President Fillmore. Simply put, the United States did not recognize Grisar's ownership claim in any way; his land and improvements (home) were confiscated. In order to make the reservation stick, the title issued by the city of San Francisco was challenged.

The route to the Supreme Court was not entirely direct, but this dispute finally got there, and the following revelations from that case are historically noteworthy.

With respect to the legality of the customary assignments made by Mexico to pueblos, the court made this observation:

"These laws provided for the assignment to the pueblos, for their use and the use of their inhabitants, of land not exceeding in extent four square leagues. Such assignment was to be made by the public authorities of the government upon the original establishment of the pueblo, or afterwards upon the petition of its officers or inhabitants:...All lands within the general limits stated, which had previously become private property, or

were ***required for public purposes, were reserved and
excepted from the assignment***." (Emphasis added)

In tracing the history, the court added:

"Until the lands were thus definitely assigned ***and
measured off***, the right or claim of the pueblo was an imperfect
one. It was a right the government [Mexico] might refuse to
recognize at all, or might recognize in a qualified form; it might be
restricted to less limits than the four square leagues, which was
the usual quantity assigned. Even after the assignment the
interest acquired by the pueblo was ***far from being an indefeasible estate*** such as is known to our laws." (Emphasis added)

Continuing:

"The interest...amounted to little more than a restricted
and qualified right to alienate portions of the land to its inhabitants for building or cultivation, and to use the remainder for
commons, for pasture lands, or as a source of revenue, or for
other public purposes. ***And this limited right of disposition and use was, in all particulars, subject to the
control of the government of the country [Mexico]***."
(Emphasis added)

The court recognized that the boundary of the city of San Francisco
had never been finitely established; it was neither confirmed nor recorded
by the Mexican government. This then was the cloud upon the title. By
ascendancy, any grant to the city of San Francisco would pass to the United
States, the successor to Mexico, to grant.

But California entered the Union before any such grant occurred.
However, this did not invalidate San Francisco's claim to "city land." This
forced the city of San Francisco to present their claim to the Board of Land
Commissions for its adjudication. To this board, the United States also
presented their objections. The board agreed with neither of them
completely. This led to an appeal to the Circuit Court of Appeals by both
parties. Before the Court could rule on the case, the federal government
withdrew their objection. This left the court the role of determining the
validity and extent of the city of San Francisco's claim. This was finally done,
and it confirmed title to the city of San Francisco.

This was not the end, however. In 1866, Congress passed an act "to quiet the title to certain lands within the corporate limits of the city of San Francisco." Remember that Grisar had been ousted from possession of what he thought was his property in 1855 by the federal government, who had literally confiscated his property, upon which a military installation had been or was being built. This act of Congress was probably for the purpose of clearing up this conflict of interest. Grisar was to lose. It is how he lost that is important with respect to this summary.

Scarcely anyone is going to deny that the United States has an obligation to defend the continental limits of the United States by the installation of certain military posts. Along with the obligation goes the implied right to acquire land for such an installation. This is covered by the Constitution (Art. I, Sec. 8, par. 17). Because of its strategic location, the Presidio of San Francisco would certainly be one of them; the federal government thought so.

The Supreme Court's rationale for hearing the case at all after it had been decided by the Circuit Court of Appeals—to which the United States was neither a party nor an appellant—is extremely interesting reading. At this date, it makes little difference.

The Supreme court noted the cloud upon the title that San Francisco had that has been previously pointed out. The court had this to say:

> "It is not a claim to a tract which had been specifically defined; it was a claim only to a specific quantity, embracing, it is true, the city of the pueblo and adjoining lands, **but which had yet to receive its precise limits and bounds from the officers of the government. Until this was done, the government was not precluded from setting apart and appropriating any portions of the lands claimed, which might be necessary for public uses. Until then the claim of the city was subservient to the right of the government in this respect**." (Emphasis added)

In other words, if it has no finite boundary, it is not a defensible claim. On two counts this boundary was indefeasible: It had not been recorded in Mexico prior to the cession of the land to the United States; the land had not been surveyed by the General Land Office to determine its exact location so that it could be conveyed by patent.

One could and should ask, "How does the entry into the Union by California enter into this? Did President Fillmore have the right and power to reserve Public Domain land in a state after statehood?"

The court said, "Yes," and cited the Pre-Emption Act of May 29, 1830 (4 Stat. at L. 421) as their authority.

"The right of pre-emption contemplated by the act shall not 'extend to any land which is reserved from sale by act of Congress, or by order of the President, or which may have been appropriated for any purpose whatever.'"

An examination of the Act of 1830 clearly points out that this is a vast stretch of powers extended to the President *after* 1830. The President had no such power.

Why?

It is taken out of context.

The Act of 1830 was specifically directed at settlers or occupants of the public lands who were in possession of the land prior to the passage of that act. Quoting from the act itself:

"Be it enacted...That every settler or occupant of the public lands, ***prior to the passage of this act***, who is now in possession, and cultivated any part thereof in the year one thousand eight hundred and twenty-nine, shall be, and is hereby authorized to enter, with the register of the land office...Provided, however, That no entry or sale of any land shall be made, under the provisions of this act, which shall ***have been*** reserved for the use of the United States, or either of the several states, in which any public lands may be situated."
(Emphasis added)

In other words, the act was directed, as pointed out above, at land already occupied. Absolutely nothing was directed to future land. Further, we are talking about land in a territorial state of being, land that was clearly in federal ownership. This was not the case in San Francisco in 1866.

At Section 4 of that act, the following is particularly noteworthy, for it is from this section that the court in this case quotes:

"...this act shall not delay the sale of any of the public lands of the United States[247]...on which the right of pre-emption is claimed; nor shall the right of pre-emption, contemplated by this act, *extend to any land, which is reserved from sale by act of Congress, or by order of the President, or which may have been appropriated, for any purpose whatsoever*." (Emphasis added)

Again, note that this was applicable to land that had *been* appropriated: Past tense.

This extract from the act of 1830 as quoted by the court in Grisar v. McDowell is taken well out of context. It simply does not apply to San Francisco at all—36 years later. However that may be, the act of March 3, 1853 (5 Stat. at L. 453) was brought into play. This act provided for the survey of the public lands in California and extended the pre-emption system to them. With respect to that act, the court stated the following:

"...it is declared that all public lands in that state shall be subject to pre-emption, and offered at public sale, with certain specific exceptions, and among others of 'lands appropriated under the authority of this act, or reserved by competent authority."

The only question that could be raised—that was not—was the issue of title to the public lands. Did the Equal Footing Doctrine pass this title (even in trust) to the state upon statehood? This issue was never brought up; it was not argued, and, as such, it was not pivotal.

This case became one of the cornerstones of a list of cases to follow; that involve assumptions that have repeatedly been made by the court: the title to the public land has slipped from state to federal after statehood. Here we see that slipping process at a relatively early date.

247-Land of the United States was territorial land only. After statehood, this land passed to the state in conformance with the Equal Footing Doctrine. Its title was held by the federal government in trust for the state. It had to be surveyed before it could be conveyed by patent.

IRVINE v. MARSHALL (1858)

61 US 558; 15 L Ed. 994

This case is about unappropriated lands in the territories of the United States before statehood. Can a person acting for another, as his de facto agent or otherwise, take title to land in his own name and ignore the person for whom he was acting? By whose law is title conveyed or forfeiture declared, federal or territorial? Can the acts or customary practice of a governmental land department control the action or opinion of the court?

Territorial land in Minnesota was purchased by one party as an agent for another, using the other's funds. The title to that land was issued in the name of the agent and so recorded with the General Land Office of the United States, irrespective of the fact that the funds for its purchase were not his own. Later, the agent refused to relinquish title. This refusal was the subject of a suit brought before the territorial government, and by a technicality (a time-limit of 20 days expired in which to amend the complaint), title remained in the name of the agent. This iniquitous situation was the subject of a suit brought before the Supreme Court of Minnesota, which had no other option than to rule in favor of the agent whose name appeared on the patent; certain Minnesota statutes stated that title and possession are vested in the person named. This decision was appealed to the U.S. Supreme Court. Can the territorial or state government act as a medium for forfeiture of title to land, or does that lie with the federal government?

That is all that this case is about: Who has the final authority to convey title or authenticate a forfeiture of that title.

This case also touches upon the establishment of a trust relationship between the agent and the person for whom he was acting, inasmuch as this was the core to the problem in the first place.

There is much that the court observes as underlying information in finding that the court is not bound by the acts of federal governmental departments.

The following quotations are noteworthy:

"It cannot be denied that all the lands in the Territories, not appropriated by competent authority before they were acquired, are in the first instance the exclusive property of the United States, to be disposed of to such persons, at such times, and in such modes, and by such titles, as the government may deem most advantageous to the public fisc, or in other respects most politic."

Further:

"That within the provisions prescribed by the Constitution and by the laws enacted in accordance with the Constitution, the Acts and powers of the Government are to be interpreted and applied so as to create and maintain a system, general, equal, and beneficial as a whole."

And:

"The system adopted for the disposition of the public lands embraces the interest of all the States, and proposes the equal participation therein of all the people of the States. This system is, therefore, peculiarly and exclusively the exercise of a Federal power."

In short, only the federal government may convey title to, or settle matters concerning title of federal lands while such land is a part of a territory.

With respect to one party acting for another—a de facto trust in effect—the court cites Massie v. Watts, reported in the 6th vol. of Cranch, p. 148:

"According to the clearest and best established principles of equity, the agent who so acts [takes title in his own name and takes possession of the land] becomes a trustee for the principal. He cannot hold the land under an entry for himself, other wise than as a trustee for his principal."

As an aside, in a qualified way, this is what occurred in the West. Following the acquisition of the Louisiana Purchase, as well as the Mexican lands acquired by war and solemnized by the Treaty of Guadalupe Hidalgo, the United States became the trustee of the public lands to be held in trust for the future states.

The court reinforces what was said before in Wilcox v. Jackson (see the summary of that case), cites that case and makes the following statement:

"...an attempt to control, by the authority of the laws of the State of Illinois, the effect and operation of a right or title derivable from the United States to a portion of the public lands, this court thus emphatically declares the law: 'It has been said that the State of Illinois has a right to declare, by law [State law], that a title derived from the United States, which by their laws [State] is only inchoate [incipient] and imperfect, shall be deemed as perfect a title *as if a patent had issued from the United States*." (Emphasis added)

"But in this case no patent has [been] issued; and therefore, by the laws of the United States, the legal title has not passed, but remains in the United States. Now if it were competent for a State Legislature to say, that not withstanding this, the title shall be deemed to have passed, the effect would be, not that Congress had the power of disposing of the public lands, and prescribing the rules and regulations concerning that disposition but that Illinois possessed it. That would be to make the laws of Illinois paramount to those of Congress in relation to a subject confided by the Constitution to Congress only."

In short: Without a patent to the state, there was no transfer of title regardless of statehood, and the state of Illinois could not presume such transfer of title by virtue of statehood.

However interesting this may be, it is dicta as far as this case is concerned. This case hinges upon equity and righting of a wrong that was developed out of a technicality. Who has final jurisdiction to right that wrong? The court found a way to reverse the Supreme Court of Minnesota and did.

The Land Office recognized the certificate of purchase as evidence of title which was in the name of the agent. The court said:

"...they [officers of the Land Office] could by no means control the action or the opinion of this court in expounding the law with reference to the rights of parties litigant before them.... The reception of the certificate of purchase as evidence of title may be regular and convenient as a rule of business, but it has not been anywhere established as conclusive evidence, much less has it been adjudged to forbid or exclude proofs of the real and just rights of claimants."

In other words, the court found that the "real and just rights" were really established by the de facto trust, and that equity dictated that the agent, as a trustee, could not preempt the rights of the trustor or, more accurately in this case, eliminate them.

This case does not in and of itself establish ownership of the land by the federal government. That is not the subject matter of this case at all, even though it refers to and quotes extracts from Wilcox v. Jackson.

It does address itself to a trustee-trustor relationship and relies upon a violation of this relationship in this case in order to find for the plaintiff as well as find that a department of the government may not control or influence the opinion of the court.

With respect to the trustee-trustor relationship, this is of parallel importance, for it is this exact trustee-trustor relationship that is in question between the advocates of federal ownership of the public lands in perpetuity and those who claim that this land is owned by the states.

Other than the question directly before the court, all else is in dicta. This includes the extract from Wilcox v. Jackson.

KLEPPE v. NEW MEXICO (1976)

426 U.S. 529, 49 L.Ed. 2nd 34

This case is about the constitutionality of the Wild Free-Roaming Horses and Burros Act.

The act itself was enacted,

> "[to protect] all unbranded and unclaimed horses and burros on public lands of the United States from capture, branding, harassment, or death."

> [and] "they are to be considered in the area where presently found, as an integral part of the natural system of the public lands."

> [The animals are to be protected and managed] "as components of the public lands.... in a manner that is designed to achieve and maintain a thriving natural ecological balance on the public lands."

What this case is **not** about is equally important. It is not about ownership of the public lands inside the boundary of a given state. Ownership of this land by the federal government was stipulated to by the state of New Mexico. It is not a question for the court to decide. That question was not asked. It was not argued. In fact, by agreeing that the animals had been captured on "federal land," the defendant agreed, further, that the land was, indeed, in federal ownership. This made it unnecessary for the court to consider the ownership of the land at all. It was not a part of the controversy.

The defendant, New Mexico, argued that Congress lacked the power to control the animals on the public lands of the United States unless the animals were somehow migrating from state to state thus bringing the animals under the umbrella of interstate commerce or that they were damaging the public land. In other words, under the Powers Clause of the Constitution, Congress lacked the power to make rules and regulations relative to the animals in question unless the animals were engaged in migration that would place them under the powers granted to Congress by the Commerce Clause of the Constitution (interstate commerce) or the rights of a land owner to protect his property from damage.

The court found that Congress did indeed have the power to pass this Act and that it was within its power to do so under the Powers Clause of the Constitution.

However, in finding this conclusion, the court made some momentous observations, which are outlined below. These observations are important because this single case is a cornerstone for those who claim that the United States is the owner of the public lands.

It is certainly clear that in writing this opinion, Justice Marshall makes the assumption that all public lands within a state are federally owned. This case went beyond a previous case, New Mexico v. Morton,[248] which found that Congress' power under the Property Clause of the Constitution limited Congress to **protection** of the land from damage. The court noted that this act went beyond protection of the land; it extended protection to the animals themselves and reversed this earlier ruling.

With respect to the Property Clause, the court had this to say:

"...we must remain mindful that while courts must eventually pass upon them, determinations under the Property Clause are entrusted primarily to the judgment of Congress." The court cited U.S. v. San Francisco, Light v. United States, and U.S. v. Gratiot."

Further:

"...the [Property] Clause, in broad terms, gives Congress the power to determine what are 'needful' rules 'respecting' the public lands..... And while the furthest reach of the power granted by the Property Clause have not yet been definitively resolved, we have repeatedly observed that *'the power over the public lands thus entrusted to Congress is without limitation.'*" (Emphasis added)

The underlined quotation directly above comes from U.S. v. San Francisco, which, in turn, got it from U.S. v. Gratiot. The "without limitation" phrase comes from Gratiot, and that phrase is taken out of context here as elsewhere. The complete phrased is as follows:

248-New Mexico v. Morton, (1975) 406 F. Sup. 1237.

"...and this power is vested in Congress without limitation, and has been considered the foundation upon which the territorial government rests."

The "without limitation" phrase refers to land while it was in a territorial condition—not land after the state had entered the Union. See the appendix condensation of United States v. Gratiot.

In Kleppe v. New Mexico, there is no limitation with respect to the use of the word "territory."

"The decided cases have supported this expansive reading. [granting to Congress broad powers to make rules and regulations regarding public lands of the United States.] It is the Property Clause, for instance, that provides the basis for governing the Territories of the United States."

What the court had to say in Dred Scott v. Sandford about the limits of what "territory" means in the Constitution is ignored completely. Dred Scott v. Sandford states that the meaning and reference to territory in the Constitution is only that land ceded by the original thirteen colonies to the United States as a "common fund." Dred Scott was decided in 1856, well after the partial settlement of the land acquired by the Louisiana Purchase and the more recently acquired land included in the Treaty of Guadalupe Hidalgo: Land acquired as the spoils of war with Mexico. Land in both of these areas was commonly called "territory," but it is not the same and is *not* the territory as mentioned in the Constitution, even though the name is the same.

The following quotation is a direct refutation of the requirement that state legislative consent with respect to federal ownership of public lands within a state is necessary.

"The argument appears to be that Congress could obtain exclusive legislative jurisdiction over the public lands in the State only by consent, and that in the absence of such consent Congress lacks the power to act contrary to state law. This argument is without merit."

This certainly does not jibe with my reading of the Constitution. See Art. I, Sec. 8, Cl. 17.

It is assumed by the court that the public land within the state of

New Mexico is federally owned. How it became federally owned without the cession of the state no one has said. To be consistent with the Constitution, it cannot simply be commandeered in perpetuity. None of the original colonies had any such thing happen to them. They ceded only their "waste" land to the West. In any event, Justice Marshall assumes that the federal government is the titular owner of the public land inside the state of New Mexico, and he clearly indicates this in his findings.

An important point in this case is that New Mexico did not challenge ownership of the land. New Mexico claimed that the United States had only rights—"only the rights of an ordinary proprietor" as pointed out in Fort Leavenworth R. Co. v. Lowe (114 U.S. 525, and Paul v. United States, 371, U.S. 245.)

The court gave broader powers in this case.

"Appellee's [New Mexico] claim confuses Congress' derivative legislative powers, which are not involved in this case, with its powers under the Property Clause. Congress may acquire derivative legislative power from State pursuant to Art I, Sec. 8, Cl. 17, of the Constitution by consensual acquisition of land, or by non-consensual acquisition followed by the State's subsequent cession of legislative authority over the land...."

The court branded as unfounded the claim that consent of the legislature of the state was required for federal sovereignty of land within a state. The court did, however, leave the state free to enforce its criminal and civil laws on those lands.

"But where those state laws conflict with the Wild Free-roaming Horses and Burros Act, or with other legislation passed pursuant to the Property Clause, the law is clear: The state law must recede."

It is hard to envision anything broader than this. Congressional power under the Property Clause is indeed unlimited.

Some limiting of the Property Clause did occur in this case.

"While it is clear that regulations under the Property Clause may have some effect on private lands not otherwise under federal control, we do not think it appropriate in this declaratory judgment proceeding to determine the extent, if any, to which the Property Clause empowers Congress to protect animals on private lands or the extent to which such regulation is attempted by the Act....and [we] leave open the question of the permissible reach of the Act over private lands under the Property Clause."

While this case is clearly about the limits, or, more accurately, the lack of limits, of the Property Clause of the Constitution, it assumes without doubt that the public lands within a state are Federally owned.

However, the most telling extension of power given to the federal government with respect to Congressional power comes from U.S. v. Gratiot as quoted above.

This cannot be. Gratiot, in its full context limits the powers of Congress in the Property Clause to land while it was in a territorial condition. Everything other than the fact that this act is constitutional and not inconsistent with the Powers Clause of the Constitution is a matter of dicta. Dicta would extend to the assumption of federal ownership of the public lands within the state of New Mexico. This was not asked; this was not argued; this was not decided and as such it is not law. Nevertheless, attorneys take it as one of the cases that lays the foundation for their belief that these public lands are indeed federally owned.

LIGHT v. UNITED STATES (1911)

220 U.S. 523; 55 L. Ed. 570; 31 Sup. Ct. Rep. 485

This case is about trespass—trespass upon forest reserve land that is adjacent to public land which is, in turn, adjacent to 540 acres belonging to the plaintiff, Light. Light's 540 acres is about 2 miles from the forest reserve land, and it was his 500 head of cattle that he is accused of allowing to roam, unrestrained, upon this forest reserve land without having first secured a permit to do so.

Light declared that he did not need a permit and refused to secure one, claiming that the 1891 Forest Reserve Act that established the Holy Cross Forest Reserve in Colorado (the forest reserve land in question) was unconstitutional. On the other hand, the federal government declared that a permit was required in order for cattle to graze "in a national forest," and to graze upon that land without one was an act of trespass.

Besides, Light further declared, federal ownership of the land placed the owner in no different position than an ordinary property owner, and, as such, the federal government was required to fence its land as required by the laws of the state of Colorado. Failing to do this, Light claimed, the federal government was enjoined by the Colorado Statute from recovering any damages occasioned by cattle or other animals going thereon. Further, he claimed that the proclamation creating the reserve without the consent of the state of Colorado is contrary to and in violation of the trust granting the public lands "in trust for the people of the several states." Or, in other words, he declared that the Forest Reserve Act of 1891 was unconstitutional.

It is interesting to note that Light was really making two rather opposite claims: One, that if the property was a Federal Forest Reserve, it should be fenced like any other property of a private citizen consistent with the statutes of Colorado, and second, that it wasn't a forest reserve at all, inasmuch as the Forest Reserve Act of 1891 was unconstitutional. As we shall see in this case, he gave the court an out. It could rule on one issue and duck the other. This it did.

The court found only that Light was, indeed, trespassing upon federal land.

In the course of the court's finding, the following quotations are noteworthy:

"...it is argued that the act of 1891 providing for the establishment of reservations was void, so that what is nominally a Reserve is, in law, to be treated as open and uninclosed land as to which there still exists the implied license that it may be used for grazing purposes."

Here the court quotes Butte city Water Corp. v. Baker, 196 U.S. 126:

"...the Nation is an owner, and has made Congress the principal agent to dispose of its property,...Congress is the body to which is given the power to determine the conditions upon which the public lands shall be disposed of."

The court then quotes from Camfield v. United States, 167 U.S. 524, which is summarized in the appendix:

"The Government has with respect to its own land the rights of an ordinary proprietor to maintain its possession and prosecute trespassers. It may deal with such lands precisely as an ordinary individual may deal with his farming property. It may sell or withhold them from sale."

Then the court adds a short comment of its own and quotes from United States v. Beebee, 127 U.S. 342:

"And if it may withhold from sale and settlement it may also as an owner object to its property being used for grazing purposes, for 'the government is charged with the duty and clothed with the power to protect the Public Domain from trespass and unlawful appropriation.'"

Then, more germane to the issue of withholding the land indefinitely—an obvious retort to Light's claim that the Forest Reserve Act of 1891 is unconstitutional, the court refers to Stearns v. Minnesota (summarized in the appendix) in making the follow statement:

"The United States can prohibit absolutely or fix the terms on which its property may be used. As it can withhold or reserve the land it can do so indefinitely, Stearns v. Minnesota."

Read Stearns v. Minnesota. That case is about a contract between the state of Minnesota and certain railroads regarding taxation of the railroad and the grant-land they were given as an inducement to build the railroads. The court in that case makes the statement, in dicta, that Congress possessed the power to withdraw all the public lands in Minnesota from private entry or public grant.

It appears that the court was convinced that Light had willfully driven his cattle onto the reserved land, and in connection with that conviction, the court pretty well settled Light's claim that the federal government had no continuing rights on the forest reserve land in question or that Congress had no right to establish a reserve.

"'All the public lands of the nation are held in trust for the people of the whole country.' U.S. v. Trinidad Coal Co., 137 U.S. 160. And it is not for the courts to say how that trust shall be administered. That is for Congress to determine. The courts cannot...interfere when in the exercise of its discretion, Congress establishes a forest reserve for what it decides to be national and public purposes. In the same way and in the exercise of the same trust it may disestablish a reserve, and devote the property to some other national and public purpose. These are rights incident to proprietorship, to say nothing of the power of the United States as a sovereign over the property belonging to it. Even a private owner would be entitled to protection against willful trespasses...."

Continuing:

"Fence laws do not authorize wanton and willful trespass,...This the defendant did, under circumstances equivalent to driving his cattle upon the forest reserve."

The court then avoids the decision of constitutionality of the Forest Reserve Act of 1891 in the following manner by upholding the judgment of the lower court:

"The judgment was right on the merits, wholly regardless of the question as to whether the Government had enclosed its property. This makes it unnecessary to consider how far the United States is required to fence its property *or the other constitutional questions involved*." (Emphasis added)

The court then cites Siler v. Louisville & Nashville R.R., 213 U.S. 175:

"...where cases in this court can be decided without reference to questions arising under the Federal Constitution that course is usually pursued, and is not departed from without important reasons."

This is the only case that I am aware of that ever raised the issue of the constitutionality of the Act of 1891. Light's claim of the unconstitutionality of that act was really the basis of his claim that the federal government lacked the power to allow him to graze his cattle on public land adjacent to his property and at the same time to prevent him from grazing those same cattle on Forest Reserve Land immediately adjacent to the public land.

The court apparently did not think these reasons were important enough! Further, it is important to note that this case does not decide ownership of the public land. That was not the issue before the court. However, there is no doubt that the court certainly did assume that the ownership of the land was indeed federal. And it would be a presumption that a trust relationship existed between the federal and the state. This trust relationship has become foggier and foggier as the years have gone by, but that only makes it harder to see; it does not negate its existence.

As an aside, I do not know whether Light had filed for any water rights upon the forest reserve land. I presume not, inasmuch as it is not mentioned. It would be interesting to know if anyone had done so prior to this case. It is mentioned that water was better or more plentiful on the forest reserve land, leading to my supposition that the water may have been filed upon by someone.

STATE OF MONTANA v. UNITED STATES

(1981) 450 U.S. 544, 67 L Ed 2d 493, 101 S Ct. 1245

This case is about the right of the Crow Indian Tribe to regulate hunting and fishing by non-Indians on land within its reservation; namely, the bed and banks of the Big Horn River, which is entirely within the Crow Indian Reservation.

The related treaties with the Indian tribes were cited wherein their land was reduced from 38.5 down to 2.3 million acres. The ownership of this final 2.3 million acres was the issue inasmuch as the Crow Indian Tribe had disposed of, by sale, certain areas—28 percent to non-Indians. It was the regulation of this 28 percent of former reservation-land that brought about the suit. Who had the jurisdictional authority over its regulation, the Crow Indian Tribe or the United States? The specific area of dispute was the Big Horn River and its banks.

The Indians understood and assumed it was theirs and related the testimony of their original understanding. The District Court, in short, stated that the "language and circumstances" of the relevant treaties was insufficient to rebut the claim by the United States; that the United States does not and did not intend to divest itself of its navigable waters, (citing Holt State Bank); that only an Act of Congress could give the Tribe authority to regulate hunting and fishing by non-Indians; that all authority to regulate non-Indians resided in the state of Montana. After a reversal on appeal, the Supreme Court upheld the findings of the District Court as related above.

The reason:

> "[The District Court] thus concluded that the bed and banks of the river had remained in the ownership of the United States until they passed to Montana on its admission to the Union."

The time-line is interesting here.

1. 1851: Treaty of Fort Laramie (with Indians)

2. 1868: Treaty of Fort Laramie (with Indians)

3. 1889: Montana enters the Union as a State

Montana was a territory at the time of the two treaties, and, as such, the land was owned by the United States. The court stated that the bed and banks of the Big Horn River was not included in the two treaties, but instead was a de facto withholding of title because the waters under the Big Horn River were, in reality, navigable waters, and would not pass to the Crow Indian Tribe unless that intention to do so was "made very plain."

To justify this conclusion the court had this to say:

"...conveyance by the United States of land riparian [next to] to a navigable river carries no interest in the riverbed.

"Rather, the ownership of land under navigable waters is an incident of sovereignty....

"As a general principle, the Federal Government holds such lands in trust for future States, to be granted to such States when they enter the Union and assume sovereignty on an 'Equal Footing' with the established States. [The court cites Pollard's Lessee v. Hagan]

"After a State enters the Union, title to the land is governed by state law."

This is clear evidence that the court believed that "Equal Footing" extended to land ownership and not just to an equality to "Federal Councils." The totality of the Equal Footing Doctrine does dictate the transposition of title of federal (territorial) land to the state upon entry into the Union.

There is even more in this case than the issue of land under navigable waters being transferred to the state upon entry into the Union. "Uplands," even though small in amount, are also mentioned. The following from footnote number 1 (67 L.Ed. 2d 493 at 501) is as follows:

"...although the complain[t] in this case sought to quiet title only to the bed of the Big Horn River, we note the concession of the United States that if the bed of the river passed to Montana upon its admission to the Union, *the State at the same time acquired ownership of the banks of the river as well.*"
(Emphasis added)

Of additional importance in this case is the amount of reliance the court placed upon the notice of intent when withholding title, or, as was the case in this suit, the conveyance of such title. The court cited Martin v. Waddell[249]/ and U.S. v. Holt State Bank,[250] and said the following:

> "...nor was an intention to convey the riverbed expressed in 'clear and especial words.' [or] 'definitely declared or otherwise make very plain.'"

It was in the case of Utah Division of State Lands v. United States[251] that Sandra Day O'Connor used the same reference to Holt State Bank and said in that case:

> "...we simply cannot infer that Congress intended to defeat a future State's title to land under navigable waters 'unless the intention was definitely declared or otherwise made very plain.'"

Even though in each of these cases we are dealing with land under navigable waters, one instance is to withhold the conveyance of title and the other to issue it, the implication is clear: Conveyance of the title to territorial land does take place when a state is admitted to the Union "unless the intention was definitely declared or otherwise made very plain" that title was not to pass. In other words, the title to the land at that time cannot be withheld from the state unless the intention to withhold it is indicated in "clear and especial words," and/or the intention to withhold title is "definitely declared or otherwise made very plain."

The major importance of this case to this book is that it is a recent opinion that recognizes the Equal Footing Doctrine, and in conformance therewith, the passage of title from the United States of territorial land to the separate state upon statehood.

However, there is a difference in this case that clouds the simple issues: This case is about a treaty granting land to the Crow Indian Tribe, not about land destined for statehood. I think it was this difference that gave the court their justification for their seemingly adverse ruling.

249-Martin v. Waddell, 16 Pet. 411, 10 L Ed 997.

250-U.S. v. Holt State Bank, 270 US, 55; 70 L Ed 465; 46 S Ct 197.

251-Utah Division of State Lands v. United States: 482 U.S. 193; 96 L.Ed. 2d 162; 107 S Ct. 2318

NEVADA v. UNITED STATES (A.K.A.)

STATE OF NEVADA ex rel. NEVADA STATE BOARD OF AGRICULTURE v. UNITED STATES

(1981) 512 FS 2nd 166
(1983) 699 FS 2nd 486.

This case was first brought to trial by Nevada to question the authority granted the Interior Department of the United States by the Federal Land Policy Management Act of 1976 (FLPMA) from placing a moratorium—which had been done—on the disposal of the public land within the state of Nevada. Nevada alleged that the Land Policy Management Act of 1976 was unconstitutional, that it infringed Nevada's 10th Amendment rights and that it constituted a violation of the Equal Footing Doctrine. Declaratory relief was sought.

In spite of the above, it should be noted early on that at no time did Nevada claim ownership of any of the land. That was not what the case was about. It was about constitutionality and the Equal Footing Doctrine. In fact, in the 9th circuit, to which the Federal district decision was appealed, Justice Schroeder observed that Nevada **agreed** that eighty-eight percent of the land within the borders of Nevada was federally owned. Ownership was, therefore, not an issue.

Justice Schroeder observed:

"...this action did not claim title to any land; it challenged only the moratorium."

Continuing:

"...the amended complaint sought no additional or alternative relief to that sought in the original complaint."

And:

"Nevada agrees that this case does not involve a claim of title to land."

The reason there is a reference to an amended complaint is because the federal government withdrew its moratorium, in effect leaving Nevada nothing over which to sue. The court offered Nevada an opportunity to amend their complaint and continue the litigation. This Nevada did.

Nevada, in its amended complaint, expressed no further concern that a new moratorium would or could be instituted and inasmuch as the moratorium had been lifted, Schroeder said:

> "...all cases illustrative of the general rule that when action complained of have been completed or terminated, declaratory judgment and injunctive actions are precluded by the doctrine of mootness."

In other words, there was nothing the court could do under those circumstances but to affirm the 9th District Court's dismissal of the action.

In concluding, Justice Schroeder had this to say:

> "Any further challenges to actual or anticipated federal action with respect to Federally **held** lands will arise in a different legal and historical context from that surrounding the 1964 moratorium, which prompted this suit." (Emphasis added)

In reviewing the above and previous quotations, I find that this is about as close as the court could come to saying that the decision would have been different if a different question had been asked.

Inasmuch as the Supreme Court upheld the 9th District Court's decision, much emphasis has been placed upon the verbiage in that decision. In fact, any research on the subject of the Equal Footing Doctrine and state ownership of land upon entry into the Union is eventually going to lead to this case and beg a conclusion that the ownership of the land is unequivocally federal. However this may be implied, no such decision came from this case.

Nevada raised the issue, and admitted that the United States held the public land in trust and argued that the states were to be admitted on an "Equal Footing," and said in their argument:

> "...that Equal Footing is a constitutional condition of all states of the Union."

Nevada did not argue that, as a result of the Equal Footing Doctrine, the land became State land. To the contrary, Nevada admitted that the federal government owned "eighty-eight percent" of the land within the state of Nevada. In the absence of a claim of ownership to the land by the state of Nevada, the court had no alternative but to agree and quote from Alabama v. Texas:[253]

> "The Equal Footing Doctrine does not affect Congress' power to dispose of Federal property."

Of course not. It never did. The question is what is it that is federally owned. Does this include the public land after statehood? This last question was not asked, and was left up to the reader to assume. It was not decided.

Further, the court adds:

> "Federal Regulation which is otherwise valid is not a violation of the "Equal Footing" doctrine merely because its impact may differ between various states because of geographic or economic reasons."

All that says is that if something is valid for another reason it is not a violation of the "Equal Footing" doctrine.

And finally, the court cites United States v. Texas:[254]

> "The doctrine applies only to political rights and sovereignty; it does not cover economic matters, for there never has been equality among the states in that sense."

The court is saying that regulation, where it is in conformance to the Constitution, is not a violation of the "Equal Footing" Doctrine; that the doctrine applies to political rights and sovereignty, not economic equality. Sovereignty was not argued by Nevada with respect to ownership of the land.

The court does interpret Pollard v. Hagan in an interesting manner and makes this observation:

> "...there are no such limitations on territory subsequently acquired by the federal government by treaty or conquest. Thus it can be seen that the trust (to sell the public lands) found

---

253-Alabama v. Texas, (1954) 347 U.S. 272; 74 S.Ct. 481; 98 L.Ed. 689.
254-United States v. Texas, (1950) 339, U.S. 707; 70 S.Ct. 918; 94 L.Ed. 1221.

in Pollard's Lessee would not apply to such land owned by the United States within the borders of Nevada."

Take this reference to territory and compound it by the observation in Dred Scott v. Sandford that the Constitution, in referring to territory, talks about and refers to only the territorial land trust set up by the Northwest Ordinance, and one comes up with two separate trusts. The court is saying that no such trust existed for Nevada to sell the land and that the trust only existed for the Northwest Territory. My interpretation of the Treaty of Guadalupe Hidalgo is that a trust did exist, even though it was de facto in nature. And what are the implied trust provisions? Sell the land and make states out of that territory. Read again the quotation from the Treaty of Guadalupe Hidalgo itself in the section entitled, TREATIES.

The court summarizes several cases and makes the following observation:

> "No state legislation may interfere with Congress' power over the Public Domain;...the act of admission usually contains an agreement by the state not to interfere.... Nevada was admitted to the Union subject to such an agreement."

While the court cited one section of Pollard's Lessee, it ignores another observation in that case which declares that the disclaimer of ownership in the Enabling Acts, to which the court is referring, is null and void. I quote that portion of Pollard's Lessee as follows:

> "The right of Alabama and *every other new state* to exercise all the powers of government which belong to and *may be exercised* by the original states of the Union, must be admitted and remain unquestioned except so far as they are temporarily deprived of control over the public lands." (Emphasis added)

The court continues:

> "...the Constitution [Art. 4, Sec. 3 Cl. 2] entrusts Congress with power over the public lands without limitation; it is not for the court to say how that trust shall be administered, but for Congress to determine."

This is lifted exactly as it appears in the case of U.S. v. San Francisco. As I have already pointed out, this quotation from United States

v. San Francisco come directly from a quotation, taken out of context, in U.S. v. Gratiot. The "without limitation" has to do with territorial land only. See the summary of U.S. v. Gratiot in the appendix.

The court adds:

"Thus the consent of the state is not required for Congress to withdraw large bodies of land from settlement."

This was certainly true when the land was in a territorial state of being. However, as quoted in this case, the quotation, out of context from Gratiot, gives immense power to Congress that it clearly does not grant when taken in context.

This case did not decide ownership of the land. But it has been taken to imply exactly that: that the ownership of the land resides in the federal government. That question was simply not asked, and as such it was not answered.

NEW YORK v. UNITED STATES: (1992)

505 U.S. 144; 120 L. Ed. 120; 112 S.Ct.

This case revolves around radioactive waste and its disposal. Can a state be compelled by the federal government to accept waste from another state simply because it has a radioactive waste disposal site? This case has to do with federal mandates issued to the state to comply with their regulations. New York did not agree with the dictum and sought a clarification via this law suit. All powers given to Congress by the Constitution are explored in this case.

After all the exploring, the court found that two of the three provisions of the Low-Level Radioactive Waste Policy Amendments Act of 1985 were constitutional, while the last one, a matter of coercion, was not.

As Justice O'Connor put it:

"The constitutional question is as old as the Constitution: It consists of discerning the proper division of authority between the Federal Government and the State.... Congress has substantial power under the Constitution to encourage the States to provide for the disposal of the radioactive waste generated within their borders, the Constitution does not confer upon Congress the ability simply to compel the States to do so."

This case draws upon the provisions of the 10th Amendment and has this to say:

"It is in this sense that the Tenth Amendment 'states but a truism that all is retained which has not been surrendered.' United States v. Darby, 312 U.S. 100, 124; 85 L. Ed. 609; 61 S. Ct. 451, 132. As Justice Story put it, 'this amendment is a mere affirmation of what, upon any just reasoning, is a necessary rule of interpreting the construction. Being an instrument of limited and enumerated powers, it follows irresistibly, that what is not conferred, is withheld, and belongs to the state authorities.'"

Justice O'Connor quotes United States v. Butler, 297 U.S. 1; 80 L. Ed. 477; 56 S. Ct. 312:

"The question is not what power the Federal Government ought to have but what powers in fact have been given by the people."

Federal power has expanded and Justice O'Connor makes this observation:

"As the Federal Government's willingness to exercise power within the confines of the Constitution has grown, the authority of the States has correspondingly diminished to the extent that federal and state policies have conflicted.... We have observed that the Supremacy Clause gives the Federal Government 'a decided advantage in the delicate balance' the Constitution strikes between State and Federal power." [Gregory v. Ashcroft, 115 L. Ed. 2nd 410]

Adding:

"Congress may not simply 'commandeer the legislative processes of the State by directly compelling them to enact and enforce a federal regulatory program.'" [Hodel v. Virginia Surface Mining and Reclamation Ass. 452 U.S. 264, 288]

More:

"...the Constitution has never been understood to confer upon Congress the ability to require the States to govern according to Congress' instructions."

Justice O'Connor points out that our federal government is a government of all the people of the United States, and she quotes Hamilton in the *Federalist No. 15:*

"...we must extend the authority of the Union to the persons of the citizens—the only proper objects of government."

And in the *Federalist No. 16:*

"The government of the Union, like that of each State, must be able to address itself immediately to the hopes and fears of individuals."

Samuel Spencer, a delegate to the Constitutional Convention, is quoted by O'Connor:

> "...the framers explicitly chose a Constitution that confers upon Congress the power to regulate individuals, not States."

The following seems particularly apropos regarding federal mandates:

> "If state residents would prefer their government to devote its attention and resources to problems other than those deemed important by Congress, they may choose to have the Federal Government rather than the State bear the expense of a Federally mandated regulatory program, and they may continue to supplement that program to the extent state law is not preempted. Where Congress encourages state regulation rather than compelling it, state governments remain responsible to the local electorate's preferences; state officials remain accountable to the people."

With respect to the limits placed upon the federal government to encourage or compel a State to act, O'Connor makes this observation:

> "No matter how powerful the federal interest involved, the Constitution simply does not give Congress the authority to require the States to regulate. The Constitution instead gives Congress the authority to regulate matters directly and to pre-empt contrary state regulation. Where a federal interest is sufficiently strong to cause Congress to legislate, it must do so directly; it may not conscript state governments as its agents."

With respect to Congress exceeding its authority, the court had this to say:

> "Where Congress exceeds its authority relative to the States, therefore, the departure from the constitutional plan cannot be ratified by the 'consent' of the state officials"

In other words, each is responsible to comply with the limits placed upon them by the Constitution. One cannot add to the authority of the other if such added authority is counter to the provisions of the Constitution—even if one wanted to.

On the same subject:

> "The constitutional authority of Congress cannot be expanded by the 'consent' of the governmental unit whose domain is thereby narrowed, whether that unit is the Executive Branch or the State."

With a general view of the Constitution and its enumerated power, O'Connor added this:

> "But the Constitution protects us from our own best intentions; it divides power among sovereigns and among branches of government precisely so that we may resist the temptation to concentrate power in one location as the expedient solution to the crisis of the day."

All in all, this case is a plethora of observations and insight into the limitations and division of the powers of two sovereigns: The United States and the state.

POLLARD'S LESSEE v. JOHN HAGAN (1845)

(a.k.a. POLLARD v. HAGAN)

44 U.S. (3 How) 212; 11 L. Ed. 565

This case is about title to city lots in the city of Mobile, Alabama, whose property lines commence at the edge of a street on the shore of the land and extend outward into a canal off Mobile Bay, a large bay off of the Gulf of Mexico. How far out into the bay is the other boundary? Does the boundary of the lot(s) extend(s) into a canal beyond the high water mark of the tide? The questions asked of the Supreme Court: Which party owns the lots? Both parties have an issued title, one from the United States Government as a patent, the other coming ultimately from the state of Alabama as a deed. Which title is valid and which is not?

This case was considered by the court to be of great importance: In their words, "importance to all the States of Union, and particularly the new ones."

Because: The court was being "called upon to draw the line that *separates the sovereignty and jurisdiction of the government of the Union, and State government*." (Emphasis added)

Alabama was declared a territory in 1817 and became a state in 1819. Alabama was a territory carved out of what was originally a part of Georgia land that was ceded to the United States in 1802 for "a common fund," in trust, to pay debts incurred by the American Revolution—similar in principle and stipulations to those of the cession by Virginia to the United States for the same purpose.

The court restated the purpose of the stipulations of cession:

"...that all the lands within the territory ceded, and not reserved or appropriated to other purposes, should be considered as common fund for the use and benefit of all the United States, to be *faithfully and bona fide disposed of for that purpose, and for no other purpose whatsoever*." (Emphasis added)

The court paraphrased the Enabling Act that admitted Alabama to the Union and said:

"That the people of Alabama disclaimed all right and title to the waste or unappropriated lands lying within the State, and that the same should remain at the sole disposal of the United States, and that all navigable waters within the State should forever remain public highways, and free to the citizens of that State and of the United States, without any tax, duty, impost or toll therefor, imposed by said State,"

The court went on to add an important observation:

"That by these articles of the compact, the land under the navigable waters, **and the Public Domain above high water**, were alike reserved to the United States, and alike subject to be sold by them." (Emphasis added)

Note that the court drew no distinction between land under navigable waters and Public Domain land above high water. Note further that the purpose of retention of the land was that it was to be sold.

At this point the court makes a momentous declaration:

"We think a proper examination of this subject will show that the United State *never held any municipal sovereignty, jurisdiction, or right of soil in and to the territory, of which Alabama or any of the new States were formed; except for temporary purposes, and to execute the trusts created by the acts of Virginia and Georgia Legislatures, and the deeds of cession executed by them to the United States, and the trust created by the treaty with the French Republic, of the 30th of April, 1803, ceding Louisiana.*" (Emphasis added)

The court is making a point of "temporary municipal sovereignty" and the existence of a "trust" for a purpose and "for no other use or purpose whatsoever." The purpose is to divide the land into states.

Adding to this point, the court said:

"...it was the intention of the parties to invest the United States with the eminent domain of the country ceded, both national and municipal, for the *purposes of temporary government, and to hold it in trust for the performance of the stipulations and conditions expressed in the*

deeds of cession." (Emphasis added)

Further:

"...and to invest them with it, to the same extent, in all respects, that it was held by the States deeding the territories." [Meaning, Georgia, in this case.]

Alabama was admitted on an Equal Footing with the original states:

"...she succeeded to all the rights of sovereignty, jurisdiction, and eminent domain which Georgia possessed at the date of the cession, except...the public lands remaining in the possession and under the control of the United States ***for the temporary purposes provided for in the deed of cession, and the legislative acts connected with it***." (Emphasis added)

At this point, the court specifically limited the rights of the United States and said:

"Nothing remained to the United States...but the public lands. And if an express stipulation had been inserted in the agreement [stipulations in the ceding], granting the municipal rights of sovereignty, and eminent domain to the United States, such stipulation would have been void and inoperative; because, ***the United States have no constitutional capacity to exercise municipal jurisdiction, sovereignty, or eminent domain, within the limits of a State or elsewhere, except in the cases in which it is expressly granted [in the Constitution].***" (Emphasis added)

Further, with respect to public lands the court said:

"The rights of Alabama and every other new States to exercise all the powers of government which belong to and may be exercised by the original States of the Union, must be admitted, and remain unquestioned, except so far as they are, *temporarily*, deprived of control over the public lands."

Then the court reiterated the object of the cession and the limits this placed upon the parties.

"The object of all the parties to these contracts of cession was to convert the land into money for the payment of the debt, and to erect new States over the territory thus ceded; and ***as soon as these purposes could be accomplished, the power of the United States over these lands, as property, was to cease***." (Emphasis added)

The important point above is that there was a purpose for the trust, and that it had a termination point in time: Payment of the debt and the establishment of states. There was no other.

Importantly, the court then limits the power to be exercised by the United States within a state.

> "...the United States hold the public lands within the new States by force of the deeds of cession, and the statutes connected with them, ***and not by any municipal sovereignty which it may suppose they possess, or by compact with the new States*** [a referral to the disclaimer of title to land in the state's Enabling Act], ***The provision of the Constitution above referred to*** [Art. I, Sec 8, Cl. 17: "Forts, Magazines, Arsenals..."] ***shows that no such power can be exercised by the Unites States within a State***." (Emphasis added)

That is pretty clear. The United States may ***suppose*** that it has power of municipality and sovereignty within a state, but it does not exist unless it is authorized by the Constitution or unless it is there for a ***temporary*** purpose to fulfill the obligations of a trust.

With respect to the disclaimer to the land contained in the Enabling Act, the court said:

> [This] "cannot operate as a contract between the parties, but is binding as a law. Full power is given to Congress 'to make all needful rules and regulations respecting the territory or other property of the Unites States.' This authorized the passage of all laws necessary to secure the rights of the United States to the public lands, and to provide for their sale, and to protect them from taxation."

The phrase above, "binding as a law," sounds like a refutation, but it is not. The court is talking about holding the public land for sale and for establishing states out of the territory, nothing else. In other words, the federal government of the United States was designated, by law to become the exclusive sales agent for the land belonging to the individual state. As a matter of contract, this exclusive sales agency would last just as long as the provisions of the contract (spelled out in the treaties) were being faithfully pursued. The purpose of the contract? Sell the state land.

[There was another compelling reason for maintaining this exclusive sales contract: The sale of the public land was a major source of revenue.]

With respect to the Enabling Act and the public lands, the court had this to say:

> "The proposition submitted to the people of the Alabama territory, for their acceptance or rejection, by the act of Congress authorizing them to form a constitution and State government for themselves, **so far as they related to the public land within that territory, amounted to nothing more nor less than rules and regulations respecting the sales and disposition** of the public lands. The supposed compact [Enabling Act and its disclaimer]...conferred no authority, therefor, on Congress to pass the act granting to the plaintiffs the land in controversy." (Emphasis added)

Note the emphasized portion above. This certainly adds credence to the implied exclusive sales agreement to sell state land. In other words, the Enabling Act and its contained disclaimer by the state of Alabama to ownership of the land "conferred no authority...[for] Congress to pass the act granting [title to the land] to the plaintiffs..." Why not? Because the federal government did not own the land; it had become the property of the state of Alabama upon statehood.

The court then goes into a lengthy analysis of the history of the land mass, history of cession, the different treaties that affected it and its disposition. Finally, the court drew this conclusion:

> "Alabama is therefor entitled to the sovereignty and jurisdiction over all the territory within her limits, subject to the common law to the same extent that Georgia possessed in before she ceded it to the United States. To maintain any other doctrine, is to deny that Alabama has been admitted into the Union on an Equal Footing with the original States, **the constitution, laws, and compact, to the contrary notwithstanding.**" (Emphasis added)

With specific reference to navigable waters, the court cites several cases and concludes that even the Commerce Clause[255] did not give the United States powers to dispose of land under navigable waters and goes on to say:

> "For, although the territorial limits of Alabama have extended all her sovereign power into the sea, it is there, **as on the shore**, but municipal power, **subject to the Constitution of the United States**, 'and the laws which shall be made **in pursuance thereof**.'" (Emphasis added)

After the next phrase the court makes its finding. That phrase is either ignored by the proponents of ownership of the public lands in perpetuity by the federal government or misunderstood. That phrase:

> "By the preceding course of reasoning we arrive at these general conclusions:"

I would rather the court had said: "As a result of the foregoing," but the court did not. The difference is minimal, but even so, its absoluteness is minimized or ignored.

The court found that:

> "First. The shores of navigable waters, and the soils under them, were not granted by the Constitution to the United States, but were reserved to the States respectively."

That is an answer to the direct question of this case.

The reason:

> "Second. The new States have the same rights, sovereignty, and jurisdiction over this subject [land under navigable waters] as the original States."

This is an expression of the degree and extent to which the Equal Footing doctrine is to apply.

> "Third. The right of the United States to the public lands, and the power of Congress to make all needful rules and regula-

---

255- "to regulate commerce with foreign nations, and among the several States."

tions for the ***sale and disposition* thereof, *conferred no power to grant to the plaintiffs*** [title to land issued by the United States] ***the land in controversy in this case***." (Emphasis added)

The finding of the court is limited to land under navigable water, but all of the "preceding course of reasoning" draws no such distinction between land under navigable waters and dry land above the high water mark.

The proponents for the continuance of federal ownership of the public lands after statehood contend, rightly, that all of this—short of the actual finding—is in dicta and as such cannot be the basis for law. I find it most interesting that, to them, this dicta has no force and effect while the same kind of dicta that is found in case after case that "assumes" ownership by the federal government is not dicta and is "law." This is a startling incongruity. By using this criteria of logic and reasoning, this "assumed" ownership is no more law in this case than is the tracing and "preceding course of reasoning" in this case! I prefer to think that some "course of reasoning" by the court is far superior to none at all. In short, the big difference is that in this case the court has traced the history of ownership and burdens placed upon the transfer of title carefully and in detail. The history of "assumed" ownership has no such tracing in cessions, treaties, or historical basis at all.

The dissenting opinion to the decision of the court by Justice Catron is quite interesting. In his dissenting opinion, he points out that in an earlier opinion the court drew no distinction between "high lands of the United States as to the low lands and shores." While it was his belief that the Act of 1836 gave Congress the power to convey title he carefully points out that in that earlier opinion, the entire court unanimously agreed in that case, Pollard's Lessee v. Files (2 How., 602), concurred that there was no distinction between "highlands of the United States as to the low lands and shores."

SCOTT v. LATTIG (1913)

227 U.S. 229

This is one of the cases that comes closest to centering upon the central theme of Part Two of this book; who has dominion and sovereignty of the public lands when a state joins the Union, the United States or the new state?

I wish I could say that that particular issue was decided in this case, but it is not. Unfortunately, that very issue was not argued. The defendant in this case relied upon another route of law in his endeavor to establish his ownership of land in the middle of the Snake River. He lost. But then, from the perspective of sheer justice and equity and not law, he should have lost.

This case is about the ownership of a rather large island in the middle of the Snake River, which at that point was the border between Idaho and Oregon. Lattig received title to his land on the Idaho side of the river in 1894, and his neighbor to the south, Green, received his in 1895; both were parcels received by patent from the United States. How long either of them had been living on their parcels was not stated. The island in question in this case was near the center of the Snake River, a navigable river. In 1904, 10 years later, Scott settled upon the island. He wanted to homestead the island and discovered that for some reason it had not been surveyed. He requested that it be surveyed so that he could gain title to the island. This was done in 1906 by direction of the Commissioner of the General Land Office. This survey was filed, and Scott tendered his application to enter the island as a homestead. His application was accepted, and in due course, Scott received a patent from the United States.

After all these years, Lattig now entered the picture. Lattig claimed that he owned the entire island, the 55 acres directly opposite his land on the bank of the river as well as the remaining 83 acres directly opposite the land of his neighbor to the south, Green. The basis for his claim? By state law, (Idaho joined the Union in 1890, four years prior to Lattig's gaining title to his land) he contended that to its thread (navigable center) an island in a stream belonged to the party whose property abutted the shore on the side of the thread. That took care of his claim to the smaller portion of the island. As for the larger portion, he claimed it by adverse possession: The doctrine of I-got-there-first-and-I'm-strong-enough-to-keep-it. Both have a foundation in English Common Law, and it was this foundation upon which he relied for his claim of title, not that the land passed to the state upon statehood. That was not brought up and it was not argued.

The island had remained unsurveyed while all the surrounding land had been surveyed in 1868. Based upon this lack of survey, Lattig claimed an additional reason why his common law claim was valid.

It would be difficult for most fair-minded people to have much sympathy for Lattig's claim. It would appear as though Lattig had found a loophole in the law and wanted to take advantage of it. If this was the case, and from the information contained in the case it appears to be so, most fair-minded people are going to try to find a way to thwart such an action. And the court did. But to do it the court had to find that the patent issued to Scott was valid. This they did. Without going into a lot of detail about the difference between land adjacent to a navigable stream as differentiated from land adjacent to a stream that is not navigable, the following quotation sums up the courts finding on the issue of ownership of the island.

> "But the island, which we have seen was in existence when Idaho became a State, was not a part of the bed of the stream or land under the water, and therefore its ownership did not pass to the State or come within the disposal influence of its laws. On the contrary, although surrounded by the waters of the river and widely separated from the shore, ***it was fast dry land, and therefore remained the property of the United States and subject to disposal under its laws, as did the island which was in controversy in Mission Rock Co. v. United States***, 109 Fed. Rep. 763, 769-770, and U.S. v. Mission Rock Co., 189 U.S. 391." (Emphasis added)

As for the lack of survey, the court simply dismissed this by saying:

> "Of course, the error in omitting it from the survey did not divest the United States of the title or interpose any obstacle to surveying it at a later time."

The court found for Scott.

The fundamental issue still remains without a definitive decision: confirmation or refutation that the ownership passes to the state upon statehood. It is true that the court says that title to fast dry land does not pass to the state upon statehood, but unfortunately, this is based, not upon argument, but upon assumption by the court. It is not a basis for law. Assumptions are not decisions.

STEARNS v. STATE OF MINNESOTA (1900)

179 U.S. 223; 45 L Ed 162; 21 Sct 73

This case is about contract law and the right to tax: A contract born out of the bilateral agreement between railroads to build a railroad in exchange for grant-land issued to these same railroads, a percentage of the gross revenue derived from the operation of the railroad companies, and an agreement to not tax the property of the railroads. How binding was this contract? Did it go on forever? Did this exemption from taxation extend to all the other property not connected with the actual operation of the railroad? Was not the percentage of revenue in reality a tax? Those were the questions raised in this case.

In answering those questions, the court delved into the history of the land granted to the railroad and the de facto trust covering the land granted (the land was granted by the United States to the state for a purpose not specifically including the construction of railroads across their lands). This, then, touches upon trusts and the obligations imposed by those trusts, and Congressional power to make rules and regulations.

In another respect not associated with this case specifically, the court's findings reinforce the conditions of entry into the Union by each state as stipulated in the respective Enabling Act for that state.

The history of "taxing," granting agreements, or entering contracts authorized by Minnesota law had been addressed by the court earlier and found to be unconstitutional until a subsequent Minnesota law had been passed. This prior method affected the railroads.

The court then addressed the fact that all railroads were not treated exactly the same, however minor that difference happened to be.

With respect to the subject-matter of this book, the court then examined the land grant to the state, its purpose, and the limitations of that grant.

> "...the state could take and dispose of lands upon precisely the same terms which it took and disposed of the lands to the present plaintiffs...."

The court did not find a narrow path for changes initiated by the state legislature, but did insist that a contractual arrangement did exist, and said:

"...contractual exemptions of the property of the rail-road company in whole, upon consideration of a certain payment, cannot be changed by the state so as to continue the obligation in full, and at the same time deny to the company, either in whole or in part, the exemption conferred by the contract."

The court added:

"But there is another matter of significance. The lands in controversy were granted by Congress to the state as trustee."

And:

"These lands were not donated by Congress to the state, to be used by it for its own benefit and in its own way, but were conveyed to the state in trust with the understanding that, as trustee, it should use them in the best possible manner for accomplishing the purpose of the trust."

While the court addresses its comments directly to the issue of taxation, it has this to say:

"It is true that Congress might act so as in effect to keep withdrawn a large area of the state from taxation. Under reservation in the act of admission and the acceptance thereof by the state of Minnesota the right of Congress to determine the disposition of public lands within that state was reserved, and.... lands belonging to the United States are exempt from taxation by the state."

And without pause the court adds this important statement:

"So that Congress should determine that the great body of public lands within the state of Minnesota should be reserved from sale for an indefinite period it might do so, and thus the lands be excepted from taxation; and yet it cannot be imputed to Congress that it would discriminate against the state of Minnesota, or pass any legislation detrimental to it interests. It had the power to withdraw all the public lands in Minnesota from private entry or public grant, and, exercising that power, it might prevent the state of Minnesota from taxing a large area of its lands...."

With obvious reference to the Enabling Act of admission, the court adds the following:

"...the state expressly agreed that no tax should be imposed on lands belonging to the United States, that it should never interfere with the primary disposal of the soil within the state by the United States, or with any regulations Congress might find necessary for securing the soil to bona fide purchasers thereof. These provisions are not to be construed narrowly or technically, but as expressing a consent on the part of the state to the terms proposed by Congress; and among these terms were that the full control of the disposition of the lands of the United States should be free from state action. Whether Congress should sell or donate; what terms it should impose upon the sale or donation; what arrangements it should make for securing title to the beneficiaries—were all matters withdrawn from state interference by the terms of the enabling act and the Constitution."

Then the court adds this limiting statement:

"...until such time as all interests of the Unites States in the lands had ceased, but also until they had been used to fully accomplish the purposes for which Congress was selling or donating them."

This last statement certainly recognized the existence of another obligation: Purpose. The purpose of these lands is defined in the treaties by which they were obtained. For Minnesota, it was the Louisiana Purchase, solemnized by the Treaty of Paris in 1803.

"The inhabitants of the ceded territory shall be incorporated in the Union of the United States and admitted as soon as possible according to the principles of the federal Constitution..."

Disposition of land was a necessary adjunct of this treaty, otherwise the land could not become a state, and the purpose of the treaty would not have been fulfilled.

The Equal Footing Doctrine required equality. Rules and regulations regarding how the land was to be disposed of was a federal matter, but disposition—not retention—was the avowed purpose as defined by the treaties regarding what was to happen to the land. Retention was never a defined purpose.

It is with some irony that I must point out the demands of the treaties with respect to the trust relationship between the trustor and trustee as pointed out above: Note the breach of trust that has occurred primarily in the western states by the federal government's retaining, in perpetuity, the public lands—a clear violation of the de facto trusts created by the Treaties of Paris and Guadalupe Hidalgo.

It is quite obvious that a de facto trust was established. Further, equity dictates that when the purpose of the trust has been accomplished, the trust is to be extinguished. However, the avowed purpose of the de facto trust was never consummated. It was stalled in perpetuity for the altogether too obvious purpose of retention of the public land in federal control. If this were a civil matter today, such a stalling would render the trust null and void.

With all of the above having been said, the court declared that a contract did in fact exist, that it could not be changed by subsequent state legislation, which, in effect, raised the "taxation" (tax) of the property of the railroads.

That, after all, was the subject of the case: Contract and taxation.

Being outside of the issue of the subject matter of the case itself, there is nothing in this case that says that the land is the property of the United States. It was not decided. If anything, it is in dicta.

UNITED STATES V. CALIFORNIA (1947)

332 U.S. 19; 91 L. Ed. 1898

This case is about ownership of the offshore submerged land off the coast of California between the low-water mark and the three-mile limit.

The United States and California both presented their arguments for their singular ownership, tracing the precedent for such ownership, back to the original thirteen colonies and to the jurisdiction and ownership of that land that was a part of the original cession from Great Britain to the separate, sovereign colony states.

The two compelling arguments were divergent:

California claimed that the off-shore submerged lands were theirs because the original colonies acquired it by cession from Great Britain as separate, sovereign states, and, as such under the Equal Footing doctrine, those lands belonged to them. The United States claimed that the colonies did not acquire the off-shore submerged land as a part of the cession, and the court agreed with them. The following statement sums up their reasons for finding that the submerged lands beyond the low water mark to the three-mile limit belong to the United States.

> "From all the wealth of material supplied, however, we cannot say that the thirteen original colonies separately acquired ownership to the three-mile belt or the soil under it, even if they did acquire elements of the sovereignty of the English Crown by their revolution against it."

Adding:

> "Those who settle this country were interested in lands upon which to live, and waters upon which to fish and sail. There is no substantial support in history for the idea that they wanted or claimed a right to block off the ocean's bottom for private ownership and use in the extraction of its wealth."

California had alleged that there was no arguable controversy. The court decided otherwise. Further, California argued that the Attorney General of the United States had not been granted power either to file the suit or to maintain it. The court decided otherwise, and in so doing had the following to say:

> "...Article IV, Sec. 3, Cl. 2 of the Constitution vests in Congress 'Power to dispose of and make all needful Rules and Regulations respecting the Territory or other Property belonging to the United States....' We have said that the constitutional power of Congress in this respect is without limitation. United States v. San Francisco, 310 U.S. 16, 20-30. Thus neither the courts nor the executive agencies could proceed contrary to an Act of Congress in this congressional area of national power."

Note the reference to U.S. v. San Francisco. It is here in U.S. v. San Francisco that the earliest use of the condensed phrase taken out of context from Gratiot, "without limitation," is used by the court referring to Congressional power in this area. This same condensed phrase appears in New Mexico v. Kleppe as well as others.

See U.S. v. San Francisco, which is summarized in the appendix. That quotation is out of context. The actual complete quotation in Gratiot is as follows:

> "And the Constitution of the United States (article four, section three) provides, 'That Congress shall have power to dispose of and make all needful rules and regulations respecting the territory or other property, belonging to the United States.' The term 'territory,' as here used, is merely descriptive of one kind of property, and is equivalent to the word 'land.' And Congress has the same power over it as over any other property belonging to the United States; ***and this power is vested in Congress without limitation, and has been considered the foundation upon which the territorial government rests***," (My emphasis added)

The quotation from United States v. San Francisco is shortened. It is the same as the one above except that it stops after "without limitation" and continues with the following additive which substantially alters the original meaning in Gratiot from which it is taken:

> "And it is not for the courts to say how that trust shall be administered. That is for Congress to determine. Thus, Congress may constitutionally limit the disposition of the Public Domain to a manner consistent with its views of public policy."

The phrase "without limitation" is limited to **territory** and does not include public land after the state entered the union.

Note that all of the above with reference to "without limitation" has to do with the authority of the Attorney General to file the case. This is dicta as far as the subject matter of this case is concerned. This case is about ownership of land, not Congressional power to make rules and regulations.

With respect to the Equal Footing doctrine and the original states, the court had the following to say:

> "In the Pollard case it was held, in effect, that the original states owned *in trust for their people* the navigable tidewaters between high and low water mark within each state's boundaries, and the soil under them, as inseparable attribute of state sovereignty. Consequently, it was decided that Alabama, because admitted into the Union on 'an Equal Footing' with the other states, had thereby become the owner of the tidelands within its boundaries. Thus the title of Alabama's tidelands grantee was sustained as valid against that of a claimant holding under a United States grant made subsequent to Alabama's admission as a state." (Emphasis added)

Note the use of the "an Equal Footing" phrase. In commenting on the Pollard case, the court is calling attention to the fact that Alabama was admitted on an Equal Footing with the other states, and that incidental to this admission to the Union, Alabama acquired title to the tidelands in order to be on an Equal Footing with the other states.

This is a very important point to remember because the Supreme Court clearly includes title to land, even though it is submerged—a geographical and physical element—goes along, part and parcel, with political equality as an integral part of the Equal Footing Doctrine.

In earlier cases, the Equal Footing Doctrine has been restricted to mean political equality only. Here we see, in a recent case, that this equality is extended beyond political equality to another element, sovereignty and dominion over land as well.

However this may be, note the following quotation:

> "[The court] does question the validity of the rationale in the Pollard case that ownership of such water areas, *any more*

than ownership of uplands, is necessary incident of state sovereignty contemplated by the 'Equal Footing' clause. The court cites U.S. v. Oregon, 295 U.S. 1, 14. (Emphasis added)

In a way this seems to place a certain amount of emphasis on "ownership of uplands" and questions this as a part of what was contemplated by the Equal Footing Doctrine. In other words, the court questions—without deciding—that the Equal Footing Doctrine may extend to "uplands."

As a result, the phrase "with other states" becomes the key issue as a state enters the Union on an Equal Footing with the other states. Does that mean that, in order to be equal, the state has a right of sovereignty over its lands, as did all the other states? I think that it certainly does.

The dissenting opinion of Justice Reed is important to note. While it is not a part of the opinion, it does, nonetheless, indicate a view held by a minority of the court.

"The original states were sovereignties in their own right,...Any part of that territory which had not passed from their ownership by existing valid grants were and remained public lands of the respective states. California, as is customary, was admitted into the Union 'on an Equal Footing with the original States in all respects whatever.' 9 Stat. 452. By Section 3 of the Act of Admission [Enabling Act], the public land within its borders were reserved for disposition by the United States. ***'Public lands' were used in its usual sense of lands subject to sale under general laws***." (Emphasis added)

This is an important point to take into consideration when viewing the present policy of withholding land from sale and claiming its federal ownership in virtual perpetuity. The states entered the Union on one basis, and after having entered, that basis was changed: The land was withdrawn from sale. In other words, a contract or provision of a de facto trust was broken.

Justice Reed makes this observation is a letter from Jefferson to the British Minister in early 1793 regarding waters and land out to the three-mile limit:

"This distance can admit of no opposition, as it is recognized by treaties between some of the powers with whom we are connected in commerce and navigation, and is as little, or less, than is claimed by any of them on their own coasts. H. Ex. Doc. No. 324, 42d Cong., 2d Sess., pp. 553-54.

Then Justice Reed makes this observation:

"If the original states did claim, as I think they did, sovereignty and ownership to the three-mile limit, California has the same rights in the lands bordering its littoral."

Continuing:

"While no square ruling of this Court has determined the ownership of those marginal lands [referring to lands under the sea], to me the tone of the decisions dealing with similar problems indicates that, *without discussion, state ownership has been assumed*." (Emphasis added)

In reverse, *without discussion*, federal ownership has been assumed regarding ownership of uplands after statehood.

In another dissenting opinion, Justice Frankfurter makes the telling observation that a Court's decree may not be the last word and had this to say with respect to an implied government interest in the land:

"...it implies that the Government has some proprietary interest. That has not been remotely established *except by sliding from absence of ownership by California to ownership by the United States*." (Emphasis added)

Such has certainly been the case with respect to the public lands.

UNITED STATES v. CALIFORNIA (1978)

436 U.S. 32; 56 L. Ed. 2d 94; 98 S Ct 1662

The subject of this case has to do with the title and control over the submerged lands and waters within the Channel Island National Monument, which are situated within the three-mile limit off the California mainland. Who has the sovereignty and dominion over this land—the United States or the state of California?

The court first cited the Antiquities Act of 1906:

"The President of the United States is authorized, in his discretion, to declare by public proclamation historic landmarks, historic and prehistoric structures, and other objects of historic or scientific interest that are situated upon the lands owned or controlled by the Government of the United States to be national monuments,..."

Note that this act is directed toward ruins and buildings and not land.

[As an aside, it was this same Antiquities Act that President Clinton evoked when he recently set aside 1,600,000 acres in Utah—a land set aside, not buildings.]

In 1938, President Roosevelt appropriated most of Anacapa and Santa Barbara Islands for this national monument relying upon the disclaimer clause of California's Enabling Act for his authority to claim that this land was federally owned and that it had not passed into state ownership upon California's acceptance into the Union in 1850, nearly 90 years earlier.

In 1949 President Truman issued another proclamation enlarging the monument to encompass "the area within one nautical mile of the shoreline of Anacapa and Santa Barbara Islands..."

The court clarified the dispute thus:

"What is disputed in this litigation is dominion over the submerged lands and waters within the one-mile belts

363

surrounding Anacapa and Santa Barbara Islands."

While the case of U.S. v. California (1947) held that the submerged lands off the coast of California were indeed federal land and did not pass to the state of California upon statehood, the court in this case concluded that the Submerged Lands Act of 1953 was intended to undo the effect of the court's 1947 decision (U.S. v. California (1947).

In enacting the Submerged Lands Act of 1953, Congress:

"...recognized, confirmed, established, and vested in and assigned to the States '(1) title to and ownership of the lands beneath navigable waters within the boundaries of the respective States...[and] (2) the right and power to manage, administer, lease, develop, and use the said lands and natural resources....'"

This included the submerged lands and waters within one mile of Anacapa and Santa Barbara Islands.

There was one catch with which the court had to deal.

The United States, in their pleading, claimed they were exempted from the grant by the Submerged Lands Act and they still owned the land because the United States actually occupied the land under "claim of right."[256] The court rejected their claim and declared that the operation of the Submerged Land Act was binding and that "the Government's proprietary and administrative interest in these areas passed to the State of California in 1953."

The effect of this case was to confirm that once land had passed into state ownership at statehood, it could not be incorporated into the Channel Island National Monument by Presidential proclamation. In other words, at the time of statehood, the federal government lost jurisdiction and proprietary interest over the land and no incremental ownership by the federal government remained. Further, the court rejected the federal government's "claim of right:" Even though you have occupied the land and claim that it is yours by adverse possession, that is not so. "Claim of Right" is not a valid claim for the federal government. It would be contrary to the Constitution.

256-"Claim of Right" is covered in that section titled PRESCRIPTIVE LAW AND THE "CLAIM OF RIGHT."

UNITED STATES v. GRATIOT (1840)

39 U.S. (14 Pet) 526; 10 L. Ed. 573

This case is about a contract to purchase and smelt lead from a United States lead mine in a territory which later was to become part of the state of Illinois. Illinois was admitted to the Union in 1818. The United States retained the lead mine and operated it as a government-owned mine under the authority of the President of the United States.

The basic question raised in this case was this: Does the President, alone, have the authority to operate, lease, or contract services or function of a government owned lead mine under authority delegated to him by an Act of Congress (3rd March, 1809, a date that pre-dated the entry of Illinois into the Union, and as such a date when the land was in a territorial state)?

The case brought was specifically about collection on a bond for services the United States considered unperformed. The defendants (Gratiot, et al.) claimed that the President had no such authority to enter into the contract—that the President of the United States had no such power under the Act of Congress, March 3, 1807 to make a contract. The court found that Congress did in fact have the power to delegate to the President such authority.

At the time of this Act of Congress, the location of the mine was located in the territory of Illinois and, as such, federal land. The state had not yet been accepted into the Union. The lead mines were within the Northwest Territory, ceded by Virginia to the United States in 1784 for a "common fund." A consequence of that cession in 1783 was that the Continental Congress passed the ordinance of 1785, which stated, in part, that the land would be surveyed and sold, and further, that all springs and mines would be noted and reserved for the United States, along with "one third part of all gold, silver, copper, or lead mines, to be sold or disposed of as Congress should afterwards direct."

Congress did "afterwards direct." In 1796, Congress directed that the surveys note "all mines, salt licks, salt springs, and mill sites," and a mile square around it be "reserved for the future disposal of the United States." In 1800 Congress added "that the land of the United States reserved for future disposition, might be let on leases by the surveyor-general for terms not exceeding seven years." In 1807 Congress passed another act. This act withdrew parts of the land that remained unsettled from settlement and allowed the settlers to remain as "tenants at will" with the approbation of the President. However, if on this land a spring or mine existed, the "tenant" was not allowed to work the mine without the "approbation" of the President. In that same act, the President was authorized to lease such springs and mines "for a term not exceeding five years."

It was argued by the defendant that this act limited the "reservation" or lease to five years, and that this limit was not to be defeated by any renewals thereof. Further, it was argued that in another territorial area (by that time the state of Missouri), the lead mines had become the jurisdictional property of the state of Missouri upon its entry into the Union and that: "the whole system was driven out of the State of Missouri. In that state there is no longer a body of tenantry, holding under leases from the United States." In other words, when Missouri entered the Union, federal authority ceased.

Congress had been reserving land within the territory (established by the cession of the original colonies) by successive acts, certain lands for "future disposition." The term of the reservation, or lease for an "indefinite period for future disposition" did not exceed seven years.

The court, in this case, was clear in pointing out that

"...the only point here submitted is, whether or not the contract in question is a lease."

By saying this, the court demurred on the issue that the defendant raised:

"...that the Constitution confers no power to make such a contract, under the authority given to Congress to dispose of, and make rules and regulations respecting, the public territory; that the power of sale, and of such previous measures as are necessary for that purpose, and for ascertaining the value of the lands, is all the Constitution confers; and that the grant leases might have the effect of establishing a permanent tenantry within the State."

This was the background which the court considered.

The court pointed out that the title of the Act of Congress on the 3rd of March, 1807 was as follows:

"An Act making provision for the disposal of the public lands situate[d] between the United States military tract and the Connecticut reserve, and for other purposes."

The land referred to above was what we know of today as "West Point:" A military post. Two other purposes were outlined: Lead mines in the Indiana territory and authorization for the President to lease such lead mines as outlined above.

The court made the following statement:

"And the Constitution of the United States (article four, section three) provides, 'That Congress shall have power to dispose of and make all needful rules and regulations respecting the territory or other property, belonging to the United States.' The term 'territory,' as here used, is merely descriptive of one kind of property, and is equivalent to the word 'lands.' And Congress has the same power over it as over any other property belonging to the United States; **and this power is vested in Congress without limitation, and has been considered the foundation upon which the territorial government rests**." (Emphasis added)

This is one of the most important—and quoted, even if out of context—findings of the Supreme Court. It has been repeatedly taken out of context and its meaning slanted or even perverted by its reduction. The portion used in many following cases eliminated the last phrase in its entirety, to wit: "and has been considered the foundation upon which the territorial government rests."

A careful reading of this entire quotation makes it clear that what the court is addressing is land that is property of the United States—territorial land, not public land belonging to the state after its entry into statehood.

This elimination of the last phrase of this emphasized paragraph above changes the entire meaning of the court's finding in U.S. v. Gratiot.

Note that this entire subject is about land that was in a territorial condition—territory established by session of land to the United States from Virginia for "a common fund."

This fact alone limits the finding of this case to territorial land from Virginia or the like and cannot—or more accurately, should not—infer that this finding is universal and applies to all other territorial land later acquired from France or from Mexico. It is not the same kind of territorial land at all.

Based upon this fact, the finding that "this power is vested in Congress without limitation" means that it applies solely to territorial land (specifically, land by cession such as from Virginia). The rest of that quotation suggests this as well: "and has been considered the foundation upon which the territorial government rests."

Without doubt, this misquoted section has been used to give to Congress powers the judge in this case never, ever intended it to have.

UNITED STATES v. MISSION ROCK CO. (1903)

189 U.S. 391

This case is about the ownership of two relatively small rocks in the San Francisco Bay, as well as the submerged, now filled land adjacent to the two rocks. The question was asked of the court in 1903, "Who owns them, now?" And, "Who had the right to convey the submerged tidelands in 1870, well after the state of California joined the Union?"

In 1870, the state of California granted, by patent about 14 acres of the submerged land around these two rocks. The submerged land was filled to the extent that by 1890, the fast land area had been increased to about 4 acres, upon which dry-docks, extensive wharves and warehouse building had been built.

In 1899, the president issued an order declaring the islands permanently reserved for naval purposes. In their court action that followed this declaration, the United States claimed all the filled land and compensation for its past use.

To my knowledge, the issue of state of California's ownership of the two rocks was neither raised nor argued. Ownership of these two rocks was **assumed** to be federal inasmuch as neither of them had been claimed, and as such they were **assumed** to remain a part of the Public Domain, with the right of disposal remaining with the federal government.

Circuit Court of Appeals Justice Ross, whose finding in this case was upheld by the Supreme Court, had this to say about the history of the two rocks:

> "...the title thereto [of the two small island-rocks] is still in the United States, *unless the same passed to the state of California by virtue of the admission of that state into the Union under act of congress of September 9, 1850 [the date California joined the Union],* or unless the United States relinquished its title thereto under subsequent acts of congress." (Emphasis added)

However, he went on to quote the disclaimer clause of the California Enabling Act that states:

"...the people of the state shall never interfere with the primary disposal of the public lands within its limits, and shall pass no law and do no act whereby the title of the United States to, and right to dispose of...shall be impaired or questioned."

Of particular importance and note in this Circuit Court's finding is a reference to the upland:

"...the...court held in Weber v. Board, 18 Wall. 57, 65, 21 L. Ed. 798, that although such title was acquired by the United Stated by the cession from Mexico, equally with the title to uplands, *they held it only in trust for the future state*." (Emphasis added)

Emphatically, the Circuit Court went on to state that California became the titular owner of all the "soil under the tide waters of the Bay of San Francisco, subject to the paramount right of navigation over the water...."

After considerable explanation as to why, the Circuit Court said:

"...we are of the opinion that the United States is not entitled to recover from the defendant any of the submerged land included in the grant from the state of California...."

Then Justice Ross went on to add this statement with respect to the two rocks:

"We are further of the opinion, however, that that grant did not include the two rocks or island above mentioned, for the reason that *neither of them ever passed to the state*...." (Emphasis added)

In other words, the United States retained title to the two small islands, but the filled land surrounding them was not theirs; title to this submerged land was subject to the disposal rights of the state of California.

This finding, however, was not acceptable to the United States; they wanted it all. And, as such, they elected to appeal the decision to the Supreme Court.

The Supreme Court upheld the lower Court.

This case is of particular importance inasmuch as it does the following: It gives particular weight to the disclaimer contained in the California Enabling Act quoted above (ignoring what Pollard v. Hagan and Coyle v. Smith had to say about such disclaimers); it assumes—again without deciding—federal ownership of the public land after statehood; it ignores the Equal Footing Doctrine; but it does recognizes that a trust relationship does exist with respect to this public land, to wit, "...they held it only in trust for the future state."

Of course, this last quotation begs the question: Doesn't the trust expire when the "future state" become a state and joins the Union?

UNITED STATES V. CITY AND COUNTY OF SAN FRANCISCO (1939)

310 U.S. 16; 84 L. Ed. 1450

Essentially, this case has to do with this question: Does the city and county of San Francisco have the right to sell power (electric energy) generated or water stored for its exclusive use to a private utility as a commodity for resale? The location of the dam and generating facility is the Hetch-Hetchy Dam inside Yosemite and Stanislaus National Parks—federal lands.

These lands were acquired by the federal government strictly in accordance with the U.S. Constitution: The land was ceded to the U.S. by the legislature of the state of California and accepted subsequently thereto by Congress, thus becoming federal land.

Justice Black, in finding that the intent of the legislation permitting San Francisco to develop power and water was for its exclusive use and for distribution to the ultimate consumer, not to another utility, had this to say germane to the issue of Part Two of this book:

> "Article 4, Sec. 3, cl. 2 of the Constitution provides that 'Congress shall have the Power to dispose of and make all needful Rules and Regulations respecting the Territory and other Property belonging to the Unites States.' The power over the public land thus intrusted to Congress is without limitation. [The court then cites U.S. v. Gratiot, 14 Pet (U.S.) 526, 527, 10 L ed 573, 574.] 'And it is not for the Courts to say how that trust shall be administered. That is for Congress to determine.' [The court then cites Light v. U.S., 220 US 523, 537, 55 L. Ed. 570, 574, 31 S Ct 485.] Thus, Congress may constitutionally limit the disposition of the Public Domain to a manner consistent with its views of public policy."

There is no question about this ruling. The land was legally, in all respects, federal. And as such, the federal government had the right "like any other private citizen" to enter into a contract. They did.

Note the reference to U.S. v. Gratiot. This 1840 decision rears its head as pivotal. See the appendix condensation of U.S. v. Gratiot. Note therein that the quotation cited is out of context: namely, "And this power is vested in Congress without limitation, ***and has been considered the foundation upon which the territorial government rest.***"

In other words, correctly interpreted from Gratiot, Congressional power is coincidental with ***territorial government***, inasmuch as the territorial government was directly established by Congress. And further, Congress could make whatever changes in that territorial government it saw fit: The territorial government was an extension of Congressional power. This power included power over territorial land as well, but it was limited to that time before the territory became a state. It did not and does not extend to state lands after admission to the Union. At that time, Congressional power over the land ceased to exist. It was transferred to the state.

The reference, as used by Justice Black, gives a much enlarged meaning to Congressional power than that which was intended in Gratiot.

Further, while compelling and reinforcing to the idea of expanded congressional power, Justice Black's reference to Gratiot is dicta. And as such it cannot be used as the basis for law. That subject was not argued; it was not an issue in the case.

The quotation above, "Thus Congress may constitutionally limit the disposition of the Public Domain to a manner consistent with its views of public policy," comes from the reference to Light v. U.S. The following is from the reference on page 537 cited by Justice Black:

As cited in Light v. U.S. (a direct quote from U.S. v. Trinidad Coal Co., 137 U.S. 160):

"All the public lands of the nation are held in trust for the people of the whole country."

The court continues in Light:

"And it is not for the courts to say how that trust shall be administered. That is for Congress to determine. The courts cannot compel it to set aside the lands for settlement; or to suffer them to be used for agricultural or grazing purposes; nor interfere when, in the exercise of its discretion, Congress establishes a forest reserve for what it decides to be national and public purposes. In the same way and in the exercise of the same trust it may disestablish a reserve, and devote the property to some other national and public purpose. These are rights incident to proprietorship, to say nothing of the power of the United States as a sovereign over the property belonging to it."

This direct quote from U.S. v. Trinidad Coal Co. indicates a recognition of a trust relationship with respect to land held by the federal government. The National Parks are no such trust. The two National Parks involved in this case (U.S. v. City and County of San Francisco) are Yosemite and Sequoia National Parks, and they are held by the federal government "like any other private person." On the other hand, land held by the federal government after a state has entered the Union is, at the very least, held in trust for the state, and at most, it is a withholding of recognition of state ownership after the state's entry into the Union. Light v. U.S. certainly evidences the trust relationship. See the summary of Light v. U.S. in the appendix.

UNITED STATES V. TEXAS (1950)

339 U.S. 707; 94 L.Ed. 1221

This case is about title (ownership) of land under the sea for a distance of 3 miles from shore. Is it federal land or state of Texas land?

Texas, an independent nation recognized by the United States as such, joined the Union in 1845 on an "Equal Footing" with the other states, by treaty, retaining "all the vacant and unappropriated land lying within its limits," (L. Ed. p. 1225). No land was delivered to the federal government. Intent: Sale of this land was to be applied to payment of Texas debt, inasmuch as none of this debt was assumed by the federal government.

The question of state title to land from high-water line to low-water line was never questioned; Pollard v. Hagan was cited and title to that land was reaffirmed to be that of the state.

The basic question was this: Exactly what was required by the Equal Footing Doctrine to equate Texas with the other states? Did this mean that the land of a sovereign nation—which Texas was—must be forfeited from the low-water line to the 3-mile limit in order to be equal?

The court decided in the affirmative; Texas must give up that land in order to be on an Equal Footing with the other states.

The following quotations are noteworthy:

"The 'Equal Footing' clause has long been held to refer to political rights and to sovereignty."

Note the word "sovereignty." See that section entitled DOMINION AND SOVEREIGNTY for a definitive meaning. Sovereignty means ownership and the right of disposition.

The court cited Stearns v. Minnesota (179 US 223, 245; 45 L. Ed. 162, 174).

"It does not, of course, include economic stature or standing. There has never been equality among the States in that sense. Some States when they entered the Union had within their boundaries tracts of land belonging to the Federal Government;

others were sovereigns of their soil. Some had special agreements with the Federal Government governing property within their borders."

The court cites Stearns v. Minnesota (179 US pp 243-245; 45 L. Ed. 173-175).

Continuing:

"The requirement of Equal Footing was designed not to wipe out those diversities but to create parity as respects political standing and sovereignty. Yet the "Equal Footing" clause has long been held to have a direct effect on certain property rights. Thus the question early arose in controversies between the Federal Government and the States as to the ownership of the shores of navigable waters and the soils under them. It was consistently held that to deny to the States, admitted subsequent to the formation of the Union, ownership of this property would deny them admission on an Equal Footing with the original States, since the original States did not grant these properties to the United States but reserved them to themselves."

The court cites Pollard v. Hagan.

The important part of the above quotation is that it relies upon Pollard v. Hagan. That, then, requires a refocus of exactly what Pollard v. Hagan says. The finding in that case was limited to land under navigable waters. In dicta, the history related in that decision is ignored, for it *did not limit the history to soil under navigable waters*.

Therefore, by indirection, the implied, assumed ownership of the land by the federal government in this case must be taken in the same light: Dicta cannot be taken as the basis for law. It has not been argued. History, as recited in cases in dicta, is no more or less than a recitation of history, and must be taken that way. It is history—albeit probably quite accurate—and it should receive attention. But it is not law.

Continuing:

"The 'Equal Footing' clause prevents extension of sovereignty of a State into a domain of political and sovereign power of the United States from which the other States have been excluded, just as it prevents a contraction of sovereignty"

The court cites Pollard v. Hagan.

It is interesting to note that the court seems quite selective as to what is an expansion of sovereignty and what is a contraction of sovereignty.

If the court can deny Texas its off-shore land in order for it to be equal with the original states, by the same reasoning the soil of a territory belongs to a state after it became a member of the Union. To consider otherwise it is surely a "contraction" of a state's sovereignty as compared with the original states, and thus generates inequality.

"For equality of States means that they are not 'less or greater, or different in dignity or power.'"

The court cites Coyle v. Smith (221 US 559, 566; 55 L. Ed. 853, 857).

UTAH POWER & LIGHT V. UNITED STATES: (1917)

243 U.S. 389

This case has to do with commercial electric power companies building and operating power generating facilities on unappropriated public land prior to their being set aside as forest reserves. Later, this same land became forest reserve land by executive order, as authorized by Congress' enactment of the Forest Reserve Act of 1891.

Following that date, permits to operate on or use Forest Reserve Lands had to be obtained from either the Department of Interior or the Department of Agriculture, depending on the location of the generating facilities. The power companies refused to request a permit or secure a license for the operation of the facilities. The United States filed suits to evict the users or require that they secure permits.

In defense of their action, the power companies said in essence the following: We got here first; the land was not being used by anyone; the land was unappropriated, even though it was open to settlement when we got here; the land is now state of Utah land; the state has the right of eminent domain, and the ownership of the land by the United States is no more than that of an ordinary owner; this land is not being nor was it ever being used by the federal government in the operation of their legal duties as outlined in Art. I, Sec. 8, Cl. 17 ("Forts, Magazines, Arsenals,..."); the reservation of this land later as a national forest was not a declaration that the land was needed for governmental purposes as outlined in Art. I, Sec. 8, Cl. 17 of the U.S. Constitution; the power to dispose of territory belonging to the United States should not interfere with the governmental powers of any state which is essential to the exercise of its proper function under the Constitution upon an Equal Footing with the original states; the operation of the electric power generating facilities falls under existing state statutes to which we are adhering.

In short, The United States said not so; Congress passed the law delegating such power to manage the federal lands to both the Secretaries of the Departments of Interior and Agriculture; a license and a permit are required by the secretaries: Get the license or get off the land.

It is interesting to note that at no time did the power companies claim that the land was owned by the state. To the contrary, they tacitly admitted federal ownership by claiming that the federal government's ownership of the land was no more nor less than that of an ordinary proprietor; that the United State, in their power to dispose of the land, should not interfere with the power of the state—an admission that the federal government had proprietary rights.

The court agreed with the United States and found that the power companies did indeed need a license or a permit to operate upon federal land, but the court did not find that the power companies were required to pay for past use of the land.

Important: This finding was not a declaration of ownership by the federal government; it was an assumption. Ownership was not asked and as such it was not answered.

However that may be, it is abundantly clear that the court believed the land to be federally owned. Note the following quotation:

> "We are concerned here with three suits by the United States to enjoin the continued occupancy and use, without its permission, of certain of its lands in forest reservations in Utah as sites for works employed in generating and distribution of electric power, and to secure compensation for such occupancy and use in the past. The reservations were created by executive orders and proclamations with the express sanction of Congress. ***Almost all the lands therein belong to the United States*** and before the reservations were created were public lands subject to disposal and acquisition under the general land laws."
> (Emphasis added)

This certainly says that the land belongs to the United States. That was the assumption of the court—not its decision.

The question certainly should be asked here (as elsewhere where such statements occur as to federal ownership of the land) as to why this isn't a final statement as to ownership. This statement is an observation as differentiated from an opinion. An opinion comes from the subject matter of the case and is a final finding by the court. The subject matter of ownership was not an issue in this case, and as such it was not argued and decided. Besides, ownership was tacitly admitted to be federal.

This case was about more than license and permit. As the court said:

"The principal object of the suits, as is said in one of the briefs, is to test the validity of these asserted rights and, if they be found invalid, to require the defendants to conform to the legislation of Congress."

The court found that when lands of the United States are within a state and not being used for forts or other governmental purposes, they rise above the status of the lands of similar land owners; jurisdiction, powers, and laws of the state are subordinate to federal jurisdiction, powers and laws.

This is a modification of the concept as earlier declared that the federal government is like any "ordinary proprietor" with respect to land ownership. Not so, said the court.

The following is noteworthy:

"...repeated decisions of this court have gone upon the theory that the power of Congress is exclusive and that only through its exercise in some form can rights in lands belonging to the United States be acquired."

In other words, the court is saying that only Congress has the power to change the manner in which land is disposed of or acquired by others. However, note that Congress is drawing on Art. IV, Sec. 3, cl. 2 of the Constitution—and quotes that section—"to dispose of and make all needful rules and regulations respecting" the lands of the United States. This quote is out of context. It should have been completed, for this clause refers to territory and other property. It does not refer to land. Please refer to the summary of Dred Scott v. Sandford in the appendix. In detail, in that case, the court recites what the Constitution means when it is referring to territory: Namely the Northwest Territory *and no other*. Keep in mind that much of what the court is assuming in this case is dicta.

Here comes a quotation that has major implications. In a way, it almost implies that there is such a thing as prescriptive law even with respect to Constitutional matters:

"From the earliest times Congress by its legislation, applicable alike in the States and Territories, has regulated in many particulars the use by others of the lands of the United States, has prohibited and made punishable various acts calculated to be injurious to them or to prevent their use in the way

intended, and has provided for and controlled the acquisition of rights of way over them for highways, railroads, canals, ditches, telegraph lines and the like. ***The States and the public have almost uniformly accepted this legislation as controlling, and in the instances where it has been questioned in this court its validity has been upheld and its supremacy over state enactments sustained.***"
(Emphasis added)

In a way, this underlined part of the quotation implies that if you don't object to something, it becomes a fact or a reinforced law.

The court then said:

"And so we are [of the] opinion that the inclusion within a State of lands of the United States does not take from Congress the power to control their occupancy and use, to protect them from trespass and injury and to prescribe the conditions upon which others may obtain rights in them...."

Then the court quotes Camfield v. United States:

"A different rule would place the Public Domain of the United States completely at the mercy of state legislation."

One final quotation:

[With respect to decrees,] "The defendants have not complied with any, or really offered to do so, but have proceeded upon the theory that the act and all the regulations are without application to their situation. In this they have been mistaken, and so are occupying and using reserved lands of the United States without its permission and contrary to its laws."

There is no question but what the court assumes and even concludes that the public lands within the state are federally owned even after statehood.

In this case, as in all the others I have examined, this was not decided; it was assumed.

UTAH DIVISION OF STATE LANDS V. UNITED STATES: (1987)

482 U.S. 193; 96 L. Ed. 2nd 162; 107 S. Ct. 2318

Oil and gas were discovered under the bed of Utah Lake. Utah claimed the land and filed this lawsuit to have their ownership confirmed since the federal government had claimed ownership too, and of course, the oil and gas royalty that went with it.

This case was brought to determine the title to this land—land under navigable water (Utah Lake) as well as a strip of land (fast-land) 2 miles from the shore of this lake that had been reserved from settlement by the federal government.

These questions were asked: After entry into the Union, who owns this land, the federal government or the state? Did the reservation from settlement placed upon this strip of land prior to Utah's entry into the Union constitute a withholding of title passage from the United States to the state of Utah upon statehood?

Now for the background.

Utah Lake was declared to be a site for a reservoir, as authorized by Act of Congress in 1888 while Utah was still a territory. In 1890, Congress, in effect, repealed the 1888 Act with respect to reservoir sites, but added a provision that reservoir sites previously located or selected under the 1888 Act would remain segregated and reserved from entry or settlement. However, in 1989, in accordance with the then-in-effect Act of 1888, Major John Wesley Powell, the Director of the United States Geological Survey, submitted a report to the Secretary of Interior which in part stated:

> "[the] site of Utah Lake in Utah County in the Territory of Utah is hereby selected as a reservoir site, *together with all land situated within two statute miles of the border of said land at high water*." (Emphasis added)

The Land Office at Salt Lake City was notified of this proposed reservoir site and instructed to "refuse further entries or filing on the lands designated, in accordance with the Act of October 2, 1888." This they did.

Later, this selection of Utah Lake as a reservoir site was confirmed in the official reports of the Geological Survey to Congress.

With the discovery of oil and gas under the lake bed, ownership of that land was claimed by the state of Utah as well as the United States. Settlement of that ownership issue was finally brought to the Supreme Court by Utah after first losing their suit in the District Court as well as in the Tenth Circuit.

Keep in mind that there were two issues involved; land under the lake bed as well as ownership of a strip of land 2 miles wide surrounding that lake.

The Supreme Court declared, in a split decision, that Utah did indeed own the land under navigable waters as a result of the Equal Footing Doctrine and that a reservation of land by the federal government does not defeat a state's title to that land upon statehood.

The court explained the historical background of ownership of land under navigable water: The Crown held sovereignty of that land; the separate thirteen colonies claimed title to that land, and because they did, this became an integral part of the Equal Footing Doctrine: If the colonies possessed a right or dominion and sovereignty, then so would any state entering the Union thereafter. It was that simple.

> "Because all subsequently admitted States enter the Union on an "Equal Footing" with the original thirteen states, they too hold title to the land under navigable water within their boundaries upon entry into the Union."

Further:

> "We have stated that '[a] court deciding a question of title to the bed of a navigable water must...begin with a strong presumption against conveyance by the United States, and must not infer such a conveyance **unless the intention was definitely declared or otherwise made very plain, or was rendered in clear and especial words.**" (Emphasis added)

Much of this comes directly from U.S. v. Holt State Bank.[257]

With respect to "conveyance" of land to a third party, as well as the effect of a federal reservation of land upon its title passage, the Court stated:

257-U.S. v. Holt State Bank: (1926) 270 U.S. 49; 70 L. Ed. 465; 46 S. Ct 197.

"Although this Court has always spoken in terms of a 'conveyance' by the United States before statehood, we have never decided whether Congress may defeat a State's claim to title by a *federal reservation* or withdrawal of land under navigable waters. In Shively,[258] this Court concluded that the only *constitutional* limitation on the right to grant sovereign land is that such a grant must be for a 'public purpose appropriate to the object for which the United States holds the Territory."

(The court's emphasis)

Note the underlined "federal reservation" and its context within the sentence. There are two ways of interpreting the meaning. First, a Federal reservation of land under navigable water, and second, Federal reservation of any land. If the strip of land 2 miles wide was not also involved, the meaning would be singular; namely, a Federal reservation of land under navigable water. The court spent considerable effort to explain, in what might appear to be superfluous, that what Powell was really asking was that the land surrounding the lake be set aside and reserved from settlement, not just the lake bed itself. In other words, he was asking for an extension of land that was already reserved. In support of this contention, the court says as much on page 206 of 482 US 193:

"Given that the bed of Utah Lake was already 'segregated' from public sale, the United States Geological Survey Reports are best understood as reporting the *further* segregation of the lands *adjacent* to the lake which, until the reservation of Utah Lake in 1889, had not been segregated and thus had been available for public settlement. In the Eleventh Annual Report, for example, the Geological Survey's announcement that "the segregation" of Utah Lake 'includ[ed] not only the bed but the lowlands up to mean high water' in our view simply announced an increase in the segregated portion of Utah Lake. Because the bed of Utah Lake had been segregated as early as 1878, the Geological Survey's statement that the lakebed was segregated need not be taken as a statement that the bed was included within the reservation."

This focuses the decision of the court upon the strip of land 2 miles wide, and, as a result thereof, I must conclude that the term "federal reservation" as used herein is speaking to all Federal reservations of land.

With respect to the object for which the United States held the territory (of Utah), that object was defined in the Treaty of Guadalupe Hidalgo.

258-Shively v. United States: 152 U.S. 48; 38 L.Ed. 331; 14 S. Ct. 548.

That object? To form a state or states on an Equal Footing with the original thirteen states.

The court then closes the issue of holding land under navigable water:

> "....we simply cannot infer that Congress intended to defeat a future State's title to land under navigable waters 'unless the intention was definitely declared or other wise made very plain.'" (From U.S. v. Holt State Bank)

The court then touched upon the Equal Footing issue:

> "Given the longstanding policy of holding land under navigable waters for the ultimate benefit of the States, therefore, we would not infer an intent to defeat a State's Equal Footing entitlement from the mere act of reservation itself. Assuming arguendo that a reservation of land could be effective to overcome the strong presumption against the defeat of state title, the United States would not merely be required to establish that Congress clearly intended to include land under navigable water within the federal reservation; the United States would additionally have to establish that Congress affirmatively intended to defeat the future State' title to such land."

Here you have a clear statement, in converse, that the title to the land goes to the state upon statehood **"unless the intention was definitely declared or other wise made very plain"** by Congress.

It was argued that the mere fact of "reservation" was notice enough that title was not to pass to the state. The Court rejected this argument and in so doing made the following statement.

> "When Congress reserves land for a particular purpose, however, it may not also intend to defeat a future state's title to the land. The land remains in federal control, and therefore may still be held for the ultimate benefit of future States."
> (Emphasis added)

The court does make an interesting distinction between conveyance and reservation as means or methods of granting or withholding title. Relying upon Shively v. Bowlby, the court confirms that Congress prior to statehood could convey title to a third party for a "public purpose appropriate to the Territory." But it could not, however, accomplish the same result by reservation. Note the following quotation on page 201 of 482 US 193:

>"The Property Clause grants to Congress plenary power to regulate and dispose of land within the Territory, and assuredly Congress also has the power to acquire land in aid of other powers conferred on it by the Constitution.... [However,] the United States could not accomplish the same purpose by a means that would keep Utah Land under federal control. We need not decide that question today, [Meaning: deciding how the United States could accomplish that objective.] however, because even if a reservation of the bed of Utah Lake could defeat Utah's claim, it was not accomplished on these facts."

What were the facts? The notice of a reservation of land by the official reports of the Geological Survey to Congress. The court is saying that this report is not an "intention...definitely declared or otherwise made very plain."

In other words, the notice of a reservation cannot keep the land in federal ownership or sovereignty.

This is a momentous decision that impacts all federally reserved land—including National Forest and BLM land.

But what about the strip of land 2 miles wide? That land was not land under navigable water. This case settled that issue as well. The title to this strip of land went to the state of Utah upon statehood. If anything, the United States retained *only* the right to dispose of it as pointed out in Part Two in the section entitled, THE DISCLAIMER CLAUSE: AN EXCLUSIVE SALES CONTRACT. The sovereignty of that land went to the state upon statehood, in accordance with the Equal Footing Doctrine.

The court makes an issue of the fact that the original thirteen colonies laid claim to submerged lands, and as a result thereof, all submerged land of a new state was to become state land upon entry into the Union. Can it be that the original thirteen colonies did not lay claim to any and all of the Crown land within their borders? I think not. In fact, I find that it is a preposterous presumption that they might not have done so. While I cannot identify this land, I am certain that it was there. The Crown land could not all have been unappropriated waste land to the west.

389

If this is so, I find that the restriction to just navigable waters is too narrow and that the "Equal Footing" basis with the thirteen colonies must assuredly include title to dry (fast) land as well.

However, I must make this observation. The court is saying that title to all land that is under navigable waters passes to the state immediately upon statehood and that sovereignty is theirs immediately. No such finitely defined finding with respect to the fast-land was spelled out. That was done inferentially only as a necessary observation and finding of the court: Reservations of land by the federal government cannot defeat a state's title to land unless it is done in clear unmistakable language (my terminology). The court found that a mere reservation did not withhold title.

The next compelling question: Is that part of the decision dicta? No, it is not.

Why? Because the question of ownership of the strip of land was raised by the federal government in their argument. They were the ones who brought it up; that the reservation of land that appeared in the United States Geological Report to Congress was a notice of intent to withhold title. The fact that this so-called "notice" was really about the 2 mile strip of land makes the ownership of this strip an issue, and as a result thereof, subject to the decision of the court. And the Supreme Court did decide: 1)Title passes to the state immediately upon statehood, in conformance with the Equal Footing Doctrine, all land underlying navigable water, and 2)A reservation of land by the federal government does not defeat a state's title to the land.

With respect to the subject matter of Part Two of this book, this case confirms that the federal government does not possess title to the public land after statehood. If anything at all, the federal government retains only the continuing right to sell that land and collect the proceeds from the sale. Dominion and sovereignty (limited though it may be with respect to its sale) passed to the state upon statehood.

An examination of the minority opinion is in order inasmuch as this was a 5 to 4 decision.

The minority did concur that title of land underlying navigable waters passed to the state upon statehood unless Congress' intention to convey the land to a third party during the territorial period

"was definitely declared or otherwise made very plain, or was rendered in clear and especial words, or unless the claim confirmed in terms embraces the land under the waters of a stream."

However, in this case they conclude the question is whether a congressional **reservation** of land unto the United States during the territorial period has defeated a state's claim to title under the Equal Footing Doctrine. They assert that it has and point out that the Report to Congress by the United States Geological Survey is such a notice to withhold title—presumably "definitely declared or otherwise made very plain."

I must observe that it was the Geological Survey that reported to Congress their desire to reserve the land; **not** Congress' independent notice to withhold title from the state as a result of the reservation. These are two issues, not one. The question, therefore, was clearly before the court: Did the act of reserving land under navigable water constitute a withholding of title upon statehood, and secondarily, did the reservation constitute a notice "definitely declared or otherwise made very plain to withhold title upon statehood?"

The majority said the reservation did not defeat a state's title to the land in accordance with the Equal Footing Doctrine (inferentially including the strip of land 2 miles wide), and they did not consider a report to Congress to suffice as a notice "made very plain" to withhold such title passage. The minority opinion disagreed.

The minority stated, in clear terms, their opinion about the status of reserved land after statehood. Note the following quotation from page 210 of their dissenting opinion:

"In the case of reservation, the submerged lands retain their sovereign status."

Meaning: Sovereignty is retained by the United States.

WILCOX v. JACKSON (1839)

13 PET 498

This case is about title to land that at one time had been appropriated for a fort. The fort was abandoned; the Department of Indian Affairs wanted the land; the land was preempted by a squatter who filed upon the land and then passed his title to another.

The questions asked in this case are: When could title pass to another? Who passes title? Does preemption of land and recognition of that preemption by a federal land office mean that title has passed?

Note the following quotations from this case:

"...whensoever a tract of land shall have once been *legally* appropriated to any purpose, from that moment the land thus appropriated becomes severed from the mass of public land; and that no subsequent law, or proclamation, or sale, would be construed to embrace it, or to operate upon it, although no reservations were made of it." (271) (Emphasis added)

"But the property in question was a part of the Public Domain of the United States: Congress is invested by the Constitution with the power of disposing of, and making needful rules and regulations respecting it. Congress has declared, as we have said, by its legislation, that in such a case as this a patent is necessary to complete the title." (273)

Illinois had argued that an inchoate (imperfect) title could be perfected by state legislation in such effect as to be deemed "as perfect a title as if a patent had issued from the United States."

On that subject the court had this to say:

"...if it were competent for a State Legislature to say that notwithstanding this [no patent issuance], the title shall be deemed to have passed; the effect of this would be, not that Congress had the power of disposing of the public lands, and prescribing the rules and regulations concerning that disposition, but that Illinois possessed it. That would be to make the laws of Illinois paramount to those of Congress, in relation to a subject confided by the Constitution to Congress only." (273)

"We hold the true principle to be this, that whenever the question in any court, State or federal, is, ***whether a title to land which had once been the property of the United States has passed, that question must be resolved by the laws of the United States***." (273) (Emphasis added)

Note the verbiage, "had once been the property of the United States." This makes the total statement highly limiting: Land formerly federally appropriated for a legal purpose. In other words, a federal patent is required, inasmuch as they had been the former owner of the land.

Wilcox v. Jackson also cites Elliot et al v. Peirsol et al.
(1 Peters, 340)

"Where a court has jurisdiction it has a right to decide every question which occurs in the cause, and whether its decision be correct or otherwise, its judgment, until reversed, is regarded as binding in every other court. ***But if it acts without authority, its judgments and orders are regarded as nullities. They are not voidable, but simply void***." (270) (Emphasis added)

The question remains: Does the declaration that each state shall enter the Union upon an Equal Footing (the basis of admission of additional states to the Union by the Continental Congress) constitute a lawful act? The Constitution says that it is (in Art. VI, Sec. 1). Congress, doubting that this verbiage was adequate inasmuch as it was a referral—perhaps too vaguely to suit them at the time—reenacted the Ordinance of 1787 in which Equal Footing among other things is set forth. This they did in 1789—after the adoption of the Constitution of the United States.

This then raised the operability of the quotation above cited from Elliot et al v. Peirsol et al.

"...if it acts without authority, its judgments and orders are regarded as nullities. They are not voidable, but simply void."

Note the emphasized word in the first quotation: ***Legally***.

The Constitution lays out, in strict form, how Federal Land may be acquired (Art. I, Sec. 8, Cl. 17). Countless hundreds of thousands of acres have been acquired or withheld without the "consent of the legislature of the state," not to mention what for.

There is nothing in this case that declares that title to the public lands within a state after statehood is federal. That is assumed. It is not decided.

Left open are the issues of the Equal Footing Doctrine and the trustor-trustee relationship of the public lands following their acquisition resulting from treaties.

CASES

VARIOUS SELECTED QUOTATIONS

"...shall not create any right, title, interest, or estate in or to the lands."   33, 39

"...a sliding from absence of ownership..."   121, 229

".... Congress may not simply commandeer the legislative processes of the States..."   167

".....this Court never has sanctioned explicitly a federal command to States to promulgate and enforce laws and regulations."   166, 167

".....That the State of California shall be one, and is hereby declared to be one, of the United States of America, and admitted into the Union on an Equal Footing with the original States in all respects whatever"   75

"....there are no such limitations on territory subsequently acquired by the federal government by treaty or conquest. Thus it can be seen that the trust (to sell the public lands) found in Pollard's Lessee would not apply to such land owned by the United States within the borders of Nevada." 335

"....That the said State of California is admitted into the Union upon the express condition that the people of said State, through their legislature or otherwise, shall never interfere with the primary disposal of public lands within its limits,..."   75

"....this action did not claim title to any land; it challenged only the moratorium."   196, 333

"...it implies that the Government has some proprietary interest. That has not been remotely established except by sliding from absence of ownership by California to ownership by the United States."   361

"...it obviously does not confer [upon Congress the] power to admit a new State which shall be any less a State than those which compose the Union."   215, 298

"...it was the intention of the parties to invest the United States with the eminent domain of the country ceded, both national and municipal, for the purposes of temporary government, and to hold it in trust for the performance of the stipulations and conditions expressed in the deeds of cession."

344

"...she succeeded to all the rights of sovereignty, jurisdiction, and eminent domain which Georgia possessed at the date of the cession, except......the public lands remaining in the possession and under the control of the United States for the temporary purposes provided for in the deed of cession, and the legislative acts connected with it."   345

"...the Constitution protects us from our own best intentions:..." 61, 167, 168, 229

"...the government has, with respect to its own lands, the right of an ordinary proprietor,..."   295

"...the party who brings a suit is master to decide what law he will rely upon."...   245

"...the president of the United States may, from time to time, set apart and reserve, in any state or territory having public land bearing forest, in any part of the public lands."   20, 173, 231, 235

"...the United States hold the public lands within the new States by force of the deeds of cession, and the statutes connected with them, and not by any municipal sovereignty which it may suppose they possess, or by compact with the new States..., The provision of the Constitution above referred to...shows that no such power can be exercised by the United States within a State."   76, 363

"...there is to be found no sanction for the contention that any State may be deprived of any of the powers constitutionally possessed by other States, as States, by reason of the terms in which the acts admitting them to the Union have been framed."   201, 299

"...where cases in this court can be decided without reference to questions arising under the Federal Constitution that course is usually pursued, and is not departed from without important reasons."   328

"'All the public lands of the nation are held in trust for the people of the whole country.'"   327, 374

"an ordinary proprietor...[and] is subject to the legislative authority and control of the states,..."   175

"and nothing in this Constitution shall be so construed as to Prejudice any Claim of the United States, or of any particular State."   67, 108, 116, 168, 195, 286

"A different rule would place the Public Domain of the United States completely at the mercy of state legislation."   296, 384

"Alabama is therefor entitled to the sovereignty and jurisdiction over all the territory within her limits..."   347

"All the public lands of the nation are held in trust for the people of the whole country."   327, 374

"And it is not for the courts to say how that trust shall be administered. That is for Congress to determine. Thus, Congress may constitutionally limit the disposition of the Public Domain to a manner consistent with its views of public policy."   282

"Any policy or action to which the executive order applies that, upon examination by the decision-maker...appear to have an effect on private property sufficiently severe as effectively deny economically viable use or any distinct legally protected property interest to its owner, or to have the effect of, or result in, a permanent or temporary physical occupation, invasion, or deprivation, shall be deemed to have a taking implication for the purposes of the executive order and these guidelines."   55

"Because the federal government now intends to retain ownership of almost all its lands, the basic public land legal conflicts are over use, not disposition, of the public resources."   211

"But the Constitution protects us from our own best intentions; it divides power among sovereigns and among branches of government precisely so that we may resist the temptation to concentrate power in one location as the expedient solution to the crisis of the day."   352

"But the island, which we have seen was in existence when Idaho became a State, was not a part of the bed of the stream or land under the water, and therefore its ownership did not pass to the State or come within the disposal influence of its laws...it was fast dry land, and therefore remained the property of the United States and subject to disposal under its laws, as did the island which was in controversy in Mission Rock Co. v. United States, 109 Fed. Rep. 763, 769-770, and United States v. Mission Rock Co., 189 U.S. 391."   352

"Congress may not simply 'commandeer the legislative processes of the State by directly compelling them to enact and enforce a federal regulatory program.'" [Hodel v. Virginia Surface Mining and Reclamation Ass. 452 U.S. 264, 288]   167, 340

"For equality of States means that they are not 'less or greater, or different in dignity or power.'"   379

"It should first be borne in mind, however, that in this bill, if passed, makes no disposition of the Public Domain. It merely regulates a use to which it is now being put..."   41

"Nevada agrees that this case does not involve a claim of title to land."   196, 333

"No matter how powerful the federal interest involved, the Constitution simply does not give Congress the authority to require the States to regulate..."   168, 341

"No state legislation may interfere with Congress' power over the Public Domain...the act of admission usually contains an agreement by the state not to interfere...Nevada was admitted to the Union subject to such an agreement."   336

"Nor can it [Article IV, Sec. 3,], upon any fair construction, be applied to any property but that which the new government was about to receive from the confederated States...."   68, 69, 305

"On her [California] admission into the Union, she [California] became the owner of all the public land not disposed of by law of Congress."   132, 227

"Preference shall be given in the issuance of grazing permits to those within or near a district who are landowners engaged in the livestock business, bona fide occupants, or settlers, or owners of water or water rights as may be necessary to permit the proper use of lands, owned, occupied or leased by them..."   37

"So that Congress should determine that the great body of public lands within the state of Minnesota should be reserved from sale for an indefinite period it might do so, and thus the lands be excepted from taxation; and yet it cannot be imputed to Congress that it would discriminate against the state of Minnesota, or pass any legislation detrimental to it interests. It had the power to withdraw all the public lands in Minnesota from private entry or public grant, and, exercising that power, it might prevent the state of Minnesota from taxing a large area of its lands..."   354

"State officials thus cannot consent to the enlargement of the powers of Congress beyond those enumerated in the Constitution."   167, 168

"That all the lands within the territory so ceded to the United States, and not reserved for or appropriated to any of the before-mentioned purposes...shall be considered as a common fund for use and benefit of such of the United States...and shall be faithfully and bona fide disposed of for that purpose, and for no other use or purpose whatsoever...." 5, 124, 343

"The 'Equal Footing' clause has long been held to refer to political rights and to sovereignty."   377

"The 'Equal Footing' clause prevents extension of sovereignty of a State into a domain of political and sovereign power of the United States from which the other States have been excluded, just as it prevents a contraction of sovereignty."   378

"The argument appears to be that Congress could obtain exclusive legislative jurisdiction over the public lands in the State only by consent, and that in the absence of such consent Congress lacks the power to act contrary to state law. This argument is without merit."   321

"The argument that Congress derives from the duty of 'guaranteeing to each State in this Union a republican form of government,' power to impose restrictions upon a new State which deprives it of equality with other members of the Union has no merit..."   87, 201, 298

"The constitutional authority of Congress cannot be expanded by the 'consent' of the governmental unit whose domain is thereby narrowed, whether that unit is the Executive Branch or the States."   86, 166, 258, 342

"The doctrine applies only to political rights and sovereignty; it does not cover economic matters, for there never has been equality among the states in that sense."   197, 335

"The Equal Footing Doctrine does not affect Congress' power to dispose of Federal property."   335

"The Government has with respect to its own land the rights of an ordinary proprietor to maintain its possession and prosecute trespassers. It may deal with such lands precisely as an ordinary individual may deal with his farming property. It may sell or withhold them from sale."   326

"The immunity of the Federal Government from suit extends to all federal officers and agents acting within the scope of their duties as such."
246

"The inhabitants of the ceded territory shall be incorporated in the Union of the United States and admitted as soon as possible according to the principles of the federal Constitution..."   131, 355

"The object of all the parties to these contracts of cession was to convert the land into money for the payment of the debt, and to erect new States over the territory thus ceded; and as soon as these purposes could be accomplished, the power of the United States over these lands, as property, was to cease."   184, 345

"The President of the United States is authorized, in his discretion, to declare by public proclamation historic landmarks, historic and prehistoric structures, and other objects of historic or scientific interest that are situated upon the lands owned or controlled by the Government of the United States to be national monuments..."   363

"The Property Clause provides that 'Congress shall have Power to dispose of and make all needful Rules and Regulations respecting the Territory or other Property belonging to the United States.'"   290

"The powers delegated by the proposed Constitution to the Federal Government, are few and defined. Those which are to remain in the State Government are numerous and indefinite...."   208

"The question is not what power the Federal Government ought to have but what powers in fact have been given by the people."   61, 166, 205, 340

"The requirement of Equal Footing was designed not to wipe out those diversities but to create parity as respects political standing and sovereignty...."   378

"The right of Alabama and every other new state to exercise all the powers of government which belong to and may be exercised by the original states of the Union, must be admitted and remain unquestioned except so far as they are temporarily deprived of control over the public lands."185, 336

"The rights of Alabama and every other new States to exercise all the powers of government which belong to and may be exercised by the original States of the Union, must be admitted, and remain unquestioned, except so far as they are, temporarily, deprived of control over the public lands.   345

"There is nothing in this language which intimates that treaties do not have to comply with the provisions of the Constitution..."   189

"This action flew in the face of accepted ideas regarding the functions of the Federal Government. It involved a reversal of the course which had been pursued with relation to the Public Domain from the foundation of the Union. It conflicted with the whole American tradition of individualism and preference for private property ownership."   30

"Thus the consent of the state is not required for Congress to withdraw large bodies of land from settlement."   337

"Today's action is firm but restrained. It should send a message, loud and clear, that the United States does indeed own and manage federal lands."   258

"We, therefor, think the United States hold the public lands within the new States by force of the deeds of cession...and the statutes connected with them, and not by any municipal sovereignty which it may be supposed they possess, or have received by compact with the new States, for that particular purpose. The provisions of the Constitution above referred to show that no such power can be exercised by the United States within a State."   76, 346

"Whatever the limitation upon her powers as a government whilst in a territorial condition, whether from the ordinance of 1787 or the legislation of Congress, it ceased to have any operative force, except as voluntarily adopted by her, after she became a State of the Union."   88, 202, 299

"Whenever a federal officer or agent exceeds his authority, in so doing he no longer represents the Government and hence loses the protection of sovereign immunity from suit."   246

"Where Congress exceeds it authority relative to the States, therefore, the departure from the constitutional plan cannot be ratified by the 'consent' of the state officials"   165, 259, 341

"Where Congress exceeds its authority...departure from the plan of the Federal Constitution cannot be ratified by the consent of state officials..."   165, 259, 341

"[Admission of California into the Union is subject to the] express condition that the people of said state shall never interfere with the primary disposal of the public lands..."   75, 223, 370

"[The purpose of this clause] was to exclude the conclusion that either party, by adopting the Constitution, would surrender what they deemed their rights...The union of the two provisions in the same clause shows that they were kindred subjects, and that the whole clause is local, and relates only to lands, within the limits of the United States; and that no other Territory was in the mind of the framers of the Constitution, or intended to be embraced in it."   70, 305

A treaty is "to be regarded in courts of justice as equivalent to an act of the legislature, whenever it operates of itself, without the aid of any legislative provision."   187

"...It applied only to the property which the States held in common at that time, and has no reference whatever to any territory or other property which the new sovereignty might afterwards itself acquire...the design and meaning of the clause to be such as we have mentioned. It does not speak of any Territory, nor of Territories, but uses language which, according to its legitimate meaning, points to a particular thing. The power is given in relation only to the territory of the United States—that is, to a Territory then in existence, and then known or claimed as the territory of the United States."   304

"...Nor can it, upon any fair construction, be applied to any property but that which the new government was about to receive from the confederated States."   69, 305

"...The new States have the same rights, sovereignty, and jurisdiction over this subject...as the original States."   348

"...The power over the public land thus intrusted to Congress is without limitation...Congress may constitutionally limit the disposition of the Public Domain to a manner consistent with its views of public policy."
                              192, 264, 282, 290, 358, 373, 374

"...The right of the United States to the public lands, and the power of Congress to make all needful rules and regulations for the sale and disposition thereof, conferred no power to grant to the plaintiffs [title to land issued by the United States] the land in controversy in this case."   348

"...The term 'territory,' as here used, is merely descriptive of one kind of property, and is equivalent to the word 'lands'...and this power is vested in Congress without limitation, and has been considered the foundation upon which the territorial government rests."   367, 373

"...This "cannot operate as a contract between the parties, but is binding as a law. Full power is given to Congress 'to make all needful rules and regulations respecting the territory or other property of the Unites States.' This authorized the passage of all laws necessary to secure the rights of the United States to the public lands, and to provide for their sale, and to protect them from taxation."   184, 300, 346

"'...And it is not for the courts to say how that trust shall be administered. That is for Congress to determine.'"   282, 328, 358, 373, 374

"'...the power over the public lands thus entrusted to Congress is without limitation.'"   142, 192, 264, 282, 290, 320, 373

"...associating the power over the Territory in this respect with the power over movable or personal property—that is, the ships, arms and munitions of war, which then belonged in common to the State sovereignties..."   68, 69, 304

"...Being an instrument of limited and enumerated powers, it follows irresistibly, that what is not conferred, is withheld, and belongs to the state authorities.'" 166, 339

"...Bowman, The Question of Sovereignty over California's Off-Shore Islands..." 218

"...Congress 'may deal with such lands precisely as a private individual may deal with his farming property. It may sell or withhold them from sale.'" 281

"...Congress has declared, as we have said, by its legislation, that in such a case as this a patent is necessary to complete the title." (273) 393

"...deprived of territory for the benefit of the United States." 126, 162, 165

"...forever disclaim all right and title to the waste or unappropriated land lying within the said territory..." 76, 184

"...It was not ceded because it was inconvenient to the State to hold and govern it, nor from any expectation that it could be better or more conveniently governed by the United States." 303

"...if an agency does not speak to the question of pre-emption, we will pause before saying that the mere volume and complexity of its regulations indicate that the agency did in fact intend to pre-empt." 291

"...in trust until California gained statehood in 1850. At that time, they passed to the state under the 'Equal Footing' doctrine. See Borax, Ltd. v. Los Angeles..." 219

"...it is so admitted with all of the powers of sovereignty and jurisdiction which pertain to the original States..." 202

"...jurisdiction extends to certain enumerated objects only, and leaves to the several States a residuary and inviolable sovereignty over all other objects." 114

"...On her admission she at once became entitled to and possessed of all rights and dominion and sovereignty which belonged to the original States." 88, 202

"...on an Equal Footing with the original States, in all respects whatever..." 75, 85, 89, 95, 96, 182, 200, 202, 203, 228, 258, 345, 347, 360, 373, 381

"...power to impose restrictions upon a new State which deprives it of equality with other members of the Union, has no merit." 87, 201, 299

"...require the States to govern according to Congress' instructions." [Coyle v. Oklahoma] 166, 340

"...State government would clearly retain all the rights of sovereignty which they before had, and which were not, by the act, exclusively delegated to the United States." 113, 118

"...so far as they related to the public land within that territory, amounted to nothing more nor less than rules and regulations respecting the sales and disposition of the public lands..."   347

"...stipulated that such land should remain subject to the sole disposition of the United States...[the United States] can derive no force from the consent of the State."   201

"...that what is not conferred, is withheld, and belongs to the state authorities."   166, 339

"...the constitutional power of Congress in this respect is without limitation."   358

"...the Constitution does not confer upon Congress the ability simply to compel the States to do so."   339

"...the departure from the constitutional plan cannot be ratified by the "consent" of the state officials."   168, 259, 341

"...the Framers explicitly chose a Constitution that confers upon Congress the power to regulate individuals, not States."   204, 341

"...the land under the navigable waters, and the Public Domain above high water, were alike reserved to the United States, and alike subject to be sold by them."   344

"...the lands within the territory ceded, and not reserved or appropriated to other purposes, shall be considered as common fund for the use and benefit of all the United States, to be faithfully and bona fide disposed of for that purpose, and for no other purpose whatsoever."   3, 184, 343

"...the power there given, whatever it may be, is confined, and was intended to be confined, to the territory which at that time belonged to, or was claimed by, the United States, and was within their boundaries as settled by the Treaty with Great Britain, and can have no influence upon a territory afterwards acquired from a foreign government..."   67, 302

"...the two rocks or island above mentioned, for the reason that neither of them ever passed to the state..."   370

"...the United State never held any municipal sovereignty, jurisdiction, or right of soil in and to the territory, of which Alabama or any of the new States were formed; except for temporary purposes, and to execute the trusts created by the acts of Virginia and Georgia Legislatures..."   183, 265, 344

"...the United States have no constitutional capacity to exercise municipal jurisdiction, sovereignty, or eminent domain, within the limits of a State or elsewhere, except in the cases in which it is expressly granted [in the Constitution]."   183, 345

"...title was acquired by the United Stated by the cession from Mexico, equally with the title to uplands, they held it only in trust for the future state."   370

"...whatever be the limitations upon the power of a territorial government, they cease to have any operative force, except as voluntarily adopted after such territory has become a State of the Union."   202, 352

"And the same power of making needful rules respecting the Territory is, in precisely the same language, applied to the other property belonging to the United States—associating the power over the Territory in this respect with the power over movable or personal property..."   68, 69, 204

"It could not be expected that those possessing Sovereignty could ever voluntarily part with it."   100

"The clause in relation to the territory and other property of the United Stated provide for the first, and the clause last quoted provided for the other. They have no connection with the general powers and rights of sovereignty delegated to the new government..."   71, 306

"the State government would clearly retain all the rights of sovereignty which they before had, and which were not, by the act, [of agreeing to the provisions of the new Constitution] exclusively delegated to the United States..."   113, 118

"[the Federal Government's] sphere is limited. Certain subjects only are committed to it; but its power over those subjects is as full and complete as is the power of the States over the subjects to which their sovereignty extends."   119

INDEX

WORDS, NAMES AND SHORT PHRASES

E

Earth First, 47

Eastex Aviation, Inc. v. Sperry & Hutchinson Co., 88n

educational trust lands, 28

electric power companies, 381

Eleven Western States, 1, 2, 28, 121

Elko, Nevada, 46

Elliot et al v. Peirsol et al, 394

Eminens, 90

eminent domain, 90-91, 176, 236n, 266, 344-45, 381

Employment Act of 1946, 44

enabling acts, 14, 35, 73, 165, 166, 177, 179-80, 183, 185, 199-203, 228, 232, 297-300, 353, 355

endangered species, 230

Endangered Species Act, 47, 52

End of American Exceptionalism, The (Wrobel), 24n

Engdahl, David E., 119, 160

England, 98, 90, 96, 110, 161, 174

English Common Law, 351

Enlarged Homestead Act of 1909, 6n

Environmental Defense Fund, 47

Environmental Policy Act, 47

Environmental Protection Agency, 47-48

equal footing, 75, 79, 85-86, 88-89, 91-92, 96-99, 104, 153, 197-99, 202-3, 216, 223, 233, 258, 265, 330, 334, 345, 347, 359-60, 377-78, 381, 386, 388, 390, 394

    doctrine applies only to political rights, 197, 335

Equal Footing Doctrine, 4, 66, 77-78, 80-83, 106-7, 121, 125, 131-32, 140, 159, 165, 173-74, 176-77, 178-79, 180-83, 195, 197-98, 199, 202-3, 211, 215, 219, 229, 233, 235, 240, 265, 272, 314, 330-31, 333-37, 348, 356, 357, 359-60, 371, 377, 386, 389-91, 395

erosion, 46

Escanaba Co. v. Chicago, 88-89, 91-92, 95, 97, 175, 202, 299

Estoppel, 73

Executive Order 12630, 52, 53, 54, 56, 170-172, 240, 381

F

Fallini v. Hodel, 49

Fallon, Nevada, 53

fauna, 46, 187, 230

Fauske v. Dean, 39

ADDENDUM NUMBER ONE

RECENT INFLUENTIAL ACTIONS AND EVENTS

July 15, 2000

CONTINUED INTEREST AND CHANGING EVENTS REGARDING R.S. 2477

- - - - - -

CHALLENGE TO THE CONSTITUTIONALITY AND USE OF THE ANTIQUITIES ACT OF 1906 TO SET ASIDE VAST TRACT OF LAND BY EXECUTIVE ORDER

- - - - - -

OPPOSITION TO THE NEW PROPOSED CONGRESSIONAL LEGISLA-TION TO PROVIDE FUNDS FOR THE PURCHASE OF PRIVATE LAND: THE CONSERVATION AND REINVESTMENT ACT

- - - - - -

The interest in all the items listed above have one thing in common that is noteworthy: They all sound the alarm that the federal government through its agencies and bureaus is or has been acting in a capacity beyond the enumerated powers outlined and set forth in the Constitution.

In review: Our Founding Fathers, the framers of the U.S. Constitution, set up the basic framework for a limited government—the only one of its kind today—that empowered the federal establishment to do only those things, generally speaking, that state governments would be unable to do or be able to accomplish. Keep that simple fact in mind. These powers are enumerated. They are outlined in specific terms in Article I, Section 8 of the U.S. Constitution. Rather than enumerate them here, it should suffice it to say, that they are powers that allow the federal government to coordinated the actions between the different states as well as allow the federal govern-ment the latitude and authority to function by and between different foreign governments. They are about what you would think they should be when you look at them with that objective in mind. But the Founding Fathers went a step further: They specifically noted in the Constitution that all other

437

powers not so enumerated would be the powers reserved to the different states. That is the catch that we now find is the focus of the items listed above.

CONTINUED INTEREST AND CHANGING EVENTS

REGARDING R.S. 2477

R.S. 2477 has been around for a long time—since 1866 to be exact. But before we can examine the attention it has been getting in recent years, we must understand exactly what it is and what it was intended to accomplish in the first place.

R.S. 2477 was first enacted by the 39th Congress, Session I. Chapter CCLXII (262), Section 8 in 1866. It was a part of a rather long list of items that dealt with mining and titled, "An Act granting the Right of Way to Ditch and Canal Owners over the Public Lands, and for other Purposes." Section 8 of that act, now known as R.S. 2477, reads as follows:

"Sec. 8. And be it further enacted, That the right of way for the construction of highways over public lands, not reserved for public uses, is hereby granted."

This is an unconditional grant of a right of way over public lands "not reserved for public uses." This last phrase means that if a reserve has not been placed upon a parcel of land prior to the road becoming a matter of fact, then the right of way is valid in every degree. It is noteworthy that nothing is said about how, where, or under what conditions such a right of way was to be granted. Nor was anything said about the road's physical characteristics, its use, appearance, destination or even the date for its construction. It was an open grant of a right of way that had no termination date contained or implied in its original form. In 1866, there was a lot of public land that had not been pre-empted, claimed or patented, and this act was obviously passed to provide continuity and uniformity for the development of mineral resources at that time—a time that was only 14 month after the Civil War between the states had ended.

Section 8 was later separated for indexing and identification purposes and became known as Section 2477 of the Revised Statues, 43 U.S.C. 932. There were no changes or modification to R.S. 2477 until 1976. At that time, it was repealed in its entirety by adoption of Public Law 94-579, better know as the Federal Land Policy and Management Act (FLPMA). Of interest, the following notation accompanied the repeal:

"Saving Provision"

"Repeal by Pub. L. 94-579 not to be construed as terminating any valid lease, permit, patent, etc., existing on Oct. 21, 1976, see section 701 of Publ L. 94-579, set out as a note under section 1701 of this title."

The repeal could not affect any right of way, no matter where it might have been, that was a matter of fact prior to 1976 provided that it was not on reserved land. R.S. 2477 was a perpetual grant of a right-of-way over public land. What Congress did by executing the repeal was to say that this perpetual grant of a right of way is no longer valid after 1976. However, as to any "highway" (road) that was in existence prior to 1976, the right of way was valid. This would include any and all roads, even a footpath, over public lands–even if they were no longer in use.[1] Disuse never cancels out a right of way or easement any more than disuse cancels an easement a power company may have over a portion of your land. The right-of-way or easement can only be canceled by permission of the grantee–the person who received the right-of-way or easement in the first place.

However that may be, the verbiage in FLPMA is quite interesting. FLPMA did not just repeal R.S. 2477, it repealed portions of a whole host of other statutes as well that dealt with ditches, canals, surveys and plots of right-of-way, etc. In the case of R.S. 2477, the repeal specifically mentions "lease[s], permit[s], patent[s], etc." Presumably, a right-of-way would be included in the "etc." inasmuch as a right-of-way is not a lease, a permit, nor a patent. Recognition of this fact is contained in one portion of FLPMA that says, to wit, that an existing right-of-way may be canceled with the approval of the grantee and a permit issued in its stead.

I must point out that there is scarcely any equity in this provision. The permit subjects the permittee to exclusive Federal law and to any changes that might occur, as well as, I suppose, a cancellation provision.

Nye County in Nevada relied upon this perpetual right-of-way and reopened a road that the Forest Service had closed after it had washed out. The Forest Service would not grant permission for the reopening of the road, ostensibly because it was on National Forest Land. The Forest Service claimed a permit was required for its reopening. Nye County disagreed, stating that the road had been there for years, and that it was a county road. Dick Carver, a Nye County commissioner drove a caterpillar tractor over the route of the washed-out road and reopening it to travel. The issues were

---

1 - It is rather meaningless to differentiate the two words "highway" from "road." Today a highway might mean a four lane or two lane paved road. In 1866, a highway was nothing more than a dirt road that was free to everyone's use. Black's Law Dictionary defines "highway" as follows: "A free and public roadway, or street; one which every person has the right to use."

clear-cut. The Forest Service claimed that permission had to be obtained prior to the reopening inasmuch as the land over which the road extended was on Forest Service National Forest land. Germane to the Forest Service objection in that case was supposed damage that might occur to a stream bed adjacent to the road. On the other hand, Nye County took the position that the road was ages old, that it predated the Forest Service, that it was in truth a R.S. 2477 right-of-way and that as a county road–which it was, Nye County had every legal right to maintain and keep the road open. From the foregoing information, this should have been the end of the matter, but it has not proven to be the case. In addition to supposed damage to adjacent land, federal sovereignty of the land has been raised by the Forest Service. Further, they contend, Congress delegated the authority over the public lands to them and that federal sovereignty of the land is a matter of fact. This, of course, flies in the face of the Equal Footing Doctrine of state sovereignty after statehood. The Forest Service cite Kleppe v. New Mexico and U.S. v. Gardner as their authority to claim sovereignty for the federal government. The Forest Service ignores the host of cases that indicate otherwise–they must in order to justify their position.

Be that as it may, the basic question with reference to R.S. 2477 is really this: How binding is the right-of-way? Does sovereignty (ownership of the land) really have anything to do with the issue? To the first question, Absent a voluntary release of the right-of-way, I believe the right-of-way is completely binding and cannot be changed by anyone other than the sovereign owner of the land and only in that case if the sovereign exercises his right of eminent domain and pays for the release of the right-of-way in accordance with the Fifth Amendment. To the second question, I believe that the determination of who is actually the sovereign owner of the land, the federal government or the state is immaterial; the right-of-way was executed by a duly authorized government who at that time was the sovereign owner of the land at the time of its granting. There is no cancellation clause.[2]

The issue of R.S. 2477, its continuance or affect, seems to have not been totally put to bed. Exactly why, I don't know, but on September 30, 1996 Congress passed another law[3] that reads as follows:

> "No final rule or regulation of any agency of the federal Government pertaining to the recognition, management or validity of a right-of-way pursuant to Revised Statute 2477 (43 U.S.C. 932) shall

---

2 - Several informative articles of importance with reference to R.S. 2477 and other subjects may be obtained from Bill Redd, San Juan County Commission, P.O. Box 9, Monticello, UT 84535.

3 - Pub. L. 104-208, Div. A, Title 1, Section 101(d) [Title 1, Section 108], September 30, 1996, 110 Stat. 3009-200

take effect unless expressly authorized by an Act of Congress subsequent to the date of enactment of this Act [Sept. 30, 1996]."

In essence, this says: "Hands off, bureau or agency, this is our [Congress'] issue to deal with, not yours."

I cannot help but wonder if the opening of the Jefferson Canyon road by Dick Carver of Nye County, Nevada on July 4, 1994 had anything to do with this. The book, *The Battle of Jefferson*, by Don Bowman gives a detailed history of Nye County's reopening of the Jefferson Canyon road. Of additional interest, that book contains a great deal of substantive information with reference to R.S. 2477 rights-of-way.[4]

I must point out at this juncture, that if there were no other cases than Kleppe[5] and Gardner, the Forest Service would be correct with reference to federal ownership of the public lands. But there are a whole host of cases that are clearly in conflict with the position taken by the Forest Service. In other words, there is truly a conflict in the opinions rendered by the Supreme Court on this issue of federal sovereignty. However that may be, there would be no conflict if the judgment were left up to the framers of Constitution. Land ownership for purposes not enumerated in the Constitution was not on their agenda; they would not have approved of it.

The problem is simply this: How do we get others to recognize the limits placed upon our federal government by the constitution? Further, is Congress authorized to delegate the determination of sovereignty to a federal agency or bureau? I think not. This is a clear violation of Article IV of the Constitution as well as the 14th Amendment. As a matter of fact, if Congress itself had determined sovereignty by passage of a law, that too would be a violation. It is simply worse to have an agency or bureau do it in the stead of Congress.

Governor Leavitt of Utah seems to want to compromise the issue of state ownership and control of the public land and strike some kind of bargain with the Forest Service that recognizes federal authority to negate a contract. This is not an act that is consistent with the Constitution: The state cannot give nor accept anything which is not theirs to give or accept as provided for in the Constitution. Conversely, the same thing is true from the federal government's side as well. If it is not authorized by the Constitution, it cannot be done. It's that simple. All the negotiating in the world cannot change that fact—unless you change the Constitution!

4 - *The Battle of Jefferson*, by Don Bowman. Published by Spur, Inc.

IBSN 0-9652738-0-6. Library of Congress Catalog Number 96-92273.

5 - Kleppe seems to be receiving some attention as to its consistency with the Constitution. This subject is taken up in the last section of this addendum.

CHALLENGE TO THE CONSTITUTIONALITY AND USE OF THE
ANTIQUITIES ACT OF 1906 TO SET ASIDE VAST TRACT OF LAND BY
EXECUTIVE ORDER

As I point out in the text of the book in the section entitled, THE
ANTIQUITIES ACT OF 1906, this act has been used by a number of presidents to set aside certain public lands into "national monuments" that he
believes are qualified for such set aside because of the their importance as
"historic landmarks, historic and prehistoric structures, and other objects of
historic or scientific interest." In that section, I raise the question about the
misuse of that act as authority to set aside vast stretches of land that clearly
go well beyond the confines of the verbiage in the act itself. Congress has
done nothing about this over-stretching even though they are aware of it.
Apparently, the constitutionality of this over-stretching has not been important enough for them to do something about it.

But first a review of how the act has been used in the past.

Its first use was to set aside the Devil's Tower in Wyoming, a set
aside of 1,153 acres. Teddy Roosevelt used the act to set aside 800,000 acres
of the Grand Canyon area of Arizona. The size of the set aside did not bother
Congress. President Jimmy Carter used the act to set aside 55,000,000
acres in Alaska. Again Congress did not challenge the use of the act.
Presidents Nixon, Reagan and Bush did not use the act. No executive order
employing the Antiquities Act of 1906 has ever been overturned. It would
appear that acquiescence on the part of Congress to such set asides has been
a green light to the Clinton Administration, and President Clinton has used
the act extensively to set aside a number of tracts of substantial size. The
only limiting, if you could call it that, occurred when the Grand Teton
National Park was established; Congress attached a rider to prevent any
further appropriation of Wyoming land.

Clearly, the use of the act has been outside the purview of the
authors of the bill in 1906, and finally the act is being challenged upon
constitutional grounds, not, ironically, by Congress, but by private citizens
in southwestern Utah and legislators in Arizona!

Their specific grievance? The set aside into a national monument of
a vast stretch of land known locally as the Arizona Strip , located just south
of Kanab, Utah, extending southwesterly to the Grand Canyon National
Park and to the Lake Mead Recreational Area, the Utah border on the north
and the Nevada border on its west–an area of about a million or so acres.
Historically, this land has been used by ranchers for grazing purposes, and

grazing permits issued by the BLM or the Forest Service cover most, if not all of it. Additionally, water rights in effect for over 100 years are a matter of fact on this land, such water rights belonging to these same ranchers. Keep in mind that these water rights may also include–and probably do–certain physical improvements such as tanks, ditches, wells, pipe, and other improvements to store or transport water. We are talking about the change or confiscation of use of vested private property or private property rights of a lot of people.

The grounds for their suit? Deprivation of their Federal Constitutional Rights. They are not claiming that the Federal Government does not possess authority to make rules and regulations with respect to public lands, but that these rules and regulations deprive them of the their Constitutional Rights. This is an interesting departure from past challenges such as Kleppe, and particularly Gardner, where federal authority over the public land was challenged largely on the basis of federal ownership of the public land. This time it is Constitutional Rights of individuals as well as duly constituted public officials of a state.

The case: Esplin v. Clinton (CIV 00 0148 PCT PGR). It was filed on January 25, 2000; a Motion to Dismiss was filed on March 27, 2000 by Clinton; a Response to Defendant's (Clinton) Motion to Dismiss was filed by Esplin on May 19, 2000; and a Reply to Plaintive's Response to Defendants' Motion to Dismiss was filed on June 16, 2000. It all makes for very interesting reading as to the reach of federal power, not only over public land, but over constitutional rights of the individual.

In essence–and in oversimplified terms–the complaint by Esplin, et al, says that their rights are or are about to be abridged by the set aside of the land into national monument status; that their grazing rights–not to mention their water rights–are about to be confiscated, reduced, or eliminated; that their right and duty to govern as members of the Arizona legislature are eliminated; that the Antiquities Act of 1906 is unconstitutional in that there is no constitutional foundation for its being; that Congress may not delegate such authority to the president that unilaterally impinges or preempts a state's duty and authority to govern. These last item are of material significance, while the first items are really a fear of what might happen in view of the history of the Clinton Administration. While it is too early to tell, I suspect that the defendant (Clinton) will not be able to obtain a dismissal on the abrogation of a state's right to govern. This one will go to trial!

My disappointment is simply this: Where is Congress? Why does it take a group of private citizens to do what our Congressmen and Senators should be doing–looking after the continuity and conformance to the Constitution of governmental acts?

OPPOSITION TO THE NEW PROPOSED CONGRESSIONAL LEGISLA-
TION TO PROVIDE FUNDS FOR THE PURCHASE OF PRIVATE LAND:

THE CONSERVATION AND REINVESTMENT ACT

On the surface this proposed legislation sounds like it is exactly what this country needs, a fund to purchase private property so that it may be conserved or set aside for laudable conservational or ecological reasons. The amount of the fund is enormous, billions of dollars.

If it is so good as to its supposed intent, then what is wrong with it?

Consider the following:

Whose property are we talking about and who is it that will determine its need for a supposed higher and better use? Will it be a bureau or agency? What review of the their determination will there be? Will the purchase damage or impact the remaining property in the area as to its then in place use? How will compensation for this possible damage be handled? Is the purchase of private property on a grand scale for purposes not enumerated in the Constitution constitutional? And lastly, how would our Founding Fathers react to such legislation? Would this act be consistent with their views of federal power?

These questions can develop a lot of doubts as to the appropriateness of such legislation.

Rather than take these questions in the order of their presentation above, let us first look at the possible constitutionality of the proposed act. In order for it to pass the test of constitutionality, this act must be associated with or be one of the enumerated powers granted to the United States as a federal government. I don't see that it is. There is no provision in the constitution for the purchase of land as such; it must be connected to an enumerated grant of power as provided for in Article I, Section 8 of the Constitution such as a post office, federal roads, federal building, military bases, etc. This isn't. This is for the sole avowed purpose of conservation. While it is true that the Act of 1891, the Forest Reserve Act, was for the purpose of conservation of a natural resource, this act, it seems to me, goes well beyond the confines of the Act of 1891, whose constitutionality I seriously doubt even though it has been over 100 years in place.

This proposed act almost says that the land already set aside across the nation is insufficient to preserve or conserve this nation's natural resources even if this represents 60 percent of the land of the western eleven states (not including Alaska). Be that as it may, this does not dampen the enthusiasm to conserve–especially if the conservation does not affect something you personally hold dear or own.

In addition, the tenor of this proposed bill strikes me as an invasion of a state's right to govern its sovereign territory and quite possibly the provisions of the 14th Amendments dealing with a citizen's right to the due process and protection of the laws. Quoting from the 14th Amendment:

> "No State shall make or enforce any law which shall abridge the privileges or immunities of citizens of the United States; nor shall any *State* deprive any person of life, liberty, or property, without due process of law; nor deny to any person within its jurisdiction the equal protection of the laws." (Emphasis added)

This refers to a State depriving a person of life, liberty, or property, without due process of law. A recent court decision, Saenz v. Roe,[6] adds the United States to this admonition. The Lawyers Edition summarizes this finding as follows:

> "The protection afforded to a citizen by the Fourteenth Amendment Citizenship Clause *is a limitation on the powers of the federal government as well as the states.* U.S.C.A. Const. Amend. 14, Section 1." (Emphasis added)

The actual language in the court's decision is as follows:

> "Moreover, the protection afforded to the citizen by the Citizenship Clause of that Amendment is a *limitation on the powers of the National Government as well as the States*." (Emphasis added)

Further, condemnation is authorized by failure to protect against it.

Also, the bill states that a willing seller is required. A willing seller can and is often bludgeoned into become a "willing" seller when confronted with the alternatives to his not becoming "willing." Take the man in the San Joaquin Valley who was forced to sell a portion of his land to a governmental agency so that the remaining portion of his land would not be impacted by the designation as a habitat for an endangered species. He became a "willing" seller. The protection in the bill regarding a willing seller is patently hollow. Selling in desperation does not constitute a "willing" seller.

I hate to raise this specter: Will the federal government do what they say they will do on a continuing basis? And if they don't, who will enforce the enforcers? I would hope that it would not be to designate the fox to look after the chicken coop.

Another dangerous provision of the bill is the establishment of the Wildlife Conservation and Restoration Program. This program sets up the

Saenz v. Roe, (1999) 119 S. Ct. 1518.

federal agencies that will be responsible for the enforcement of the program to become veritable commissars with extensive authority and control over a rather vast stretch of private property that could and probably would restrict private property rights as well as access—all in the name of protection of a whole new list of species which are not now under the Endangered Species Act. This goes too far.

Another facet of the bill raises a red flag in my mind. It provides for the funding–government funds–to non-government organizations to secure conservation easements. This is patently wrong. A federal government has no business funding a non-governmental organization for anything. This opens the flood gates to a sub-rosa non-governmental organization to do the bidding of a governmental agency or official. This simply should never be allowed to happen.

While the following is admittedly quite hypothetical, it is nonetheless something to consider. Suppose that the concentration of purchases should somehow be directed to a state in which a vast amount of public lands are now located. Let us take Nevada as our extreme example. If, by chance, these purchases of private property were directed toward Nevada which is already composed in excess of 86 percent federally owned or controlled land, it surely would not take long with the vast funds available to render the State of Nevada the smallest state in the Union in terms of private property, if indeed there was any left.